Lords
of the
LAND

Lords
of the
LAND

The War Over Israel's Settlements
in the Occupied Territories,
1967–2007

IDITH ZERTAL   AKIVA ELDAR

TRANSLATED FROM THE HEBREW BY VIVIAN EDEN

Nation Books
New York
www.nationbooks.org

LORDS OF THE LAND:
The War Over Israel's Settlements in the Occupied Territories, 1967–2007

Copyright © 2005, 2007 Idith Zertal and Akiva Eldar

First published in the Hebrew language by Dvir publishing house, Israel, 2005

Published by
Nation Books
A Member of the Perseus Books Group
116 East 16th Street, 8th Floor
New York, NY 10003

Nation Books titles are available at special discounts for bulk purchases in the United States by corporations, institutions, and other organizations. For more information, please contact the Special Markets Department at Perseus Books Group, 2300 Chestnut Street, Suite 200, Philadelphia, PA 19103, or call (800) 255-1514, or e-mail special.markets@perseusbooks.com

Nation Books is a copublishing venture of the Nation Institute and the Perseus Books Group.

Library of Congress Cataloging-in-Publication Data is available.

ISBN-10: 1-56858-370-2
ISBN-13: 978-1-56858-370-9

9 8 7 6 5 4 3 2 1

Interior design by Bettina Wilhelm

Printed in the United States of America

Contents

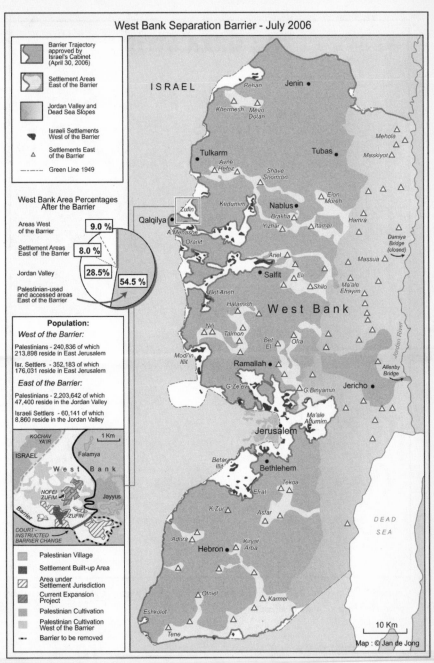

West Bank Separation Barrier - July 2006

Barrier Trajectory approved by Israel's Cabinet (April 30, 2006)

Settlement Areas East of the Barrier

Jordan Valley and Dead Sea Slopes

▸ Israeli Settlements West of the Barrier

△ Settlements East of the Barrier

Green Line 1949

West Bank Area Percentages After the Barrier

Areas West of the Barrier — **9.0 %**

Settlement Areas East of the Barrier — **8.0 %**

Jordan Valley — **28.5%**

Palestinian-used and accessed areas East of the Barrier — **54.5 %**

Population:

West of the Barrier:

Palestinians - 240,836 of which 213,898 reside in East Jerusalem

Isr. Settlers - 352,183 of which 176,031 reside in East Jerusalem

East of the Barrier:

Palestinians - 2,203,642 of which 47,400 reside in the Jordan Valley

Israeli Settlers - 60,141 of which 8,860 reside in the Jordan Valley

KOCHAV YA'IR 1 Km

ISRAEL — Falamya

West Bank

NOFEI ZUFIM — Jayyus

ZUFIN

Barrier

COURT-INSTRUCTED BARRIER CHANGE

Palestinian Village

Settlement Built-up Area

Area under Settlement Jurisdiction

Current Expansion Project

Palestinian Cultivation

Palestinian Cultivation West of the Barrier

Barrier to be removed

ISRAEL

Rehan

Jenin

Khernesh Mevo Dotan

Mehola

Tulkarm Tubas Maskiyot

Avne Hefez

Shave Shomron

Elon Moreh

Qalqilya Zufin Kedumim Nablus Hamra

A.Menashe Braklia

Oranit Yizhar Itamar

Damiya Bridge (closed)

Ariel Massua

Salfit Eli

Shilo Ma'ale Efrayim

Bet Arieh

Halamish **West Bank**

Nili Bet El Ofra

Talmon

Modi'in Illit Allenby Bridge

Ramallah Jericho

G.Ze'ev G.Binyamin

Ma'ale Adumim

Jerusalem

Betar Illit Bethlehem

Tekoa

Efrat

K.Zur Asfar

DEAD SEA

Adora Kiryat Arba

Hebron

Otniel Karmel

Eshkolot

Tene

10 Km

Map : © Jan de Jong

Courtesy of the Foundation for Middle East Peace
http://www.fmep.org Mapmaker: Jan de Jong

The Gaza Strip

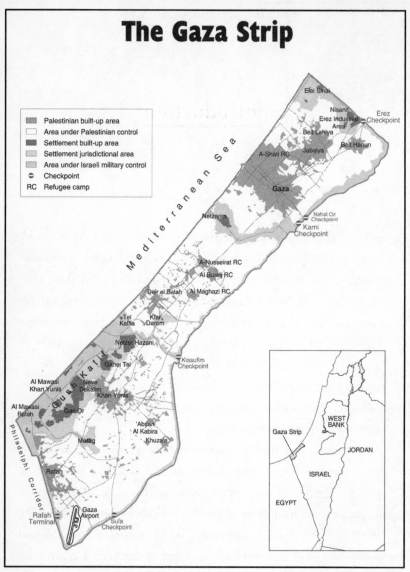

Legend:
- Palestinian built-up area
- Area under Palestinian control
- Settlement built-up area
- Settlement jurisdictional area
- Area under Israeli military control
- ⊖ Checkpoint
- RC Refugee camp

Mediterranean Sea

Elei Sinai
Nisanit
Erez Industrial Area
Erez Checkpoint
Beit Lahiya
Beit Hanun
A-Shati RC
Jabalya
Gaza
Netzarim
Nahal Oz Checkpoint
Karni Checkpoint
A-Nusseirat RC
Al Bureij RC
Deir el Balah
Al Maghazi RC
Tel Katifa
Kfar Darom
Netzer Hazani
Gush Katif
Kissufim Checkpoint
Ganei Tal
Al Mawasi Khan Yunis
Neve Dekalim
Khan Yunis
Al Mawasi Rafah
Gan Or
'Absan
Al Kabira
Khuza'e
Morag
Philadelphi Corridor
Rafah
Rafah Terminal
Gaza Airport
Sufa Checkpoint

WEST BANK
JORDAN
Gaza Strip
ISRAEL
EGYPT

Courtesy of B'Tselem (The Israeli Information Center for Human Rights in the Occupied Territories) http://www.btselem.org/ UN's OCHA

Introduction

From a light plane flying over the West Bank, the view is beautiful. Stretching from the lush green of Samaria in the north, southward toward Jerusalem and over the yellowing Judean Hills that slope eastward down to the Jordan River and the Dead Sea, the landscape modulates from Tuscan green to stony gray to desert. It is, from this height at least, a land of few people and much scenery. Small aggregates of life, like interlinked clusters of grapes or beehives, nestle in a valley or clamber up a hillside, strewn in clumps over wide empty spaces. White roads and shiny asphalt highways carved into the chalky rock extend from one settled hive to another.

As the Cessna flies at a lower altitude, greater details emerge. Brown wooden houses, red-tiled roofs, and here and there a blue splash of swimming pool in the midst of luxuriant foliage almost mingle with the small, light-colored stone cubes crowded around the tall minaret of a mosque, surrounded by expanses of wheat fields and olive groves. And then suddenly, as if out of nowhere, a larger place materializes: a town, a pile of houses jumbled together with no discernible logic, climbing and descending a mountainside and surrounded by rocky land or cultivated groves.

But beneath the serene, colorful picture seen from the window of the cruising Cessna, the ideological grid of the territories reveals itself, as in an old and faded painting in which the layers of color on the canvas peek through and tell their story.[1] This is the outline of the grand plan of the Jewish presence that determines the configurations and the reality on the ground. Gradually the subtext is exposed and the drama of the Jewish settlers' state, of the Israeli occupation, of the destruction and plunder, and of the lawbreaking unfolds in the deceptive landscape. The seemingly random patches of Jewish settlement become more meaningful, part of the pattern of renewed Jewish possession of "the land of the Fathers," at the expense of millions of Palestinians and of the wholeness of the Palestinian national body.

Four decades have passed since the 1967 war, after which Jewish citizens of Israel began to settle beyond the border of their state in contravention of international law, which prohibits an occupying state from transferring population into occupied territory.[2] For approximately two-thirds of its history, Israel has been an occupying state. The State of Israel has been free of the malignancy of occupation for only nineteen of the fifty-nine years of its existence. The vast majority of the 7 million Israelis do not know any other reality. The vast majority of the 4 million Palestinians who live under occupation do not know any other reality. The prolonged military occupation and the Jewish settlements that are perpetuating it have toppled Israeli governments and brought Israel's democracy and its political culture to the brink of an abyss. They have transformed the very foundations of Israeli society, economy, army, history, language, moral profile, and international standing. A state that emerged out of the catastrophe of the destruction of European Jewry, and from it drew the legitimacy for the means of its establishment and for the very fact of its existence, is being crushed from within and is increasingly the subject of bitter controversy abroad because of the settlements.

When this book was first published in Hebrew, in early 2005, the Israeli proposal for "disengagement" from the Gaza Strip and the dismantling of the Jewish settlements there was still a raw idea within a foggy thicket of unknown and unexpected factors. Yet another of the grandiose unilateral acts designed by Ariel Sharon, Israel's prime minister from 2001 to 2006, the disengagement plan led to a confrontation between the concepts of the State of Israel (the political, legal, and civic entity established and internationally recognized in 1948) and the Land of Israel, or *Eretz Yisrael* (the embodiment of millenarian, religious, and national aspirations and myths), and between their historical representatives, and seemingly threatened to break Israeli society in two. The most extreme members of the settler community have long declared the nullity of the State of Israel and of Israeli democracy, while most of them have vowed uncompromising resistance to what they see as the destruction of the Home (*Hurban HaBayit*, or Temple). However, despite the harsh scenes of collective hysteria, and the Judgment Day threats that went along with it, the actual disengagement, carried out in August 2005, has already nearly sunk into historical oblivion. To a large extent it was the settlers themselves who paid for their repeated apocalyptic prophecies and their going to the brink too many times. There is a limit to the catastrophic traumas that the overflowing collective Israeli memory can contain.

The disengagement operation seemed to some like the start of a new era in relations between Israel and the Palestinians: a first step in the painful and lengthy process of undoing the settlement project and Israel's return to the 1949–1967 borders. This was more wishful thinking than anything else. Others saw it as no more than yet another of Sharon's cunning and brilliant maneuvers, of sacrificing the handful of indefensible settlements in the Gaza Strip for the sake of winning the greater campaign for control of the West Bank and the settlements that Sharon himself had sown there. As for the settlers, who since the very beginning have been fighting for every house and every outpost they built on every godforsaken hill as though it were a replica of the Temple, and as if each one of them held the secret of their being and its raison d'être—they saw the disengagement as a kind of world war of Holocaust-like dimensions. In Sharon's unexpected collapse into a deep coma, which occurred just a few months after the destruction of the Gaza settlements, the settlers were able to see, with the spiritual guidance of their rabbis, a divine punishment of someone who dared to challenge them and their God.

Insofar as can be asserted today, Israel's withdrawal from Gaza was none of these. It did not inaugurate a new era of Israeli withdrawal from the occupied territories, it did not ensure the settlements in the West Bank, and it did not bring Sharon's punishment down on him. Nor did it release Gaza for even a single day from Israel's military grip or from the price of the occupation that its inhabitants pay every day, nor did it bring quiet and security to the communities on the southwestern border of Israel, or even to its other borders. It gave rise only to more hatred, more destruction, and more hopelessness.

Under cover of the uproar over the disengagement, followed by the political upheavals in Israel that derived from it and then by the second Lebanon War in the summer of 2006, the settlement fever and all it involves continues. Almost out of sight and out of mind, it is going on with the full cooperation of the State of Israel and its institutions, as though it were an involuntary, unconsidered movement of a body that has lost its mind. Tenders for building new neighborhoods in the settlements, mainly in the Greater Jerusalem area, continue to be published, and new houses are rising steadily. In 2005 alone construction began on 1,666 housing units in the West Bank. The number of Jewish settlers beyond the Green Line,[3] which was long ago erased from Israel's textbooks and many of its history books, continues to rise at a steady rate. At the end of 2006 the number of settlers stood at 270,000 (to this number should be added some 220,000 settlers living in neighborhoods surrounding Jerusalem, beyond the Green line), and since the withdrawal from Gaza nearly 20,000 new settlers have been added in the West Bank. Two-thirds of them were babies born in the settlements and the rest were newcomers, from Israel or other countries.

In November 2006, the Peace Now movement published a report based on official data of the State of Israel. This report found that more than 40 percent of settlement land in the occupied territories had been private lands owned by Palestinians and that 130 settlements were established wholly or in part on lands that the state itself had determined to be "private." The settlers took control of these lands, but it was the state that had confiscated them and enabled the settlement of its citizens in contravention of international law, of some government decisions and in many cases of court orders. It is in this context that one must interpret the theatrical display on February 1, 2006, when the government took down nine structures in the "illegal" outpost of Amona, on the outskirts of the flagship settlement of Ofra. This action did not express the government's desire to impose the law on the settlements; the show, during the course of which more than a thousand Israeli soldiers and police confronted several thousand screaming and kicking settlers, did in fact reveal the state's role in the settlement project. Indeed, while the government put its organized, legitimate force into action in order to take down a few houses of no importance in a bogus settlement that was barren from its inception, it continues to enable the expansion of the large, ostensibly legal settlements and in so doing deepens their grip and their ostensible legality. It was achieved by means of the demonstrative distinction the state made between the negligible, "illegal" outposts and the main, consensual settlements that are the heart of the problem, the *aporia* of the entire settlement project and in effect of the State of Israel since 1967.

Along with the expansion of the settlements, the annexation to Israel of part of the West Bank continued by means of the separation wall, which butchers the land. By the end of 2006 more than 50 percent of the route of the wall had been completed and put into operation (about 400 of the 790 kilometers planned, or 250 of 490 miles). An additional seventy-seven kilometers (forty-eight miles) were in various stages of construction, and the rest were in the planning stage, in legal proceedings, or in the process of authorization. Together with the roadblocks in the territories—several hundred of them, some huge and fixed, others smaller and mobile—this wall— the articulation, birth, and planning processes of which are extensively surveyed in the final chapter of this book—has become the most crucial factor in this twilight zone. The wall and the roadblocks are thwarting the movement of Palestinians in their land and their ability to work. They are separating people from their fields, their relatives, and their neighbors, and children from their schools. Not only have the wall and the roadblocks made the Palestinians' lives less and less tolerable, but they are also collapsing the foundation on which Israel has based its policy since 1967 and undermining its legitimacy as well as its moral and security claims.

On the face of it, the Jewish settlement project is an impressive geopolitical achievement. Scores of settlements are scattered in the large blocs around Jerusalem and on the western and eastern slopes and hilltops of the Samarian Hills. Settlements and outposts are sown in the Jordan Valley and in the Hebron Hills, Jewish neighborhoods are invading the heart of the town of Hebron, and Jewish suburbs are touching Nablus and Ramallah, creating a human and urban mix so volatile that any attempt to draw a border through it in order to separate the two peoples will entail bitter struggles and agony. During the years of the occupation, Israel has built approximately 120 "legal" settlements and countless "illegal outposts." Yeshivas, religious schools that provide premilitary training, industrial zones, gas stations, and quarries, have been established in the occupied territories. Even a large college has sprung up in the heart of Samaria, which is attended by both Jewish and Arab students from within the Green Line.

Nevertheless, and this too is a possible perspective, the vast majority of settlers live in large urban concentrations such as Ma'aleh Adumim, Ariel, and Karnei Shomron. This is less than 10 percent of the Palestinian population that lives in the territory and less than 5 percent of the Jewish population in Israel. As surprising as this may seem, forty years of Jewish settlement in the territories have not filled the occupied land with Jews, despite the might that the settlers project and their massive presence on the Israeli agenda. Both from the perspective of the airplane and through the window of a car traveling through the West Bank, the overriding impression is of a land that is still relatively empty, and the further one goes from the ring of settlements to the north and south of Jerusalem, and from the settlements along the Green Line in central Israel, this impression grows stronger. Most of the settlements, including ones established more than twenty years ago as well as outposts just a few years old, look fragile, neglected, ephemeral, as though they lack vitality of their own. The network of infrastructures that link the settlements—the electricity grid, the water system, the formidable military forces that move around in the territory—are the elixir of life for the settlements, the secret of their power. Remove them from the equation and this project collapses like a house of cards. If Israeli society ever finds the courage to separate itself from the territories it occupied in war forty years ago, the country might finally restore its place in the region, and among the community of nations.

———

The obsession with Jewish settlement in the territories has altered over the years but has not subsided. Its high price can be seen daily on the ground and in the news. Both societies have been ravaged and are torn within themselves, though to differing extents, and the destruction is testimony not only to the disaster of settlement but also to a hubris that knows no bounds, of fanaticism that rises up against the fanatic and destroys both occupier and occupied, both settler and he whose land has been taken from him and has become the settlement of the other.

The history of the Jewish settlements, like the history of the establishment of Israel from the ashes of the Holocaust, is Israeli history, but it has always been a drama that has fascinated the entire world. The world sees itself as a partner and a player in that drama. Nevertheless, even though the settlements have been engaging governments, the media, and scholars here and abroad for four decades, to this day not a single comprehensive book has been written in Hebrew or in any other language about the Jewish settlements. The tale of the territories that were conquered by Israel in 1967, which in turn have conquered Israel's history, has not yet been told in full.[4] This book attempts, for the first time, to do so. (It should be understood that it is comprehensive from the Israeli perspective only; we make no attempt to convey the forty-year occupation from the perspective of the Palestinians.) *Lords of the Land* was written during the years of the second Palestinian intifada, those agonizing years that revealed the price in horrors that is being paid for the occupation by both societies. Inevitably, this book has been influenced by the time of its writing. The present discussion has also been informed by the manner in which a modern power, unable to turn an impressive military victory into peace, has sunk into the endless human, moral, social, military, and political morass of occupation and domination of another people. This perspective also affords the authors the wisdom of hindsight, of a type that is never at the disposal of the history makers.

Lords of the Land charts a two-pronged development. On the one hand there is the settlement movement, which from its very inception was imbued with a sense of sacred national-religious mission. On the other hand we have seen the gradual collapse of the state's institutions, whether by choice or out of weakness in the face of the messianic zeal that burst into the public sphere after June 1967. Thus, this is the intertwined story of the settlers and of the State of Israel over the past forty years. The expansion of the settlements would not have been possible without massive aid from various state institutions, without legal sanction, and without the expedient and affective ties woven between the settlers and the military. The settlements flourished not only with the authorities' seal of approval but also with official encouragement and at the government's initiative.

The authorized, "legal" settlements began in the era of the Labor-led governments, from 1967 to 1977. They flourished in the days of the Likud governments that followed and during the subsequent period of the Labor, Likud, and unity governments. In the course of the negotiations that engendered the September 1993 Oslo agreement, and in the period following it, the settlements saw an unprecedented building boom. All the subsequent governments have made a point of approving new construction, ostensibly only within the boundaries of the existing settlements, but they have always supported—by political and budgetary deed and by failing to enforce the law and deter violations—the establishment of new settlements in the guise of new neighborhoods and "illegal" outposts. Thousands of elected officials and civil servants—politicians, magistrates, attorneys general, army commanders, academics—have lent a hand over the years, some openly and some discreetly, to the Jewish settlement project. At the same time, very few intellectuals and media people, along with human rights organizations, have sounded alarm bells in regard to the expansion of the settlements, the continuing seizure of lands, and the ever heavier oppression of the Palestinians. Yet there has been no reckoning. To this day, no one has assumed responsibility or has been called to account for his part in the settlement project. Perhaps Israeli society has been relatively silent about it because, even as it has become less democratic, less humane, less rational, and at the same time poorer, more divided, and more hateful, the lives of most Israelis have continued unhindered while the settlements have been conquering Israel and destroying the lives of the Palestinians.

The story of the settlements and the occupation is huge: complex and elusive in its first years; wild, tragic, and omnipresent as the occupation has deepened. It spreads, as we have said, over forty years, and there are innumerable individuals who have been allies and partners to it, to one degree or another, both on behalf of the state and on the part of the settlers. It has had its many moments in the spotlight, as documented in this book, but it is also made up of the routine and relatively quiet process of settling and expansion, composed of myriad details. This story has not yet ended, and its denouement is not known. Part of it, then, is history, part of it is current events, and part of it is hidden in an unknown future. To cover this complex history in its various facets, the book was divided into three sections: the first, containing the first three chapters, covers the narrative; the second, containing the four subsequent chapters, which constitute the core of the book, offers the analytical, thematic study of the settlement phenomenon. The concluding chapter links the chronological to the thematic discussion.

Thus the first section of the book, titled "The Forty-Year War," sets forth the political infrastructure of the events, from their beginnings to the end of the year 2000. The first chapter in this section covers the years between 1967 and 1977: the first settlements in the Etzion Bloc and Hebron; the vacillation of Labor governments in the face of the first settlers; the role played by personalities like Yigal Allon, Israel Galili, Moshe Dayan, and Shimon Peres in the development of the settlements; and the first steps of the settler movement Gush Emunim (Bloc of Faith). Chapter 2, from 1977 to 1992, covers the years during which the state was administered by Likud or national unity governments. Those were the years of Menachem Begin, who turned out to be a great disappointment for the settlers, but also the years of Ariel Sharon, the powerhouse behind the expansion of the settlements and their spread throughout the West Bank in order to thwart evacuation and return of the land to the Palestinians. This chapter also deals with the increasing violence on both sides and tells the story of the Jewish terror group that was active in the early 1980s as well as the period covered by the first Palestinian intifada, which began in December 1987. Chapter 3 covers the 1990s, with the expansion and development of the settlements under the umbrella of the Oslo agreements as an accompanying leitmotif to the 1994 massacre in Hebron of twenty-nine Palestinians by settler extremist Baruch Goldstein, and the 1995 assassination of Prime Minister Yitzhak Rabin by the extremist Jew Yigal Amir. This chapter also follows, for the first time, the thread that led from the massacre in Hebron to the murder in the heart of Tel Aviv.

The second, thematic section, titled "From Redemption to Destruction," begins with Chapter 4, which is devoted to the study of the historical and ideological origins of Gush Emunim and to the unique modes of action developed by this organization, which, because of its nature, its heritage, its discourse, and its people, turned into the most sophisticated and influential political movement since the establishment of the state, and also the most dangerous. Chapter 5 examines the culture of death and the cult of death in the settler community, and the way that death and the dead became a powerful political tool in the hands of the settlers. Chapter 6 probes the special relations and complicity that developed between the settlers, on the one hand, and the higher echelons of the military forces and the security establishment, on the other, and analyzes the intimate and fruitful connection between the two parties. Chapter 7, which concludes this section, is an inquiry into the legal dimension of the settlement project. It tracks the ways in which the various legal authorities—from the Judge Advocate General in the Six-Day War and afterward, through attorneys general, state prosecutors, courts, and scholars—sanctioned and legitimized the occupation and the settlements. This chapter analyzes the legalization of the basic illegality of the civilian Jewish presence in the occupied territories, which has enabled constant violation of the law by the settlers and nonenforcement of the law with regard to them. It demonstrates the norm of blatant inequality before the law, as law professor and parliamentarian Amnon Rubinstein said in the Knesset, that in the territories "there are Israeli citizens with full rights, and there are non-Israeli non-citizens with non-rights."[5] Chapter 8, which concludes the book, tells the story of the years 2000–2007, the years of the cruel war for the settlements, of Palestinian terror, and of the separation wall, with a spotlight on Ariel Sharon's role in the perpetuation of the occupation and the settlements until his unexpected, fateful disappearance from the public eye, which already bears the signs of a mythical event.

It is no accident that a chapter on the full economic price of the settlements and their consequences is absent from *Lords of the Land*. These pages do contain a great deal of information about the cost of the successive phases of the settlement project. Such information is abundantly available in the public domain, buried in the state budget books, and documented frequently in parliamentary questions in the Knesset, in the press, in reports of social organizations, in State Comptroller's Reports, and elsewhere.[6] However, we have not succeeded in calculating a sufficiently precise exposition of this matter and a comprehensive price tag for the entire four decades of the settlement phenomenon. This is the result of the systematic way in which unfathomable amounts of state funding have been directly and indirectly channeled to the settlements through innumerable tracks and under various guises and disguises. It was purposely done via government ministries and other state agencies, as well as with the help of the World Zionist Organization and the Jewish Agency, with the money's ultimate destination intentionally concealed.[7]

Deception, shame, concealment, denial, and repression have characterized the state's behavior with respect to the flow of funds to the settlements. It can be said that this has been an act of public duplicity in which all of the Israeli governments since 1967 have been partner. This massive self-deception still awaits the research that will reveal its full magnitude. The citizens of Israel are not only entitled to know the full economic price of the settlements; they also owe themselves an answer to the question of why their state has been involved for many decades in a political project with inestimable historical implications, all the while blurring the tracks of its involvement. Why have we done everything possible to conceal our deeds, from ourselves and from the world? Is this dissimulation evidence of knowledge and awareness of the sin? Thus the question must also be asked as to what Israel's statesmen and politicians in this era were thinking, and what Israel's citizens were envisioning, as they invested themselves ever more deeply in such an enormous project of occupation and settlement during the last third of the twentieth century. This was, after all, the era of postcolonialism, marked by the bitter aftermath of the crumbling of the world's last occupying regimes and by the awareness of the lethality of any occupation anywhere, not only for the occupied but also for the occupier.

Although we conducted scores of interviews and conversations with government officials, the military, jurists, economists, and settlers, some of whom appear in the book by name and others who asked not to be identified, *Lords of the Land* is based primarily on written sources, official papers, and documents both open and classified, transcripts of court proceedings, State Comptroller's Reports, Knesset proceedings, and reports and studies from human rights organizations and Internet sites. Beyond that, we have had recourse to the abundant work of the Israeli and foreign media, which have closely followed the settlement project in all its facets from its very inception. Newspaper archives have proved to be a large and rich source of knowledge and insight, and the use of many and varied journalistic sources, often contradictory in outlook, has rounded our perspective and added to the subtlety and complexity of the portrait. The work of certain journalists in particular in covering the settlements over the years, such as Nadav Shragai of *Ha'aretz*, has aided us greatly and has been a crucial source of information for us. The settler society, on the whole a highly ideological community that is imbued with a sense of mission, speaks and writes extensively both within the community and to the surrounding society. We have therefore referred extensively to its publications, such as

Nekudah and *Besheva*. We have also made use of the relatively limited secondary research literature that exists on the subject. These materials are cited where appropriate. But *Lords of the Land* is based for the most part on primary sources, and the responsibility for what is written is entirely ours.

Finally, this book, as we have said, is a first attempt to comprehend the entire phenomenon of the Jewish settlements, which is both very well known and very unknown, in all its complex and less obvious facets. The book's aim, among other things, is to expose what was meant to be concealed from us, or what for years we have not wanted to see, and to stimulate a more informed public debate on the subject at a time that is so critical for the settlements, and even more so for Israel and for the entire region.

Part One

The Forty-Year War

I

Blindness

In late September 1967, shortly before the Jewish New Year, a small convoy led by a handsome, bright-eyed young man made its way from the religious cooperative community of Nehalim in central Israel to the Etzion Bloc in the southern West Bank.[1] That evening the first stake of Kfar Etzion was hammered into the rocky land, a first step in a fateful journey into which the first settler, Hannan Porat, and his friends swept all of Israeli society.

It is the wont of such history-revolutionizing stories to probe backward and find themselves mythological beginnings. Thus the legend has it that when Porat was a little boy, he climbed the guard tower of Kfar Etzion and the night watchman aimed the spotlights for him at the Arab villages that surrounded his kibbutz. "So many Arabs all around, and we're all alone?" cried the child in alarm. "The darkness is where they are, and the light is where we are," the watchman soothed him.[2] Nineteen years after he was evacuated from his home, together with the other children and the women of his religious kibbutz, as well as those from three other nearby kibbutzim, Porat, now 24, saw the light again. On June 7, 1967, the 29th Brigade of the Jordanian Infantry, which had been deployed in the Hebron Hills, was ordered to retreat to the eastern side of the Jordan River.

The Israeli army, in which Porat was a soldier, was the only armed force that remained to the west of the Jordan. The breakthrough to the eastern, Arab quarters (the Old City) of Jerusalem with the Paratroops Brigade was for him the first move in his campaign for the return to Gush Etzion. The myth that he wove around the return to his home in Kfar Etzion is reminiscent of the "key stories" of the 1948 Palestinian refugees from Jaffa and the Galilee, and their mythic dream of return.[3]

The image that flashed through the mind of the Jewish refugee of the 1948 war who had returned to settle in his natal, abandoned village was, paradoxically, Palestinian poet Mahmoud Darwish's text about the return to his own village, al Birwa, in western Galilee. Aghast at the very fact of the comparison, Porat hastened to eradicate the lines of similarity between everyday, routine longings of Palestinian refugees for their land and the burning faith that is nourished by the divine promise of the Jewish people's right to their land. "An Arab who returns to his village is human and touching," wrote Porat, "but a Jew who returns to his village is something beyond nostalgia. This is history. This is meta-history."[4] Later, when a Jewish settler from Kiryat Arba killed twenty-nine Muslim worshipers at the Tomb of the Patriarchs in Hebron, Porat explained that for him, a dead Arab is as anonymous as a dead Bosnian.[5] "Hannan felt like someone who was leading the camp and had seen the light," said Aviezer Ravitzky, a professor of Jewish philosophy and an expert on national religious Zionism. "When you are in the midst of a divine process, and God is on your side, you gradually lose your sensitivity to the suffering of the other. You become impervious, you see the big picture and little things like human beings disappear. A person with a redemptive outlook like that is satisfied only by the whole and the perfect. Anything that is not whole is perceived as treason."[6]

Hannan Porat and his allies saw the establishment of the state by secular Zionism as "the beginning of redemption." These young members of the national religious camp identified the Six-Day War as the Big Bang that afforded religious Zionism the opportunity to take part in the next phase of redemption, the Jewish settlement of the Greater Land of Israel. It was only natural that the Etzion Bloc was selected as the bridgehead from the basically secular and pragmatic State of Israel, the boundaries of which had been demarcated by the end of the 1948 war, to the national religious Land of Israel, the boundaries of which had been extended by the battles of the 1967 war. The "Bloc" was unlike all those Arab areas that had "fortuitously" fallen into Israel's hands on the three fronts. In the 1948 war, 141 local Jews had been killed there and many others had been taken prisoner by the Jordanians. The battle for the Etzion Bloc and its fall were also connected to the heartbreaking tale of the thirty-five young soldiers, the golden boys of the secular pioneering Zionist dream, who were massacred in February 1948 on their way to rescuing the besieged Etzion Bloc. This was an open wound that needed healing. The exiles from Kfar Etzion had in fact established new homes at Nir Etzion inside the Green Line, but many carried with them the memory of their abandoned home. Every year the original settlers' descendants from all around the country held a reunion at the cemetery plot for the Gush Etzion dead at Mount Herzl in Jerusalem. Among them were orphans of the War of Independence and those whose parents had been Jordanian prisoners of war.[7]

Upon the completion of his military service, the paratrooper Porat went to study at the Merkaz HaRav Yeshiva in Jerusalem, where he and his colleagues shared the redemptive outlook of their mentor, Rabbi Zvi Yehudah Kook. The young yeshiva students looked with despair at their weak, disoriented, elderly government in the wake of the war. Indeed, the pragmatic, sober vision of the representatives of the historic Labor Zionist movement, fatigued by decades of bearing the burden of building a nation and a state, did not stand a chance against the messianic burst of energy to which the war had given rise among the religious youth. The extensive territories that had fallen into Israel's hands almost overnight confronted Israel's leadership with dilemmas beyond its capacities. From the very first days of Israel's rule in the West Bank and the Gaza Strip, as in the Golan Heights and the Sinai Peninsula, it was clear that Israeli settlement in these territories would have far-reaching implications. Some believed that settling territories on all the fronts would serve as a political card in negotiations with the Arab states, if and when this happened in some unknown future. Others saw the settlements as a way to tie the government's hands in any such negotiations, and there were some who conceived of the settlements as an infrastructure for Israeli-Palestinian cooperation.[8] The official government line, particularly for international purposes, was that Israel's military presence in the territories was not an end in itself and that the territories were a deposit— an asset for political bargaining in peace negotiations. The decision to annex only East Jerusalem emphasized, ostensibly, the different attitude toward the areas of the West Bank adjacent to Jerusalem, which have not been annexed to this day.

On June 19, a few days after the war ended, the government announced a decision reflective of this position. The official releases stated that "united Jerusalem will remain within the territory of the State of Israel (special arrangements will be made for the sites that are sacred to the various religions); as an interim stage, a military situation will remain in the West Bank; an effort will be made to seek a constructive solution for the long term; Israel is prepared for talks with King Hussein with the aim of building a good neighborly relationship and arriving at economic union between the two states; the agreement will be based on self-government (autonomy) for the local inhabitants."[9] There was no mention of the Etzion Bloc in the government's announcement.

Presumably, at the time of the June 19 decision, Prime Minister Levi Eshkol had already seen the proposal for the solution to the Palestinian problem that had been written by some officials of the Mossad, Israel's foreign intelligence service. At the behest of the Israel Defense Forces Intelligence Division, the officials had surveyed Palestinian attitudes in the West Bank and submitted a document to the head of military intelligence on June 14. The authors, experienced intelligence officers, recommended that an independent Palestinian state should be established as quickly as possible "under the auspices of the IDF" and "in agreement with the Palestinian leadership." The Palestinian state would be established in the territories of the West Bank and the Gaza Strip within borders based on the 1949 truce lines, with minor adjustments in Jerusalem, the Latrun Salient northwest of Jerusalem, and the Gilboa area at the northern edge of the West Bank. "In order to enable an honorable agreement," the document said, Israel would "examine the possibility of relinquishing some Arab villages in its territory." In the framework of the proposed plan, Israel would "take upon itself the initiative to solve the [refugee] problem once and for all" and head an international project to rehabilitate and settle the refugees. This revolutionary proposal, which stressed that it was necessary to act quickly and in agreement with the Palestinians, and which, had it been accepted and implemented, could have changed the history of Israel and the entire Middle East, was based, according to its authors, on an inquiry they had conducted among the political leadership in the West Bank. They found that "the vast majority of West Bank leaders, including the most extreme among them, are prepared at this time to reach a permanent peace agreement" on the basis of "an independent existence for Palestine," without an army.[10]

But the voice of sanity and the long-sightedness of the four Mossad men were lost in the clamor of the euphoria of those days. On June 16 Defense Minister Moshe Dayan was still writing, in a proposal he submitted to the ministerial committee on defense matters, that "we are not settling Jews in the West Bank, in Hebron, in Etzion and in the Jiftlik [in the Jordan Valley]."[11] A month later, when he met with Hannan Porat and his friends from the Kfar Etzion settlement group, Dayan was still insisting that there should be settlement only at the "five fists" along the hilltops that overlook the Coastal Plain, in accordance with his pronouncement right after the war. However, a short while later he changed his mind, and in the plan that he formulated and that bore his name, he added the Etzion Bloc to one of the "five fists" at the core of his plan.[12]

The government's wavering, changing, and contradictory plans certainly did not deter Porat. He established a fact when he set September 23 as the date for moving onto the land, whether with the government's or with God's blessing. Porat often equated himself with the earlier generation of pioneers who had settled Palestine before the founding of the state, and he liked to cite from memory the meaning of "pioneer" as defined by Yosef Trumpeldor, the one-armed martyred hero of the legendary 1920 battle of Tel Hai: "A pioneer is an individual who is prepared for everything. If he is told to carry bricks, he carries bricks; if he is told to plow, he plows; if he is told to teach, he teaches. In short, he is like a piece of iron, which is wrought as needed." From time to time Porat would close his eyes and recite: "'Here am I,' just as Abraham had replied to God, 'Here am I—for priesthood, for kingship, to kill, to be killed. Lord of the Universe, here am I for all that is required. . . . This, with thousands upon thousands of differences, is how I understand the true meaning of the concept of pioneer."[13]

In his biography and charismatic personality, the young man who not long ago had folded away his paratrooper's uniform and returned to civilian life exemplified traits and values that the secular Labor leaders, themselves former pioneers, could not resist. They perceived the blue-eyed fighter, paratrooper, and religious settler of the land as a new incarnation and avatar of the soldier-tiller of the land, the cherished icon of national movements that fight for territory. The ritual fringes dangling beneath his shirt and the skullcap on his head constituted for them added value of Jewishness that they had extirpated from themselves in the fervor of their revolutionary past. For his part, Porat made a point of adopting the external appearance of an ascetic pioneer. As time passed and he became a key political figure in religious Zionism and a leader of the settlement movement, Porat demonstratively maintained this look: a faded blue shirt of the sort that in the past had been one of the symbols of the Labor movement in Israel, shabby trousers, scuffed sandals, and a khaki carryall always hanging from his shoulder. "His appearance, as it is reflected in his pictures in the newspapers, is like that of an eternal group-leader of the Bnei Akiva [national religious] youth movement," noted a reporter.[14]

The Gush Etzion people and their supporters laid siege to the prime minister. On August 16, 1967, their first delegation came to a meeting with Eshkol at his office in Jerusalem and urged him to renew the Jewish settlement in the Bloc.[15] Two days later the prime minister reported to his party's policy committee that the Etzion representatives were pressuring him. "Youngsters from the Etzion Bloc have been coming to see me," he said, "and telling me that they want to settle there." He added that his advisers were asserting that "there is nothing there to be clung to." Eshkol tossed out a typical comment about Dayan, who "tends towards some kind of settlement there." Ministers Yigal Allon and Israel Galili confirmed that Dayan "had changed his mind" and now supported settlement.[16]

Restoring Former Glory

The triple "no" published on September I by the Arab states in the wake of their summit held in Khartoum, Sudan—no to peace, no to recognition of Israel, and no to negotiations with it—came to the aid of those who opposed viewing the territories as bargaining chips in peace negotiations. At the Israeli government meeting that was held just over a week later, on September 10, after well-orchestrated public activity and an organized campaign of pressure on the prime minister by the movement for the Greater Land of Israel, the National Religious Party (NRP), and the Etzion Bloc people themselves, Eshkol had softened. Despite the opposition of his close associate Agriculture Minister Haim Gvati to any settlement without a serious policy debate of the future implications,[17] Eshkol in effect gave his reluctant approval. Not ten days had gone by since the Arab summit, when Yigal Allon, in his capacity as coordinator of settlement issues in the territories, had requested a discussion of the establishment of settlements in the Jordan Valley and the Etzion Bloc. At the same time, the Settlement Department of the Jewish Agency submitted to the prime minister an operational plan for the creation of "workplaces" for settlers in the Bloc.[18]

On September 22, the Etzion Bloc people, among them Hannan Porat, came to the Prime Minister's Office and appealed to him to allow them to "restore the former glory of the Etzion Bloc." The group was already prepared to settle, they told Eshkol, and they were determined to rebuild the Bloc from which their parents had been expelled. The seventy-two-year-old Eshkol, who for them was the embodiment of the gray Mapai politico in his ways and in his manner of speaking, listened to what his visitors had to say and made it clear to them that the future of the West Bank and the territories had not yet been decided. However, he promised that he would put the settlement institutions and the Agriculture and Defense ministries to work, and that within a week there would be an "authoritative answer."[19]

The issue came up at the government meeting two days later. Dayan suggested expropriating lands suitable for cultivation in the area of the Etzion Bloc and planting military-agricultural settlements and army bases there. He proposed "connecting the Etzion Bloc to the earlier State of Israel so that it would be a separate island, a kind of complete enclave. A road 15 kilometers [9.3 miles] in length should be paved from the Etzion Bloc to the Lachish Region. . . . Gradually this will become something more permanent."[20] The government took note (in Decision 839) of the prime minister's statement that "in the near future a settlement will be located in the Etzion Bloc." Eshkol knew that the settlers were planning to claim the territory within a day or two, but for his own reasons he decided to keep the details of this move and its date from his government colleagues. The ministers, most of whom had reservations about the idea, assumed that they would still have the chance to express their opinions before the formal authorization was granted. The next day the members of the Kfar Etzion settlement group were again invited to the Prime Minister's Office. "We were prepared for the possibility of settling at Kfar Etzion without authorization, with the backing of the Greater Land of Israel movement people and others," Hannan Porat related later. "We organized everything we needed on a truck that was parked at Moshav Nehalim. . . . Eshkol asked us when we wanted to move there and we replied that we wanted to pray there on Rosh

Hashanah [October 5–6]. Eshkol replied: 'Go ahead.'" Despite the permission, a few members of the group pressed for going to settle that very day, without waiting for the agreed-upon date.[21]

This is how the decision to establish the first settlement in the West Bank was taken, without the government having discussed principles of a comprehensive settlement policy and all the short- and long-term implications, thereby setting a precedent of immeasurable importance. The establishment of "facts on the ground" and cunning, sophisticated play with the powers that be and with time—forcing the ending on the one hand, and waiting patiently for the ripe moment on the other, until the walls of resistance weakened or fell—provided more significant historical impetus than any government decision. Eventually, Rabbi Moshe Levinger, who was the first Jewish settler in Hebron seven months later and who also played a part in the settlement of the Etzion Bloc, said that "this was our strategy: not to bang our heads against the wall but rather the opposite, to drag out the action so that in the end it would be accepted when the moment was propitious. We always knew how to use the time factor in the democratic game. Timing is always important to us, because the amplitude of time worked to our benefit. They simply got used to the facts on the ground."[22]

Eshkol, his government, and their ideological colleagues were not blind to the squatters' plans to settle in the territory, but while they were agonizing about the tremendous diplomatic and security issues and the demographic and political outcomes of any move they made, Porat and those who shared his beliefs exempted themselves from such considerations and moral doubts. The Labor movement adopted the Etzion Bloc and transformed it into one of those "security settlements" that, unlike "political settlements," were embraced by the consensus and that profited from the generous public funding that derived from this status.

As early as September 1967, prior to the meeting of the central committee of Rafi—the political party of David Ben-Gurion, Moshe Dayan, and Shimon Peres, which was slated to discuss a proposal to merge with Mapai and Ahdut Ha'avoda—party secretary Peres, who always nurtured an inclination for historical grandeur, formulated a fourteen-point plan. In this document he set forth the policy lines for the party in the wake of the war that had "deepened the connection between the Jewish people and its past." The recipe for Jewish settlement in the territories—the source of Israel's military, legal, moral, and political embroilment in the territories over four decades—was embodied in full in this early document. The intentions perhaps were good, but the myopia that went along with them was no less impressive. Provision 8 of the document stated that "a Jewish settlement shall be established in the east, north and south of Jerusalem without displacing Arab inhabitants," and Provision 9 stated that "places that had been left [in 1948] will be renewed." The places that Peres listed were Beit Ha'arava, Qalia, Hebron, and the Etzion Bloc, all of them on Palestinian land.[23]

At that same meeting at which the merger of the parties was discussed, a vociferous argument developed between Peres and Dayan. Peres said that the moral aspect of the occupied territories should not be ignored, while Dayan replied that it should be admitted that Israel does not have a solution to the refugee problem and that if the refugees wanted to they could "continue to live like dogs," and anyone who so desired could leave. "Let us tell the truth: We want peace and there is no peace. . . . We will maintain a military government in the territory for four or five more years and see what happens. Anyone who wants to leave can leave. And thus it could happen that we will be left with fewer [refugees] and this will be a great thing." To Peres's point about the moral considerations, Dayan riposted that "Ben-Gurion had said that anyone who approaches the moral aspect of the Zionist problem is no Zionist."[24]

For the members of Ahdut Ha'avoda, colleagues and disciples of Yitzhak Tabenkin, the outcome of the Six-Day War was a crucial historical correction. Ever since the 1930s Tabenkin's movement had rejected the idea of the partition of the land, and at the first debate on the 1937 partition plan, at the Twentieth Zionist Congress, they refused to join the compromise proposal suggested by the heads of the Labor movement. They subsequently formed a separate faction, which led in 1944 to the split between Mapai and Ahdut Ha'avoda. Throughout the 1940s Tabenkin and his people clung to this position, refusing to accept the Labor leadership's readiness, declared at the 1946 expanded Jewish Agency meeting in Paris, to discuss the establishment of a Jewish state in a "suitable territory of the land of Israel," meaning in a part of the entire land.[25] For Tabenkin, settlement activity was the primary goal of Zionism, while state and army were by-products of the settlements and mostly instrumental for their defense. Military control and diplomacy are not sufficient, he said toward the end of the 1950s; the state's independence derives from the extent of settlement.[26] In 1953 Tabenkin said that the partition of the land was a temporary situation and that the wholeness of the land would be achieved either in peaceful ways or through war: "If they force a war upon us we shall restore the wholeness of the land."[27] He repeated these ideas in various ways during the 1950s and '60s. One year before the war, in June 1966, Tabenkin said that "everywhere the war will make this possible we shall go to restore the wholeness of the land."[28]

The Etzion Bloc Precedent

The wholeness of the land was thus an article of faith, to be achieved by any means, by the strength of the sword as well as by the classical

Zionist combination of settlement and its defense, of the tiller and the soldier, of land and blood. The representatives of this outlook in the government, Ahdut Ha'avoda ministers Yigal Allon and Israel Galili, not only became the advocates for the settlers inside the government but also helped them with advice, material aid, weapons, and, most important, the seal of approval of the pioneering Labor movement. Their militant, constructive sense of vocation combined with the settlers' godly sense of mission. Allon, the handsome offspring of Zionism and legendary commander of the Palmach, the elite strike force established before the founding of the state, believed only in territory, even if it was populated by a million Arabs, and had no faith in a peace treaty. "A peace treaty," he said at the government meeting on June 19, "is the weakest guarantee of the future of peace and the future of defense." He warned against returning a single "inch" of the West Bank and added that if he had to choose between "the wholeness of the land with all the Arab population . . . or giving up the West Bank, I am in favor of the wholeness of the land with all the Arabs."[29]

Many saw the return to Kfar Etzion as a one-time gesture to the Jewish refugees and the families of those who were killed in 1948, and not as a precedent. Yet this modest move proved to be but the first step in a long march and a huge project, creating an entire world. Not only the people of the Greater Israel idea but also the government and the governments that came after it were encouraged by the relatively mild international reaction and the response of the Israeli left to the settlement in the Etzion Bloc. And when the first crack in the dam appeared, the continuation was just a matter of time. It came with a mixture of arrogance and blindness, as though there were no outside world and no other factors to be taken into account along with the advocates' own strength, desires, and interests. Even at the historic government meeting of June 19, Prime Minister Eshkol remarked in reply to Allon's plan that "some colleagues . . . have reinforced my sense that we are formulating what is good for us, what we want, and playing chess with ourselves."[30] However, despite his misgivings concerning settlement in the territories, he did nothing to stop it. On November 9, 1967, the prime minister contacted the chairman of the World Zionist Organization and requested that the Settlement Department help the government of Israel establish new settlements in the territories. He committed the government to bearing the costs of these settlements.[31]

Once the offspring of the Kfar Etzion people were permitted to return to the homes that had been left in 1948, the country's leaders found it difficult to explain to the descendants of the victims of the massacre in Hebron in 1929 (see Chapter 5), and also to themselves, why the Jews of Hebron should be shortchanged. And indeed, the idea of settling in Hebron began to be bandied about less than two weeks after the settlement at Kfar Etzion. Nothing succeeds like success. It is no coincidence that the key figure in the Hebron story was Rabbi Moshe Levinger, Hannan Porat's admired teacher and the rabbi of Moshav Nehalim, from which the first small convoy of settlers had set out to the renewed Kfar Etzion. During the Sukkot holiday, about a month after the move to Kfar Etzion, Rabbi Levinger received a phone call from attorney Elyakim Haetzni, one of the most prominent nonreligious disciples of the idea of Greater Israel, who asked him to come urgently to his office. Haetzni was and remains to this day an idiosyncratic figure among the settlers. Born in Germany, the radical young idealist was an oppositionist by nature, a vociferous and determined fighter for principles and a partner to many anti-establishment efforts in the 1950s. In 1957 a group of people, among them Haetzni, Professor Yeshayahu Leibowitz, and Shmuel Tamir, who eventually became justice minister in a Likud government, founded a short-lived movement called the New Regime. This movement aspired to change the nature of the regime in Israel, to break the monopoly on rule by Ben-Gurion and his Mapai Party and the huge power structure that the historical Labor movement had established. The New Regime movement called for passing a constitution that would establish the citizen's basic rights; for the annulment of the laws and regulations that restrict the liberty of the individual; for freedom of speech, freedom of movement and organization; for the abolition of the military government over the Arabs of Israel; and more. In geopolitical terms, the New Regime movement supported the uniting of the entire land of Israel in peaceful ways, the establishment of federative treaties with Jordan and Lebanon, and a solution to the problem of the 1948 Palestinian refugees.

Haetzni, then, was no stranger to the question of the Land of Israel and the people of the Greater Israel movement. He told Levinger that the head of the Hebron Yeshiva in Jerusalem said that Ben-Gurion had asked him "why we haven't yet gone there [to settle in Hebron]" and had said that "we must do so at once."[32] Confirmation of this can be found in Ben-Gurion's remark at the meeting of the Rafi secretariat on June 8, 1967. To his surprised colleagues, Ben-Gurion said: "We now control Jerusalem, and that is one of the greatest of events—one of the first things that must be done is build neighborhoods . . . to immediately settle the Jewish Quarter. If there are empty Arab houses, we'll put Jews into them as well. The same is true for Hebron . . . I am sure that with the current mood, the people will go."[33]

Betrayal of Trust

Imbued with a double sense of mission, religious and military (a winning mixture in a belligerent nationalist society), Levinger and a group of young soldiers who had fought in the Six-Day War, among them

Israel Harel, Benny Katzover, Rabbi Haim Druckman, and Rabbi Eliezer Waldman—who eventually became key figures in Gush Emunim—contacted the military governor of Hebron in the spring of 1968 and asked to hold the Passover seder and spend the night there. They promised to leave the city the day after the holiday. As at that time Israeli civilians were prohibited from staying in the West Bank after nightfall, Levinger's group needed the army's permission. This group of people and their friends drew the claim of the Jewish people's right to return to Hebron and settle there from the biblical era, as it was generally believed that this was the burial place of the patriarchs and matriarchs of the Jewish nation. Along with that primordial source of right, the settlers also clung to the trauma of 1929.

The seder celebrants' intention to break their commitment and remain in Hebron could have been inferred from various signs. Paid announcements that were published in the newspapers before Passover urged believers in the settling of Hebron "to contact without delay" a certain post office box in Tel Aviv. Levinger's people tried openly to purchase apartments in the town and rented rooms in the Park Hotel only after the attempt to purchase did not go well.[34] The clues were completely obvious, and there is reason to believe settler Hagai Segal's claim that when the army and the government officials permitted holding the Passover seder in Hebron, they knew that Levinger and his friends did not intend to leave the town the day after the holiday.[35] The mayor of Hebron, Sheikh Muhammad Ali Jabari, was deceived into believing that the rented hotel rooms were evidence of the Jews' intention to leave Hebron as they promised, and did not object to them lodging in his city. Equipped with a permit that bore the seal of Uzi Narkiss, head of the Central Command, the settlers arrived at the Park Hotel on the night between April 12 and April 13. This is how, in the presence of sixty men and women, the first Jewish neighborhood was ceremoniously and festively stabbed into the heart of an Arab town. The very next day, after Passover night, the celebrants announced that they were "the first group of settlers that has come to renew the Jewish settlement in Hebron."[36] As their entry into the town had been done legally, under the 1945 Emergency Defense Regulations, it was possible to get them out only under those same regulations.[37]

A few days later Yigal Allon had already honored the Hebron settlers with a ministerial visit, which was contrary to the spirit of the government's decisions. He saw to arming them with weapons that were brought from the Etzion Bloc and provided them with a small car and other items to ease their organization. In his wake came other members of the government, from the religious parties, for semiofficial visits to the new settlers. This first seed that sprouted and sent out tendrils was the beginning of the violent conflict between Jews and Palestinians in Hebron. It swiftly enflamed tempers in the town and moved Sheikh Jabari to demand the removal of the settlers.[38] Though the demonstration outside the Park Hotel by a handful of Hebrew University professors who carried placards against the settlement and saw Rabbi Levinger's move as the dangerous beginning of a messianic-political trend did attract media attention, it was devoid of any influence. Thus a long-lasting pattern of events was created: well-intentioned intellectuals protest in a polite, barely audible voice, and the convoy of settlers moves forward unhindered.

Prime Minister Eshkol continued to evade making committed decisions in the matter of Jewish settlement in Hebron.[39] Defense Minister Dayan's proposal—to host the settlers in an installation of the military government until such time as a final decision was taken and a solution found for the group[40]—was already an expression of "explicit government auspices" for the small settlement, and the settlers saw it this way as well.[41] On orders from the chief of staff, the settlers received weapons from the army and were trained to use them, without being inducted into the Israel Defense Forces.[42] According to the plan, the Hebron settlers were supposed to work in the Etzion Bloc and later also to find work in services connected to the military government, a linkage that eventually shaped the character of the settlement and the creeping occupation in the territories under the auspices of the Israeli army.[43]

In reply to a parliamentary question in the Knesset, Dayan said that the settlers were "yeshiva students, joined by a number of other people who belong to their group." He claimed that he did not know who had funded the settlers' stay in Hebron and that his ministry had no plans concerning them. In response to Knesset Member Uri Avnery's question as to whether it was true that the group of settlers had lied to the army authorities concerning their stay in Hebron for only forty-eight hours, and had not kept their commitment, Dayan replied that he "did not examine innermost thoughts." According to him, the members of the group had filled out an application form for recognition as permanent residents of Hebron, "and the [military] administration had approved their request in accordance with the government's decision."[44] Thus the government's indecisiveness and ambiguous handling of the issue was tantamount to authorization for the settlers to clinch their hold, step by step. A first school was established at the Park Hotel. A yeshiva sprouted alongside the school, with ten students from the Merkaz HaRav and a group of students who came from the Or Etzion Yeshiva, all funded by the "Movement for the Greater Israel" and a wealthy American Jew named Shmuel Wang.[45] This was the pattern, molded in Hebron, that was to serve as a model of action for future generations of settlers. The pattern was in effect copied from the days prior to the establishment of the state, when the illegality of the actions of the Jewish community in the land of Israel had become an ethos, a worldview, and a daily practice vis-à-vis the "foreign" British rule.

At the end of September 1968, half a year after the government had allowed a handful of settlers to celebrate Passover night in Hebron, a ministerial committee on Hebron and the Etzion Bloc decided to establish a Jewish neighborhood in the town. The committee determined that the possibility of making use of other plots of land owned by Jews should be examined. From that point the way was paved for recognized settlement in the center of the city. The settlers received permission to set up small workshops and a yeshiva and to build housing units inside the administration complex. The kiosk near the entrance to the Tomb of the Patriarchs developed into a restaurant and shop for souvenirs and religious items.[46] On the ground, the model of hostile, violent relations with the Palestinian inhabitants and the quasi-automatic response of the Israeli military began to take shape. First, the settlers inserted themselves into the heart of an Arab locale. As the town's inhabitants, whose ancestors had lived there since ancient times, did not look kindly on the Jews' penetration of their hometown and tried to repel the unwanted intruders, clashes broke out. Large military forces were required to protect the handful of settlers; to ensure this protection, veteran Palestinian Hebronites were evicted from their homes and their places of business.

Heavenly City

It was, however, Yigal Allon, of the Labor movement, who was the main propellant force behind the settlement in Hebron. Even before the first of the settlers came to the town, he had already voiced the idea of establishing a Jewish neighborhood there. On January 14, 1968, Allon submitted to the government secretariat a proposal for a decision to "encourage the building of a Jewish neighborhood" in Hebron. Three months later he reiterated the proposal. When it was rejected, Allon decided to help the settlers without authorization. Parallel to that, Menachem Begin, a right-wing leader and minister with no portfolio, made a proposal in the government to "plan and build townships with Jewish inhabitants in Jericho, Hebron, Bethlehem, Nablus, Tul Karm, Jenin and Qalqilya."[47] The inevitable violent hostility that was inherent in the very fact of the settlement inside an Arab town known for its religious fanaticism led Allon to consider the possibility of establishing a kind of Upper Hebron that would overlook and keep surveillance on the crowded Arab city. A group of secular people headed by Elyakim Haetzni, which wished to distinguish itself from the zealously religious Levinger group, also demanded the establishment of a separate township on the outskirts of Hebron.[48]

The government dithered. On September 25, 1968, a special team appointed by Defense Minister Dayan for the examination of the possibilities for establishing a Jewish settlement in the Hebron area submitted its recommendations. They suggested the establishment of an urban center to the northeast of Hebron, which would be adjacent to the town's municipal jurisdiction, or the establishment of an urban settlement in the Etzion Bloc, about fifteen kilometers from Hebron.[49] At a meeting at the beginning of October of the ministerial committee on Hebron and the Etzion Bloc, chaired by Prime Minister Eshkol and consisting of the ministers of defense, justice, and religious affairs, it was decided rather to establish a Jewish neighborhood in the heart of Hebron itself, "taking into consideration the army's needs and exploiting plots of land that are Jewish-owned."[50] On December 10, 1968, Allon submitted to the ministerial committee a proposal for a resolution that would mean giving up Jewish settlement inside Hebron and instead adopt a model like Upper

Nazareth, a Jewish town overlooking that Arab city in Israel's Galilee region. Following Allon's proposal, the committee decided to locate land that could be appropriate for a separate Jewish neighborhood outside of Hebron, and "at a reasonable distance from it." The committee also decided to continue negotiations that had already begun with the Russian Church to purchase 150 dunams (37.5 acres) in the Hebron area, to examine the economic projects planned for Mount Hebron, and to determine who would be directed to the Etzion Bloc and who to the new Hebron, in accordance with their social profiles.[51]

On the previous day, Allon had said at the government meeting that Israel had accustomed itself "and the entire world to relate to the act of settlement as facts that carry unique weight. This has become one of the weapons of our national revival movement. Presumably, therefore, they will make no mistake in understanding the importance of this act."[52] Allon's plan was accepted by the government and became part of a larger plan "to connect to the state of Israel, in addition to greater Jerusalem, all of Mount Hebron, with its population, the southern West Bank, including the Arabs there, with a status similar to that of the Arabs in the Arab Galilee and the Little Triangle." The expansion of Jerusalem, argued Allon, "brings many Arabs into Israel, so that the addition from Mount Hebron isn't all that fantastic. . . . We need this both to expand our territory and to better ensure Jerusalem's future in the territory as a whole . . . and we are not burdening ourselves with an Arab population of an order of magnitude that threatens the demographic balance."[53]

This tried-and-true Zionist outlook, which was now copied into the context of Hebron, dated back to the days of the "tower and stockade" settlements of the 1930s—the establishment overnight of controlling Jewish settlements like elevated observation points surrounded by fences and walls in the heart of an Arab population. A historic religious right and the concern for security, two pillars of activist Zionism, were the firm arguments on which Jewish Hebron was established under the name of Kiryat Arba. On February 5, 1970, the ministerial committee on Hebron decided to set about planning the configuration of "Upper Hebron." The decision included authorization to build 250 housing units at the permanent site of the planned settlement for those who were already in Hebron.[54] On March 25, 1970, by a large majority of forty-eight in favor, five against, and seven abstentions, the Knesset approved the government's decision to establish Kiryat Arba. Before the vote, Knesset member Uri Avnery moved to strike the proposal from the house's agenda on the grounds that the government's decision "damages the chances for peace in the region." His motion was rejected. Allon, who by then was already minister of education and deputy prime minister, said in reply to Avnery: "The fact is that in the settlement by the group at that hotel, there was no violation of the law. . . . We must not come to terms with the fact that because of the murderous pogrom in 1929, we of our own volition will make Hebron empty of Jews."[55]

Eventually, when Kiryat Arba and Hebron had become a fact, as well as the hothouse of the entire settlement project, with its subversion and defiance of the law and of Israeli democracy, some who in their official capacity had been involved from the beginning admitted that the move had been a tragedy of errors and that the government had been dragged after the settlers' lies and tricks. "Kiryat Arba was a tragedy," said Shlomo Gazit, the first coordinator of activities in the territories, fifteen years later.[56] And Uzi Narkiss, who in his capacity as head of the Central Command allowed the settlers to hold their Passover ritual in Hebron, wrote about "the cunning manipulation of the political situation" by the settlers and about "the little trick" they played on him that was "destined to go very far."[57] It was a poor attempt to rewrite history and conceal the full cooperation of the government and army with the wild settlement.

Occupiers' Idyll

Overlooking ancient Hebron from the east, the ninety-dunam (22.5-acre) tract of land that was selected for the new township was spread over a high hill partly covered in vineyards and fruit trees. It is located about a fifteen-minute walk from the Tomb of the Patriarchs and commands a view of the entire area of Mount Hebron. The lovely hill was first seized by the military government "for military purposes." The vineyards were uprooted and the homes of the Palestinians who lived on the hilltop and the slopes were confiscated, evacuated, and razed. The owners of the land and the houses received nominal compensation. Before the first apartment houses were built, a military camp was set up, which was dismantled once the construction of the first 250 housing units was completed and the settlers moved in, leaving the civilian township behind on the hill.[58] The claim of "military purposes," which the High Court of Justice in Jerusalem recognized far too late as false, commenced its long history here. And as the construction of the first 250 apartments was proceeding at a rapid pace, Levinger demanded that the government expand it further to establish the Jewish settlement in "the city of the Patriarchs" and prepare plans for hundreds of additional apartments. He claimed that more than 300 families were ready to move in the moment the housing units were ready.[59]

In mid-June, the ceremony was held for the transfer of the first residential building at the site, and on the eve of Rosh Hashanah, 1971, the first fifty families moved into the new Jewish town-settlement.[60] Everything was done with the government's approval and with the taxpayers' money. And it was a Labor-led government. As the lands of Kiryat Arba had been expropriated from local owners, and this expropriation had no legal validity as long as the formal political status remained unclear, the tenants did not purchase the apartments but rather deposited a symbolic sum at the Ministry of Housing and paid monthly rent, also symbolic.[61] The veteran settlers in Hebron, who claimed that they had been "agonizing," as they said, for more than three years in the "prison" in the heart of the town, now preferred the spacious new apartments, and moved in without complaints. This original nucleus was joined by twenty families; altogether, the township was inhabited by fifty families.

From the very outset the Kiryat Arba settlers aimed at presenting a picture of a local idyll, of serenity between their religious and secular members as well as between them and the Arab inhabitants of Hebron. But tensions seethed beneath the surface. The disharmony was both internal, over the image and character of the community, and external, over political control of the settlement; there was discord in the government between the Labor ministers, who saw themselves as its founders and guardians, and the national-religious ministers.[62] Finally the Labor minister of housing informed the Knesset that a team from the Housing Ministry would be managing Kiryat Arba, as had been done successfully in the new Jewish towns of Upper Nazareth, Arad, and Carmiel within the Green Line. He added that Kiryat Arba was located in territories held by the IDF, and therefore that establishing any form of local governance was a matter for the military government.[63] A month later, on January 30, 1972, the government decided that Kiryat Arba would continue to be managed by the military.[64]

A story similar to the tranquil and peaceful coexistence within the boundaries of the new settlement was also recited in the Jewish-Arab context. "Security overrides all the difficulties. It is quiet in Hebron," reported *Ma'ariv.* The Arabs of Hebron did the construction work on Kiryat Arba. Local industry in Hebron assisted the Jewish building project, and was nurtured by it. Palestinian businesses thrived for a while on the new Jewish inhabitants, whose numbers increased. Something of an economic boom was felt, and the settlers began to take pride in the friendly relations they developed with local notables. It appeared as though good neighborly relations were developing with the families that lived close to the buildings of the Kirya.[65] But this was an occupiers' fictitious idyll. The State of Israel continued to expropriate Hebronite lands on the grounds of "military needs," and incidents between the Jewish settlers and the Arab inhabitants became commonplace.[66] Responding to the claim by the inhabitants of Hebron that they were not hostile to the settlers, Hebron Mayor Jabari said in February 1972 that the Jewish settlement had been greeted by strong protests from the inhabitants and owners of land that was expropriated. "If there have not been violent incidents by armed individuals against the [Jewish] settlement, this is only because the Arabs know that resistance of this sort will lead to the demolishing of the adjacent Arab neighborhoods."[67] The mayor's words were prophetic. As the years passed, this order of things became Hebron's claim to fame. Entire Arab neighborhoods in the heart of the town were abandoned as the result of the settlers' harassments and the Israeli army's idleness or cooperation.

The settlers' truth in regard to Arab Hebron and its inhabitants was exposed in a letter they sent to the prime minister. "Adjacent to an Arab town of 50,000 inhabitants (including many hostile people) there is the need for a Jewish town of 100,000. Therefore we call upon the government to decide on the transition from neighborhood to city and to set about immediately to build 5,000 housing units in Kiryat Arba. A small neighborhood surrounded by a fence and watchtowers does not make an impression in the midst of a population of 50,000. Only a Jewish locality of 100,000, with industrial projects, a broad road and electricity, will put the Arab town in the shadow of the Jewish town."[68]

The first large settlement in the territories did not attract the thousands they had expected, despite the wonderful climate, the inexpensive housing, and the commendable religious and national mission. Less than five years after the entry of the first Kiryat Arba settlers into the apartments in the large buildings clad in Hebron stone, it emerged that the vision had outpaced the reality. The government kept its word and built a fortified town in the desert, and the apartments stood empty. Of the 877 apartments that were built in Kiryat Arba by the end of 1977, only 400 were tenanted. The small, isolated community turned more and more inward. Kiryat Arba became a shabby development town where life was hard and bitter.[69] Seventy families who had been among the first settlers departed for other places. "I didn't see the ranks of Gush Emunim filling the vacant apartments in Kiryat Arba," said Israel Galili, head of the ministerial committee for settlement affairs and the disappointed patron of the settlers, in May 1976. "If only there could be found in Gush Emunim potential with the pathos of personal fulfillment. So far, a strange fire [Leviticus, 10:1] is burning there."[70] During daytime hours, most of the people visible in the streets of Kiryat Arba were Arab laborers. They carried out most of the work there, were employed in most of the services and in contributing to the redemption of Greater Israel, on the scaffoldings, while the Jews continued to earn their living in Jerusalem. "When Kiryat Arba is completed," said a senior officer, "the men will work in Jerusalem and the IDF will have to protect the place so that the Arabs won't harass the women and children."[71]

It seems that the only industry that flourished in Kiryat Arba was the yeshiva industry. Yeshivas and study houses of various sorts and leanings settled in the Kirya, and with them their rabbis and instructors, and their students, a large horde that fed off the Ministry of Religious Affairs and other government ministries. Of the 640 adults in the population in 1977, 140 were yeshiva students, and dozens more were employed in various capacities at the yeshivas.[72] Moshe Levinger and Rabbis Eliezer Waldman and Dov Lior, who headed the Kiryat Arba Yeshiva, set the tone in the new settlement, which became increasingly fanatical. The approaching days of the Messiah and the redemption were part of this community's routine menu. When Waldman, who had been a celebrant at the Passover night at the Park Hotel in 1968, was asked about his fears of a forced withdrawal, he replied that this fear was nonexistent for him. "It has never crossed my mind that there could be a withdrawal. . . . I believed then [in 1967] and I believe now that what has been fulfilled before our very eyes has been done according to the divine plan. The impetus to settle in Hebron arose mainly from the desire to be a part of the Holy Name's deeds and to have the privilege of taking part in the activity of redemption."[73] Later on, from the study houses headed by Waldman and Lior, emerged the people of a Jewish terrorist group, who cited their rabbis and teachers in their testimony to the police. After the 1994 massacre by Kiryat Arba resident Dr. Baruch Goldstein of Arab worshipers at the Tomb of the Prophets, that same Rabbi Lior raised Goldstein to the status of a just man and saint, comparing him to the martyrs of the Holocaust. From the yeshivas of Kiryat Arba also came rabbinical rulings to refuse to obey orders for the evacuation of settlements.

The Disgrace of Samaria

Within the ranks of the original Kiryat Arba settlers, the idea of settling Samaria (the northern West Bank) took shape along with the idea of the primary nucleus of Elon Moreh, the progenitor of the massive settlement in Samaria. The group was conceived in long discussions between two of the first Kiryat Arba settlers, Benny Katzover and Menachem Felix. They were a study pair at a yeshiva there, and the days of routine and dullness of Kiryat Arba that followed the excitement of its establishment led them to consider that the time had come to take further action. Katzover, a graduate of the national-religious yeshivas, had served in the Air Force and married his wife under a wedding canopy erected in the courtyard of the military government in Hebron, the first Jewish wedding in the newfound land. His friend Felix was a graduate of the Noam Seminary in Pardess Hannah and a student of the Merkaz HaRav Yeshiva in Jerusalem, the elite, obligatory trajectory of those who would eventually lead Gush Emunim. The two concluded in 1973 that the task in Judea in the southern West Bank had been accomplished, and that the time had come to launch an assault on the hills of Samaria, in the northern part of the territories. "There was talk among us about how 'something' in the leadership and the direction of the leadership of the crochet skullcaps wasn't right," related Katzover a decade later. "For about an entire year before the word *emunim* [faith] was mentioned, the decision was simmering inside us to set up a settlement nucleus for Nablus. . . . We closed our Jewish study books [*Gmarot*] and decided: We are going for the struggle for a Jewish hold on Samaria."[74]

The two began to gather around them families that were prepared to leave their homes in Kiryat Arba and head for the hills, and they sought a leader. Levinger was essential for Kiryat Arba and Hebron. Hannan Porat was "prepared to enlist in the battle, but not prepared ever to leave Kfar Etzion." The Yom Kippur War (October 1973), with its devastating effects on Israeli society and on these young believers in particular, reshuffled everything, and was the opening shot in the big move. When they returned from the war and the reserve duty that followed it, there was already talk about interim agreements in Sinai. "At that time we came to the realization that the games were over," said Katzover. "No more political negotiations and no more love affair with Israel Galili—we're heading for the territories!"[75]

The struggle for the hills of Samaria had begun. This time it swept up hundreds of people from all over the country. We plucked "a real string," said Hannan Porat. This was during the transitional period between Golda Meir and Yitzhak Rabin as prime minister. The members of the settlement nucleus assembled in the Jordan Valley, and from there they planned to set out for Hawara, just south of Nablus. Defense Minister Shimon Peres was "summoned" to Rabbi Zvi Yehudah Kook, who tried to persuade him to allow the group to settle at Hawara by agreement. Peres said that the entire government would have to decide on any settlement near Nablus. But in early June 1974 the convoy set out with the blessings of the rabbi; General (Res.) Ariel Sharon, who had just achieved hero status during the 1973 war and was making his way into politics on the shoulders of the settlers; and religious members of the government, who came to express solidarity with the settlers.[76] The evacuation at Hawara following the government's decision was swift and relatively calm, but the pictures of the young skullcap-wearing settlers struggling with the soldiers found their place in the archive of the collective consciousness and had their effect. "Do you really think that the government is going to go after every caprice of every hundred guys?" demanded Yitzhak Rabin, who had recently become prime minister.[77]

The second settlement attempt, at the old train station at Sebastia at the end of July 1974, was already a different story. Many Knesset members and journalists and thousands of supporters accompanied it. After the traumatic evacuation from the old Turkish train station, to the stones of which the settlers clung as though they were the building blocks of the Temple, the heads of Elon Moreh met for the first time with the heads of Gush Emunim. The two groups merged, agreeing that the movement would not be affiliated with any political party and that their joint mode of action was decided—"actual, physical settlement in the territory."[78] All the activities, settlement actions (four times to Sebastia, as well as Ma'aleh Adumim, Shiloh, and Ofra) in 1975 and 1976, the *hakafot* (circumnavigations with Torah scrolls), the marches, and the demonstrations that attracted more and more supporters were thenceforth organized under the banner of Gush Emunim.[79]

The barrier that impeded settlement attempts in the heart of the Palestinian population in the West Bank was smashed in April 1975, with the establishment of the settlement of Ofra in the Benjamin region.[80] Ofra was the first big Gush Emunim project and a successful model for the mode of political-messianic action that had just taken shape. It arose in the midst of the struggle for Elon Moreh and created the precedent for the Sebastia compromise and thence to settlement throughout the occupied territories. The settlement takes its name from a biblical site that is located about eight kilometers (five miles) southwest of the site that is considered to be ancient Shiloh. Ofra was the capital of the region that had been transferred from the Kingdom of Samaria to the Kingdom of Judea in the year 145 B.C., and an important settlement during the Hasmonean period.[81] The home of the settler nobility, Ofra is located on the mountain ridge on the road from Ramallah to the Jordan Valley, in a particularly lush and beautiful landscape at one of the highest elevations in the area of southern Samaria. Inflexible membership rules, strict adherence to uniform construction, and advanced and sophisticated community management created a model settlement in Ofra both in its external appearance and its human and ideological quality. Its inhabitants define it as "a mission-oriented religious communal village."[82]

The biographies of the two rather symbolic settlements, which represent the two extremes of the varied settler populace, Kiryat Arba and Ofra, and which were established close in time to each other, testify to the extent to which the ramified story of the settlements could not have been predicted in advance. Kiryat Arba, which was established openly, by the decision of a government that was led by the Labor movement, planned in advance and with generous budgets, was supposed to have been a true "city in Israel," part of a larger plan of occupation and control. Instead it became a small town, somnambulant and failed, full of religious institutions but godforsaken and awash with cults of graves and death, where the inhabitants live in the shadow of murderous terror attacks. Ofra, on the other hand, which was established in trickery and on false pretexts, flourished into the heart of the Israeli consensus because of its respectable appearance, the settlers' flagship institutions that were established there, and the mellifluous discourse of some of its better-known inhabitants.[83]

The story of Ofra began like so many other settlements that came after it. A nucleus from the newly established Gush Emunim movement decided to settle in the heart of a densely populated Palestinian area. Three unauthorized attempts at settling on the land ended in evacuations. Yehuda Etzion, who was eventually to become a member of a Jewish terrorist group, began to enlist support for the idea of setting up a work brigade, like those of the mythological third *aliyah* (immigration wave) in the early 1920s, as a means for advancing the settlement. The plan was to obtain work in the region, preferably in the service of the army, and later on to find a way to sleep overnight at the workplace, thus creating facts on the ground. The work brigade that he formed found employment with a contractor from Jerusalem who was carrying out work on the military camp in Samaria. The defense minister's adviser on settlement affairs, who came from the Labor movement, signed the official permit for the Gush Emunim work brigade to be hired for the job. It was Hanukkah time then, and the permit was perceived as a small miracle. For eight months the group excavated the rocky hill and at night returned home to Jerusalem.[84] On the eve of Israel's Independence Day, 1975, they decided that the time was ripe. They were sent hints that Defense Minister Shimon Peres was looking for a way to approve their settlement in the area, and that if they made their move quietly and without publicity, and the settlement was called a "work camp," with no mention of a "permanent settlement," there was a chance that they would be allowed to stay. The project of sleeping at the work site was planned down to the smallest detail and in coordination with well-connected people at the Defense Ministry who supported the idea: At 5 P.M. exactly, the time when they would enter the houses, these officials would report to the defense minister about the move. The timing was critical for the success. Too early a report to the minister, they feared, was liable to give rise to postponement and procrastination, whereas a later report might mean that the army would report on it to the minister first. On April 20, 1975, at the agreed-upon time, the members of the group entered the houses. They numbered twenty men and three women.[85]

To the Israeli military governor of Ramallah, who demanded that they leave, the settlers replied that they would do so only "on condition that he report right up to the level of the defense minister." Peres's response was a demand to evacuate. "You want to crush and oppress," Hannan Porat lamented angrily to the senior army officer who brought Peres's response. "Don't you understand that you cannot but give an outlet to the cry of the land of Israel?" Later, the governor of Ramallah received an instruction not to touch the settlers, either way, until the next morning. The following day the governor received a renewed instruction not to help them—but not to hinder them either.[86]

Behind the scenes a small drama was under way. Hannan Porat, the Gush Emunim liaison to Shimon Peres, hastened together with Uri Elitzur, one of the original Ofra settlers, to the Defense Minister's headquarters in Tel Aviv. The two requested Peres to permit ten to twelve members of Gush Emunim to sleep overnight in the area. Peres, whose mind was on other matters, was not alert enough to the future significance of Porat's request. In his book *Dear Brothers*, Hagai Segal described the meeting between Porat and Peres, as reported by Porat himself. "Minister," demanded the thirty-year-old settler of the experienced, rather blasé defense minister who was many years older than him, "whether you agree to our position or not, you will not be able to deny the true spirit of awakening that is at the foundation of our repeated attempts to settle in Samaria. You must give some release to this wakening, some kind of positive outlet. Otherwise, a sharp clash will not be long in coming." "How can I ensure," asked the minister, who had seen a few political tricks in his long career, "that you will not trumpet this as a victory over the government?" Porat promised the defense minister that the move would be made "with the lowest of profiles."[87] Peres gave in. "What am I supposed to do? Send out forces at 9 or 10 at night to evacuate them by force?" asked Peres of his advisers in one of those rhetorical questions at which he became so expert during his years in politics. "So let them stay there, but allow them to bring a generator. If, God forbid, they are attacked and something happens to them, there will be an outcry in this country that 'ten Jews were abandoned'—give them a minimum of security." After a consultation with Prime Minister Rabin, Peres authorized Gush Emunim to remain at the site, on condition that they see to a generator themselves and follow instructions from the army.[88]

Diligent in Their Business

This is how the soldiers of the Messiah, people diligent in their business, leapt over secretaries, officials, and advisers, cut corners, and shortened political corridors in order to appear before ministers and the top people. One of the first commentators on Gush Emunim, journalist Danny Rubinstein, wrote in 1982 in his book *On the Lord's Side* that no minutes were kept of the dozens of conversations that settler leaders held with government ministers, Knesset members, and politicos of all the parties in the spring and summer of 1974. They were Moshe Levinger, Hannan Porat, Haim Druckman, Yoel Bin-Nun, Benny Katzover, Gershon Shafat, and other Gush Emunim activists. All became household names. Both sides preferred to preserve secrecy and vagueness about the meetings. Along with a great many reprimands and criticism, the settlers also heard words of praise and admiration, and received good "tactical" advice. The dark times in the wake of the Yom Kippur War apparently needed a refreshing phenomenon such as this group of young, dedicated people, who were willing to thrust themselves, body and soul, on the sacred land, cling to it and love it in an unrestrained way, and on behalf of the entire nation. "The mixed feelings, opposition and even revulsion on the one hand, nostalgia and closeness on the other, towards this group, gave rise to consternation, running around and ultimately—to the absence of an unambiguous government position," wrote Rubinstein.[89]

From the moment the defense minister's initial authorization was given to sleep over at the place, Gush Emunim organized itself quickly. Groups and individuals from all over the country came to help, bringing along whatever came to hand—tents, old rifles from the heroic days of 1948, a small generator, a water tanker, and camp beds. The first women joined their husbands, and by the time the Ofra camp had been there for one week, the wails of the first baby could be heard.[90] At the gate a sign was put up that said "Ofra—Work Camp," and at the camp mobile dwellings were refurbished, roads were paved, water and electricity lines were brought in, and primary public services were put in place. All of this was done, according to the settlers, out of "joy and devotion," with no help from the official settlement institutions.[91] The existence of a new Jewish settlement in the heart of Samaria was revealed only at the beginning of June 1975 in *Ha'aretz*. "A permanent Gush Emunim settlement has existed for a month and a half now northeast of Ramallah, without government permission and without even having been brought up for discussion by any authorized bodies. The settlement, which is known by the name Ba'al Hatzor or Ofra Camp, is populated by a few dozen people, members of Gush Emunim, among them twenty-five permanent workers of whom eight have families that live together with them at the site. . . . The settlement was established with a new Gush tactic: avoiding spectacular actions and creating facts on the ground. . . . The settlers say that they have kept the existence of the camp secret, for fear that publicizing it could lead to the failure of the idea," reported the newspaper.[92]

Knesset Member Yossi Sarid, at that time a member of the Labor Party and like most people still naïve about the settlers' doings, could not believe his eyes during the visit he made to the quasi-secret "work camp." "It is hard to understand how a settlement in every respect has arisen without a government decision," said Sarid. Following a parliamentary question he submitted, the Knesset Foreign Affairs and Defense Committee came to Ofra. "Its members were impressed and amazed by what they saw. Knesset member Meir Talmi of Mapam [the most left-wing of the Labor Zionist parties] even wondered where youth like that could be found today. The committee froze its treatment of the matter," reported the Gush Emunim bulletin that bore the title "Ofra—a fence that established a settlement."[93]

The official who played a key role in the transition of Ofra from a sleeping site for workers to a permanent, viable settlement, who granted the group the first permit to bring their wives and children, was the defense minister's adviser Moshe Netzer, who felt very kindly disposed to Gush Emunim, and who probably believed his actions represented his minister's wish, if not his declared positions. Netzer, a scion of old Labor apparatchiks, said that Peres and Galili supported turning the place into a real settlement, while Prime Minister Rabin had more reservations, although he refrained from imposing a veto. For Justice Minister Haim Zadok, it sufficed that the place would remain defined as a "military work camp," as by law and custom a military camp can always be removed. However, the accelerated development of Ofra thwarted any attempt to evacuate the "camp," an option that was not even seriously considered. When the political leaders woke up to reflect on the nature and consequences of the "work camp" that had been established in a densely populated Palestinian area, there were already fifty families living there. The Ofra outpost revealed Gush Emunim's real grand design: settlement in strategic locations, deep into the land of the Palestinians, and not necessarily at sacred sites or on the ruins of imagined patriarchal tombs.

Defense Minister Peres was the good Samaritan of Ofra. He also knew how to maneuver with time. When asked by the settlers when he intended to raise their plight in the government, he replied: "When the conditions are right."[94] And Peres saw to it that the conditions would be right. The official body that was supposed to deal with the matter was the ministerial committee for settlement issues, and the committee was not able to discuss Ofra because it was not defined as a settlement point but rather as a military work camp—that is, as far as the committee was concerned, it did not exist at all. Semantic hair-splitting of this sort continues to accompany the settlement project to this day, especially with respect to the outposts. The absorption minister from Mapam, Shlomo Rosen, demanded that the matter of Ofra be discussed in the government but heard Rabin's lament along the lines of "What can I do? I'm not responsible!" In the end, when it was no longer possible to ignore the "facts on the ground," the issue of Ofra was tossed to the ministerial committee on settlement. The committee also had reservations about supporting Ofra, mostly for economic reasons. However, the national-religious ministers, headed by the young Gush Emunim adherent Zevulun Hammer, applied pressure, and Peres himself urged that Ofra be recognized. He publicly recognized the existence of "a civilian work camp" at Ofra, stressing the importance of the camp to the regional defense of Jerusalem. In the wake of Peres's coming out of the closet and with the support of Galili and Allon, the ministerial committee recognized the settlement. This decision led in effect to the "laundering" of the phantom settlement. From the moment it was recognized as a civilian settlement, Ofra was officially entitled to government support, which until then had been given surreptitiously in indirect ways.[95]

Peres Plants a Tree

At a festive ceremony in December 1975, a dining hall and a first internal road were dedicated at Ofra. Toward the end of that winter, on Tu B'shvat (Jewish Arbor Day), 1976, Peres came to celebrate with the Ofra settlers, encouraged them, and was given the honor of planting a tree. In response to the left's accusation that with his own hands he had established a new settlement not in accordance with a government decision, Peres said from the Knesset podium that in June 1975 he had already approved the arrangement for sleeping at Ofra, "after consulting with the people I thought I should consult. . . . We informed the people there that we did not recognize this place— either as a settlement or as a residential locale." Peres added that for the decision about the sleeping arrangement in the territory, the agreement of the two or three ministers concerned was sufficient.[96] Researcher Peter Demant says that the other minister whom Peres consulted was Prime Minister Rabin.[97] As in Hebron before, the army served in Ofra as a lever and justification for the establishment of a Jewish settlement, and the paradoxical interdependence between state security needs and the interests of occupation and settlement was set in motion. Yet as history goes, what was claimed to be crucial for security became a security liability and required more and more military forces for its security.

The Ofra pioneers were in no hurry to share the bounty of their great victory with just anyone who happened along. The "mission-oriented religious communal village" took great care to preserve its homogenous human and social fabric. Its members were selective and demanding about the acceptance requirements for candidates to join their ranks, painstakingly sorting every man and woman who wanted to settle with them on the disputed land that had been given to them at almost no cost (every family at that time paid 700 Israeli pounds a month, at about six pounds to the U.S. dollar, for a new apartment of forty square meters, or 430 square feet).[98] Not everyone could board the flagship of Gush Emunim. Candidates were required to face an admissions committee and obtain a graphologist's assessment and a special permit from the Jewish Agency.[99] Anyone who had not been a member of the founding nucleus was considered a "new immigrant."[100]

Settlement vs. Racism

As the matter of the new settlement of Ofra rolled back and forth between the two sides of the Green Line, between the settlers and the authorities, on November 10, 1975, Israel's ambassador to the United Nations, Haim Herzog, stepped up to the podium of the General Assembly. The guest balcony was filled with Israeli diplomats and Jewish invitees, who by their presence meant to protest an anti-Israeli resolution. The proposed resolution invoked Resolution 3151 of December 14, 1973, which deplored "the unholy alliance between South African racism and Zionism." It also took note of Resolution 77, which had been adopted by the Assembly of Heads of State and Government of the Organization of African Unity, which had been held in Kampala, Uganda, at the end of June 1975, and stated that "the racist regime in occupied Palestine and the racist regime in Zimbabwe and South Africa have a common imperialist origin, forming a whole and having the same racist structure." The General Assembly was also asked to take note of "the Political Declaration and Strategy to Strengthen International Peace and Security and to Intensify Solidarity and Mutual Assistance among Non-Aligned Countries, adopted at the Conference of Ministers for Foreign Affairs of Non-Aligned Countries held at Lima from 25 to 30 August 1975, which most severely condemned Zionism as a threat to world peace and security and called upon all countries to oppose this racist and imperialist ideology." Seventy-two member countries voted in favor of the resolution, thirty-five voted against it, and thirty-two abstained.[101]

Herzog, a retired major general and the son of the first chief rabbi of Israel, knew a thing or two about the art of speech making. After whispering a verse from the Yom Kippur liturgy, "Our God and God of our fathers, be with the mouth of the messenger of your nation, the House of Israel," Herzog said: "It is symbolic that this debate, which may well prove to be a turning point in the fortunes of the United Nations and a decisive factor in the possible continued existence of this organization, should take place on November 10. Tonight, thirty-seven years ago, has gone down in history as Kristall-nacht, the Night of the Crystals."[102] Herzog thus made the inevitable, always effective umbilical link between Israel and the Holocaust. "The vote of each delegation will record in history its country's stand on anti-Semitic racism and anti-Judaism. You yourselves bear the responsibility for your stand before history, for as such will you be viewed in history. We, the Jewish people, will not forget. . . . For us, the Jewish people, this resolution based on hatred, falsehood and arrogance, is devoid of any moral or legal value."[103]

The spirit of what had happened at the General Assembly gave impetus to the Gush Emunim settlement attempt at Sebastia, at a time when the name of the United Nations was being eradicated from streets and squares countrywide. A special international Jewish soli-darity conference called by the government and the Jewish Agency declared that "the Jewish people has an historical right to the land of Israel." It was for just such a propitious moment that Gush Emunim had been waiting since its efforts to settle there were foiled by the army in the summer of 1974. Rabbi Kook's disciples knew well the weaknesses and soft spots of the political establishment that stood in their way, the 1948 vintage. The wearers of the crochet skullcaps knew all too well that the hearts of the bearers of the former, classic settlement ethos would not, at this perilous hour, allow them to raise a hand against young, energetic "pioneers." In these young people they saw the fervor and the hope that had faded in them since the disaster of the Yom Kippur War. Employing the army against the settlers at a time when Jews from all over the world were flocking to the capital of Israel to demonstrate solidarity and a commonality of fate would have focused attention on the disagreement and polarity among Jews in their own country—and delighted our enemies, thought Prime Minister Rabin.[104] Indeed, a statement published by Gush Emunim said that "the settlement at Elon Moreh is a direct continuation of Zionist fulfillment and persistence, like the establishment of Ein Gev, Gadot, Hulata and the other moshavim along the Northern Road."[105]

Gush Emunim did not make do with exploiting the proximity in time to the UN resolution and the historical event of *Kristallnacht*. Its members decided to wait until the Hanukkah festival, at which time Israel proudly celebrates its ancestors' heroic fight against the gentiles. This is also children's vacation from school. Could there be a more appropriate Zionist response than establishing a Jewish settlement, during the days of Hanukkah, on the ruins of biblical Samaria and the city of Sebastia, which had been built by Herod? On the eve of the Hanukkah Sabbath, Gush Emunim published in the newspapers a call to its supporters: "We call upon you, who see how the Jewish people is abandoned to the hatchets of the Palestinian Liberation Organization in the corridors of the UN, suffering the insult of portions of the land of Israel that are empty of Jews, seeing the government of Israel in its weakness and impotence in face of the plan for the Palestinian state that is simmering in Samaria: Come with us. Get out of the house, put off all your business and join the great move of the Jewish people that is returning home."[106] The paid advertisement gave detailed information about the settlement project. In contrast to previous operations that had been planned and implemented secretly, this time Gush Emunim was determined to turn Sebastia into the site of a showdown with the authorities.

"We were in the midst of the preparations for going to Sebastia, and it was like getting organized for a huge military operation," wrote Meir Harnoy, one of the heads of Gush Emunim. "There were many teams dealing with all the administrative aspects, from mapping the territory to the main thing—that is, raising funds for the operation ... transportation, preparations for an extended stay there, marching routes, alternative routes and, no less important—a rear command headquarters that would follow us and help throughout the operation."[107] But this time the masses did not flock to the hills of Samaria.[108] The army too, despite its expectations of a huge crowd and its own preparations, did not evince much determination in facing the settlers.[109] In his memoirs, Yitzhak Rabin later wrote that many of the Gush Emunim people managed to infiltrate through the IDF roadblocks even though "we knew in advance about the intention of the Gush people and their supporters and orders had been given to prevent them from going against the government's decision."[110] The prime minister was under the impression that the orders of Defense Minister Peres to the military "had been issued half-heartedly or had been carried out sloppily." In reply to the prime minister's question, Chief of Staff Mordechai (Motta) Gur said that there was a need for no less than 5,000 soldiers to evict the invaders, and that the evacuation would take "a few days." The prime minister believed that the chief of staff was unwilling to order his subordinates to evict the settlers.[111]

Only on the second day of the invasion of Sebastia, when it became known that the barriers were easily broken through, did masses of people begin to flock there. Toward evening, a convoy of about 400 supporters arrived from Jerusalem, headed by Menachem Begin, Ariel Sharon, and other right-wing leaders. Rabbis and delegations from kibbutzim came to express their support for the settlers.[112] Delegates from the Jewish solidarity conference joined in the ceremonies of affixing mezuzahs. Gershon Shafat, a Gush Emunim leader, wrote that Rabin's decision to refrain from evicting them during the solidarity conference is what gave them the time to get organized and to fortify the settlement both physically and politically.[113]

Sebastia's Blame

Choking with rage at the circumstantial contingency created by the UN event and its immediate effect on the status of the newly established Gush Emunim, Rabin decided to take other measures, and sent the defense minister to conduct negotiations with the settlers. He also delegated his adviser for security matters, Ariel Sharon, to be responsible for evacuating the settlers at Sebastia to a military camp.[114] Yet another example of those historical ironies. Seven days after the settlers dug in at Sebastia, as rumors were spreading in the temporary settlement that the eviction was scheduled for the following day, the defense minister's helicopter landed there. Peres jumped out of the helicopter and secluded himself with the squatters in the old, abandoned Turkish train station.[115] A veritable frenzy took over the settlers. They danced, sang, and tore their clothing; there were even those who flagellated and injured themselves. Rabbi Levinger came into the meeting with Peres, his face covered in blood from self-inflicted scratches.[116] Poet and *Davar* correspondent Haim Gouri, a Palmach veteran, a close friend of the prime minister's, and a prominent public figure, also joined the meeting between the defense minister and the settler leadership. Also present were senior army officers, the minister's adviser, and his bureau chief. From this point, the versions of what happened there diverge.

According to Peres's version, Sharon and Gouri proposed that the settlers leave the site immediately and that thirty people transfer to the nearby military camp to await a new discussion in the government. A similar idea, which had been brought up during the attempt to settle at nearby Hawara, had been rejected at the time by Rabbi Zvi

Yehudah Kook. This time, the settler leaders voted in favor of the compromise. "The compromise was a great achievement and tantamount to an opening for settlement in all of Judea and Samaria," predicted settlers, without knowing just how correct their prediction would prove.[117] Gouri's version was different. In an article he published many years later in *Ha'aretz*, he attributed most of the responsibility in the Sebastia affair to Peres. "I was under the impression the settlers wanted to climb down the tree they had climbed up and that the minister and the general were also looking for a way to avoid a violent clash between troops and thousands of people, including pregnant women," wrote Gouri. But in a document in the defense minister's own handwriting, says Gouri, the latter's proposal that thirty individuals be transferred to the nearby military camp became a proposal that "'The Elon Moreh group, numbering thirty families, will move to the military camp in the area and enjoy freedom of movement. . . . *Vive la différence*. From thirty people to thirty families.'"[118] Gouri also noted that at that time Peres was close to Moshe Dayan, who favored establishing six cities on the mountain ridge and was the main political force behind the settlement of Ofra. Later, Peres argued that "if the government is freezing and preventing settlement in places appropriate for settlement, then this is writing a White Paper for ourselves," noting that "the settlement in the western slopes of the hills of Samaria and Judea is what will redeem us from the disgrace of Israel's narrow hips."[119] Gouri also took some blame. "I do not absolve myself of involvement in the story. But the compromise that was 'accepted by the settlers' was all his," he wrote, with reference to Peres.[120]

Ariel Sharon, however, had no regrets about his role. Of his contribution to the precedent-setting compromise at Sebastia, he said that if indeed he did have a part in achieving the compromise it was for this alone that his stint under Yitzhak Rabin at the Prime Minister's Office had been worthwhile. This, he said, served as an incentive for him to postpone his intention to resign from his post as the prime minister's adviser.[121] Rabin convened his government to confirm the compromise proposal. Secular, rationalist, and decent almost to naïveté, Rabin hated the settler phenomenon. In Gush Emunim he saw "a very grave phenomenon—a cancer in the body of Israeli democracy." Their entire worldview and their modes of action were alien to him and, as he said, contrary to Israel's democratic basis. An ideological war must be waged against them that would expose the true significance of the Gush positions and modes of action, he said. Such a war, thought Rabin, could not be conducted only with IDF bayonets, and it would not stand a chance as long as the Labor Party was split in its attitude toward the Gush and as long as the defense minister saw its people as "true idealists."[122]

For the moment, however, Rabin proposed taking a softer tactical approach toward the settlers. "The evictions just strengthen them," he said. "Let's give them permission to go into the Qadum camp, and three weeks later they'll all go home," he added, thus testifying to the extent to which he and his colleagues in the old political guard were blind to the new sort of messianic-political energies that had erupted in Israel's public sphere. Most of the ministers had reservations about the possibility of allowing the settlers to remain in the area. Several warned that settling in Samaria would narrow Israel's room for maneuver when the time came to negotiate with the Arab side. Others warned of a precedent of submitting to pressures from lawbreakers. The compromise was authorized after Rabin threatened to resign if members of the government refused to approve it. Justly, the settlers saw the move they had forced on the government as a victory from which there was no way back. "The heads of Gush Emunim who came out to the site joined the dances and were carried on the shoulders of their friends as leaders who had succeeded in their mission and were receiving from the public the honor they deserved. . . . For many, including myself, there was a sense of another step, as a continuation of the day the state was established. Now I could understand in an unmediated experience the joy of the dancers who came out to the streets on the 29th of November," wrote Meir Harnoy.[123]

In a debate held in the Labor-led Alignment Knesset group on December 9, 1975, no vote was taken after Rabin again threatened that if the faction's decision was opposed to that of the government it would make it impossible for the government to remain in power.[124] However, the exchanges at the meeting were instructive. It was a kind of reckoning of conscience, during which issues of principle and history arise that are rarely discussed in such forums. The first speaker, Yitzhak Navon, who was later to become the president of Israel, said that he would not have been alarmed "had the government decided to establish a settlement at Sebastia. It is entitled to. So that if I'm speaking now, it's not about the political aspect, but about what is happening here in this country with respect to the regime and with respect to the government's authority. . . . The government has dangerously cast its own authority, influence and strength into question." Yigal Allon, one of the founders of the illegal Hebron settlement, spoke about the authority and obligations of the prime minister and the defense minister. They "had to decide how to proceed. . . . I think they made the correct decision. But I am very worried about how we in the government allowed ourselves to reach a situation like this, of no alternative." Allon, who had been a full partner to the disruption of proper governance and had lent a hand to the Hebron settlers' deceptions some years earlier, said now that "the problem is not only one of democracy. The problem is entirely one of statesmanship of the very first order and a problem of proper governance in Israel." Justice Minister Haim Zadok labeled the Sebastia affair "Altalena 1975," referring to the incident in 1948 when the newly formed IDF opened fire, at Prime Minister Ben-Gurion's orders, on a ship off the coast of Tel Aviv that was bringing weapons to the Irgun Zvai Leumi, which was supposed to have been incorporated into the IDF. Zadok said the Sebastia affair was aimed at undermining the government and the regime both domestically and in the eyes of the rest of the world.[125] The settlers' second in their duel with the government, Shimon Peres, repulsed the critics. "It was not just Gush Emunim," he said. "Inside the camp [in Sebastia] there were people from the established agricultural settlements and kibbutzim of all stripes. . . . A democratic regime has to respect the law, but there are laws, and there are very many of them, about which the government is authorized by the legislator to use its judgment as to how to enforce them. The law does not blindly and automatically command the government to use it [the law] alone. . . . Even though the law says that every individual must be conscripted into the IDF the defense minister, not because of provisions that exist in the law but *for reasons that reach into the very soul of the nation*, exempts certain people from conscription. . . . In my opinion, I have been given the authority, not in an unknown situation but rather on the background of what is known, to manage the issue. As someone who does not scorn the desires and pressures of Gush Emunim—I think that they are good citizens and good settlers—I do not think that Gush Emunim should dictate policy to the government."[126]

Peres's words uttered in the Knesset group quarters did not impress the young Knesset member Yossi Sarid. "The government needs to clarify to itself whether it is dealing with a political provocation or with burning faith," said Sarid. "In this case there is a trampling of the principle that no negotiations are conducted before evacuation. The

moment the principle is trampled, the dam to settlement is burst."
Prime Minister Rabin asked, "When was there a principle that there
are no negotiations?" and Sarid, who foresaw the future better than
others, replied that "in this case the settlers determined the outcome,
because they wanted to establish a fait accompli in the heart of Samaria
that had not been there before, and they did. And it does not matter in
the slightest whether they established it twelve kilometers from Sebastia
or at some other point." Do you believe, Sarid asked the prime minister, "that in three months' time, after they have settled into the army
camp, you are going to get them out of there 'without violence'? What
kind of argument is it 'without violence'? No matter how long this is
postponed, it will turn out that this was nothing but an illusion. And
it will be something many times worse."[127]

Rabin was not blind to the danger of the Sebastia compromise.
Precisely the opposite. "I see it as one of the most serious problems
of confrontation we have had to deal with," said the prime minister at
the Knesset meeting. "The group that calls itself Gush Emunim, as a
group, an outlook and a way, is threatening the democratic way of life
in the state of Israel, and confronting it must be done on all levels. . . .
I have no illusion that with the agreement we ended the confrontation
. . . because the aim is to use lawbreaking to impose a way." But the
prime minister did not summon up the determination needed to confront the dedication of Peres and Sharon, who were helping the settlers establish themselves at the military base.

On May 9, 1976, more than half a year after the settlement moved
in, the time came for the government to discuss the fact of its existence
and its future. With a majority of fourteen votes, it was decided that
"no settlement will be established at Qadum." It was also decided that
"at a date in the near future that will be determined by the government,
the nucleus will move from Qadum to a permanent settlement, which

will take into consideration the government's settlement plan. Until then nothing will be done at Qadum that would turn the site into a permanent settlement." It was clear, however, to all debating parties that the absence of a definite date for removing the settlement from its location was in fact an insurance document for future existence of the settlement and that the affair had come to an end.

Ten days later the government discussed the settlement policy in the West Bank. Yigal Allon admitted that were he able to do so, he would "try to change some decisions that were taken during the Sebastia affair."[128] Shimon Peres proposed setting up a civilian camp next to the military camp and suggested that its inhabitants would work in the center of the country. "I prefer that he [the settler] have a home in Qadum and Tel Aviv rather than in Caesarea and Tel Aviv. . . . There is nothing 'wild' about the current settlement at Qadum. Let them stay there until the government decides within a month or two on the fate of settlement across the Green Line." The head of the National Religious Party, Yosef Burg, said, "I do not think all that highly of the settlement at Qadum. Thirty settlers in one place or another are not going to change the face of Jewish history, but removing them by force is an act that runs counter to good sense and counter to the unity of the people."[129]

Seven months after the government decision that "no permanent settlement will be established at Qadum and that in the near future the nucleus of settlers will be removed from there," Benny Katzover boasted that "the Defense Ministry recognizes our existence and is even sharing with us the expenses of guarding the place." The Communications Ministry installed the first telephone at the site. On instructions from the Transportation Ministry a daily bus was instituted from Tel Aviv to Qadum, and the Histadrut labor federation health service opened a clinic there. But the young settler nevertheless had complaints to the government. "As far as the Education Ministry goes, for example, we do not exist," he said. "Another ministry that does not recognize us is the Finance Ministry. At Qadum they are 'dying' to pay income tax—and it isn't accepted from them."[130] After all, how is it possible to collect taxes from virtual inhabitants of a place that does not exist?

It was Israel Galili, the settlements' advocate and master of vagueness, who suggested the language of the decision: "The government will increase the settlement efforts on both sides of the Green Line, in accordance with the government's decision, and on the basis of this government's policy guidelines that were approved by the Knesset. . . . The government will prevent settlement attempts that do not receive its approval, which are contrary to the law and contrary to Israel's security and peace policy."[131] When Galili was asked why the government opposed settlement in Samaria, he obfuscated and said, "The government has not adopted a common and obligatory ideology with respect to non-settlement in Samaria, just as it has not taken a decision that closes off this or that region of the country." Since the war, said Galili, the government has been deciding where settlements will be established and not where settlements will not be established. When asked for his reaction to the U.S. State Department's statement of May 12, 1976, which expressed opposition to Israeli settlement in any part of the occupied territories, he said that he did not wish to attribute responsibility for the American statement to the affair of Sebastia and Qadum, but added in his convoluted way: "We must stick to a clear distinction between the basic needs that justify settlement and irresponsible initiatives or reactions that end in weighing on settlement and alarming hostile elements into taking an active policy against us, if not worse."[132] A few minutes before the vote in the government, the minutes record the prophetic words of Justice Minister Haim Zadok. "I hope that

Sebastia and Qadum will not go down in history as an example of the government relinquishing its authority," he said.

Eleven months later, on April 17, 1977, Rabin's government approved the establishment of a new settlement in the territories, adjacent to the Qadum military base. It was named Kedumim. The Sebastia affair was indeed a turning point in the history of Gush Emunim and of the entire Jewish settlement project. "Here, at this place and at this hour, the first stake of the revolution in the perception of settlement in Israel was driven in," wrote Harnoy. "Here the stake was also driven in for the political change that occurred in 1977, when the Likud came into power, for the first time since the establishment of the state."[133] This historical diagnosis was correct. Though Peres and others in the Labor movement had tried to placate the settlers, "because they were good citizens and good settlers," and "for reasons that reach into the very soul of the nation," as Peres had said, when the day for the quid pro quo came along these "good citizens" had no compunctions about turning their backs on the people who had stood by them at Ofra and Sebastia, and instead supported en masse the Labor Party's historical rival.[134] With a fair amount of justice, the Gush Emunim people attributed the Likud victory in the 1977 elections to themselves and their increasing influence on Israeli politics. On May 17, 1977, the Israeli voter handed political control to the rightist parties headed by the Likud under the leadership of Menachem Begin. The illusion that it was possible both to satisfy the settlers and to keep the option of peace and compromise intact was thrown into the face of the Labor movement.

More than that, the outcome of the elections revealed the existence of a new political force in Israel, still half-hidden and unexpected in its innovative modes of action and effectiveness. Since then, there has been no political struggle or public debate in Israel on the matter of the country's future, the fate of the territories and politicians' life expectancies that has not derived from the settlers' words and actions, even though they have remained a minority. A few days before his death, Yigal Allon, one of the fathers of settlement in the territories, told an acquaintance of his from Ofra, settler leader and publicist Israel Harel, that "we will never forgive you for removing us from power."[135] The pragmatist philosophy of "another acre and another goat," which had guided the pioneers of secular socialist Zionism and established the state, had now been confiscated by the new alliance of the Revisionists and the national-religious, and had become their tool.

2
Bad Faith

The political earthquake that occurred on May 17, 1977, was very much felt in the Jewish settlements. After years of battling the government and the army, the settlers heard the music of the Messiah's approach and celebrated. "Dancing, singing, a kind of Independence Day eve, almost November 29, 1947," rhapsodized one of them later.[1] Two days after the elections, accompanied by television crews and journalists from Israel and abroad, Prime Minister–elect Menachem Begin came to the settlement of Qadum in Samaria—a settlement that had been forced on the Labor-led government in the twilight of its rule—and was greeted with dance and song in settler style. "These are liberated territories, which belong to the Jewish people," declared Begin. "The new government will call upon young people to come and settle the land." However, the eternal oppositionist who had now been elected prime minister was well aware of the essential difference between the limitless latitude available to the leader of the opposition and a prime minister's limitations. "Judea and Samaria," he said, "must not be annexed to Israel." Then he added, with a kind of Talmudic casuistry, "because in any case it is our land and not a matter of land that belongs to others." These declarations, and the photographs that show Begin hugging a Torah scroll to his chest under a large wedding canopy surrounded by a crowd of settlers in the heart of the disputed territory, elicited sharp international reactions.

As the uproar over the prime minister–elect's demonstration continued, a delegation of six members of the Gush Emunim secretariat came to Begin's small apartment in Tel Aviv and presented him with a plan for establishing twelve new settlements in Judea and Samaria in the next few months. Still excited by the political upheaval and the revolution in his life and status, Begin welcomed the plan.[2] The expected appointment of Ariel Sharon as minister of agriculture and the minister responsible for settlement led the settlers to his office as well. The designated defense minister, Ezer Weizman, also promised his support for settlement.[3] However, reality dawned on the new prime minister just two months after he was elected. At his first meeting with the American president in the White House, on July 19, 1977, he learned that Jimmy Carter—who himself had just come into office the previous January—was sticking to the traditional position of the United States: that the settlements were illegal, constituted a violation of United Nations Security Council Resolution 242, and were an obstacle to peace. To the Bible-oriented Southern Baptist, Begin replied that the "traditional" American attitude was at most ten years old, whereas "the attitude of the Jewish people is about 3,000 years old" and anchored in divine decree. The new prime minister preached to the American president: "In your country, Mr. President, there are a number of cities that have names taken from the Bible. You have eleven places called Hebron, five places called Shiloh and another seven places called Bethlehem and Bethel. Is it conceivable that the governor of one of the states will prohibit Jews from settling in those cities? . . . In the same way, the government of Israel cannot prohibit a Jew from settling in the original Hebron, or in the original Bethlehem, or in the original Bethel, or in the original Shiloh." Carter had to content himself with Begin's promise that the Israeli government "would not surprise him" and gave his reluctant agreement to the expansion of the existing settlements in the territories.[4]

However, Begin was not indifferent to the American pressure. In September 1977, on the eve of the Jewish New Year, the prime minister summoned the first of the settlers, Hannan Porat, for a tête-à-tête. Begin explained to Porat that due to heavy pressures at home and abroad, he would have to obtain the government's approval for the twelve-settlements plan, and as the moment was not propitious for a debate in the government, Begin advised the young settler simply to act. "Settle on the land in a partisan way and get organized on the ground. After the fact it will be easy to say, 'My sons have vanquished me!'" Yet the Gush Emunim people were dumbfounded. Was the new government also going to turn its back on them?[5] Before the establishment of the "twelve settlements," Porat was again summoned to Jerusalem and heard from the prime minister that the government had decided to establish only half of the dozen. It was also decided that only men, who would be required to wear uniforms and would be housed in military camps, would be permitted to settle. Families would not be allowed. Porat accused the prime minister of breaking promises. "I haven't broken any promise," retorted Begin in anger. The settlers threatened to go ahead without permission. "Anyone who settles—will be removed by force!" responded the prime minister.[6]

But Sharon, the settlers' guardian angel ever since 1974, came to their aid this time too. The American president's objection to the settlements, the prime minister's vacillations, and the opinion of his fellow members of the government made no impression on Sharon, whose splinter party, Shlomzion, had won only two seats in the elections. Because he knew the man and his habit of disobeying and deceiving his superiors, Begin had refused to put the defense portfolio into Sharon's hands. He gave him, instead, the junior agriculture port-folio but added to this the chairmanship of the ministerial committee on settlement matters. The committee was authorized to decide on settlement activities throughout the country, but under Sharon it focused exclusively on settlement in the territories. When none of the ministers questioned the committee's decisions, they became government resolutions.[7] Sharon's stance and his control of the land and water resources through the Agriculture Ministry became a tremendous lever for formulating and implementing his own settlement ideology. The location of each settlement, its character, its extent and size in the short and long term, its employment possibilities, and the identity of the body responsible for its establishment were discussed at the committee. The committee's decisions also determined the degree of the state's participation in the allocation of land and the infrastructure and construction expenditures. Thus the committee served as a tool in Sharon's hands for gaining control over the West Bank territories, developing them, and settling them in the guise of official, legal, and government-planned activity.

The man who had incited the settlers against the previous government did not stop for even one day building in the territories under the cover of archeological digs and military camps, while taking over lands in stealthy ways with the aim of thwarting diplomatic moves. He did this, in his inimitable way, with all his might, without consulting other members of the government, and without suitable infrastructures for putting the new settlements on a firm basis. On September 29, 1977, Sharon presented his settlement map to the government and embarked on his long campaign to change the geographic, political, demographic, social, economic, and security map of the State of Israel. The plan comprised three main elements. The first dealt with the establishment of a string of urban-industrial settlements along the top of the mountain ridge that ran from north to south through the center of the northern West Bank (Samaria), the purpose of which would be, among other things, to control the coastal plain. The second element was the defense of the eastern border. To this end, additional settlements were planned along the Jordan Valley—from Beit Shean just north of the West Bank to the Dead Sea at its southern border. Until that time, the Labor government had established twenty-seven settlements in the Jordan Valley. This new chapter included east-west roads along the width of the territory and the establishment of more settlements to secure these new roads. The third main element in the plan dealt with an envelope of Jewish settlements surrounding the Arab neighborhoods of Jerusalem, "to strengthen the capital."[8]

The massive, systematic establishment of as many settlements as possible in the least possible time while scattering them over as vast a territory as possible in the West Bank was Sharon's typical pattern of action. This aim shunted aside every economic, security, moral, urban, and ecological consideration. Sharon promised the ministers that by the end of the twentieth century there would be 2 million Jews living in the territories. More modest plans were set aside or died a natural death.[9] "I'm the only Laborite [Mapainik] in this government," declared Sharon proudly, referring to the historic mainstream Labor Zionist movement that got things done. "I'm not talking here so that my words will be recorded in the minutes. Mark my words. The moment this is approved, I am going to do it."[10] To the Knesset plenum he announced: "The settlement project that is going to be carried out will be more extensive than that in the past."[11] He kept his word.

Equipped with high-resolution maps, Sharon and his aides skipped from hill to hill, from bald mountain to bald mountain, locating the settlements on high ground mostly for political and strategic reasons, so that they would both overlook their environs and limit the expansion of Palestinian villages and towns that had existed there for hundreds of years. The unconcealed intention of Sharon's "redemption of the land," as it was called in the early days of Zionist settlement, was to thwart the establishment of a viable Palestinian state that would have reasonable territorial contiguity. Throughout the West Bank, tents were pitched, roads were hacked out of the landscape, and highways were paved. Young men and women made their homes on barren hills, drew their water from water trucks, and illuminated their humble abodes with electricity provided by generators. Sharon promised the pioneers in the territories that the good, comfortable days would not be long in coming.[12] In the media there were reports of new settlement outposts that had gone up surreptitiously and of a secret agreement between Gush Emunim and the government for the establishment of a dozen settlements, the inhabitants of which would be camouflaged as IDF soldiers. Sharon made no denials. In answer to parliamentary questions, he declared that "the government plan for settlement is in accordance with Israel's political aims and moves."[13]

Within a few years—Sharon's "finest," most productive years—the stony ground of the West Bank was sown with dozens of settlements. The settlement dice were thrown seemingly at random as if by a huge sower, a mythical Zionist icon striding the expanses of the barren land.[14] But the sowing arm was aiming well at strategic junctions and at the entrails of the large Palestinian towns, and made certain that none was overlooked. Elkanah, Beit El, Halamish, Kokhav Hashahar, Migdal Oz, Salit, Kedumim, Rimonim, Shavei Shomron, and Tekoa were already established by the end of 1977. In 1978 and 1979 Sharon established eight additional settlements, among them the extremist ideological settlement Elon Moreh, the city of Ariel, Kfar Tapuah, and Karnei Shomron. During the next three years, 1980 through 1982, toward the end of which Sharon was no longer serving as agriculture minister, major settlements like Efrata, Barqan, Ma'aleh Shomron, and Psagot were built. Sharon's successor as head of the committee on settlement matters, Professor Yuval Neeman of the far-right Tehiya (Revival) movement, a nuclear physicist, followed in his predecessor's footsteps.[15]

Some of the settlements flourished and grew, but many of them did not succeed in establishing themselves and remained as sort of mirages on the ground, even after twenty years or more. But Sharon's plan was indeed successful. The territories of the West Bank were thickly sprinkled with settlements. Roads were cut through to them and bypass highways were paved, which served the settlers exclusively. The Palestinians' land was scratched up and torn along its length and breadth and stripped bare by the settlers and the Israeli government. Eventually, when the second Palestinian uprising erupted, dozens of barriers and roadblocks were erected along these roads, which were aimed primarily at protecting the settler population and prevented the local inhabitants from moving freely in their land. Thus two separate states for two hostile peoples, the Palestinians and the settlers, developed within the territories of the West Bank, and these two states had separate systems of roads, services, and laws.

Between Yamit and the West Bank

For most Israelis, President Anwar Sadat's visit to Jerusalem in November 1977 and the peace process with Egypt that began in its wake were two events that marked the start of a new and promising era of peace. For the settlers they were omens of an approaching apocalypse. Their defender in the government, Sharon, swung into action. In order to keep up with the pace of the negotiations with Egypt, and fearing that the plan for Palestinian autonomy in the West

Bank would coerce Israel to refrain from establishing new settlements, the government approved Sharon's request to establish three new settlements every month.[16] The rumors about Begin's intention to evacuate Sinai and the Rafah Salient spread immediately after Sadat's visit and were amplified with the progress of the negotiations. The settlers' leaders once again stormed the Prime Minister's Bureau in Jerusalem. "If we have to make the choice between you and the Land of Israel, then the Land of Israel is preferable," said Hannan Porat to the prime minister, a sentence that every prime minister who came after Begin had the privilege to hear from the settlers.[17] "Tell your friends in the Rafah Salient that the Prime Minister, I, Menachem Begin, declare that no Jewish settlement will ever be removed from the soil of the Land of Israel," reassured Begin. "If the subject of uprooting settlements comes up again for discussion at the negotiating table then I, Menachem Begin, will get up, pack my bags and return home." From Knesset Member Yitzhak Rabin, a delegation of settlers from Yamit heard a different tune. "The matter is closed. I have a bad feeling that they've sold the salient," said Rabin.[18]

The issue of the settlements did indeed come up at the negotiating table during the 1978 summit at Camp David, and the Israeli prime minister did not get up and leave, as he had promised the settlers. Moreover, Sharon too "betrayed" them when the moment of truth arrived. From Camp David, the prime minister phoned the minister of agriculture, who had remained in Israel, to consult him about the question of the settlements. Sharon replied to Begin that peace was preferable to the settlements, and thus released the prime minister from his vow to the settlers. A Gush Emunim activist who was at Sharon's home during the telephone conversation with Begin heard about it from the minister of agriculture himself.[19]

For its part, Gush Emunim immediately began to organize its

counterattack. While the prime minister was at Camp David trying to invent the impossible formula for a compromise between the settlements and peace, the Gush made public its own alternative peace plan, which included settling a million Jews in the West Bank by the end of the twentieth century. For the year 1978–1979 alone, the Gush planned the establishment of a settlement adjacent to the large Palestinian city of Nablus, the expansion of the settlement of Beit El, the paving of five main roads, the establishment of five additional settlements, and the preparation of the infrastructure for ten more.[20] "If the government does not deal with the urgent tasks [of creating a Jewish majority in the land of Israel], there will be no alternative to coming out against it in a harsh struggle," warned the settlers.[21]

Two days after the end of the Camp David talks and the historic agreement they produced, which included autonomy for the inhabitants of the West Bank, the lifting of the military government in the territories, and a freeze on all settlements for a period of three months, on December 19, 1978, Gush Emunim embarked on its largest and most organized operation thus far: the settlement of Elon Moreh at Hawara, south of Nablus. This time the entire settlement universe—with all the Kook-inspired yeshivas, the supportive home front, and the hothouse for the ideological settlers—enlisted en masse to help the operation. Rabbi Zvi Yehudah Kook published an "order of the day" to his past and present students, in a coded language to which only they were accustomed. It said, among other things, "It is sometimes the case that leaving the Torah is its fulfillment . . . on the special matter of the commandment to settle Israel, which is equivalent in weight to the entire Torah. . . ."[22]

This was a real battle cry. Kook's yeshiva in Jerusalem, Merkaz HaRav, was designated as the gathering point for leaving for the settlement. Hundreds of settlers, supporters, and students from the paramilitary (*hesder*) yeshivas mustered there and were taken in buses to the area for settlement. Thousands surrounded the site; hundreds tried to ascend the mountain. For three whole days the settlers stayed on the mountaintop, erected a tent and a hut on the rocks, flew a flag, and surrounded themselves with a fence. Men, women, and children demonstrated on the mountain their ferocious, uncompromising love for the Land of Israel and their determination to sabotage any agreement that the government of Israel would sign.

In the absence of Begin, who was still in the United States, but with his backing, the government decided to remove the settlement from the site. The mountain was declared a closed military zone and encircled by hundreds of soldiers. In order to break the settlers' spirits and crush the settlement, the army prevented the provision of water and food. As in previous cases, and as in cases that would come later, there was a parade of prominent public figures, ministers, Knesset members, the chief of staff, and senior army officers who came to the mountain to express solidarity with the settlers or to persuade them to disperse quietly. The chief of staff's attempt to achieve a compromise and move the settlement in its entirety to a military camp was rejected both by the settlers and by Defense Minister Ezer Weizman, who demanded total evacuation in accordance with the government's decision. "I did not promise many settlements," said Weizman, hinting at his prime minister's declaration the day after his victory in the elections.[23] The forcible evacuation of the mountain under the eyes of the Israeli and world media, the scenes of hundreds of soldiers wrestling with the help of helicopters against the exhausted settlers clinging with the last remnants of their strength to the rocks and the lone hut they had erected—these scenes were just a prologue to what happened not very long afterward on the sands of the Rafah Salient and in Yamit, and almost thirty years later in the Gaza Strip.

The descent from "Mount Shchem" was a defeat for the settlers in the battle but not in the war. Before many months went by, on the last day of 1978, 100 members of the Elon Moreh group set out from Kedumim accompanied by hundreds of inhabitants of West Bank and Golan Heights settlements in another attempt to settle on Mount Shchem. They were stopped at the army roadblock at the village of Jatt, and encamped there en masse with the media recording their moves until they received permission to pass. Countering the people from the right who had come to encourage the settlers, Defense Minister Weizman declared that "if we have decided to live here 'forever' we must learn to live in cooperation with Arabs. . . . Now is the time to engage in fortifying existing settlements and not in building new ones. There are changes in the region and they must be taken into account."[24]

But images of the settlers demonstrating with their children by the roadside in the rain and in the cold proved effective. On January 7, 1979, the Begin government made the decision to see the Elon Moreh settlement nucleus as a candidate for settlement in the near future. The settlers welcomed the government's decision, expressing the hope that this was "a first step towards the establishment of the Hebrew town of Shchem." However, they also declared their opposition to the peace moves, "to the abandonment of Sinai and the Salient settlements, the proposed agreement on autonomy and a very creeping settlement policy in Judea and Samaria."[25] Sharon wasted no time. With the government's decision in his hands, as if he needed it, he set out to find a new place to settle the dedicated Elon Moreh group. Along with his band of friends from Gush Emunim, he circled in a helicopter over the city of Nablus and the surrounding hills to find a site that would satisfy all their wishes. The lot fell to an area adjacent to the village of Rujaib. There was, however, a problem. The lands that Sharon had located were privately owned.[26]

The question of settlement at the site came up for discussion at least four times in the government and the ministerial committee on settlement matters, and fell each time because of the opposition of Deputy Prime Minister Yigal Yadin, Foreign Minister Moshe Dayan, and Defense Minister Ezer Weizman, all of them ex-generals and revered security personalities. They argued that Israel should not "push into" the heart of densely populated Arab areas, and that there was more than enough land throughout the West Bank. To this was added an existing government decision that private lands must not be confiscated for settlement purposes. Begin, the liberal champion of individual rights and property rights, demonstratively passed this decision in order to differentiate his government from the previous Labor governments, which had no compunctions about confiscating for "military needs" even private Palestinian land, whether or not this was necessary.

By this time the old, eroded "security needs" argument had lost its magic effect and was making the security establishment very uncomfortable. Weizman, who despised the settlers' demonstrations, their arrogance, and their crude attitude toward both the local Arab population and the government of Israel, held firm to the government's decision and refused to sign the order to confiscate the lands. But the pressure from the settlers and their indefatigable political lobby, both inside and outside the government, overwhelmed the voice of reason. At the beginning of June 1979, a majority in the government voted in favor of establishing a Jewish settlement in the middle of Samaria. Weizman, who repeatedly argued that such a settlement would have no security value, accepted the position of the majority in the government but did not hesitate to declare at the convention of his party and Begin's, Herut, just prior to the move to settle, that "you can't go around all your life trying to prove to the world that you are settling just because it's important for security. This is a falsification of Zionism."[27]

On June 6, 1979, twelve years after the beginning of the occupation of the Samaria area, the signal was given for its second conquest. On that day Gush Emunim received word that some 800 dunams (200 acres) in Hawara intended for their settlement were about to be confiscated. Sharon intentionally acted to postpone the signing of the confiscation order until the morning of the move, so as not to enable the owners of the land, inhabitants of the village of Rujaib, to petition the High Court of Justice. Accordingly, the Gush organized for fast action, by the "stockade and tower" method of the Jewish settlements in the 1930s, as its spokesmen put it, and at 8:30 on the morning of June 7, with the signing of the confiscation order, the Gush people were already heading for the hill. As always, they were accompanied by hundreds of noisy supporters, and this time also by heavy mechanical equipment, helicopters, and the army. By that evening, a road had been cut through to the top of the mountain, which rises to an altitude of 700 meters southeast of Nablus. By nightfall, a small settlement was already standing: tents, one prefabricated house, a flag, and a fence.[28] It seemed as though stabbing "the knife into the heart of Palestinism," as the settlers themselves called the settlement,[29] had gone well.

The settlement "in the heart of Palestinism" caused a huge uproar in Israel and internationally. The Israeli opposition, the Palestinians, international organizations, and the American administration all protested the decision to establish the settlement, as well as its location and the timing of the move, on the eve of the autonomy talks with Egypt. Even American Jewry woke up, uncharacteristically, to protest both the move and the Israeli government's policy in the territories. Their formal leadership, the heads of the Conference of

Presidents of Major American Jewish Organizations, came to Begin's bureau in Jerusalem to demand that he remove the settlement. The Peace Now movement, which had only recently been established, threatened to demonstrate against the settlement at the site and throughout the country.[30]

A week after Elon Moreh was established, the Palestinian landowners, represented by attorney Elias Khoury, submitted an appeal to the High Court of Justice. In light of previous rulings by the court, their petition did not seem to stand much of a chance. The duty justice even rejected the request by the counsel for the petitioners to issue an interim restraining order to freeze construction. But the continuation was different and completely unexpected. The security value of the settlement, which was controversial even within the government; the shallowness of the document from the chief of staff, Lieutenant General Rafael Eitan, defending the importance of the place from a security perspective; the professional opinions of retired Major General Mati Peled and former chief of staff Haim Bar-Lev as to how inessential the settlement was for the country's security and the difficulties it would cause by tying up large military forces in order to protect it from "attempted attacks"; and finally, the testimony of two settlers from Elon Moreh to the effect that it had not been security needs but rather motivations of faith and obedience to a higher dictate that had led them to the mountain, and that the settlements were not a temporary phenomenon but rather part of an eternal cosmic occurrence—determined the fate of Elon Moreh. Initially the full bench of the court issued an interim order for its "total" suspension. And at the conclusion of five stormy months of litigation and the writing and editing of the ruling, five justices handed down a resounding decision that the settlement must be evacuated and the lands returned to their owners.[31]

The settlers were given an extension of thirty days to leave the site. The court's ruling dismayed the prime minister, who at the start of the legal proceedings had celebrated the fact that "there are judges in Jerusalem." An editorial in *Yedioth Aharonoth* defined it as a "national tragedy."[32] The entire right mustered for a campaign to revile the prosecution and the Supreme Court and to remove the occupied territories from their authority. The historic decision by Meir Shamgar more than a decade earlier in his capacity as Judge Advocate General, the highest legal authority in the army, to place the territories under the authority of the Supreme Court had finally proved itself to be a barrier to the arbitrariness of the colonizing occupier. Following the declaration by Gush Emunim that it would not evacuate Elon Moreh, whatever the implications of the decision, the prime minister announced that the court decision would be honored in full and that there would not be legislation to retroactively cancel it. Various legal experts saw in this moment one of the most difficult tests, if not the most difficult, that the rule of law in Israel had ever faced.[33]

With unprecedented determination, Attorney General Yitzhak Zamir and State Prosecutor Gabriel Bach resisted attempts by the settlers' supporters in the government to thwart, circumvent, or manipulate the court's decision. The prime minister held yet another of his innumerable meetings with the heads of Gush Emunim—more than with any other group of citizens in Israeli society—in an attempt to persuade them to come down from the mountain they had climbed with the aid of his government. Finally, six months after the settlers had moved onto the land, with the authorization and permission of the government and with the help of the army, the settlement was dismantled and the settlers left the site. For a moment, at least, the rule of law was able to take credit for a victory over a group of people,

Israeli citizens, who since 1967 had undermined it very effectively, and with the help of so many senior accomplices.

In Yamit's Name

The trauma of Elon Moreh deeply scarred both the settlers and the government. At the time it was unfolding, the peace process was moving ahead on another front, on the border with Egypt. However, the bitter experience of Mount Shchem did not deter the settlers from refusing to believe that the Begin-Sharon government would indeed uproot Jews from their "permanent" homes in Sinai or from clinging until the very last minute to the hope that the Camp David decisions would not be carried out.

The connection between the settlers in the West Bank and Gaza and the settlers in Sinai, who were cut from a different cloth, was loose. The interests of the two communities of settlers were not the same. If the settlers in Sinai and the Rafah Salient were less privileged Israelis or adventurers who had gone to the golden sands to find a better life, the ideological-messianic settlers of the West Bank were guided by divine command. Their Gush Emunim leaders, however, detected in the struggle over the evacuation of Sinai a test of what was to come. They planned to make the dismantling a traumatic experience, and their well-orchestrated campaign began right after the Knesset ratified the government decision of withdrawal.

Rabbi Kook declared that the peace agreement was a "government betrayal," and that its signing had no validity.[34] Kiryat Arba Rabbis Dov Lior and Moshe Levinger distributed a bulletin in which they wrote that "the struggle for Hebron has begun. . . . We need everyone from Kiryat Arba. Let each and every one of us do all in our power in order to come to the demonstration. . . . The hour of the difficult and crucial decision has arrived."[35] At a discussion held by members of the newly established Yesha (a Hebrew acronym for Judea, Samaria, and Gaza) Council secretariat with heads of the movement to stop the withdrawal from Sinai, Hannan Porat, who was a Knesset member at the time, proposed creating "an acute, large and weighty balance of terror. A balance of terror that will force the government to come to the realization that evacuation is impossible. Only such a realization will guarantee the prevention of a civil war. However, taking a lukewarm path could lead to a clash." The settler who was so experienced in struggles against Israeli governments knew that there was nothing that deterred Israeli politicians more than the phrase "war between brothers."[36]

"In the struggle for Yamit I saw a struggle for Judea and Samaria," said Rabbi Yoel Bin-Nun later. "I did not believe for a moment that there was a chance of saving Yamit."[37] The Gush Emunim political secretary also admitted that "a large measure of naïveté was needed to believe that we would stop the withdrawal; we were there so that no Jewish settlement would ever be uprooted again."[38] Elyakim Haetzni acknowledged that the struggle for Yamit was aimed at forestalling the "evil" in the West Bank. Two weeks before the evacuation, Haetzni wondered "whether it was worth shaking up the government and bringing the end closer for a government that had annexed the Golan and established dozens of settlements in Yesha." His reply to his own rhetorical question was positive. "Indeed, quite a few of our enemies wish to see the evacuation of Sinai and the dismantling of the settlement as a precedent that will spread to Yesha, the Golan and even Jerusalem," he wrote. "With respect to these, there is value to the bitter war to stop the withdrawal in Sinai: to ensure that the putrefaction will not spread to the other parts of the body. To this end it was necessary to conduct the bold struggle in Sinai, which entailed suffering and a national trauma."[39]

The West Bank and Gaza settlers encouraged their colleagues to show determination and put at their disposal their rich experience in the battle for public opinion and in establishing facts on the ground. When inhabitants of the Rafah Salient came to an agreement with the government to evacuate their homes, the "professional" settlers, Sebastia veterans, took their places.[40] The movement to stop the withdrawal from Sinai, established for the organization of the resistance activities, engaged in lobbying, propaganda, and the tenanting of hundreds of empty homes in the Yamit area by supporters who came from all over the country. The people of the Yamit Region knew that these people were coming there mainly to fight for their homes in Elon Moreh and Ofra. "I have a feeling that some of the elements operating in the area are clearly intending to foment a civil war! Such a war could serve their interests. . . . A national trauma of a civil war in the Yamit Region could serve as a warning to any government that would sit down in the future to discuss any agreements whatsoever about evacuating settlements in Judea and Samaria," said one of them.[41] "It is easy for you, the people from Judea and Samaria, to preach to us. Every one of you has a home . . . to which you will return. But we will have to look for a new home."[42] Here for the first time the abyss gaped between the secular settlers of Yamit and its environs and the West Bank settlers. While the former had flocked at the time to the beautiful, bountiful expanses of the salient mainly in order to improve their standard of living, and were now demonstrating in order to add a few zeroes to the sum of compensation they would receive, the latter were arguing that there was no amount of money in the world that would uproot them.

The din of the protest activities swallowed up the roar of the bulldozers that were preparing ground in the West Bank for new settlements. The government itself accelerated development there at the same time that it was preparing the evacuation of Sinai.[43] Toward the end of December 1980, Rabbi Israel Ariel of Yamit came to the founding convention of the Yesha Council, to bring the blessing of Yamit Region settlements. He brought along a modest gift—a bit of rope [in Hebrew, the word for "region," as applied to Yamit, and the word for "rope" is the same: *hevel*]. "We are one *hevel*," he said. "This is the same hangman's rope that must not be mentioned in the hanged man's home. We are all living with the sense that the hangman's rope is around the neck of the Yamit Region. Just as they are evacuating settlements in Yamit here, there is a threat to evacuate settlements in Judea and Samaria too." He tried to rouse the West Bank settlers from their complacency. "Do not wait for the moment when they come to fell the settlements of Judea and Samaria, heaven forbid. And do not wait for the moment when the cranes come to Kedumim and Elon Moreh," Ariel told his listeners. "Take Yamit as an example, and the moment they come to uproot a sapling, to try to saw down houses, let every man leave his home and fight in Yamit in order to save Judea and Samaria."[44]

Mending the Rupture

The period that followed the April 1982 evacuation of Yamit was characterized by a momentum of steady construction in the settle-ments. The settlers calculated that a large number of families living in regular houses would make it difficult for the government and the army to evacuate them. In June 1982—the same month that Israel invaded Lebanon, which led to an occupation that would last eighteen years—the Judea and Samaria settlers held an emergency meeting in Ofra that was aimed at studying the lessons to be learned from the expulsion from Yamit. A hundred settlement heads came to the meeting, as well as representatives from the Golan Heights, stalwarts from the veteran settlements in the Jordan Valley and the mythical Jezreel Valley in Israel proper, the cradle of Zionist collective settlements, and other supporters. The talk was high-flown, as always, and the reckoning of conscience tempestuous and moral, as was the speakers' way. One of the Ofra settlers said: "We were forced to establish the movement to stop the withdrawal from Sinai because we had neglected continuous work on the dissemination of information and policy in ordinary times, and the awakening came only when the sword of evacuation was lying on our necks. So that we will not have to establish another movement to stop a withdrawal, we must awaken, organize, and set to work immediately."[45] This was the signal for the entire right. Pinchas Wallerstein, head of the Matteh Binyamin council and one of the settler leaders, said that "anyone who is guilty of the horrifying crime of uprooting settlements will not be absolved. We must tell the public that anyone who raised a hand to an IDF soldier must be sentenced to prison for a month, two months, or half a year, and anyone who uprooted settlements and destroyed them must be sentenced to life imprisonment. Not as pure revenge but rather as the enactment of justice for someone who has committed a crime against the land. Barely a month has elapsed since April 25 [the date of the Yamit evacuation], and the nation is already tending to forget the events of Yamit. This forgetting is liable to destine, heaven forbid, a similar fate for the inhabitants of Yesha. Therefore it is incumbent upon us to invoke day and night the uprooting and the uprooted, to say and to promise that the day will come when the uprooters will face a court and pay for their terrible crime."[46] If Wallerstein talked about crimes against the land and the nation, Elyakim Haetzni pulled from the well-worn arsenal of Holocaust memory: "Here shouting, condemnations, and cries of 'Not nice!' will be to no avail—*this scene is reminiscent of the Holocaust!*"[47]

What spared "the criminals of Yamit" from the settlers' tongues was the Lebanon War. After the bleak, pathetic scenes of Yamit, this war was intended to bring Israel an easy military victory and a bit of elation for the people. Begin also hoped to compensate for the gloom of the more distant Yom Kippur War, and even, to some extent, for the Holocaust.[48] Sharon's war aim was somewhat different, just to "establish a new order in the Middle East," and in doing so also to destroy the PLO in Lebanon in order to ease Israeli absorption of the West Bank and Gaza and prevent establishment of a Palestinian state there. For Sharon, the war for Lebanon was, in good measure, a war for the West Bank, for the territories. Thus, yesterday's "criminals of Yamit" became the heroes of today. And as the Israeli tanks stood at the gates of Beirut, Begin, who had been branded by the settlers the "Judenrat" of Yamit, became the "new Jew," the Jew "who no longer has feelings of inferiority and a psychological need to prove dignity, the pursuit of peace and suchlike."[49]

Like every collective defeat that is interpreted as such in a given society, the withdrawal from Sinai became a powerful motor, not only for embarking on the unjust and unnecessary war in Lebanon but also for the renewal and strengthening of Gush Emunim. Some in the movement spoke now of the opportunity and the necessity to "re-establish the Jewish state," of a comprehensive struggle for "the national consciousness of the Jewish people . . . and its Zionist scale of values" and of the new means that should be adopted to this end.[50] Out of the calamity of the withdrawal and the experience of the fight against the withdrawal and the peace agreements with Egypt, the Gush embarked on a renewed campaign to establish more firmly the settlements in the West Bank; the umbrella organization of the settlements, the Yesha Council, was founded; and the settlers' primary official publication, *Nekudah*, was launched.[51]

The struggle and the crisis also gave rise to the Jewish terror organization that became known as the Jewish Underground. A senior member of the terrorist group, Menachem Livni, testified that in conversations that he and his friends had held as far back as right after Sadat's 1977 visit to Jerusalem, plans had been discussed to "rehabilitate" the Temple Mount—that is to say, to blow up the Mosque of Omar, which is called the Dome of the Rock, "and this in order to stop the evacuation of the Yamit Region settlements, in fact so that no precedent would be created for evacuating Hebrew settlements and abandoning them willingly."[52] But over and above the specific, concrete plans was hovering the great and only meaningful vision for the settler extremists—the rebuilding of the Temple.

Preferential Treatment

The affair of the Jewish terror organization is deserving of attention primarily because it testifies to the hallucinatory, dangerous realms in which key people in Gush Emunim trod, in thought and deed, and because of the forgiveness that was granted them by the political establishment and by Israeli society as a whole. This preferential treatment in favor of messianic nationalists who had both conspired in murder and contrived to thwart historic state decisions by means of a series of grave crimes accorded with the preferential treatment that the settlers had always enjoyed. The people of the Jewish terror group did not arise from the murky margins of their community but in fact came from the best families of settler society and the heart of the believing establishment. They emerged from the preferred and well-funded settlements, from elite yeshivas, and from select units in the army. Most of them were funded by the government and held jobs as public officials. When the day came for justice to be applied, these people won far more than the formal pardons and decreased sentences that were granted them. They were heroes, and not only amid their own ranks.

In his statement to the police after he was captured, Menachem Livni, a resident of Kiryat Arba, a disciple of Rabbi Levinger, and deputy commander of a combat engineering battalion, said that "during the course of recent years it was explained to me by a number of rabbis that 'the Arabs are using our morality as a sword to stab in our hearts. They know us and our morality and out of this they are exploiting us in order to attack us.' It is not possible to educate and judge a human group that lives according to base moral standards to live according to other moral standards that belong to a more moral human system. For example, in order to educate a human community that lives in a primitive, pagan way in the jungle, you have to descend, understand and act according to the moral standards that are accepted in that tribe, and gradually educate the tribe toward the moral values by which the educator lives. That is, in the first stage at least, it is necessary to act against a hostile Arab population in the language they understand."[53]

Livni told his interrogators about a conference of rabbis and public leaders that was held in Kiryat Arba after the May 1980 murder by Palestinians of six yeshiva students who were returning to the Beit Hadassah compound in Hebron from prayers at the Tomb of the Patriarchs. "There was a great fear that families would leave, and an even greater fear about saving lives with regard to the future." The extremist rabbis of Kiryat Arba, the locality's administrative head, Ze'ev Friedman-Hever, and others, all of them public servants who received their salaries from the state, participated in the conference. At this meeting, the rabbis stressed that it was necessary to discourage the Arab population by means of mass attack actions. "In light of the government's weakness and the feeling of those present that the government had 'abandoned them,' it was proposed that the deterrent action be carried out by the settlers." Livni testified that after the meeting one of the rabbis, Eliezer Waldman, approached him and asked him to participate personally in the "underground" strike.[54]

Livni told of conversations he had with other people in Kiryat Arba during which the plan was drawn up. The scheme, which relied on the rabbis' opinion based in traditional Jewish law (*halakha*), was to attack "various targets, with the aim of deterring Arabs from acting against Jews." The conspirators said that they relied on halakhic opinions from the head of the Hebron yeshiva, Rabbi Zvi Liebman, and the head of the Kiryat Arba Yeshiva, Rabbi Dov Lior. "Rabbi Levinger supported it in a general way," while other rabbis, "among them Rabbi [Meir Yehuda] Getz and Rabbi [Haim] Sabato" also supported the plan.[55] Subsequently the rabbis who were mentioned in the testimony denied their involvement. Rabbi Waldman responded to *Ha'aretz* with "it never happened," while Levinger said tersely: "I am not prepared to comment on the facts."[56] During their investigation the rabbis invoked their right to remain silent. Rabbi Getz denied any acquaintance with the speakers and expressed reservations about violent actions.[57]

The first action by the Jewish terror group was carried out to avenge the murder of six yeshiva students.[58] This attack was directed against Palestinian notables of the new generation, independent national leaders, and local leaders, heads of the Palestinian Committee for National Direction. It was executed in the morning hours of June 2, 1980, exactly one month after the six were murdered. The Jewish terrorists set off explosives in the cars of the mayor of Nablus, Bassam Shaq'a, and the mayor of Ramallah, Karim Halaf. Both of Shaq'a's legs were amputated. Halaf lost one of his legs. At the same time, a charge exploded next to the garage door at the home of Al Bireh Mayor Ibrahim Tawil. Suleiman Hirbawi, a Border Police sapper who was summoned to the scene in order to dismantle the charge, was injured in the explosion and blinded.

Yehuda Etzion, one of the heads of the terror organization, testified that the attacks were planned so that they would injure the victims and not kill them. "We chose the size of the explosive charge and its placement attached to the vehicle so that people would be injured in their legs only," said Etzion. "This principle of injuring and not killing was also applied in the way the charge was placed next to Tawil's garage." The Underground, said Etzion, did not want to make the victims into martyrs by killing them but rather into "living symbols of the crime and the punishment."[59] Years later Yigal Amir, Prime Minister Yitzhak Rabin's assassin, offered a similar argument, i.e., that it had been his intention to render the prime minister incapable of any activity in order to change the course of history, and not necessarily to kill him.[60]

Purifying the Temple Mount

The Palestinian mayors were only a fleeting and incidental target. A greater vision guided Yehuda Etzion and his friends. Alongside the violent revenge against Palestinian terror, the most important aim of the Jewish terror organization was the elimination of the "defilement" from the site of the Temple, i.e., blowing up the Dome of the Rock on the Temple Mount. The bearers of this vision, Etzion and Yeshua Ben Shushan, had met before the Yom Kippur War during a tour arranged by the secretariat of the Elon Moreh settlement to locate a site for their new home. Over the years, the two met frequently at Ofra and in Jerusalem for discussion and joint learning. At one of those meetings, during the Camp David talks, Ben Shushan said to his friend that the time had come to remove the "defilement." The purpose would be to prevent the implementation of the peace agreement with Egypt and to excise the disgrace that the ancient Muslim structure brought to the Mount.[61]

Yeshua Ben Shushan was considered an outstanding figure by his friends and all who knew him. As he spoke little, his words were engraved in his listeners' minds. The son of a long-established and traditional Jerusalemite Sephardic family, he insisted on serving in an elite unit in the army. He was refused at first, until the commander of the Shaked Special Operations Unit, Binyamin Ben-Eliezer, agreed to accept him. Ben-Eliezer, later a Labor leader, did not regret this. Ben Shushan excelled as a soldier, completed officers' training course, fought bravely in the Yom Kippur War, and was gravely wounded. After his discharge from the hospital he went to study at the Merkaz HaRav Yeshiva, the ideological hothouse of Gush Emunim. It is said that the esteemed rabbi of the yeshiva used to rise to his feet when Ben Shushan entered the room. In his quiet way, his scholarliness, and his unusual biography, he captivated all who saw him and moved with natural ease in political circles. With the establishment of Gush Emunim he became the organization's man in the field, leading soldiers and sympathizers to sites of demonstrations and settlement, helping to circumvent army roadblocks and establishing settlements. When Ben-Eliezer was appointed commander of Judea and Samaria, he re-recruited Ben Shushan and appointed him to the position of regional defense officer in Samaria. Whether or not this appointment was aimed at keeping Ben Shushan under control and whether or not the full implications of it were understood at the time, his main mission was the establishment of new infantry units made up exclusively of settlement residents.[62] Thus with the help of the army and with its weapons, the settlers' militias arose in the territories.

Yehuda Etzion was no less colorful. A student of the Elon Shvut Yeshiva, determined and zealous in his faith, he was among the "professional settlers" during the first years of Gush Emunim, spending long periods on the hilltops, moving constantly from one to another. Etzion did his military service as a paramilitary yeshiva soldier in combat engineering, a unit that provided him with the training in explosives that he later used in terror group activities. He was a partner to the first settlement attempt by the Elon Moreh nucleus in Samaria, in the spring of 1974, and was among those who were forcibly evacuated while Sharon was endeavoring to protect him with his own body and instructing the evacuating soldiers to refuse to obey orders.[63] Afterward Etzion headed the work brigade out of which the settlement of Ofra grew. During the days of Camp David he took part in demonstrations all over the country and organized protest settlements. However, the failure of the settlement attempt at Rujaib near Nablus right after the signing of the Camp David agreements led him to cut himself off from Gush Emunim and to a period of isolation and thought. Settling the land no longer looked to him like the most important course of action. He set out to seek a "personality of spiritual stature, who would put himself at the head of an initiative that would march the Jewish people toward the fulfillment of its destiny."[64]

The books of his relative, Shabtai Ben-Dov, and the conversations that he conducted with his friend Yeshua Ben Shushan gave him ideas about the ways of accelerating the process of the Redemption. They both debated the crisis in Zionism, the blindness of the state to its own mission and destiny, its futile efforts to be like all the other nations, and the struggle, both spiritual and practical, that must be conducted in order to bring complete Redemption to Israel.[65] When Etzion asked his relative Ben-Dov whether removing the Dome of the Rock from the Temple Mount would start a dynamic of Redemption, the latter replied, in the last days of his life, "If you want to do a deed that will solve *all* of the problems of the Jewish people—do that!"[66] Etzion and Ben Shushan turned for advice to Rabbi Zvi Yehudah Kook, the spiritual leader of Gush Emunim, and the rabbi directed them to Ariel Sharon.[67]

"It was my right to participate in cutting short the legs of a few murderers," said Yehuda Etzion at his trial, five years later, referring to his actions as a member of the terror group. "However, I will never lend a hand to the apparently simplistic direction of the prosecution . . . to turn the deeds into criminal charges. . . . It is clear to everyone that these deeds were the product of a certain outlook whose aim and system of visions are the system of visions of the Jewish people in its land in this generation, the revival generation. This is the same faithfulness to all the history of the Jewish people since the Holy One chose Israel." Etzion then added that he therefore decided not to remain silent, "in order to say that I indeed saw for myself the obligation to prepare an action, which I would call the purification of the Temple Mount. . . . As for cutting short the murderers' legs, I insist that this action was taken justly. So justly that in my humble opinion the law existing in the State of Israel recognizes its justness or ought to recognize its justness, as it was clearly a defensive action."[68]

The immediate need to avenge the blood of the six yeshiva students postponed for a while the redemptive mending of the entire course of history. At the wedding in Hebron of a daughter of Moshe Levinger and his wife, Miriam, two weeks after the bloodshed, and subsequently, more people were secretly recruited for the terrorist organization, one by one and unseen. Among them were some who had already joined the Temple Mount Campaign, and they came from various settlements. A friend brought a friend, without superfluous talk—they joined without asking questions. A voice called them and they came. "I don't want to know. Just tell me what has to be done," they said.[69] No more than one or two were recruited from any given settlement. It was a small, scattered, compartmentalized group—not all of them knew one another—imbued with the urge for revenge and a desperate faith in their rightness. Their preliminary discussions were about technical and operational issues, and did not raise many moral questions.[70]

"One of the dangers that lies in wait for every extremist movement that adopts a practice of illegalism, and an explicit rationalization of this practice, is the decline of the movement or some of its members into directed violent action," wrote Ehud Sprinzak, a renowned scholar of extremist movements. His study of extremism distinguishes the "phases" into which even the greatest idealists sink without noticing.[71] Indeed, amid the pervasive illegality of the settlement project, which was both rationalized and obscured by the settlers' fervent belief in the approaching Redemption, violent injury to human beings was a negligible detail.

The response among the settlers and the heads of Gush Emunim to the terrorist attacks on the Palestinian mayors, for which no one claimed responsibility, was mainly tactical. It was guided by the fear of strong negative reactions from the Israeli public and of violent counter-responses by the Palestinians. Shlomo Aviner was the one rabbi among the spiritual leadership of Gush Emunim who came out publicly against the action. He said he opposed it because of the harm it did to "Israeli statehood in its current embodiment." The shattered Yoel Bin-Nun, from whose settlement of Ofra three of the conspirators came, wrote in his diary the word "Sabateans!"—referring to the mystical followers of the seventeenth-century false messiah Sabbatai Zevi. Bin-Nun knew that his friend Yehuda Etzion was involved, but he kept his thoughts to himself for many years.[72] It is said that Hannan Porat took to his bed and in his despair did not emerge from it for twenty-four hours.[73] These reactions were damning indications that most of the settlement leaders knew the attacks on the Palestinian mayors could only have come from their midst. The fact that the usually effective Israeli security services, which also knew this, tracked down the group and exposed it only four years later also demonstrates the immunity that the state authorities granted the settlers.

The success of the organization's first action, and the lack of response from the authorities, brought to the fore the plan to blow up the Dome of the Rock, a deed that in Etzion's opinion promised "the only way for Israel to become, ultimately, the proper Kingdom of Israel, worthy of the one that is promised."[74] Menachem Livni, the mechanical engineer from Kiryat Arba who had become a disciple and admirer of Rabbi Levinger, was the third man whom Yehuda Etzion and Yeshua Ben Shushan brought into the secret of their original plan. The trio would meet nearly every week, during the night between Thursday and Friday, to discuss issues of the Redemption of Israel and its realization. According to Etzion, blowing up the Dome of the Rock was intended to be the start of an extensive educational campaign by the Redemption movement to conquer the hearts of the entire nation. Livni, however, held that blowing up the Dome of the Rock was essential in and of itself, especially as this was likely to prevent the withdrawal from Sinai. Livni argued that Israelis who had no understanding of the essence of Redemption would not understand the act.[75]

Both Etzion and Livni wanted to focus on the main thing, the Big Bang, the reversal of world history and the bringing of Redemption by means of erasing the Dome of the Rock from the face of the holy Mount. A first meeting at Givat Shaul in Jerusalem, at which Rabbi Levinger was also present, ended without practical decisions. Another meeting was held in an avocado grove on the eastern shore of the Sea of Galilee, where Livni and Etzion tried to recruit rank and file for the mission, all of whom had served in the Israeli army, among them a demobilized fighter pilot. But the feeling was that the plan was too big for them, and there was no chance they could carry it out. There were also some who feared that blowing up the Islamic structure would expose Jews all over the world to violent attacks and other dangers. Etzion, the leading force in the Temple Mount plan until it finally faded away, believed on the other hand that the Jewish people were not vulnerable to disaster from such an act and that "the craziness of a few individuals" would gradually be accepted by the majority.[76]

During the course of the following months the terrorists gathered intelligence information, reconnoitered on the Temple Mount, and prepared the explosive charges. The trio of founders, Etzion, Ben Shushan, and Livni, discussed the formulation of an advance announcement to the press, public figures, and rabbis, which would forestall the "distorted and hostile" versions that would be spread immediately after the attack.[77] But the completion of the withdrawal from Sinai, and especially last-minute dithering, put a stop to the plan. Eventually Livni claimed that it was only his illness, hepatitis, that stood between him and carrying out the mission. Etzion, however, claimed that it was Livni's doubts that led him to reconsider the idea.[78]

Beloved Lost Sons

With the abandonment of the Temple Mount scheme, the group turned its attention to more "conventional" aims. Their next terror attack was carried out on October 29, 1982. The group placed two booby-trapped hand grenades on the stairs leading to the soccer field at the Hussein School in Hebron, as a match was under way. In the explosion two youngsters were injured. Less than a year later, on July 7, 1983, Palestinians shot and killed eighteen-year-old Aharon Gross, a student at the

Shavei Hebron Yeshiva, in the market square. A group of youngsters from Kiryat Arba took out their anger on the dozens of vegetable stands of the Arab merchants in the marketplace. Three weeks later, in the early afternoon, a car with forged license plates stopped near the building of the Islamic College in Hebron. Two members of the Jewish terror organization, one of them a demobilized paratrooper who had married a daughter of the Levingers and settled in the Jewish Quarter, emerged from the vehicle, entered the college courtyard and started shooting. The first bullets hit two students who were strolling there. One of the terrorists ran in the direction of the college building with a primed hand grenade at the ready in one hand and an assault rifle in the other. He let a group of girl students flee, lobbed the grenade into a side room, and fired a round in the direction of the main gate. Scores of panicked students jumped from the windows of the upper floors. The Israeli terrorists escaped in the car that was waiting for them, leaving behind three killed and thirty-three wounded. Later Livni testified that there had been a delay of "about ten minutes" in the strike.[79] Under the plan, the attack had been scheduled for the noon recess, when most of the students would have been in the courtyard.

A prisoner deal in late 1983, in which six Israelis were freed in exchange for nearly 5,000 Palestinian prisoners, among them the killers from the ambush at Beit Hadassah, and the capture by Palestinian terrorists of an Israeli bus in the south the following spring engendered the next Jewish terror plan. The target was buses of the Juliani Company, which operated mainly along the Jerusalem-Atarot route. The intention was to blow up six buses packed with Arab passengers. This would have been intentional mass murder. But some of the heads of the organization, among them Yehuda Etzion, were opposed to the plan. On Friday, April 27, 1984, at 4:30 A.M., the brothers Barak and Shaul Nir from Hebron-Kiryat Arba, together with Levinger's son-in-law, completed the booby-trapping of the buses and set out for the Western Wall to pray. On the way they were surrounded by people from the General Security Services (Shin Bet) who had been keeping them under surveillance the entire night.[80] On that same day all of the members of the organization were arrested. Rabbi Eliezer Waldman, who headed the paramilitary yeshiva in Kiryat Arba, and Rabbi Moshe Levinger were also summoned for questioning by the police. On May 2, 1985, the Justice Ministry issued a statement about the exposure of "a Jewish terror organization" and a decision "not to take legal steps against Rabbi Moshe Levinger and Rabbi Eliezer Waldman."[81]

The arrested suspects confessed to some of the acts of terror but did not express remorse. Etzion called upon the arrested men to insist proudly on the justice of the deeds. "Dear brothers," stated a document that he distributed, "if our Lord brought us to this point, it is our duty to address the nation courageously and, at the heart of the matter, to found a popular Redemption movement that will guide our nation to complete Redemption and elevate its spirit."[82] Etzion's chief collaborator, Menachem Livni, made a fiery defense speech to his interrogators: "The State of Israel in a slow and graduated process has become accustomed to the cheapening of Jewish blood. The fight against the terrorists and the population that gives them moral and practical support has taken on the form of passive defense only.... The community that lives in Hebron is an 'idealistic' community that feels the pain and hurt of the people and the nation for every single terror attack anywhere in the country. As a result of this, it wants to rectify the situation and prevent more terror attacks throughout the land." Livni demanded that he and his friends be seen as freedom fighters and Israeli patriots. "We reject in disgust the desire to bring us to trial like criminals. We are no worse than Yitzhak Shamir, Menachem Begin, and their colleagues who went forth to defend their people and their homeland in the 1930s and the 1940s."[83]

About a month after the organization was exposed, indictments were filed against twenty-five members of the terror group at the Jerusalem District Court.[84] A few of the accused, the more junior among them, later signed a plea bargain with the prosecution. The bench of judges at the court was headed by Judge Yaakov Bazak, an observant Jew, on the wall of whose chambers hung a portrait of Rabbi Zvi Yehudah Kook. The other judges were Zvi Cohen, a new judge at the court and eventually chairman of the right-wing Likud elections committee, and Shmuel Finkelman, who had been a judge in the military court that deliberated the case of the Palestinian terrorists who killed the yeshiva students in Hebron. The prosecution was represented by the deputy state prosecutor, Dorit Beinish, who eventually became president of the Supreme Court. Facing the prosecution was a battery of some of the most prominent and expensive lawyers in Israel, Dan Avi-Yitzhak, Yaakov Weinrot, and Shlomo Toussia-Cohen.

There was no disagreement about the facts. The indicted members of the terror group admitted to the acts that were attributed to them and gave detailed statements to their interrogators. Not only did they admit to their deeds; they took pride in them and aspired to turn the proceedings into a political trial. Their attorneys, however, preferred an ordinary criminal trial that would deal with trivia and thus anesthetize public opinion and lead to an easier sentence.[85] That was mainly the approach of attorney Avi-Yitzhak, who believed that the last thing his clients needed was a platform for political speeches. He intended to "put the trial to sleep" and indeed succeeded in breaking down the affair of Jewish terrorism into myriad technicalities. The endless procedural debates in court and the plea bargains led to the waning of public interest.[86]

However, another of the defense attorneys, Yaakov Weinrot, an observant Jew and a scion of the national religious movement, chose a different way. His closing speech was much more than a concrete defense of his clients' deeds or a legal treatise on matters of procedure. It was a far-reaching, uncompromising prosecutorial foray that represented the collective opinion of the settlers about the decadent and corrupt Israeli bourgeoisie that had lost its way and about the Israeli left, their arch-rival. And from Weinrot's indictment, his explanation—and a kind of a justification—for the phenomenon of Jewish terrorism emerged. The onus was thus transferred from the criminals to those Israelis who were not smitten by the settlers' charms, and directed at anyone whose secular way of life and support for an open and pluralistic society contrasted with the values of those of the men who were now facing trial.

"The first question that every reasonable person must ask himself," said Weinrot in the court, "is how religious youth has come to be where it is; how it has happened that it is running forward and placing at the forefront of its values the Land of Israel that is beyond the Green Line. How it has happened that of all the 613 Commandments, one specific commandment is observed most courageously and tenaciously. And indeed we have always aspired to mend the world of the heavenly King . . . and indeed it is uniformly agreed that the settlement of Israel does not cancel out other Commandments. . . . Such was religious Jewry at the establishment of the state. Everything that was religious was clerical, primitive, and archaic. . . . Of a hundred measures of hypocrisy, the Zionist left has taken ninety-nine. It has left the religious a small living space, like the nature reserves for the Indians. Gradually the left eroded the heartstrings and distanced the religious youth. It was then that the seeds were sown and sprouted that would establish Elon Moreh and Ofra and Beit El. . . . Why should you complain of the 'normative alienation' of these people? They see the hatred of the elite in the State of Israel, of the fashionable and phony intellectualism . . . that each time strikes at religious Jewry in wild competition. . . .

"The State of Israel was established by often anti-religious pioneers and freemasons, and the guilt feelings engendered by the Holocaust also nested deep in the heart. . . . And then, when religious youth was wondering and probing its way, the Six-Day War broke out. And it broke out opening all the apertures and the world was full of singing and for a moment all of Creation rose up and thousands of suns burst before the gate of heaven, which seemed to have opened to a revelation of grace. And together with the singing came the opportunity. New stretches of land cried out for settlement. Secular Zionism was in crisis, and at long last an opportunity was given to national religious youth to run forward ahead of the camp. It ran first and thought afterward. . . . It was impossible that an energy like this would not deviate here and there into bullying and that the unrestrained emotions would not lead to epiphenomena, and then came the great crises of the Yom Kippur War, and the despair reappeared within us, and there was not a home in which someone had not died. In order to overcome gnawing doubts the fire in the heart was fanned hugely, and an aperture to the danger that there is in alien fire was opened. . . .

"And you can remove worry from your hearts. This disease of the defendants cannot be a nationwide plague. The State of Israel today is bourgeois and disgruntled . . . whereas the entire essence of these people is constant sacrifice and giving, and on the basis of this sacrifice the deviation exists. Indeed, even today, behind bars, disappointed, frustrated, hurting, and becoming wiser, they will be the first to answer any call, and it is they who will ascend the mountain."[87]

A Merciful Jewish Heart

On July 10, 1985, the verdict was handed down. Those who were charged in the case of the attack on the Islamic College in Hebron were convicted of premeditated murder, a crime that carries a compulsory sentence of life imprisonment; others were convicted of manslaughter. In the case of the attacks on the Palestinian mayors, eleven defendants were cleared of attempted murder but convicted on the charge of causing grave damage. In the Temple Mount case, the president of the court, Judge Bazak, decided that the defendants should be found not guilty, but the other judges convicted the ten defendants in this case of conspiring to commit a crime. Six more were convicted of activity in a terror organization. In the matter of booby-trapping the buses, two were unanimously convicted of attempted murder and two others were convicted by only a majority opinion.

The heart of Judge Bazak was captivated by the "good people imbued with faith" who stood before him as defendants. Of the Temple Mount case, Bazak wrote that "even though they believed that it was proper to remove this building from the site, they, or at least a considerable number of them, had doubts as to whether this should be carried out, and this because of the grave consequences that the blowing up of the structure could have and because of the fear that afterward the government would have to rebuild the structure, something that with respect to *halakha* is far worse than the existing situation."[88] Judge Bazak's ruling with respect to the other crimes was also empathetic. Attacks on Jews in Hebron, he wrote, "have increased the feeling of helplessness and fear in the small Jewish settlement."[89] He explained that "the Islamic College [in Hebron] teaches with great fanaticism hatred of Jews. Many teachers and students from the college have had a past of action against Jews."[90] He mentioned the prisoner exchange deal and the "government's failings" as reasons for the defendants'

psychological distress. He expanded on a description of the terrorists' soul-searching before the deed, stressing their "great regret for
the souls that might be hurt during the course of the action" and the
decision "with a heavy heart to carry out the action."[91]

In sentencing the defendants, Judge Bazak evinced a degree of
mercy that is far from typical of trials of terror crimes in Israel—
terror crimes committed by Palestinians, that is. "There is scope for
additional leniency in the sentencing of some of the defendants," he
said. This was for humanitarian and personal reasons, and because at
the end of the arguments for sentencing the defendants had admitted
their "mistake" and said they would not repeat their acts.[92] With
respect to Yeshua Ben Shushan, the person who had proposed and
planned the demolition of the Dome of the Rock, Judge Bazak wrote
that "crucial weight must be given to his splendid past as a brave
officer in the special operations unit. It seems to me it is the nation's
obligation to requite its heroes on the day of reckoning."[93]

Another judge was also charmed by the defendants, their devotion, and their modest ways, arguing that they numbered among "a
unique collective of people," all of whom were "graduates of yeshivas
and had an academic education as well. Most of them have served in
the IDF and took part in Israel's wars. Among them are army officers
and heroes of Israel's wars who were wounded during the course of
their military service. Most of them are people of Torah and work
who left behind them a comfortable way of life and set out with their
families to establish a Hebrew settlement, work it, and guard it." He
did speak about the "alien fire" that inflamed them but added that
their sin did not at all resemble "the crimes of others, who wish to
destroy, kill, and cause to perish."[94] Of Ben Shushan, the judge said
that he was a man of "the book and the sword, a hero of Israel's battles," and noted that he had been wounded in the Yom Kippur War.[95]

In favor of one of the planners of the explosion on the Temple Mount was his past as a fighter pilot with many combat missions in Israel's wars to his credit.[96] The testimonies of prominent character witnesses, most of them senior army officers, also helped mitigate the crimes in the eyes of the indulgent court.

Unlike his colleagues, the third judge, Zvi Cohen, did see the "conspiracy to destroy the Dome of the Rock Mosque, which is religiously motivated and means opening a new account with more than 300 million Muslims all over the world, in addition to the existing, blood-soaked account, between the Jewish nation and the Arab nation," as an unprecedentedly dangerous threat to Israel's very existence. "This plot imposes on the Jewish people the payment for the desires of those who wish to realize the vision of the Kingdom of Israel. As it endangers the entire people, there is no mitigation in the religious motivation at its base."[97] However, even this judge was not impervious to the defendants' creditable past, especially their army service, the launderer of all crimes. "Among them are those who have written glorious pages in settlement, defense, and help to the needy. It is untenable that these should not stand them in good stead at this difficult hour of theirs," he wrote.[98]

Very Important Prisoners

Though the prosecution argued for a stern punishment, the judges handed down light sentences for all of the convicted men, contrary to what the law stipulates. This was a huge victory for the entire settler community, and it was perceived as such and greeted with great rejoicing. The convicted embraced their families and their lawyers and sang on hearing the sentences in the courtroom. "Those who harmed the mayors were convinced that the authorities had wanted this but were unable to carry it out," said Dan Avi-Yitzhak, articulating what many in the courtroom thought but would not say out loud.[99] Whatever their "grave acts" may have been, "they are our pioneers," said the attorney. "They were no less able than the prosecutors who went to make a career in the State Prosecutor's Office, but they preferred to earn their living as farmers in Judea and Samaria."[100]

The prosecution's appeal of the sentences of those who received less than seven years' imprisonment woke the dormant political genie. The people of the right and the religious parties competed among themselves as to who would give the most stalwart and raucous support to the convicts. Deputy Prime Minister and Foreign Minister Yitzhak Shamir, a former terrorist himself as a prominent member of the LEHI/Stern Gang before 1948 and as a senior Mossad agent after statehood, declared that the prosecution's appeal was "a serious mistake, which is liable to be interpreted as a challenge to a large segment of public opinion." Members of the government made embarrassing statements. "The attorney general and the people of the State Prosecutor's Office . . . err in wanting to act in Israel like in other Western countries," said one. Another saw the submission of the appeal as evidence of "the impotence of the leaders of the regime," who have not learned to deal with those elements that have "developed hatred and hostility to the settlement in Judea and Samaria." The chairman of the Likud Knesset faction initiated moves toward the passage of a special amnesty law for the prisoners.[101]

The Supreme Court, although it did believe that some of the sentences were too light, rejected the prosecution's appeal. The punishments do not suit the gravity of the crimes, wrote the justices, and had we been on the first bench we would have handed down a more stringent punishment, but now it is too late, they ruled. This was a sad display of the Supreme Court's weariness and its surrender to the public hysteria.[102]

The combined political and rabbinical pressures that were openly applied to the president of the country and other authorities bore admirable fruit. Very quickly, publicly, and with not the slightest embarrassment, the convicted men began to be released from prison after impressively abbreviated sentences.[103] In December 1985, the president pardoned two of the prisoners without making public the reasoning that had led to his decision. In April 1986, two more prisoners were pardoned. On May 4, 1986, three members of the terror group were released from prison after having served two out of the three years of what had been a very lenient sentence in the first place. A week later, on May 13, 1986, two more were released after the president converted the remaining year of their three-year prison sentence into a year on probation.[104] Seven of the Underground members remained in prison, among them three who had received life sentences.[105]

Those who remained in prison enjoyed exceptionally good conditions and went home on furloughs on the weekends. The attempts by Knesset members from the left to rescind the prisoners' rest-home conditions lest they encourage "every future underground organization" were to no avail.[106] From the time the terrorists first came to light, the political structure did not stop interfering in procedures. As early as 1980 a *Washington Star* correspondent reported that Shin Bet head Avraham Achituv was about to resign from his position in protest against the fact that Prime Minister Begin was preventing him from properly investigating the attack on the mayors and from arresting the heads of Gush Emunim or sending agents to infiltrate groups that belonged to or were close to the organization.[107] At the end of the trial, a cohabitation, rotation government headed by Labor (Alignment) and the Likud was already presiding in Israel, and the two parties grappled with each other unrestrainedly in the matter of amnesties for the prisoners. To Deputy Prime Minister and Foreign Minister Yitzhak Shamir's demand for the early release of the prisoners,[108] the justice minister said that "we are on the brink of sinking into rule by the street and the destruction of the legal system. Never has a court in Israel been required to carry out its work in such a hysterical atmosphere."[109] The chief rabbis pressured Prime Minister Shimon Peres and Defense Minister Yitzhak Rabin to urge the president to pardon the convicted men. The Prime Minister's Bureau denied this, but few took the denial seriously.[110] In a report submitted to the prime minister, Attorney General Professor Yitzhak Zamir was strongly critical of political elements that were demanding the release of the convicted, saying that they were damaging the independence of the judiciary and the public's confidence in it.[111]

A proposal for legislation to grant pardons to the prisoners was brought before the Knesset in July 1987. The new incumbent Prime Minister Yitzhak Shamir voted in favor of the law, along with Minister Ariel Sharon and another thirty-eight Knesset members. By a vote of ninety-six against, the proposal was stricken from the agenda. Before Israel's fortieth Independence Day, the justice minister from the Likud recommended to the president of Israel, who a year earlier had cut the assassins' sentence to twenty-four years, that he pardon them. At first President Chaim Herzog refused the request, until in June 1989 he decided for the third time to reduce their punishment and cut the life sentence to ten years. The meaning of this decision was that the three who had been sentenced to life imprisonment were released after six years and six months. The president justified his decision by saying that the men who had been found guilty of planning and making a real attempt to blow up the Temple Mount and kill innocent people had expressed remorse for their deeds.[112]

Land Bank

In July 1982 the ultra-right-wing Tehiya Party joined the government. The leader of the party, Professor Yuval Ne'eman, became head of the settlement committee.[113] Ne'eman and his team were undiscriminating as to the kinds of settlements, their locations, or the financial outlays they entailed. At the first discussion held by the committee, in August 1982, while the Israeli Air Force was bombing Beirut, it approved the establishment of four new settlements. One month later the committee formulated a master plan for the settlement of southern Judea and approved the establishment of another five new settlements and the consolidation of the bases of two existing ones. The meeting was held a few days after U.S. President Ronald Reagan had demanded that Israel cease settlement entirely. Ne'eman declared that the committee's decision constituted an appropriate response to the American demand.[114] By the spring of 1984, after less than two years as head of the committee, Ne'eman had approved decisions concerning eighty-two settlements (of them, only seven or eight observations locales in the Galilee and the Negev). Ne'eman's devotion to the mission of settlement in the occupied territories knew no boundaries and became his new claim to fame. He exhausted the members of the committee and reduced them to a marginal factor in the discussions, to the point that many of them simply stayed away from the meetings. Often Ne'eman himself was the only one to show up for a meeting. Thus, with his one vote he approved the establishment of more and more settlements.

The State Comptroller's Report for 1983 found that from the time the Likud came to power in mid-1977 to the end of 1983, the government had approved the establishment of 103 settlements (as compared with only twenty-two approved during the first decade of occupation). The report also found that "the establishment of the settlements in Judea and Samaria had been done without proper attention to the obligatory planning procedures," and noted that "this situation is not only deleterious to proper administration, but is also liable to lead to flaws in the work of the construction and development of the settlements and the allocation of resources and means unnecessarily." The "grab as much as you can" method promulgated by Sharon and Ne'eman has no place in a properly run country, observed the comptroller. "Most of the construction in Judea and Samaria," the report stated, "has been carried out without regional and local master plans that will ensure the orderly development of the settlements and their integration into the regional infrastructure systems and land uses for building, industry, and services. . . . Priorities have not yet been determined for allocating resources in the establishment of the settlements." The comptroller did not find explicit procedures for the decision-making processes whereby the budgets for the settlements were determined and warned that "setting the budget and the aid for establishing the settlement is done largely on the basis of contacts with bodies that have an interest in the settlement and in effect the budget is influenced by the results of negotiations with them."[115] The legality or morality of the entire project did not concern the comptroller. In part because of Israel's dire economic straits, a number of Knesset members attempted to freeze the settlements altogether, the budget for which came to about $250 million in 1983–84. They failed.[116]

The Comptroller's Report and the public criticism did not deter Professor Ne'eman. The approaching 1984 elections, which threatened to take the government away from the right, spurred and expanded his project. He did not even hesitate to exploit the period of transition and snap last-minute decisions after the voters had already expressed no confidence in the policy of the extreme right.[117] Among the thirty-two new settlements founded in 1983–84, the large number of isolated, ephemeral locales in eastern Samaria and the area around Ramallah stands out. These settlements attracted young people, among them fanatics who gradually took over additional lands nearby in order to establish new outposts without having to resort to the authorities for permits. With the constitution of the Likud-Labor unity government in 1984, there were dozens of new settlements scattered over the map of the territories. It was the fruit of the Herculean labors that Sharon had invested during the years he was in charge of settlements, and of the huge infrastructure he had built up, which enabled the settlement project to swell to its current dimensions.[118] This rate of growth was also made possible thanks to the cancellation of the prohibition imposed by previous governments on the purchase by Jews of Arab-owned land in the West Bank. Israeli land dealers, among them close personal associates of Sharon, worked hand in hand with corrupt Palestinian land dealers in stealing Palestinian lands. The press reported on a common phenomenon of luring elderly illiterate Palestinians into selling their land. In the course of 1983 Jews deceitfully acquired 124,000 dunams (about 31,000 acres) in the West Bank.[119]

In 1983, sixty-seven settlements in the West Bank were registered at the Interior Ministry (compared with thirty-nine in 1978), and in them were 22,800 inhabitants (compared with 7,400 in 1978).[120] But the Israelis did not rush to the Eldorado that was offered them, with the spacious homes and the green lawns at bargain prices. The goal that the head of the settlement department at the Jewish Agency, Matti Drobless, had set for the coming three years—100,000 new settlers—was achieved only more than ten years later. His vision—a million settlers by 2013—seems far out of reach in 2007. After twenty years of conflict and billions of shekels of public money, the number of settlers reached some 270,000 (the 230,000 settlers in East Jerusalem and around it not included).[121] In 1992, shortly before the elections for the 13th Knesset, when the surveys were predicting a victory for the Labor Party, led by Yitzhak Rabin, Sharon invited political commentators to a tour of the Samaria area. From an outlook on one of the hills in western Samaria, he gestured with his hands toward the small, red-roofed houses scattered all along the horizon. Then he indicated the strips of dark asphalt invading the territory and crossing its length and width, and spoke about the logic in this disorder. These settlements and roads have been scattered there, Sharon would say to journalists he took ceremoniously to the territories to vaunt his enterprise, in order to prevent any future government from drawing a border line here, along the Green Line.

The settlers and their political representatives knew very well how to exploit the weakness of the opposition from the left. The Labor Party was too identified with many key settlements in the territories that had been planted there when it was in power, among them large settlement blocs like Gush Etzion and in the Jordan Valley and Gaza, as well as Hebron, Kiryat Arba, Ofra, Elon Moreh, Ma'aleh Adumim, and Ariel. Its leadership had not yet worked out the full political, moral, and economic implications of the settlements. The Israeli left was finding it difficult to round up mainstream political forces and significant extra-parliamentary forces of protest. The Peace Now movement was founded only in March 1978, four years after the establishment of Gush Emunim. It sprouted from an initiative of a group of Jerusalem university students who became known because of the "officers' letter" they had sent to Prime Minister Begin calling on him to abandon the dream of Greater Israel in favor of peace with the country's neighbors. The movement's first year of activity was devoted mainly to demonstrations in support of peace with Egypt, especially on the eve of Begin's departure for Camp David.

Peace Now quickly identified the Jewish settlement project in the territories as the main obstacle to peace. Its first protest vigil across from the Prime Minister's Office against the establishment of new settlements and the fortification of existing ones was held in May 1978. The Peace Now struggle focused in the next months on a demand to freeze the construction of new settlements during the period of transition to the autonomy plan.[122] During the course of 1982, alongside its campaign to get out of Lebanon, Peace Now held a series of demonstrations against the West Bank settlements. Activists of the movement organized protest rallies near Kiryat Arba and at Elon Moreh and Har Berakha near Nablus. In a special brochure, the movement brought to the public detailed information about the Begin government's settlement plans and what they would cost, primarily in order to enlist the poor immigrant towns, scattered along the borders in the 1950s and '60s, and the weaker social strata against the settlements. The pamphlet made an effort to show its target audience, the needy population of "development towns" and poor neighborhoods, that the many billions that were being invested in the settlements were taken directly from them.[123] The publication went unnoticed.

Shall the Twain Walk Together?

The settlements were the main source of discord in the coalition negotiations between Likud and Labor toward the establishment of the rotation government.[124] Prime Minister Shamir and Minister Sharon met with Shimon Peres and Yitzhak Rabin, bringing a list of about thirty settlements, some of them new and others slated for expansion. Rabin presented a list of his own, which included existing settlement points that fit his definition of "security settlements" (as opposed to "political settlements"). The disagreements threatened to lead to the failure of the negotiations, and at the end of a trenchant debate it was agreed that there would be a quota of six settlements a year at most, all of them in areas thinly populated with Palestinians.[125] In the coalition guidelines that were presented to the Knesset on September 13, 1984, it was manifest that the Labor Party leaders were squirming between affection for the settlers and recognition of the price that the settlements were exacting from the state and Israeli society. Alongside agreement to develop the existing settlements, it was stated that "the extent of their development will be decided by the government." It was agreed that five or six new settlements would be built within a year, the names of which would be determined by mutual agreement within one week of the establishment of the government. At the same time, the negotiating parties arrived at a formulation whereby the implementation of decisions by previous governments to establish new settlements "will be in later years, at such times that will be determined by the plenum of the national unity government." The agreement also stated what should have been obvious: that the establishment of new settlements would require the approval of a majority of the government ministers. In an appendix to the coalition guidelines, the names of twenty-one future settlements were listed.[126]

From 1985 to 1990, fourteen new settlements were added, but the number of inhabitants almost doubled (from 46,000 to 81,600).[127] Nevertheless, the first two years of the term of the unity government headed by Shimon Peres, with Yitzhak Rabin as defense minister, were the leanest years the settlers had known. Between 1984 and 1985, the first year of the unity government, about 14,000 new settlers moved into the new settlements, and houses that had been built on the land before the government was established. From then until the end of 1989—the eve of the breakup of the government—

the rate of growth declined to about 5,000 settlers a year. An economic recession that had a negative influence on the construction industry throughout the country affected the territories as well. The flow of money for new construction ceased almost entirely. The economic crisis of the 1980s succeeded where international criticism and domestic opposition had failed.

Peres and his people wanted to have the best of both worlds. To those on the left they boasted of having placed a barrier to settlement expansion, while to their partners from the right they promised that when things got a bit better the government would implement the coalition guidelines exactly as stated. In this way they were able, as always, to avoid a moral and strategic discussion about the long-term implications of the creeping annexation policy. "Who is speaking the truth?" a Knesset member from the leftist Mapam Party demanded of Prime Minister Peres—the Peres who has said he has frozen the settlements, or the Peres who is promising to establish more settlements when things get better and there is money?[128]

The second unity government, which was established in 1986 and headed by Yitzhak Shamir, continued to grapple with the three-figure inflation that it had inherited from the Likud government and with the high costs exacted by the Lebanon War, and refrained from massive settlement expansion. Shamir preferred to focus on maintaining the status quo and thwarting the secret negotiations that Foreign Minister Shimon Peres held with King Hussein of Jordan, which culminated in London in April 1987, in an agreement that became known as "the London agreement." What particularly deterred Shamir in the draft of the agreement was his fear of the internationalization of the conflict and an American demand to freeze construction in the settlements during the course of the negotiations. Eight months later, in December 1987, the most comprehensive Palestinian civil uprising that had ever occurred under Israeli rule broke out. This has become known as the first intifada. On July 31, 1988, King Hussein announced the severance of the connection between Jordan and the West Bank. Thus the "Jordanian option"—that is, the idea that a Palestinian state or autonomous entity could be formed in a federation with Jordan, of which Peres and Sharon had been proponents—was in effect rendered irrelevant and impossible.

A Predestined Death

The Palestinian uprising crushed the illusion of coexistence between the occupied and the occupier, and shattered the false vision of the benevolent, "enlightened" Israeli occupation. As always in such cases, it took a chance spark to ignite a huge conflagration. Accumulated feelings of long years of military rule, oppression, and exploitation among those who had seen their dignity trampled and their lands and their water taken from them and given to the Jewish settlers exploded all at once and slapped the complacent face of the settlers and all of Israeli society. In a special edition of the settlers' journal *Nekudah* that was devoted to the crisis, the intifada was described as "the harshest test since the settlement project began."[129]

This "harsh test" did not lead the settlers to a moral reconsideration of the tragedy of the Palestinians who had become strangers in their own home, but rather stiffened their necks even further. Even those who had been considered relatively moderate became more extreme. The first settler, Hannan Porat, who had always known how to get along with the authorities and navigate between divine commands and the constraints of reality, now proposed "massive expulsions" of Palestinians. He wrote that coexistence with the Arabs depended on settlers "suppressing with a heavy hand any attempt at terror and damaging our sovereignty." If not, he argued, the struggle "will reach a stage at which either we will be expelled, or they will. We will have to see to it that they are the ones who will be expelled."[130]

Rabbi Yitzhak Shilat of Ma'aleh Adumim declared that "anything we do as a result of distress and anger, even killing, is good, is acceptable and will help. Killing is just a matter for the Kingdom. Everything in relation to the situation, of course." He said that according to traditional Jewish law it is permissible to burn Arab shops in response to harm done to Jews, and most important, "in any case, when you do this, you should not get caught."[131] Some of the settler leaders, among them Levinger and Wallerstein, pulled out their weapons, which had been hanging on the wall in the previous acts, and shot Palestinians during the heat of the rebellion, even though in no case was there evidence that their lives were threatened. The legal proceedings for these occurrences revealed the low price tag on Arabs' lives and the twilight of law that prevailed in the territories.

Settlers allowed themselves to act as if there was no law at all, and did whatever they saw fit in the territories. A key member of the Committee for Security on the Roads in Kiryat Arba boasted that in January 1988, in the early days of the intifada, following an incident in which Molotov cocktails were thrown at Jews in Hebron, he and his friends destroyed every parked car they found in the streets: "Just four people worked during an entire night in Hebron and left no car whole."[132] An unofficial bus security man on behalf of the committee bragged that "we have a regular procedure: A driver who is stoned must stop. We get out of the bus, break things, uproot and catch the stone-throwers. I personally have apprehended three Arabs who threw stones. We put them on the bus, laid them down under the seats and stomped on them."[133] An inhabitant of the Hebron Hills defined the situation in his area as "first-rate anarchy. Everyone can do whatever he wants. It's a different planet. You are the law." He added that "they used to say 'the Wild West' as a joke. Today this is no longer a joke. We go out at night, cover the license plates, go into the nearby Arab village and the fun begins."[134]

The settlers' provocations of Palestinians, combined with an idle or nonchalant army and accident, sometimes led to disaster, and children and adolescents often paid the price of the adults' arrogance. On the morning of April 6, 1988, during the intermediate days of Passover, in the midst of the intifada, a group of sixteen teenage boys and girls set out from the settlement of Elon Moreh for a hike, accompanied by two armed adults. Even though the mood of Palestinians in the area was angry, bordering on explosive, the hike and its route had not been coordinated in advance with local army commanders. The young hikers went down to the wadi that borders on the village of Beita and stopped to eat at the Ein Rujan Spring. During the lunch break young Palestinians began to gather around them. A stone was thrown, and another. A melee began. According to some witnesses, one of the young Palestinians approached a security guard and tried to grab his weapon. The security guard fired and wounded him. The Palestinians suggested that the hikers accompany them to the village, toward the exit to the main road. When the hikers came to the middle of the village, stones were thrown at them again. One of the security guards began to fire his weapon in all directions. Two young Palestinians, aged eighteen and nineteen, were killed. Another local youth was severely wounded. One of the hikers was also killed: Tirtza Porat, fifteen, the daughter of Rabbi Yosef Porat, who had been among the first settlers in Kiryat Arba and a founder of Elon Moreh.

From this point a *Rashomon*-like story developed. The first report issued by the settlers that same day said Porat was murdered when the mother and sister of one of the Palestinians who were killed threw stones at her head. The army arrested the two women for interrogation.[135] In the midst of the tumult of the shooting and stone-throwing, one of the security guards, Romem Aldovi, twenty-six, was also severely wounded. Aldovi was considered a troublemaker in the whole region, and by the army as well. He was the first settler against whom the military had issued administrative movement restrictions, prohibiting him from entering the Nablus area. In the past he had been involved in a number of incidents with Israeli soldiers in the area of Joseph's Tomb.[136]

The press did not investigate the details of the story deeply before it came out with screaming headlines. "The Blood Hike" was the front-page headline in the mass-circulation daily *Ma'ariv*, which also showed a photograph of Tirtza Porat's body taken only a few minutes after the incident, and under it the heading: "Murder of the Girl Hiker." In another headline in the same newspaper one of the hikers was quoted: "We lay in puddles of blood."[137] The newspaper printed descriptions of the alleged lynching of the boys and girls. But right from the first testimonies another reality peeked through. "In the bloodthirsty mob there were two Arabs who did all they could to help," said a report. One girl testified that "there was one nice Arab who brought us water and hid us. It's lucky he was there."[138] The hikers themselves told of inhabitants of the village who came to their aid and fended off the attackers. The inhabitants, among them three women, shielded the Jewish girls and hid them in their homes. Other inhabitants of the village called ambulances, which evacuated the wounded and the dead.

But Benny Katzover, a leader of the settlers and chairman of the Samaria Regional Council, whose daughter was with the group of hikers, declared that the settlers' wrath was "unstoppable."[139] That evening, scores of settlers and people from the Tehiya movement came to the place where the tragedy occurred and established a "spontaneous settlement" named after Tirtza Porat.[140] While the army was still investigating the incident and already had some initial findings that did not agree with the settlers' claims, Chief of Staff Dan Shomron and Amram Mitzna, head of Central Command, met with the settler leaders. Katzover said there were already settlers on their way to a campaign of vengeance. "This will ignite unimaginable conflagrations. If there isn't something of a different order of magnitude here, something that will change the rules of the game, it won't be possible to stop people." Mitzna asked the settlers to act with restraint. "As public leaders, try to exert your influence."[141]

On April 13, at the end of the Passover holiday, the conclusions of the investigation of the incident by the military, the Shin Bet, and the police became known. Although the language of the report was exceedingly cautious, it blamed the security guards of the hike, especially Romem Aldovi, whose hasty trigger finger had sent the incident spinning into bloodshed. That morning there had already been disagreements between the two security guards, both of them residents of Elon Moreh. The elder of the two forbade Aldovi to use his weapon "except in emergency situations." But Aldovi fired "warning shots" right at the start of the incident, gravely injuring one of the young Palestinians. In the center of the village the disorder increased when word of the young villager's death arrived. The mother and the sister of the young man who had been killed fell upon Aldovi, beating him on the head with a board. Aldovi, who lost control, opened fire indiscriminately. Tirtza Porat, stated the official accounting, had not been killed by a stone that had been thrown at her by an Arab but rather "by the impact of a high-speed bullet of medium caliber" to her head. The investigation refuted the settlers' claim that a grenade or improvised explosive device had been thrown at the hikers and stated explicitly that "Tirtza Porat had been shot by Aldovi's weapon."[142]

Even before the publication of the military investigation, Chief of Staff Shomron said that the settlers "came out of there alive not because anyone rescued them with a military force, but because the people of the village did not let anyone harm them."[143]

Like the settlers and the media, the Israeli government did not wait for the conclusions of the investigation, and instead cast the full blame on the local inhabitants. Even before a thorough investigation, the people of Beita were punished. Within two days, thirteen homes were demolished.[144] The dam burst at Tirtza Porat's funeral, which was held during the intermediate days of Passover, a week that is laden with symbols and the tension of redemption. Tirtza was the first victim from among the second generation of veteran settlers. Her parents, Nehama and Yosef Porat, had met in Kiryat Arba and were on the hilltops at Sebastia and Kedumim until they founded Elon Moreh. The pain of her very unnecessary death mingled with righteous wrath at the authorities, the state, and the law, which were now all embodied in the introspective, tortured figure of the head of the Central Command, Amram Mitzna, who also came to pay his respects to the dead girl. At moments the funeral turned into a near-lynching. In the presence of Prime Minister Yitzhak Shamir, his deputy David Levy, and Minister Ariel Sharon, the settlers chanted, "Fire Mitzna!" Some pointed at the officer and shouted, "You murdered her," even though everyone was aware of their own responsibility for the disaster. The prime minister declared that "every act of murder strengthens the Jewish people, unites it, and connects it to this land, deepening its roots here." Rabbi Haim Druckman called for wiping Beita off the face of the earth. Minister of Religious Affairs Zevulun Hammer followed suit and also demanded that Beita be destroyed and that a settlement named after Tirtza Porat be established immediately in Samaria. "Lord of Vengeance our God, Lord of Vengeance appear," cried Benny Katzover.[145]

At the government meeting, Sharon attacked the military investigation. "Even if there were some hitches and things that were unclear, it is inappropriate that the explanation that comes from us creates the impression that the blame falls on the Jews," said Sharon. He proposed establishing in response a settlement named Tirtza. He also called for clearing the village of Beita of its inhabitants, apart from the families who helped the hikers. Katzover demanded that Chief of Staff Dan Shomron be dismissed because of the leak of the "superficial report" of the investigation that had been carried out by the army following the bloodshed.[146] About a month later, in an article in *Nekudah*, Katzover wrote that in the Beita affair a wicked attempt had been made to blur the main point, the Arabs' murderousness. The report, said Katzover, "burst the calumny that circles in the left and the media had been spreading about us for about a month, as though everything had happened as the result of a Jewish provocation."[147]

A Domestic Israeli Issue

The tragic occurrence at Beita did not calm things down. On the contrary, the people of the settlements raised the flag of vigilante suppression of the intifada and, in some measure, of revolt against the army. This revolt was not necessarily the exclusive realm of the inhabitants of the ideological settlements. It was led by some of the heads of the secular settlements, people from Ariel, Ma'aleh Adumim, Ginot Shomron, and others. After the body of an Israeli taxi driver was found in mid-January 1989 near the Yakir Junction in Samaria, inhabitants of Ariel blocked the trans-Samaria road. Dozens of carloads of settlers entered the village of Haris, breaking windows and harassing the inhabitants. Then they entered the village of Dir Istiya, uprooted olive trees, and lit bonfires.[148] This was a pogrom of the type that the Jews had known so well during their history in the

Diaspora. After that, nocturnal invasions of Palestinian villages by settlers became a matter of routine. Following the wounding by stone-throwers of a child from Ariel, inhabitants of Sha'arei Tikva and Ariel entered the village of Azoun-Athma, shattered windows, burned tires, broke shutters, and tried to break into homes. The incident culminated in a violent confrontation between the settlers and the army.[149]

The heads of the Yesha Council, who were aware of the severe damage to their cause done by the bullying acts of thug settlers, issued a call to desist from such actions, but it fell on deaf ears. The influence of the "quality of life" settlers whom the government had lured with cheap housing and other benefits was negligible. These settlers expected that the government would provide them both full security and close military protection on the roads. When their expectations were disappointed, they imposed their own law of violence on the territories.[150] The Kiryat Arba and Hebron settlers did not lag behind their fellows from Samaria. "We have embarked on an intifada against the Arabs. We can restrain ourselves no longer," declared Zvi Katzover, the deputy chairman of the local council.[151] In May 1989 settlers broke into Palestinians' houses nearly every night. The incursions by the Jewish militias caused extensive damage to the homes of the local inhabitants. In one of these incursions, a sixteen-year-old girl was killed.[152] The settlers' violence against the Palestinians, their harassment of soldiers, and the extreme statements by their leaders damaged their standing. A survey conducted in June 1989 found that 73 percent of the Israeli public disapproved of the settlers' acts of revenge and punishment toward the Palestinians. Eighty-five percent of the respondents believed that the exacerbation of the internal dispute could lead to a war among Jews.[153]

The fear of a civil war—"a war between brothers," in the Israeli political parlance—paralyzed Defense Minister Rabin. The forgiveness he evinced toward the Jewish pogromists brought down upon him harsh criticism from the left. It was said of him that he was forsaking the Arab inhabitants, was not giving protection to his soldiers, and was intimidated by the settlers' violence and constant threats. Avraham Burg of the Labor Party called for "expelling from the territories Jewish rabble, the rioters who are trying to torpedo the peace plan by means of pogroms and a second front against the IDF." Others accused the settlers of being the greatest collaborators with the Palestine Liberation Organization.[154] The public reaction to the violent incidents in the territories also dismayed the heads of Gush Emunim. They publicly denounced the harm to the civilian population and IDF soldiers. "We condemn outright any attempt to render struggle for our land and our home immoral by harm to innocent people." The blame was laid on isolated extremists.[155] The head of the Gush Etzion council proposed expelling stone-throwers from the territories, both Jewish and Arab.[156] There were even those who went so far as to demand "an end to Israeli rule over the Arab population in Yesha."[157]

The demarcation line between Likud and Labor with regard to their attitudes toward the settlements and the settlers was blurred. While the right-wing Likud devoted itself publicly to nurturing the settlements, Yitzhak Rabin, the defense minister on behalf of the Labor Party, completed the task by ruthlessly crushing the Palestinian civilian uprising against the creeping military occupation and the settlements (in January 1988 he said the intifada should be crushed by "force, might, and beatings").

By the end of the term of the first unity government, only eight new settlements had been established, but the total number of settlers had nearly doubled during that period. When the government was established at the end of 1984, the settler population numbered 35,300. At the end of 1988, when the second unity government was formed, the number stood at 63,600.[158] During its brief tenure—about a year and a half—the second unity government, headed by Yitzhak Shamir, achieved the settlement goals it had set for itself. In 1989 alone five new settlements were established.[159] The breakup of the unity government in May 1990 and the establishment of a narrow government of the right in its stead removed any previous brakes. Land confiscations in the territories and investments in settlements broke all records. According to Israeli and Palestinian sources, during the period between January 1988 and June 1991, more than 504,120 dunams (roughly 126,000 acres) in the West Bank were requisitioned.[160]

The distribution of Palestinian lands to anyone who wanted them, and at no price;[161] the cheap mortgages that Sharon offered, which became grants; and the water, electricity, and sewage infrastructures that were given for free brought about a change in the settlers' profile. Alongside the devotees of Greater Israel there were now new immigrants, among them some of the massive influx of some 1 million Russians as the Soviet Union was breaking up, and young couples, to whom the idea was foreign. Eventually many of them adopted the ideological justifications for living in the spacious houses that were given to them at a quarter of their real price. The huge investment in the settlements once again dug a deep deficit of about $500 million in the Ministry of Housing and Construction budget for 1991. The state comptroller called attention to incorrect administration, wastefulness, and corruption at the ministry. He recommended opening a criminal investigation against a number of ministry employees and severely criticized the minister himself, Sharon. The comptroller's revelations reverberated in the public and contributed to the Likud's defeat in the 1992 elections.[162] Basing himself on old decisions by the ministerial committee on settlement, Minister Yuval Ne'eman took advantage of the "seam period" between the two governments to expand the jurisdictional boundaries of dozens of settlements by scores of kilometers. In these snatchings it was determined that any piece of land that was not more than two kilometers (1.25 miles) away from an existing settlement boundary would not be considered a new settlement, and thus could be developed. Thousands of square kilometers were thus effectively annexed to the settlements' contours. The work of setting up mobile homes on the hills was given to private contractors, to maintain the secrecy. Prime Minister Shamir kept silent as long as the campaign did not create a public uproar.[163]

Baker's Journeys in the Holy Land

The uproar came from an unexpected place—the capital of the United States. President George H.W. Bush, who came into office in January 1989, and Secretary of State James Baker decided to impose a new order in the Middle East, promoting the issue of the settlements to the top of the public agenda. This issue was raised at the first meeting between Shamir and Bush, in April 1989, and it would cast a shadow over their relations ever afterward. Shamir depicted the settlements as "a domestic Israeli matter" and added that "you have things that concern you and we have things that concern us; don't let this concern you." Bush replied that the issue was of deep concern to the United States, as every American taxpayer contributed $1,000 to funding aid to Israel. Shamir summed up with the words, "You can rest assured, this will not be a problem." The Americans took these words literally and understood that Israel would refrain from establishing new settlements.[164] Their mistake became clear only a few weeks later, upon the report of the establishment of a series of new settlements in the midst of accelerated diplomacy toward a peace process. The president was irked by report sent by the U.S. ambassador in Israel of a conversation during which the prime minister told him that he did not believe that Bush saw the settlements as an earthshaking issue.

However, Washington interpreted Israel's massive construction of houses, which stood empty on the hills of the West Bank, as defiance of the administration and a challenge to its policy on settlements. The crisis between the American administration and the government of Israel came to a head with the constitution of the government of the right in June 1990. The new government set stringent conditions for negotiations with representatives of the Palestinians, frustrating Baker so much that in an appearance before the House Foreign Relations Committee that month, he sent Israel an exceptionally harsh message: He read out the phone number of the White House switchboard and said, "When you're serious about peace, call us."[165] Shamir greeted almost every one of Baker's trips to the Middle East by laying the cornerstone for yet another new settlement. A concrete example of Baker's frustration can be found in a dialogue he conducted with Shamir at an April 1991 meeting in Jerusalem. The two dealt with Sharon's announcement that Israel intended to build 13,000 new housing units in the territories in the coming three years. "I see this as an intentional attempt to sabotage peace," said Baker, "and I am asking you to deny these statements." Shamir, as usual, played the good cop and replied, "I am not pleased with these statements, and everyone in this country knows that." This time Baker did not hold his tongue. "I am not asking you to adopt our position," he said to Shamir, "but I am asking you to prevent this person [Sharon] from sowing mines on the road to peace." Shamir's reply, "I don't want to involve you in our internal politics," angered the American secretary of state. "I don't want us to become involved in your internal politics," Baker said, "but if the provocations in the settlements continue, that is what will happen. I'm warning you." Shamir promised to deal with the matter, but the settlements continued to expand and relations with the United States continued to worsen. They reached such a low point that the Americans pulled out what was considered the Judgment Day weapon in relations with Israel—economic sanctions.

The government of Israel continued to believe that it could both receive American aid and flaunt new settlements in the administration's face. The Israeli budget for 1992 allocated resources for the building of 5,500 new housing units, on the assumption that the treasury would have American guarantees totaling $10 billion at its disposal as a special loan for the absorption of the new immigrants from the former Soviet Union. This time the Labor Party knew how to exploit the crisis between the Likud government and the American administration: The Labor candidate for premiership, Yitzhak Rabin, promised that unlike the government of the right, his government would devote the money from the guarantees to education, health, the creation of jobs, and the development of infrastructures to benefit all of the country's citizens.[166] The expansion of settlements by the Likud continued until Election Day, even after it emerged that power would be transferred to its political rival. A few hours after the polls closed, Sharon, still the minister of housing and construction, phoned Yaakov Katz, an influential settler and Sharon's aide on settlement matters. "It will take Rabin two weeks to form a government and start to put things in order," said Sharon, who instructed that 500 families who were slated for settlement in Kiryat Sefer be moved into the unfinished apartments immediately. They were moved into the buildings, without electricity and water. "There is no hill that we haven't gone up on," was Katz's summation of Sharon's activity between 1990 and 1992. "There is no tree under which we haven't sat. . . . We put up 40,000 housing units and 20,000 mobile homes with Arik Sharon, so that it will never be possible to remove them."[167]

The crisis over the guarantees issue came to its end in the summer of 1992. On August 10 Yitzhak Rabin met with President Bush at his summer home in Kennebunkport, Maine. The new prime minister promised that Israel would refrain from constructing settlements and would not approve the creation of settlements by private citizens. He made a commitment that the government would not confiscate any more Palestinian lands for settlement purposes. On October 5, 1992, Congress approved guarantees of $10 billion to Israel. The cloud that had overshadowed relations between Israel and the United States passed with a single statement by the new prime minister.[168] From 6,200 in 1992 under Sharon as minister of housing and construction, the number of building starts in the territories declined the following year, during Rabin's term, to 980. The State of Israel would enjoy a number of years of prosperity—especially after the September 1993 signing of the Oslo agreement—the likes of which it had never known since its establishment. Education, welfare and health, culture and science, the peripheral locales, and the Arab citizens within the Green Line were now given the place they deserved in the new government's priorities, just as Rabin had promised before the elections.[169] Not for long.

3

Fire on the Hilltops

On February 25, 1994, Israel's weekend papers reported on the final preparations for the army withdrawal from Gaza and Jericho. Two weeks earlier, implementation of the Gaza-Jericho agreement had begun, after Palestinian Authority Chairman Yasser Arafat agreed at talks in Cairo to Israel's demand for military control over the three east-west roads leading to the Jewish settlement blocs in the Gaza Strip. The efforts by Prime Minister Yitzhak Rabin and Shimon Peres to ensure the well-being of the settlers did not soften the hearts of their infuriated leaders. They continued to demonstrate and block roads, defame the government, and concoct schemes to thwart its moves. The call to "stop Oslo" and the commandment to salvage the land became their most urgent aim. One settler, Dr. Baruch Goldstein of Kiryat Arba, "delivered his soul to his maker" before dawn on that wintry Friday in February for the sake of the commandment. Before the Jewish children had woken up for the Purim celebrations, and at the height of the Muslim month of Ramadan, the religiously observant doctor, a native of Brooklyn, donned his army reserve uniform, picked up an Uzi submachine gun, and set out for the Tomb of the Patriarchs in Hebron.

At 5:05 A.M. the muezzin, Jamal al-Natsche, completed his call announcing the start of the morning prayers and the fast. About 800 worshipers were crowded into the Ibrahimi Mosque. Some of them had spent the night there. Sentry Muhammad Abu Salah immediately identified the "doctor" and blocked his way. This was not the first time Goldstein had entered the place when it was closed to Jewish worship, defying the fragile service arrangements and despite the Muslim guards. The Israeli soldiers were well acquainted with Goldstein's displays of wrath. "I'm in charge here and I have to go in," Goldstein said in Arabic, shoving the sentry with his rifle butt, pushing open the door, and bursting into the mosque. While rising from the floor, the sentry heard a long burst of gunfire accompanied by cries of *Allahu akhbar.* He rushed out to call for the help of the soldiers, who seemed to have evaporated, then ran back to the mosque, where Goldstein was still firing at the worshipers. At 5:15, as Goldstein was loading the fifth magazine into his weapon, he was hit by a fire extinguisher thrown at him by a worshiper. Goldstein collapsed. Other worshipers fell upon the murderer and beat him to death.[1]

Twenty-nine people were killed and 125 wounded. Reports of the massacre spread around the world. The reactions were not long in coming. From Tunis, Arafat announced the suspension of all contacts with Israel. Prime Minister Rabin summoned his government for an emergency meeting on that same day—a Friday afternoon, when government business is not usually conducted. Attorney General Michael Ben-Yair, who was on his way to Jerusalem, turned around and went back to the Kirya, General Staff headquarters in Tel Aviv. He first went into the office of Chief of Staff Ehud Barak and said to him that this was an opportunity to evacuate the inhabitants of the Jewish Quarter from Hebron. The chief of staff mumbled something in response about the Gaza Strip settlement of Netzarim.[2] On that same day the government issued a statement condemning the murder, expressing regret for the victims, and promising to compensate the families. After a lengthy discussion and over the initial opposition of Rabin, Peres, and other key ministers, the government decided to appoint a commission headed by Supreme Court President Meir Shamgar to delve into the circumstances of the killing. The commission was asked to present its recommendations on how to prevent similar occurrences in the future. Rabin's argument that the commission's deliberations would only delay the peace process, and thus further the murderer's intentions, seemed to reflect a deeper pessimism about the futility of such state commissions, which usually unearthed the obvious and were intended mainly to restore a semblance of order.[3]

"The murderer from Hebron opened fire on innocent people, but intended to kill the making of peace. His aim was political," said Rabin in the Knesset plenum three days after the massacre. "I say here in a clear and lucid voice: Let's not be mistaken; we will continue the making of peace on the basis of the Declaration of Principles that was signed in Washington and the Cairo Document." Rabin still believed that Israeli democracy and the desire of most Israelis to achieve peace would prevail, and he would not allow the settlers and their religious mentors to thwart it. Talking passionately, he told the Knesset that the doctor from Hebron "emerged from a small and limited political sector in the people. He grew up in a swamp that has its sources in foreign lands as well as here; they are alien to Judaism, they are not part of us. To him and his ilk we say today: You are not part of the community of Israel. You are not part of the national democratic camp to which all of us here in this house are partner, and very many in the nation loathe you. You are not partner to the Zionist deed. You are a foreign body, you are pernicious weeds. Sane Jewry vomits you from its midst. You have placed yourselves out of the bounds of Jewish law. You are a disgrace to Zionism and a blot on Judaism."[4]

The prime minister's harsh and moving words resounded beyond the Knesset plenum, but it seemed as though Rabin and his colleagues did not understand, or refused to believe, that the view that sanctified the land over human life was not only the province of "pernicious weeds." And thus, the man who had promised to fight Palestinian terrorism as though there were no peace process and to pursue peace as though there were no terrorism had finally caved in under the Jewish terrorism that was nurtured in the classrooms of Hebron's extremist yeshivas. Like the best and the brightest of the Israeli elites, Rabin closed his ears to the words of praise that were uttered in Kiryat Arba for the murderer. Rabin and so many others in Israel did not know— or probably knew at some level but were repressing the bitter truth— that in the settlements, at the Bar-Ilan University campus, and in many more places throughout the country, Goldstein had become a hero. "It began after Goldstein," admitted Yigal Amir to the police investigators after he fatally shot the prime minister in the back some twenty months later. "It's then that it dawned on me that one must put down [Rabin]." Amir was among the mass of mourners who attended the funeral procession that accompanied Goldstein to his grave in Hebron. From that day on, he prepared himself for the continuation of Goldstein's project to save the Jewish people from another holocaust and to advance the process of Redemption.[5]

Yet Rabin confined himself to the impressive words of condemnation he uttered in the Knesset and was reluctant to confront the settlers directly. He could not foresee the possibility that a lukewarm government response to the slaughter of the Muslim worshipers would spur Muslim fanatics to send walking bombs into the heart of Israel. The strategic decision by Hamas to carry out mass suicide attacks against Israeli civilians was made in the wake of the massacre in Hebron, said Middle East specialist Mati Steinberg, who at the time was adviser to the head of the Shin Bet (Israel's General Security Service) on Palestinian matters. "In the Hamas writings, alongside motifs of sacrifice, there is an explicit prohibition against indiscriminate harm to helpless people. The massacre at the mosque released them from this taboo and introduced a dimension of measure for measure, based on citations from the Koran."[6] The murderous act of the Jewish physician thus released dormant demons on all sides. It not only put the assassin of Israel's prime minister on the path to his crime; the mass terror attacks in Israeli cities, from which the massacre at the mosque had effectively lifted the religious Islamic prohibitions, enraged the Israeli public and devastated the Israeli peace-seeking left, eventually souring it on the prospects for peace.

A few hours after the mass killing in Hebron, while reports of riots in the town were piling up, prominent government figures demanded that Rabin take advantage of the shock created by the massacre and finally uproot the nefarious Jewish settlement from the heart of the city. The heads of the left-wing Meretz Party, Shulamit Aloni and Amnon Rubinstein, said it openly, claiming that this would be the only possible way to mend the injury. Deputy Foreign Minister Yossi Beilin argued that ousting the settlers would strengthen both the peace process and the rule of law.[7] In a discussion held at Rabin's bureau, with the participation of Attorney General Ben-Yair, the head of the international law division at the military prosecutor's office explained that it was legally feasible to evacuate most of the settlers from Hebron. He noted that Beit Hasson, Beit Hadassah, and other houses in the Jewish Quarter of Hebron had been requisitioned for military purposes under a security order. There would be no problem with canceling the orders and evacuating the buildings, said the military jurist. Ben-Yair proposed moving the settlers to a nearby military base so that it would be possible to provide them with kosher food. Participants in the meeting said later that Rabin looked undecided.[8]

The prime minister's tormented vacillation lasted for weeks. On March 19 he informed Peres that he had decided to evacuate Tel Rumeida and the yeshiva students from the Jewish Quarter of Hebron. The date for this act was to be established in consultation with the heads of the security systems.[9] The following day a small Israeli delegation set out for Tunis to appeal to Arafat to renew the talks with Israel. Arafat told his visitors that evacuating the settlers was a crucial condition for progress. Although Rabin had authorized the heads of the delegation to inform Arafat of his decision to uproot Tel Rumeida, they decided to save the gesture for the last minute, perhaps in part because they knew how hard it was for Rabin to make difficult decisions. Instead, they proposed expanding the presence of the Red Cross unit in the town of Hebron. Arafat reacted angrily, and the Israelis retired to their hotel in an atmosphere of crisis. In the evening they were informed by the Prime Minister's Bureau that Rabin had retreated from his decision to evacuate the settlers.[10]

The rumor about the intention to liquidate the Jewish settlement in Hebron spread rapidly through the settlements and the yeshivas. The "Yesha Rabbis' Committee" met in Kiryat Arba to discuss the issue of soldiers' refusal to obey a possible evacuation order. It ruled that refusal to obey an evacuation order was a divine commandment.[11] In response to a question from the committee, Rabbi Shlomo Goren, the former chief rabbi of Israel, declared war on any Israeli government that would order the evacuation of Hebron. Moreover, Goren determined that it was incumbent upon "all of Israel" to oppose "this destructive plan" with "every ounce of their power . . . and we must offer up our souls against this dastardly plot by the government of

Israel, which rests on an Arab majority, and be prepared to be killed and not allow the destruction of Hebron."[12]

On the prime minister's desk lay a memorandum from his aide for settlement matters, Noah Kinarti. The memorandum said that the head of the "operational team" of the Yesha Council for the fight against the Oslo agreement had threatened that if the settlers were evacuated from Hebron, 10,000 supporters would invade the town. If these were expelled by force, warned this chief of operations, 50,000 settlers would come and replace them.[13] The group did not confine itself to planning actions against evacuation of the Hebron settlers. It also had a detailed scheme for expelling Arabs from Hebron "in some number or other." Noam Arnon, the spokesman of the Jewish community in Hebron, threatened to activate booby-trapped cooking gas balloons, while some women deliberated on the possibility of killing themselves on the altar of the Jewish Quarter. Everyone in Kiryat Arba knew where he had to be "in real time," said the chief of operations.[14] A petition to the prime minister against the evacuation was signed by 1,002 rabbis from Israel and the Diaspora. Chief Rabbi Yisrael Lau was the guest of honor at a large assembly for Hebron held in Jerusalem.[15]

Shin Bet head Yaakov Peri advised Rabin to take the settlers' threats seriously and warned him of a revolt. Professor Ehud Sprinzak, an internationally renowned specialist on illegalism, terror, and extreme right-wing movements, who was called in to the Prime Minister's Bureau, also advised Rabin to address the settlers' warnings with care. Already at the end of May 1993, four months before the signing of the Oslo agreement, Sprinzak warned of a clash between "Jewish antidotes to violence" and "the political sociology of increasing extremism and violence."[16] The specialist on extremism argued that this was a matter of "a terrible cleavage, the collapse of an entire world that was built with great faith, great love, and great hope. . . . This is one of the greatest crises that the State of Israel and the Zionist movement have ever faced, if not the greatest. Those who are going to pay the highest price," said Sprinzak, "ought to be given the full opportunity to convince the nation with their arguments. If there is no peace at home—any peace outside is worth nothing." The evacuation of the Hebron settlers, said Sprinzak to Rabin, "is liable to ignite a conflagration in the territories."[17]

A few days after Chief of Staff Ehud Barak imposed a curfew on the families and friends of the victims of the massacre, all of them Palestinian inhabitants of Hebron, in order to ensure the safety of the murderer's neighbors and admirers, Rabin arrived for a summit meeting at the White House. At a joint press conference with President Bill Clinton, Rabin said that evacuating the settlements was a matter that must be discussed in negotiations for the final-status agreement. In a conversation with Israeli journalists, Rabin admitted that he felt uncomfortable that tens of thousands of Palestinians, the people of Hebron, were under curfew because of the 400 inhabitants of the Jewish settlement in the town, and added that he was puzzling over how to solve this.[18] In a private exchange with Dennis Ross, head of the American peace team, Rabin wondered about the wisdom of his decision not to evacuate the 400 Hebron settlers.[19] In the summer of 1995, a period of wild settler demonstrations against Oslo and Rabin himself, numerous political and security people heard Rabin say that diplomatically it was incumbent on him to uproot the Hebron settlers after the massacre but that politically the act had not been possible. What happened to Rabin while he hesitated regarding the settlements, in Hebron as well as in other sensitive regions, is well known; he was assassinated by an ardent supporter of settlements. So far not one of the Hebron settlers has been evacuated, while large neighborhoods at the heart of the town have been gradually, as a result of the settlers' violence and harassments, emptied of their original Palestinian inhabitants.

"A Lone Perpetrator"

On June 28, 1994, Justice Shamgar issued his commission's report on the massacre in Hebron, which determined that Goldstein alone bore the responsibility for the murder of the worshipers and that because it had not been possible to expect the massacre, no one should be blamed. The report stated that Goldstein had "acted as a lone perpetrator." It had not been proved, said the report, that the murderer had been abetted by anyone or that there had been "partners to the secret." As in similar reports by similar commissions of inquiry in Israel, this commission too tried to restore some false semblance of order that the murder had supposedly disturbed. The commission did not investigate the deep background to the act. It was the murder alone that was perceived as a disturbance of order, not the ongoing culture of law breaking and aggression that had existed in the occupied territories for years, and from which the murderer came. Thus the commission did not say anything new and even helped to blur the disastrous extent of nonenforcement of the law that prevailed in the territories, and of the existence of one law for Jews and another law for Palestinians. Following the publication of the commission's report, Rabin admitted that even if the government were to implement the commission's recommendations, which dealt mainly with the security arrangements at the Hebronite Tomb/Mosque, there was no absolute certainty that a deed like Baruch Goldstein's would not recur.[20] Rabin never imagined that he would be the victim of the next Jewish murderer.

Rabin's loathing of the settlers accompanied him throughout his political career, as did his flinching from confrontation with them. As far back as the early 1970s, when he was minister of labor in Golda Meir's government, he proposed that settlers should "travel to Gush Etzion with a Jordanian visa."[21] In July 1974, at the beginning of his first term as prime minister, he said in a meeting with settler leaders, one of many to come, that the settlements did not determine the borders of Israel and did not contribute to national security. The isolated settlements even jeopardized Israel's security, he added.[22] On another occasion he asked rhetorically what the settlers were seeking in Samaria and declared that the government "would not tolerate the madness of every Jew in this country." In *The Rabin Memoirs*, he called Gush Emunim a cancer in the body of Israeli democracy.[23]

The son of Israeli Labor Zionism, a graduate of the pre-state strike force, the Palmach, and a blunt, honest military man who became a diplomat and politician, Rabin embodied the cognitive dissonance between, on the one hand, the understanding that the settlements thwart any chance for a peace agreement and normalization of Israel's collective agenda and, on the other, the persistent refusal to see the growing hold of the settlements on the territories, and thus their creeping annexation. He was not alone in this state of denial; it was shared by most of his colleagues from the Labor and the Zionist left. The belated realization of the damage caused by the settlements, of which growing segments of the Israeli public had become aware, for the first time put the settlements at the focus of the election campaign in 1992. Twenty-five years after the Labor Party had laid the first foundations for them, it used the fight against this project as a lever to lift itself back into power.

The State Comptroller's Report for 1991, which was published in April 1992, two months before the elections, and especially the chapter on the Ministry of Construction and Housing headed by Ariel Sharon, breathed life into the opposition's struggle to put an end to the settlements. The report was a harsh indictment of the ministry for its improper administration, waste of public funds, and sheer corruption in its settlement activities in the territories.[24] Yet even in this case, the public debate centered on the symptoms rather than on the disease itself. The promise to "change the national priorities" became the headline of the Labor Party campaign. The secondary headline was a promise to divert budgets from the settlements to education, welfare, and needy neighborhoods and towns within the Green Line. But Rabin's own distinction between "political settlements" and "security settlements" began to take root in the public debate. Ironically, however, the Labor Party returned to power on the shoulders of the most fanatical of settlers. Rabbi Moshe Levinger from Hebron, one of the founders of Gush Emunim, decided to challenge the right-wing establishment that had come to terms with the multilateral and bilateral talks that followed from the fall 1991 international peace conference in Madrid, which was chaired by President Bush and Russian President Mikhail Gorbachev. At the head of a new list, Levinger failed to win the necessary percentage of votes in the general elections, thus funneling away from the rightist bloc the Knesset seats it needed to prevent a Labor-Meretz victory.

Evil Regime

The new Labor-Meretz-Shas government, which was presented in July 1992, was the first government since 1977 without representatives of the worldview and interests of the settlement movement. The coalition with Meretz, the party that symbolized secularism and defeatism in the eyes of the settlers, a coalition that was furthermore supported by the Arab parties, was perceived as a declaration of war on religious Zionism and the settlement movement. Rabbi Shlomo Aviner, one of the settlers' most admired spiritual leaders, wrote after the establishment of Rabin's government that these "enemies of Zionism and settlement must be stricken from the blessing [of the state]. . . . Even though it is honored by the presence of the liberators of Jerusalem, Holocaust survivors and the like, [this government] cannot atone for its negative intentions. . . . The nihilist forces in the nation, together with our Arab enemies, [are members of the government]. And if we count the Arab Knesset members who support this government, even you will see that this government does not have a majority among the nation in Israel . . . ." By appointing an Arab as a deputy minister, Aviner claimed, Rabin was no longer heading a "true" Jewish government and had "thus defiled the entire government." Who can guarantee, he asked, that tomorrow an Arab defense minister or perhaps prime minister will not be appointed, "because in a 'democracy' anything is possible."[25]

The editorial in the September 1992 edition of the settlers' organ *Nekudah* called for the destruction of the Rabin government, which "threatens to destroy, in every sense of the word, truths in the light of which many have walked and in the name of which thousands have given their lives; [it] is aiming to put the Zionist project and Zionist belief into retreat and to replace it with the golden calf and false peace. There is only one way for such a government: It must pass from the earth."[26] The incitement in *Nekudah* and in other settler media, such as Channel Seven Radio, increasingly focused on the prime minister himself, his character and functioning. Rabin's leadership was depicted as an existential danger to Israel. In November 1992 the settlers' journal wrote that Rabin "is a (bitter and ironic) caprice of history. A mediocre chief of staff who, had it not been for the Six-Day War, would have long since sunk in the abyss of oblivion." The writer urged his readers not to be led astray by Rabin's tough appearance. "Beneath the determined mask hides a weak, limited and abashed individual, who has never known how to withstand supreme pressures. . . . Removing him from the political stage, and together with him a malevolent government that is captive in the hands of the radical left and the PLO, is therefore a supreme existential need." If we do not see fit to remove him, said the article, "we will all be deserving of Rabin, traitors to the purpose of our life, making our humble contribution to the destruction of the Third Temple."[27] The word "remove," in all of its various forms, could be construed in many ways, and indeed was interpreted in a deadly way a few years later by the prime minister's assassin and his mentors.

Another writer in *Nekudah* called repeatedly for civil revolt by the settlers and for turning the courts and prisons into additional sites for the struggle against "a malevolent and treacherous government." When the time comes, he said, "When a court sentences us to a fine of so many hundreds of thousands of shekels, or imprisonment instead—we shall choose imprisonment!"[28] Hagai Segal, a member of the Jewish terrorist group and a released prisoner who had become an accepted publicist in the national press and a popular broadcaster on the settlers' Channel Seven pirate radio station, in fact found some twisted solace in Rabin's election. In an article impressive for its daring and its diagnosis of the love-hate relationship that had developed between the settlers and Israeli society, Segal wrote that "the upheaval of 1992 will put an end to our schizophrenic attitude towards the authorities. Until now, the government was with us and not with us, for us and against us. One hand fed us carrots and the other hand slapped us in the face. Arik Sharon built Judea and Samaria and demolished Yamit. . . . It is preferable that the differences of opinion between us and the authorities be sharp, clear-cut, dazzling as the brilliance of the sky. Once and for all it must be known who is for us and who is against us. . . . In the worst case Rabin will only implement what Yitzhak Shamir has in any case already plotted—autonomy [to the Palestinians]. . . . Even if we remain only 0.02 percent of all the eligible votes, we will have no alternative but to devote ourselves solely to the command of our conscience and obey principles that we have adopted warmly since the upheaval of the exodus from Egypt. Only then the day will come when the voter will enthusiastically accept our judgment, if not in 1996 then in 2000. Forbearance. We must not wait with a stopwatch."[29]

Prophetic words. In 1996 Benjamin Netanyahu brought the right back into power, after Rabin was assassinated by the bullets of a right-wing student who "devoted himself to the command of his conscience" and the principles that his comrades had adopted "since the upheaval of the exodus from Egypt." Segal was right. The Labor government went and a Likud government came, and the settlers not only remained where they were but also flourished mightily. "We are permitted to say a good word about ourselves," wrote Segal. "From the time Rabin passed the torch of government to Begin until he received it back from Shamir, we succeeded in establishing a number of solid facts on the ground. Even in the Meretz platform there is a commitment not to evacuate settlements. Long live democracy."[30] Segal's diagnosis was right on target. The ambivalence that had always characterized the labor movement's attitude toward the settlements was now hiding behind convoluted formulas and enjoyed American approval. This approach infiltrated the coalition agreement with Meretz and the government guidelines. It was in effect an almost perfect replica of the compromise of the Labor-Likud unity governments of 1984–1990. Meretz's agreement to the formulation that "decisions on new settlements and significant reinforcement will be approved by the government" made it a partner to the granting of the blessing for a safe journey to the settlers and their collaborators in the government ministries.[31] Thus silent annexation by the method of expanding existing settlements for "natural growth" could continue unhindered, even with generous aid, under the Labor-Meretz government.[32]

The founding guidelines of the new government, stipulating that the settlement freeze would not apply to the area of Greater Jerusalem and the Jordan Valley, and the vagueness of the term "Greater Jerusalem," left ample space for the settlement project within the boundaries of the Israeli consensus.[33] Varied and creative interpretations that developed over the years transformed the term "natural growth" into a transparent fig leaf for expanding Jewish settlement and confiscating Palestinian land. All of Israel's governments subsumed under this term not only the natural reproduction of the existing Jewish population in the territories but also population growth as a result of immigration. This was at a time when the governments themselves openly encouraged migration from within the Green Line to the settlements in the territories by means of a generous package of benefits and economic incentives. Under the label "natural growth," Israel also established new settlements in the guise of "new neighborhoods" in veteran settlements. To this end, the new settlements were included in the jurisdictions or boundaries of adjacent settlements, even if there was no territorial contiguity between them.[34]

In an investigative report that was published in the newspaper *Hadashot*, it was noted that during the first year of its term the Rabin government transferred $32 million for equipment purchases by the settlers and their organizations. This money was used mainly for purchasing buses and cars for the settler organizations in which settlers were later transported to demonstrations against the government. The government also provided communications equipment for Gush Emunim activists, amplifier systems, generators, and other items for antigovernment use by demonstrators.[35] The cuts in American funding resulting from the 1991–1992 dispute over loan guarantees affected only infrastructure work at the settlements. The launching of new neighborhoods was indeed reduced, investment in new industrial plants shrank, government aid to existing plants was cut, and the rate of paving roads was decreased. During its first year the Rabin government gave the settlers tax breaks amounting to $25 million, a legacy from the previous Likud government. During that same year the settlers' local councils received more than $85 million, of this about $60 million that the Interior Ministry transferred for the payment of the salaries of council employees.[36] The sum that was reported to the Americans for purposes of deduction from the guarantees stood at $430 million. Not included in this sum were investments in East Jerusalem, which stood at $700 million. The American administration contented itself with the deduction of $437 million, of which only $7 million was for the investments in East Jerusalem—that is, 1 percent of the actual investment.[37]

On November 22, 1992, the Rabin government decided (Resolution 360) to stop the public building in the territories that was being carried out under decisions of the previous government. Rabin attributed great importance to Resolution 360.[38] He stressed, however, that there should be no mention of political motives for the resolution, but only the change of priorities in the economy and the decline in immigration. Rabin's complex attitude toward the settlements was also expressed in Provision 4 of the resolution, which permitted private residential building within existing settlements "that is not from the state budget."[39] In the same decision it was also resolved that procedures concerning master plans that had not yet been authorized would be stopped. At the same time, however, in a classic move of one step forward and two steps back, the government left a wide opening for the continued spread of the settlements even outside the master plans, as it authorized the prime minister and defense minister, together with the minister of housing and construction, to appoint an "exceptions committee" that would have the authority to recommend the expansion of settlements. A few months later Peace Now discovered that the exceptions committee headed by Noah Kinarti, an adviser to the defense minister on settlement matters and an enthusiastic supporter of the settlers, was approving construction at several sites outside the master plans. Informed by Peace Now, Meretz ministers demanded that Rabin stop the procedure. The exceptions committee was upgraded from officials to government ministers, but Meretz succeeded in thwarting building permits outside the master plans in only a few cases.[40]

All these concessions by the government did not stand a chance of softening the settlers' hearts. Their onslaught on Rabin and his government, the "evil government" and "the traitorous government," was both targeted and all-embracing and would stop at nothing.[41] Zalman Melamed, head of the premilitary yeshiva in Beit El, compared the policy of a government that approves some settlements and undermines others' right to exist to "the Nazi selection at the death camps." Had the Jews risen up, wrote Melamed, "all united against their Nazi oppressors . . . the Germans would not have been able to carry out their deeds as they had planned. This is the case with this government."[42] In an almost exact reprise of what he had written in 1982 about Menachem Begin on the eve of the evacuation of Yamit, Elyakim Haetzni now compared Rabin to Marshal Pétain, who betrayed France and joined up with the Nazis. Pétain too was an admired figure in France and was elected in a proper democratic process, wrote Haetzni. "In the end he was put on trial in liberated France, sentenced to death and because he was very old his sentence was commuted to imprisonment and he finished his life on an island of exile. . . . If, heaven forbid, the disaster that you are planning for us occurs—you will not be absolved! You will face justice and be put on trial. . . . Parallel to the internal protest, the ugly face, the monstrous face of the false peace that is purchased by national betrayal will become increasingly clear."[43] Haetzni's hints were clear: the proper punishment for traitors is death.

Rabin's blatant impatience with the settlers, his body language expressing loathing for their righteous "eye-rolling," his blunt images like "ayatollahs" and "Jewish Hamas," and his remarks about their non-Zionism and his own commitment to the security of "98 percent of the citizens of Israel" were perceived by the religious settler population as an attempt to return religious Zionism to its marginality and "the obscure corner" where it had languished until its salvation in the 1967 war. For the Gush Emunim settlers, disciples of Rabbi Kook, this was the most sensitive nerve. For decades, effectively until the late 1960s, religious Zionism had played a minor role as a negligible, sometimes ridiculed companion on the bandwagon of the Zionist revolution, and the country's Laborite leadership and elites had treated it accordingly. This was also the motive for the settlers' determined drive, since 1967, to take control of the national agenda. The coming of Rabin, very much the product of that secular and arrogant Zionism that had shunted their parents aside in the past, and the way he treated them, threatened to push them once again to the margins and to deny them what they had already achieved. The appointment of the leader of Meretz, the radical secular feminist icon Shulamit Aloni, as minister of education and culture, the silencing of their Channel Seven broadcasts, and the elimination of Shas from the coalition were perceived by the settlers as additional evidence of the secular counterattack. They saw the Oslo agreement not only as the handing over of parts of the sacred and indivisible land to an "impure gentile."

It represented a rejection of the path the settlers had been paving for a quarter of a century toward conquering the country and its basic ethos from within.

Not One Settlement

Rabin's distaste for Yasser Arafat's gestures at their first meeting on the White House lawn on September 13, 1993, reflected his complex attitude toward the agreement with the Palestine Liberation Organization, at least at the outset. He saw in the Oslo agreement an experiment that had equal chances of succeeding or failing. The doubtful, skeptical Israeli prime minister was determined to make progress in the channel of negotiations and agreements without moving even a single isolated settlement, and he clung stubbornly to the principle that the fate of the settlements would be determined only in the negotiations on the final-status agreement.[44] The unbridgeable gap between the attempts to reach a political agreement that would put an end to the occupation in the territories and the perpetuation of the Israeli presence there was blatant in the Oslo agreement. The Labor Party leadership justified this by the concern that the Israeli public would find it hard to digest a move that would include, simultaneously, recognition of the PLO and an undermining of the legitimacy of the Jewish settlements in the territories. Shimon Peres argued that the small coalition majority, which was based on parties with rightist leanings, barely allowed for circumspect steps toward an interim agreement. He assumed that when the time came for a permanent-status agreement, most of the settlements would be annexed to Israel and a few of them would be evacuated or granted special status within the territory of the Palestinian state or the confederation with Israel and Jordan.[45]

In the first round of talks in Oslo, in January 1993, Abu Ala (Ahmed Qurei), who later on became the Palestinian prime minister, called upon the government of Israel to freeze the settlements as a gesture of goodwill and as proof that it was not pursuing a policy of expansion. Addressing Yair Hirschfeld, who together with Ron Pundak had paved the way to the Oslo talks, Abu Ala asked about the future of the Gaza settlements. The issue required further study because of the problem of Jewish land ownership, Hirschfeld replied. What will unfold with the settlements in Gaza will serve afterward as a model for the West Bank, said Hirschfeld. The Israeli side refused to make any concession or gesture in the matter of the settlements, and thus the debate was closed.[46] In the second round of talks, in February, the matter of the settlements came up again. Pundak talked in general terms about redirecting resources from the settlements to locales within the Green Line.[47] Only in the eighth round of the talks, in June, did the Palestinians again raise the issue of the settlements. Rabin instructed Yoel Singer, the legal adviser for the agreement, to make it clear to Abu Ala that the government of Israel would not publish an official statement on the matter of the settlements; that the settlement project would not cease; that the settlers would continue to be under Israeli security responsibility, both within the settlements themselves and outside of them; that the government of Israel did not intend to dismantle any settlement whatsoever; and that the electricity and road networks serving the settlements and the Palestinian villages would remain under full Israeli control.[48]

It was Rabin's fears about the settlers' reactions that guided his conduct and led him to prefer the Oslo channel to the option of talks with Syria, reflected Singer. Rabin took seriously Foreign Minister Shimon Peres's warning that any peace agreement with Syria would entail the immediate dismantling of settlements in the Golan Heights—and hence the dismantling of the coalition. However, with the PLO, said Peres, it was possible to get an extension of several years before launching a negotiation on the future of the settlements in the West Bank and the Gaza Strip.[49] Rabin instructed the negotiating team to stick to the format of phases and interim arrangements as well as the terms that had served the Palestinian section of the first Camp David accord between Israel and Egypt in 1978.[50] The Labor Party leadership regarded its very consent to enter into a negotiation about the future of the settlements, at a prescheduled date for talks on a final-status agreement (together with other problematic issues, such as Jerusalem and the refugees), as a far-reaching Israeli concession. This very act enabled, in their eyes, the breakthrough in Oslo.[51]

Israel was very miserly in its talks with the Palestinians. Its representatives stated that for reasons of principle it would desist only from massive support of isolated "political settlements," and would not make this public. The Palestinians were advised that the government of Israel would not adopt a policy of evacuating settlements or inhabitants, and that the settlers themselves would have to leave voluntarily.[52] Abu Mazen (Mahmoud Abbas), Arafat's deputy and eventually his successor, sent a message saying that the PLO agreed that "the final status [of the settlements] will be discussed in the context of the final-status agreement. Current position: that they remain under the responsibility of the Israeli army. Because of the complexity of the settlements, there will be a need to formulate a special agreement about dealing with them during the interim period." Their weakness compelled the Palestinians to accept a general, noncommittal formula whereby actions that would be taken in the territories during the negotiations would have no effect on a final-status agreement.[53] Philip Wilcox, the consul general of the United States in Jerusalem from 1988 to 1991, would later say that the Oslo agreement failed because the Palestinian representatives from Tunis who conducted the negotiations were not familiar with the situation in the territories and had no knowledge of the spread of the settlements and how the balance of power had changed between the settlers and consecutive Israeli governments. Thus the "Tunisians" were not sensitive enough to the disastrous consequences of the Palestinians' relinquishing of their insistence on a freeze on the settlements and the discussion of their fate. A similar blindness also characterized politicians and officials from Washington who refrained from visiting the territories because of the policy of not crossing the Green Line.[54]

Upon their arrival in Washington in September 1993 to take part in the peace ritual on the White House lawn, Hanan Ashrawi and Faisal al-Husseini saw for the first time on Abu Mazen's desk the document of the Oslo agreement, which had been formulated behind their backs. "Total shock" was Ashrawi's reaction. She accused Abu Mazen of having no idea what occupation is, and certainly not Israeli occupation. "You postponed the discussion of the issues of the settlements and Jerusalem without getting any guarantees that in the meantime Israel will not continue to create facts on the ground, facts that will determine the nature of the final status solution," she said. The eloquent professor of English literature from Ramallah, the woman who became the outstanding voice of the Palestinian resistance, did not heed Abu Mazen's explanations of the strategic advantages that the agreement afforded the Palestinians. "At many points in the agreement there is potential for a blow-up," continued Ashrawi. "The strategic advantages [in the agreement] are indeed important," she said, predicting the future, "but we know the Israelis. We know that they will exploit their advantage as occupiers to the fullest and by the time we arrive at discussing a final-status agreement Israel will have already irreversibly changed the reality on the ground." Ashrawi argued that the Palestinian negotiators should have extracted at least some achievement with respect to Jerusalem, the settlements, and human rights. "Speak to them directly in Washington," Abu Mazen dismissed her sarcastically. "Ask them to freeze the settlements."[55]

The issue came up again less than a year later in the negotiations preceding the Gaza-Jericho agreement. Minister Nabil Sha'ath asked to include in the agreement a provision concerning a settlement freeze. Rabin directed him to the government's guidelines, but refused to give him a written version of this public document.[56] Foreign Minister Shimon Peres went even further, declaring in the Knesset that "we have ensured that in the negotiations there would be no provision entered that would commit Israel to dismantle any settlement." He promised that "the issue of evacuating the settlements will be by government decision and not as a result of the pressures of negotiations."[57]

From Murder to Murder

A former Mossad operative and later a researcher and deputy head of the Jaffee Center for Strategic Studies at Tel Aviv University, Yoseph Alpher was scrutinizing the depth of the abyss that separated Oslo from the settlements. Alpher, who at that time was directing the Middle East office of the American Jewish Committee, persuaded a group of settler leaders, among them founders of Gush Emunim, to meet with senior representatives of the Palestinian Authority. Accustomed to secretive conduct, he chose a code name for his initiative, Operation Charlie, and succeeded in keeping far from the public eye a series of meetings that were held alternately in Israel and in England over a period of a year and a half. The initiative began in May 1994, shortly after the massacre in Hebron, and ended in December 1995, a few weeks after the assassination of Yitzhak Rabin. This was not diplomatic negotiation but rather "familiarization with the other side's ideological motives," according to Alpher. The intention was to examine the extent of flexibility that each side would be willing to display while the Palestinian autonomy was establishing itself and toward negotiations on a permanent-status agreement.[58]

The participants in the talks on the settler side were Uri Elitzur, the editor of *Nekudah;* professor of philosophy Yosef Ben Shlomo of Kedumim; Israel Harel of Ofra; Eliezer Waldman of Kiryat Arba, a rabbinical authority among Gush Emunim followers; and Professor Ozer Schild of Kedumim, formerly the president of Haifa University. On the Palestinian side were Mohammed Dahlan, head of the security services in the Gaza Strip and a close associate of Yasser Arafat; Hassan Asfour, a senior representative at the Oslo talks; Dr. Khalil Shikaki, head of a Palestinian institute for public opinion research; Soufian Abu Zaideh, Nabil Sha'ath's aide; and Dr. Yezid Sayigh, a Cambridge lecturer and formerly a member of the Palestinian delegation to the Oslo talks.[59] Chosen carefully, the participants represented the intellectual and political elites of the two sides.

Israel Harel, one of the more prominent settler spokesmen, a founder of the Yesha Council and the journal *Nekudah* and a regular columnist in the daily newspaper *Ha'aretz*, opened the meeting that was held in England in June 1995 with the following words, which revealed the impossible dilemma that the supposed pragmatists among the settlers faced. "I believe that my aim, the settlement of the greater Land of Israel, is the most sublime aim in the world and that the Zionist movement is the most just national movement that has ever existed. I fear that my exposure to the legitimate beliefs of the other side is liable in some way to weaken my commitment to my aim. How can I listen to the other side without harming my aim? It is easier to know your neighbor as someone who throws stones."[60] Harel predicted that in the future the Jewish people would see the Oslo agreement as a betrayal and would overturn it. Yosef Ben Shlomo added that the Oslo agreements were perhaps the beginning of the end of the Zionist project and of the Jewish State. He asserted that the Jewish national home "will stand or fall on the issue of the settlements." Ben Shlomo asked the Palestinians if they would agree to grant his settlement, Kedumim, a status similar to the status Israel had granted to the Arab town of Umm al Fahm inside the Green Line.

"My answer is—yes to settlers who will be prepared to stay but no to the settlements," said Soufian Abu Zaideh, who added, "Unless you give us the right to settle in Haifa." Abu Zaideh also argued that "the Israeli presence would help ensure Palestinian democracy." Another Palestinian participant asked why only Jews would be allowed to live in settlements that would remain in Palestinian territory. Ben Shlomo, who had offered the Palestinians "life together," proposed the mingling of Jews and Palestinians in the cities or the universities but not in small villages like the settlements. The reason is not racist, he said, but rather social, because this involves places that are relatively small.[61]

The forum met seven times in Israel and abroad. The sides took advantage of this rare opportunity to resolve some minor, local conflicts and prevent deterioration in the relations between Palestinians and settlers. Among other things, there was talk of the need to ensure quiet during the period of the elections for the Palestinian Authority and there was discussion of the possibility of instituting a "red telephone line" between the sides, by means of which it would be possible to alert those responsible on both sides to deal with emergency situations.[62] At the end of November 1995, in the shadow of the trauma of Rabin's assassination, Alpher invited the representatives of the settlers and the Palestinian Authority to a special meeting at the American Jewish Committee's offices in Jerusalem. This time too the discussion opened with a fruitless ideological debate and then developed into a pragmatic discussion of ideas for expanding contacts at the local level. Following this meeting one of the participants, Uri

Elitzur, took an unusual step and published an article in the monthly *Nekudah* in which he called upon his settler colleagues to begin talking with their neighbors. "I propose talking with them. Directly and not by means of IDF. . . . We have a thousand matters to conclude with our new neighbors, and I propose starting to talk about this immediately. Heads of settlements with the heads of the neighboring villages, a council head with his colleague from the other side of the non-line and the Yesha Council with the Palestinian Authority."[63] The article put an end to Operation Charlie. Elitzur was forced to apologize and retract what he had said under pressure from his settler colleagues.

Following the Israeli liquidation of a top Hamas military leader, Yihye Ayash, in January 1996, Hamas ended its months-long informal truce. In revenge, the organization carried out four suicide bombings in February and March, killing fifty-seven Israelis. The terror in the streets of Israel, which blocked Peres's way to the Prime Minister's Office in Jerusalem, was also among the reasons for the suspension of talks. An attempt to renew discussions after the elections failed because of resistance from the settlers and their supporters.[64] "Today everyone is trying to be nice. Everyone is talking with the PLO. . . . Rabbis are talking with the PLO. What has happened? Have we gone crazy?" asked Ariel Sharon. Only a few people on the right in fact praised the attempt at dialogue, but the general mood among the settlers was hostile, to the point of people being shunned in synagogues.[65]

The Yesha Council's "Newsletter to the Inhabitant" started publication with the signing of the 1993 Oslo agreement. The first issue detailed the goals that the Yesha Council had set for itself for the coming years and the organization's modes of action. The settlers' struggle was not limited in time. As far as they were concerned, it was a matter of a historical struggle that had been going on "ever since the exodus from Egypt." In this first issue there was talk of "the State of Israel's entering into a prolonged battle, with many chapters and reversals, in which—through struggles, doubts, and sufferings—the new profile of the land and the state for the coming generation would be shaped. All of Israeli society will be involved in this battle," said the newsletter, "but there is no doubt that we—the inhabitants of Yesha—are at the eye of the storm."[66] The historic move by religious Zionism had thus proved successful. From "hitchhikers" on the chariot of Zionism they had become, in their own eyes and in reality, the conductors and the dictators of the agenda. The council's aims were mass "population" of the settlements; the creation of a "public home front for settlement" of about a million citizens who do not live in settlements; a "national information campaign" to deal with public opinion throughout the country; the establishment of a "referendum team" that would prepare for the case in which the government would decide on a referendum about the settlements; the conduct of "negotiations with government and military elements" to determine a comprehensive policy for the settlements; and finally "coordination of action with the opposition parties."[67] All of the principles that were formulated in this initial document were put into operation in the settlers' showdown with the state institutions during the withdrawal from Gaza and northern Samaria in August 2005.

The Yesha Council took great care to endow its struggle with legitimacy and leave to more extreme groups the dirty work of thwarting Oslo. In fact, the official settler organization managed to cloak itself in the eyes of the Israeli public as a relatively moderate body open to dialogue. This pattern of behavior was manifested in the "Doubling Campaign," which was aimed at doubling with one fell swoop the number of settlements in the territories and at being the largest project since the founding of Gush Emunim. The campaign, which was a partisan initiative by individuals from the settlement of

Karnei Shomron, won extensive coverage in the media.[68] Most of the campaign activists were immigrants from English-speaking countries, spearheaded by Moshe Feiglin, who was to become the head of the Jewish Leadership group in the Likud. The soft-spoken, pleasant-faced Feiglin was a foreign body among the Gush Emunim veterans. He had not gone through the forging events of the genesis of the settlements. However, in his personality and conduct he embodied the unique mix of the settlers—unbridled ideological extremism, total willingness to sacrifice private life for the sake of fulfilling the grand design, and all this in a wrapping of rich and eloquent speech and rational arguments, in their own way. The campaign that he conceived got under way in the fall of 1993, a few days after the Jewish New Year. In a meeting in Jerusalem with the secretary general of the Yesha Council, Uri Ariel, Feiglin, and his people presented a plan for the establishment of 130 new settlement sites. According to the principle of cell division, each existing settlement was slated to duplicate itself and establish a daughter settlement nearby. "Get the file ready," said Ariel.[69]

Feiglin and his people readied the file. They proceeded as if this were a military operation, spreading a network of liaison people and locating the places for the new, symbolic settlements that would all be established in a single day throughout the West Bank. "In this way, unnoticed, in fact an entirely extra-establishment movement began, which bypassed all of the accepted mechanisms and by its very creation threatened the existing establishment in Yesha," wrote Feiglin.[70] At an assembly held by Feiglin's group in the settlement town of Ariel on December 3, the settler leaders and the representatives of the rightist parties identified a political opportunity and tried to appropriate it. It was Feiglin's plan that gave birth to the sophisticated "illegal outpost" method, which for more than a decade has been achieving two major aims: a war of attrition against and systematic harassment of the military, which was not able to post a soldier on every hill. More important, the very definition of these outposts as "illegal" implied the legality of all the other settlements and diverted state actions and public discourse to the margins of the phenomenon. In any case, the aim, the method, the practices, the selecting of the sites, and the rules of behavior on the ground that were formulated by Feiglin have characterized the resistance activity to evacuation of settlements and outposts during the past fourteen years.[71] In their day they interfered with the Oslo process, the road map, and were also put into effect in 2005 against Sharon's plan for the withdrawal from Gaza.

Alongside Feiglin's Zo Artzenu (This Is Our Land) group, a number of other extremist groups were active in the settler community, with agendas of their own. The Yesha Council navigated among the various bodies, playing its "good cop, bad cop" game. While the Jews of Hebron sowed destruction in the Arab town and its environs and the Zo Artzenu movement took to the streets and the roads, blocked intersections, and embittered the lives of the Israelis and the government, the Yesha Council sent letters of apology. Although the council heads refrained from inviting the extremist groups to meetings with their political leadership that were held in the Knesset building, they were invited by others, among them the leader of the opposition, Benjamin Netanyahu, who was the inspiration and the driving force behind the violent demonstrations in the streets. Knesset members headed by the leader of the opposition saw nothing wrong with inviting to the tabernacle of democracy and its symbol people who systematically undermined the foundations of the state and its laws.

The Settlements Are Us

The year that stretched from the fall of 1994 to the fall of 1995 was a bitter year for the Oslo agreement and for anyone who believed in the possibility of making peace between Israel and the Palestinians, and it ended with a disaster. A series of terror attacks, which began in October 1994 with the abduction and killing of soldier Nachshon Waxman and the killing of two civilians by a Palestinian who blew himself up on a crowded bus on Dizengoff Street in Tel Aviv, increased the support for the settlers. Although Hamas claimed responsibility for the wave of terror that befell Israel during that same month, the opponents of the Oslo agreement cast the blame on Rabin, who had "given guns" to Yasser Arafat and the Palestinian Authority police, foes of Hamas. On January 22, 1995, twenty-one young Israelis, most of them soldiers returning to their units after a weekend at home, died in a terror attack at Beit Lid, which was carried out by Islamic Jihad. The toll of a suicide attack on a bus in Ramat Gan on July 24 was six killed and dozens injured.

The terror attacks fanned vicious and unparalleled incitement against Rabin and the Oslo process. They completely marginalized the settlements and the military occupation in the public discourse. The constant harassments of the extremists among the settlers—and especially the massacre of Muslim worshipers in Hebron, which loosened the demons of violence and which were the very reason for the terrorist attacks within the Green Line—were forgotten as though they had never happened. The causal triangle of the settlements, the military occupation, and terrorism was broken. History started conveniently with the Palestinian assaults on innocent Jews. Terrorism had no roots, no reasons, no past. The bereavement, the pain, and the fear, which crossed the Green Line into Israel, paved the settlers' way to the hearts of the Israelis. At long last, the settlers succeeded in fulfilling their deepest wishes, not only to settle on hilltops but also to "settle in hearts." Ironically, it was the Palestinian terrorists who transformed the territories and Israel into one entity and through death gave life to the slogan "Yesha is here." The pirate radio station Channel Seven, which the settlers had established in 1988 and where most of the broadcasters were settlers, served as an important means for disseminating incitement and organizing resistance to the government of the "Oslo criminals" and its policy.[72] Upon the Labor Party's return to power in the 1992 elections, Channel Seven had already set up a news department and placed at its head a member of the Jewish terrorist group, settler Hagai Segal. Its programs served as a daily platform for personal attacks on Rabin and violent agitation against his government.

One of the prominent broadcasters at the station, Adir Zik, formerly an employee of the official Israel Broadcasting Authority, persistently called Rabin a "traitor." He read out to his listeners the dictionary definition of the word "traitor": "one who betrays his country, his people, or friends and helps the enemy." Zik, an activist of the racist Kach Party, urged his listeners to harm the prime minister physically. "Thousands of people will burst in and drag Rabin out," he said.[73] The term "out" was open to a variety of interpretations. Only after Rabin was assassinated did the law enforcement agencies and the Israeli media take any notice of the content and the form of the broadcasts and fight the pirate station, to no avail.

Even those considered moderate among the settlers waged a dirty war against the prime minister. Knesset Member Hannan Porat, the iconic settler who had supported Rabin when his rivals in the Likud recycled the story of his breakdown as chief of staff on the eve of the Six-Day War, and who admitted that Rabin's door was always open to him, said now that "a government comes and goes, and the land of Israel stands forever. The project of settling Judea and Samaria, which is part of the project of the return of Zion, does not depend on this or that prime minister. . . . For twenty-eight years now we have been in Gush Etzion, the very place about which Yitzhak Rabin said that we would have to enter with a visa." Porat was confident about the collapse of the Oslo agreement and the fall of the government and of the man who was so often generous with him.[74] On November 9, 1993, in the midst of protests against Oslo, Rabin invited the heads of the Yesha Council to a secret meeting. The sides agreed to set up a joint team of representatives, from the Prime Minister's Office and the Council, to solve the settlers' everyday problems. Word of the meeting leaked out and angered many settlers. In the Council plenum, members demanded that the head of the Council be deposed. How could the settler leaders sit in the same room with the prime minister and consult about cooperation while discussions were going on in the Yesha directorate to plan a personal campaign to break Rabin the individual?

"I was present at the discussion," related Yoel Bin-Nun after Rabin was assassinated. "The model was the late prime minister, Menachem Begin. The aim was to topple Rabin or to hurt him, just as the left had broken Begin politically and psychologically." Bin-Nun revealed that at the end of 1993 the Yesha Council held a discussion under the heading of how to "break" Rabin. Psychologists, a public opinion researcher, an advertising man, and a public relations person took part in the planning. For the first time a legal and recognized political organization, which was funded mostly by the state, initiated an action to foment revolt against an incumbent prime minister. The actual goal of the scheme was the elimination of Rabin from the public sphere as a political actor.[75]

Yet Rabin continued meeting with the settlers and exerting himself to ensure their welfare. And they continued with their double game. In the midst of the Oslo II negotiations of 1995, as they were conducting a violent struggle against the government and against the implementation of the second phase of the Oslo agreement, the Yesha Council announced that it was "prepared to continue the dialogue with the prime minister."[76] A few days before the Israeli army completed the division of the West Bank into Areas A, B, and C, Rabin ordered the head of the "Oslo II administration," Colonel Shaul Arieli, to show the map of the areas to the settlement coordinator, Ze'ev Hever, an extremely influential figure among the settlers and a member of the Jewish terrorist group.[77] Although Rabin was not blind to the possibility that the settlers would use the maps for purposes of the struggle against him, his personal correctness prompted him to believe the promises of Hever, a close associate of Ariel Sharon's, that he would maintain secrecy. The settlers asked to introduce many adjustments, of which he accepted one. However, Rabin's willingness to let them participate in the process of shaping Israel's positions was perceived by them, again, as a sign of his weakness and an invitation to further pressures.[78]

Self-Victimization

On September 28, 1995, the Oslo II agreement was signed in Washington. This time, too, Rabin refrained from an explicit commitment to suspend construction in the settlements. The agreement stipulated only that "neither side shall initiate or take any step that will change the status of the West Bank and Gaza Strip pending the outcome of the permanent status negotiations."[79] Very quickly it emerged that the fog that enveloped the term "status" enabled Israeli governments to expand existing settlements in broad daylight, pave roads, and turn a blind eye to new, unauthorized settlement sites. The proven formula "meeting the needs of the natural growth of the existing population" provided a useful cover for every action and for ignoring the commitment that was given to the United States to suspend any further settlement activity.[80]

The concern that evacuating military bases in the territories would serve as a precedent for evacuating civilian settlements gave rise to a move of insurrection on the part of the religious establishment against the state authorities. A group of well-known rabbis followed in the footsteps of Rabbi Meir Kahane's Kach movement and issued a rabbinical ruling instructing soldiers to disobey an order to evacuate military camps. Among the signatories were the leading rabbis of the settler community and the paramilitary yeshivas, all of them public servants who received their salaries from the state.[81] "Blessed are we with rabbis made of iron," said Hannan Porat, an ardent supporter of the refusal to obey the evacuation order, which he defined as a "national crime."[82] Rabin's response was sharp but apparently too late. It is untenable that such a thing can happen in Israel, said Rabin. "It is a very grave thing that a handful of rabbis, who aren't even representing all the rabbis in Israel, could make such a decision. It is inconceivable that Israel will become a banana republic."[83] In the September issue of *Nekudah* Rabin was compared once again to Pétain, France's national traitor in World War II.[84]

The psychological-cognitive transition from representing Rabin as Pétain the traitor to depicting him in SS uniform was not difficult; in fact, it was almost natural, a typical move in the escalation of the politics of hatred and incitement. And indeed on the placards carried at the rightist demonstration on the evening of Saturday, October 5, 1995, at Zion Square in Jerusalem, a demonstration at which most of the participants were settlers who had been brought there in vehicles paid for by the government of Israel, the prime minister was depicted in an SS officer uniform. Anyone who wanted to could see the meaning of the messages that emerged from that system of non-implicit signs and symbols: the death sentence. Not one of the opposition leaders who stood on the balcony overlooking the square in a

Mussolinian posture and inflamed the crowd—among them Ariel Sharon and Benjamin Netanyahu—said a word of reservation with regard to the depiction of the prime minister as an SS officer.

Exactly a month later, on the night of Saturday, November 4, Rabin was assassinated at the end of a peace rally in the main square of Tel Aviv. The assassin was a young student of law at Bar-Ilan University, Yigal Amir, an admirer of the "saint" from Hebron, Baruch Goldstein. "A Mourning Declaration and Call for National Reconciliation" issued by the Yesha Council and published the day after the murder, immediately and in a very sophisticated way, served to delegitimize any attempt to disclose the roots of the murder and its deeper reasons, and to point an accusing finger at the religious-ideological milieu from which the assassin had emerged. The inciters of yesterday stated in their announcement that "the murderer's bullets that tore the prime minister's body have severely wounded the unity of the people," as if the nation had been united prior to the assassination. "The inhabitants of Yesha, who mourn the death of the prime minister, are calling at this moment upon the entire nation to unite and condemn unanimously the murderous violence. The inhabitants of Yesha call upon all parts of the people to maintain restraint, to lower the strident voices and to refrain from mutual recriminations. Only national unity and comprehensive reconciliation will help us at this difficult hour and extricate us from the acute crisis that now prevails in the state."[85]

The false slogan of national unity was intended to cover up the sources of the assassination and the fundamental split that had been tearing Israeli society apart for a generation, and to stop any sober reckoning and analysis of the historical process that had led to the assassination. The settlers conveniently announced that they were suspending their protest activity for the duration of the days of mourning. In a virtuoso reversal of meanings that transformed the assailant into the victim, one of their leaders added: "We will not be able to accept a generalizing campaign of incitement against an entire public, first of all because this is one of the determining factors in the disaster that has occurred." There is wild incitement against us, which heaven forbid could lead to yet another terrible disaster, complained the settlers.[86]

Four days after the assassination the religious parties and the Yesha Council held a "Eulogy and Reckoning of Conscience" convocation. The left was the main culprit, according to the speakers, and the victim—religious Zionism. "All of us . . . sat this week as accused in the same dock. All of the wearers of crochet skullcaps, all of religious Zionism, and above all religious education in all its nuances. Do not deceive yourselves. We do have reason to beat our breast, but this is among ourselves," said Israel Harel. In order to clear himself and his friends of the moral turpitude of incitement, Harel annexed to his camp people of integrity like professors Aviezer Ravitzky and Uriel Simon from the moderate religious camp, who for years had been waging a determined intellectual struggle against the path of Gush Emunim, and whom nobody blamed for the assassination. On the one hand, Harel demanded recognition of himself and his colleagues as part of the nation that was mourning the disaster, and on the other, he conceded nothing of his worldview and did not beat his breast. "Not only has our way of life not been proven mistaken," he said, "but it is the way. The king's road of religious Zionism."[87]

Hannan Porat, too, harshly condemned the murder and the murderer, and moved along immediately to an equally harsh condemnation of the victim: "A person who lifts his hand to uproot Jewish settlements from their land . . . is not raising his hand against Hannan Porat and Rabbi Druckman; he is raising his hand against the word of God that ordains 'that thy children shall come again to their own border' (Jeremiah, 31:17). . . . Anyone who wants to do a reckoning of conscience must stand in that place, regard the dark abyss and say: Anyone who walks in this abyss, and anyone who thinks that in this way he can save the people—is simply stupid and wicked."[88] In a recorded interview, Rabbi Nachum Rabinowitz defined Prime Minister Rabin as a *moser*—one who intends to turn a Jew over to non-Jewish authorities—and, basing himself on Maimonides, said that the prime minister "owed his life."[89]

Only a handful of settlers faced the terrible murder with their eyes open and pointed to the culprits: their own camp. Yehuda Amital, one of the founders of Gush Emunim and now the head of the moderate movement Meimad, did not let his colleagues in religious Zionism and the settlements evade responsibility. "This assassin came from our midst. . . . Those rabbis who are not beating their breast have not thus far evinced the courage to face their public. . . . In educational institutions and in yeshivas the students are exposed to the atmosphere created there by the religious and political leadership, with the help of the media and public opinion. . . . It is not that an authority in religious law came and said to the murderer that it was necessary to murder Rabin according to that law. It is extremism that brought this about." Amital's closing words hinted at a connection he saw between the massacre of the Arab worshipers in Hebron and the murder in the city square of Tel Aviv. "The deterioration began when many chose to ignore, or close a blind eye to, the harassment of Arabs that in the end also led to an act of murder."[90]

Yoel Bin-Nun was determined not to let the Yesha rabbis who had issued the *din rodef* ruling (in fact, a sort of death sentence against whoever "threatens" Jewish life) evade responsibility for the assassination. On November 12, eight days after the assassination, Bin-Nun met with the chief rabbis and asked them to set up an investigating committee to examine the role played by Dov Lior of Kiryat Arba and Nachum Rabinowitz of Ma'aleh Adumim in the incitement to the assassination. Bin-Nun blamed those two rabbis directly, claiming he had evidence proving that a number of suspects in the assassination had been in contact with them. The rabbis denied the accusations and attacked their accuser.[91] Rabbis and public figures threatened Bin-Nun with excommunication, libel suits, and harm to the educational institution that he headed. Less than a week after Bin-Nun gave the names of the inciters to the chief rabbis, he asked their forgiveness.[92] He and his family had to leave their home in Ofra, one of the most distinguished settlements, where many members of the intellectual and spiritual leadership of the settler movement live, and move to another settlement, in the Etzion area.

Yet the first to betray the meaning of Rabin's assassination and the memory of the murdered were those who shared his outlook and his political party. Following the assassination, the Labor Party's election campaign, headed by Shimon Peres (who had assumed the role of prime minister), "sterilized" itself from any reference to the calamity, and rejected any "undesirable" element of a disturbing and divisive memory. Shortsighted election considerations overwhelmed the moral, historical reckoning that the party should have undertaken both with the settlers and with itself.[93] As the date of the elections approached, the Labor candidate for prime minister, Peres, attempted a rapprochement with settlers who were considered moderate in order to win their support. He invited eight council heads, most of them Likud people, who had established a new forum of heads of Jewish local councils in the territories in protest against the excessive "politicization" of the Yesha Council. At the same time, the Labor minister of construction and housing, Yossi Beilin, promised the heads of settlements in the Jerusalem area that he would bring before the ministerial committee for construction exceptions requests to approve the building of about 3,000 housing units in northern Ma'aleh Adumim, about 500 in Giv'at Zeev, about 1,000 in Betar Ilite, and about 800 in Alfei Menashe. The settlers expressed the hope that Prime Minister Peres, who headed the ministerial committee, would act to renew construction in the Jerusalem area, especially in Gush Etzion, to which the Labor Party had always been committed.[94]

At the beginning of April 1996, some sixty days before Election Day, the Israeli press published rumors that Peres, Ehud Barak, and Yossi Beilin were in contact with Yoel Bin-Nun concerning the possibility that Peres would declare, before the elections, that even in the final-status agreement with the Palestinians no settlement would be evacuated and that most of the settlements in the "blocs plan" would remain under Israeli sovereignty. There was also talk of increased budgeting for the settlements and recognition of their master plans. Peres indeed confirmed that his government would not dismantle settlements and would refrain from dividing Jerusalem. "There is no need to remove settlements," he said. In return for this, a group of prominent individuals from the settlements, headed by Bin-Nun, were to support Peres. The Knesset Finance Committee authorized an additional 20 million shekels (some $5 million) for the settlements.[95]

In mid-May 1996, about two weeks before the elections, an agreement was signed between Bin-Nun and heads of the Labor Party. The agreement stipulated that in the framework of the permanent-status agreement no settlement would be uprooted and that "Israeli sovereignty in essential parts of Judea and Samaria would be ensured." The document also spoke of Israeli control of settlements that would not be under Israeli sovereignty. Bin-Nun declared that the agreement expressed his recognition as well as that of his colleagues of the Oslo agreement, which was now a reality that could not be overturned. On the other hand, the agreement contained Peres's as well as his political allies' recognition of the settlements as a reality that could not be questioned. As a result, Bin-Nun called upon the religious Zionists to vote for Peres. Very few of them did, as could be expected. But the meaning of Rabin's assassination was betrayed.

Despite all the gifts he had bestowed on the settlers, and despite Arafat's concession to Peres to postpone the implementation of the withdrawal under the second Oslo agreement until after the elections, it was no longer Peres who was in a position to lead the country and resume negotiations. The settlers positioned themselves as one man behind the Likud candidate, Benjamin Netanyahu, and put their huge and sophisticated organizational infrastructure at his disposal.[96] "Between the vision of a bright future and the values of the Jewish past—the voters chose the Jewish past," wrote *Nekudah*.[97] When, in his capacity as prime minister, Netanyahu began to direct the negotiations on withdrawal from Hebron, which Peres had fled, the new head of the settlers council, Pinchas Wallerstein, pulled out an astonishing figure. According to him, in the first half of 1996, following Rabin's assassination and during the short period Peres served as prime minister, Peres approved the allocation of 350 million shekels (some $85 million) for paving roads in the West Bank.[98] Wallerstein boasted that "despite all the attempts to dry out the Jewish settlements," the number of settlers in the West Bank had soared during the periods of the Rabin and Peres governments by more than 40 percent, from approximately 100,000 in 1993 to 141,000 in 1996.[99] What guided Wallerstein in his revelations was not in fact the desire to praise Peres, but rather the urge to challenge Netanyahu.

Going Beyond the Fence

From the settlers' point of view, the beginning of the new partnership was encouraging. But the end of the relationship with Netanyahu was no different in essence from the end of their relationships with previous prime ministers who had dared to resist them. And faster than expected, Bin-Nun's prediction that Netanyahu would be far less resistant than Peres to domestic and foreign pressures, and that he would not hesitate to harm settlements in the areas of the West Bank and the Golan, proved correct.[100] The first meeting between the heads of the Yesha Council and the new prime minister was held in an atmosphere of elation. Netanyahu promised to "talk with steam shovels and not with ram's horns." Wallerstein challenged the new government with a growth goal of 50–70 percent over a period of four years, "which means we will stand at about 250,000 souls." He called for harnessing the economic distress and social fashions of the secular and the ultra-Orthodox, who do not choose their place of living according to "Zionist" considerations in order to tempt more Jews to the settlements.[101] He revealed his friends' plans to establish themselves and demonstrate their presence all along the length and breadth of the West Bank and thus thwart any possibility for the creation of a Palestinian state with viability and territorial contiguity. "Our mission during the coming four years is *going beyond the fences*," declared Wallerstein. He called for building along the roads and linking up with the Green Line. It would be the civilian rather than the military presence that would determine the fate of the territory, he said. "We shall be your soldiers," he said to Netanyahu.[102] Members of the new government began to visit the settlements, which became genuine sites of pilgrimage. There was talk of a "new wind" blowing through the government ministries.[103] The honeymoon was short.

Less than half a year elapsed before the settlers became soldiers in a front against Netanyahu. At the urging of Jerusalem Mayor Ehud Olmert (who would become Israel's prime minister in 2006), the government decided, in September 1996, to open an archeological tunnel under the Dome of the Rock/Temple Mount, an act that led to Palestinian rioting, which was joined by Palestinian police. Fifteen Israelis and seventy-five Palestinians were killed. These bloody incidents forced Netanyahu to accept President Bill Clinton's invitation to meet with Arafat at the White House. The force of the events and America's strength compelled Netanyahu to declare his commitment to the Oslo agreement and to discuss the redeployment of the military in Hebron. Under these pressures, Netanyahu had to slow down the rate of fulfillment of the settlers' expectations. "I can't recall a period of drought as difficult as the past four months," said Wallerstein a month later.[104] "People are continuing to move into the half-built houses like thieves in the night," said the head of the Samaria regional council.[105]

Once again the extremist organizations that had embittered the life of the previous government—Zo Artzenu, Moledet, Women in Green, and Matteh Maavak—threatened to do the same to the new one. They were joined by representatives of the right-wing coalition parties. Netanyahu's people warned the settlers not to repeat the mistake of fighting a government that supports settlement in order to bring back a "leftist" government.[106] The Yesha Council was not impressed. It decided to renew its frozen building plans in places where it thought "the government has no problem approving construction." The new justice minister promised that the government would cancel its previous decisions and see to it that by the end of the four and a half years of its term the number of Jewish inhabitants of the West Bank would at least double.[107] Government Resolution 150, which formally rescinded the Rabin government's decision to freeze construction in the settlements, gave the defense minister extensive authority in the area of planning and construction in the territories. Ostensibly, construction was permitted again. In fact, the resolution obligated the defense minister to issue permits at each and every stage—planning, allocation of land and earthworks to prepare for construction on "state lands." The settlers, who understood the sting in the resolution, demanded its cancellation.[108] The new defense minister, Yitzhak Mordechai, a military man who had become a politician and joined the Likud, apparently had not adopted with appropriate alacrity the rules of the game between the government and the settlers and their lobby, and did not give an inch. He instructed his aides on settlement matters to examine carefully every request to establish a new settlement. He supported in principle construction in the territories, he said, but noted that security and political timing were problematic and that he had other matters to deal with apart from the settlers' requests.[109]

In November 1996, Netanyahu caved in. He amended Resolution 150 and from then on only one authorization was needed from the defense minister—the validation of the construction plan. The amended resolution was accompanied by a commitment from the prime minister to the settler heads that he personally would deal with advancing building projects in the settlements.[110] The settlers' "steam shovels" ran over the defense minister. Throughout the West Bank the areas of the settlements were expanded. The army saw and took note of what was happening and refrained from conflict with the settlers, for whose security it was responsible. "The commanders in the field knew that they would not get backing from the government officials or the politicians," said one of them to the authors of this book. The violent evacuation of the outpost of Yizhar in 1996, which reached the point of a bloody, ferocious conflict between the army and the settlers, left the government mute and helpless. The frightened government and military response to the settlers' violence encouraged them, and wild, "illegal" outposts sprang up like mushrooms. The turning of a blind eye by the government and the army was in effect full backing for the lawbreakers.[111] The shrinking of the defense minister's powers calmed the settlers to some extent, and pushed them to increase their activities against Oslo and bring them to the level of the riots they had carried out on the eve of Rabin's assassination.[112]

The Conquest of Area C

Both sides, state institutions and the settlers, understood that any permanent-status agreement would have to take notice of the facts that had been created on the ground over the years. The "facts" had been established in what was specified as Area C by the Oslo II agreement of 1995, in a territory that encompassed about 60 percent of the West Bank, about whose fate the Oslo agreement had postponed discussion until negotiations on the final-status agreement. Most of the Jewish settlements are located in this area, alongside a few Palestinian villages. Thus the Oslo II agreement triggered a wild land grab, the likes of which had not been seen since the Likud came into power in 1977. The plan for the preservation of Area C that was drawn up by the military was in effect aimed at preventing the "illegal takeover" of these lands by Palestinians, strengthening the Israeli grip on the territory and creating Israeli territorial contiguity in advance of the opening of final-status talks. To this end, it was decided to reinforce existing settlements as much as possible by enlarging their jurisdictions and their master plans. In the race for lands, suddenly many settlements were granted new lands "for agricultural purposes," such as farms and water reservoirs. Others were awarded gas stations or "an educational services center." Farms and other construction exceptions were aimed at creating a base for settlement contiguities from the east and from the west to the mountain ridge.[113]

More than 500 cases of illegal building and trespassing on state lands at 170 sites in the West Bank were filed from 1996 to 1999. The cases tell the stories of the erection of innumerable mobile homes and temporary structures. In the Gaza region, the Guardian of Abandoned Government Property reported on twenty-six cases of trespassing on state lands for purposes of expanding settlements. A report that was distributed on August 25, 1998, stated that the extent of trespassing amounted to about 2,000 dunams, or 500 acres. The author of the report, a high official, proposed "laundering" this trespassing by means of expanding the jurisdictions of the settlements. The legal adviser in the Gaza region command headquarters wrote on September 3 that "for a number of years now no action has been taken in the region to eliminate trespassing in the Jewish settlements beyond issuing orders to the trespassers." The adviser noted that apparently a directive existed not to take action against trespassing by Israelis without prior authorization from "various elements in the Defense Ministry."[114]

The frantic chase by the government and the settlers after every bit of available land in the West Bank deprived the Palestinians not only of their land but also of their money. In February 1998 the Judge Advocate General's Office ruled that a condition for requisitioning land is compensating the owners and that the army must be prepared for that in terms of budgetary resources. Six months later the deputy head of the Civil Administration wrote that the matter of compensation claims and usage fees for carrying out confiscation orders was stuck for a long time "with no solution." He pointed to "prolonged oppression of the rights of inhabitants who have been hurt by the requisitioning of their lands" and noted that the nonpayment of the monies would increase the inhabitants' resistance to "legal land actions that will be taken in the area." Three weeks later, the head of the Civil Administration wrote to the deputy minister of defense that an essential element of proper administration requires the payment of use fees and compensation to landowners whose property has been requisitioned for military use. He added that the Civil Administration did not have an available budgetary source for the payment of use fees and compensation and that the claims submitted against the Civil Administration were not being dealt with for that reason. In September 1998 it was estimated that the sum that the Civil Administration owed Palestinian inhabitants, as the result of scores of confiscation orders that had been issued since 1995, stood at approximately 38 million shekels (close to $10 million), and for use fees, at about 4 million shekels annually.[115]

Even though the land grab in the West Bank and the Gaza Strip was taking place in broad daylight and was reported extensively in the Israeli media, the Palestinian Authority negotiators shunted the issue to the margins of the agenda in its contacts with Israel and with the United States. The biggest crisis erupted over the settlement of Har Homa, on the southeastern outskirts of Jerusalem, on the way to Bethlehem. At the end of February 1997 the Netanyahu government decided to build 6,500 housing units in the new neighborhood.[116] This was preceded by pressure from the settlers and the right, and especially from the mayor of Jerusalem, Ehud Olmert. Olmert, who would later become one of the most determined supporters of Sharon's plan for the withdrawal from Gaza and his successor at the head of the new political party Kadima and as prime minister, saw the construction at Har Homa as a test of the government's staunchness and leadership, and defined it as tantamount to a "casus belli."[117]

The Palestinians saw the initiative as a plot to build a new settlement, the whole purpose of which was to cut their capital off from the southern West Bank. Arafat claimed this was a crude

Israeli violation of a key provision in the Oslo agreement, in which the sides undertook to refrain from establishing any facts on the ground during the interim period that would prejudge the final-status agreement.[118] In all the discussions that were held in Oslo and afterward between Israeli and Palestinian representatives on the territorial issue, it was agreed that the Jewish neighborhoods that were built in Jerusalem after the decision by the government of Israel in June 1967 to annex the eastern part of the city would remain under Israeli sovereignty. The Palestinians' attitude toward the Jewish Quarter in the Old City and the neighborhoods around it was similar to their position regarding the settlements adjacent to the Green Line. In the negotiations on the final-status agreement with representatives of Barak's government after the Camp David summit in 2000, the Palestinians demanded territorial compensation for the Jewish neighborhoods in East Jerusalem, under the same principle as the exchanges of territories that would occur in the West Bank and in the Gaza Strip.

Despite their strong opposition, the United States, the European countries, and especially Egypt and Jordan, which continued to view East Jerusalem as occupied territory, came to terms with the existence of Israeli neighborhoods there and showed restraint with respect to their expansion. This reluctant acceptance was based on the assumption that in the final-status negotiations, these neighborhoods would not be an obstacle to peace. However, this assumption was accompanied by the understanding anchored in the Oslo agreement that the sides would refrain from changing the status quo and from establishing facts in all the controversial areas. In this respect, the plan to establish a new neighborhood on the border between Jerusalem and Bethlehem was a resounding slap in the face to the Palestinians.

Faisal al-Husseini, a member of the PLO steering committee and the holder of the Jerusalem portfolio in the Palestinian Authority, warned that "the construction at Jabal Abu Ghanaim [Har Homa] is liable to bring about an explosion, especially when there is no diplomatic progress."[119] Arafat threatened that he would respond to the building of the neighborhood with a unilateral declaration of a Palestinian state. Netanyahu warned that such a step would put an end to the peace process. On that same day, the Palestinian Legislative Council convened in Ramallah for an emergency meeting and declared a protest strike throughout the territories. The Palestinian cabinet secretary called for the world community to isolate Israel.[120] The international reaction boiled down mainly to verbose dissatisfaction. As with regard to the entire issue of the settlements, in the case of Har Homa the American government confined itself to lip service. The administration's treatment of the crisis put an end to the Palestinian leadership's hopes that President Bill Clinton would rein in the Israeli lust for land.

The Har Homa crisis was the main issue that was discussed at Arafat's meeting with Clinton on March 3, 1997. For the first time, the Palestinian leader entered the portals of the White House in his own right, unaccompanied by an Israeli leader. Arafat hoped that President Clinton would stand by him, as he had in the wake of the tunnel crisis of the previous September, and force Netanyahu to freeze the plan to establish the new neighborhood. Har Homa, said Arafat to the president, is a plot aimed at raising a barrier between the southern West Bank and East Jerusalem and surrounding the city with Jewish neighborhoods. This has cast into doubt Israel's willingness to abide by the spirit of Oslo. The entering of Israeli bulldozers on the ground, he added, would harm the popular support for the Palestinian Authority and its policy. President Clinton retorted that he understood Arafat but immediately added that Netanyahu's coalition constraints must be taken into account, as the fate of his government depended on the parties of the far right. Arafat urged the president to demand of the Israeli prime minister that he at least postpone the implementation of the decision.[121]

Har Homa became a symbol of the Palestinian struggle. "Is one more settlement more important than the whole peace process?" Arafat asked at a press conference at the Press Center in Washington. He told the reporters that both Rabin and Peres promised him that there would be no demographic change in Jerusalem and the territories during the interim agreement.[122] While waiting for his plane at Andrews Air Force Base on his way back to New York, feeling that his talks on the issue of Har Homa had been fruitful, Arafat was called into the base commander's office. The United States consul in East Jerusalem, Ed Abington, on whose impressions this section is based, handed Arafat the telephone. Dennis Ross was on the line. The conversation did not take long. "Dennis has informed me that Netanyahu is refusing to freeze the construction," said Arafat. According to Abington, "Arafat realized that we didn't understand, or did not want to understand, the extent of troubles that the settlements were causing him at home. He realized that he was alone in the fight."[123]

In a letter to Netanyahu sent at the beginning of March, Clinton asked him to postpone the start of construction work at Har Homa. Netanyahu tried to tempt Arafat with glass beads and announced that he would allow him to use the airport at Dahaniyeh in Gaza earlier than planned. Immediately thereafter the Israeli prime minister declared: "I am building at Har Homa this week, and nothing is going to budge me from that."[124] Dr. Saeb Erekat, the Palestinian liaison with the Netanyahu government, consulted with the government secretary in a last-minute attempt to rescind the decree. Erekat warned that the peace process would be crushed under the treads of the bulldozers.[125] Four days later the work began. Security forces prevented Palestinian and a handful of Israeli demonstrators from reaching the construction site. "We are here with enough force to take the wind out of the sails of anyone who thinks that there should not be quiet," said Deputy Chief of Staff Matan Vilnai, later to become a Labor Party politician.[126] A short while later, approval was given for the building of 132 dwelling units at Ras al-Amud in East Jerusalem. The Palestinians broke off the negotiations on the interim agreement and the permanent-status agreement. The United States imposed a veto on a UN Security Council resolution condemning the settlements. America lost the last drop of its pretensions to being a fair mediator.[127]

Netanyahu's Torments

Like Rabin and then Peres, Netanyahu could not have satisfied the settlers' entire appetite. The building of the Har Homa neighborhood did not stand him in good stead at the hour of the great test, when he was asked to pay the debt of his commitment to act in accordance with the Oslo agreement. The threats by the settler heads were his travel companions in October 1998, on his way to the summit meeting with Arafat and President Clinton. Before leaving for the United States, Netanyahu placed his hand over his heart and declared: "If I, Benjamin Netanyahu, have come to the conclusion that there is no alternative, then there really is no alternative."[128] It was a reversed paraphrase of Begin's oath, before going to Washington some twenty years earlier after his election as prime minister, never to raise a hand against even a single settlement. In order to please the settlers, however, the prime minister appointed one of their leaders, Uri Elitzur, as his bureau chief. "I am with you. I am of your opinion, but you cannot ignore the fact that the nation is weak and evincing flabbiness," Netanyahu told Hannan Porat. "Not everyone is prepared to pay the price that you and I are prepared to pay, and I am everyone's prime

Prime Minister Levi Eshkol (center) visits Gush Etzion, the area south of Jerusalem where the first settlement was established in September 1967, December 19, 1967. *Photo: Moshe Milner, Government Press Office.*

Moshe Levinger (left) and Hannan Porat (right), leaders of the newly created Gush Emunim, in a frenzied dance in Sebastia, December 8, 1975. *Photo: Moshe Milner, GPO.*

Opposition leader Menachem Begin gives public support to illegal settlers in Sebastia, July 26, 1974. *Photo: Yaakov Sa'ar, GPO.*

Yeshiva students and members of the Elon Moreh group studying Gemara in Sebastia, December 8, 1975. *Photo: Moshe Milner, GPO.*

Prime Minister Yitzhak Rabin and Defense Minister
Shimon Peres visiting the Jewish settlement in Hebron,
October 15, 1976. *Photo: Yaakov Sa'ar, GPO.*

A demonstration march organized by Gush Emunim, near the newly established settlement Ofra, April 8, 1976. *Photo: Moshe Milner, GPO.*

Chief of Staff Mordechai (Motta) Gur (right) and Head of the Army Central Command negotiating with settlers in Sebastia for a peaceful evacuation, July 29, 1974. *Photo: I.P.P.A.*

Defense Minister Shimon Peres tries to persuade the residents of Ofra to leave their illegal settlement, which has since become the flagship of the settlements, August 4, 1974. *Photo: Shaia Segal.*

After the evacuation ruling of the Supreme Court, the settlers cross Palestinian villages near Nablus on their way to their new settlement, January 29, 1980. *Photo: Hanania Herman, GPO.*

Minister without Portfolio Israel Galili (right) with first settler Hannan Porat (left) in the first settlement, Kfar Etzion, September 29, 1976. *Photo: Moshe Milner, GPO.*

Prime Minister Begin, Minister of Agriculture in charge of the settlements Ariel Sharon, with other ministers and settlers in the Elon Moreh area, February 27, 1981. *Photo: Hanania Herman, GPO.*

Last-minute prayers of settlers in Yamit to stop the evacuation order given to Israeli soldiers, April 18, 1982. *Photo: Benny Tel-Or, GPO.*

Members of the Jewish terrorist group in the territories on their way to the courthouse, June 17, 1984. *Photo: Rahamim Yisraeli.*

A violent confrontation on the roofs of the town of Yamit between resisting settlers and IDF soldiers, April 22, 1982. *Photo: Benny Tel-Or, GPO.*

Interior of the grand synagogue in the settlement of Beit El, east of Nablus, June 6, 1989. *Photo: Meggy Ayalon, GPO.*

"The Secret of Redemption is Remembering": A mourning ceremony on the first anniversary of the Yamit evacuation, Jerusalem, April 11, 1983. *Photo: Gil Goldstein, GPO.*

minister. I don't want to find myself in the next war with half an army that stays home and refuses to report to the front."[129] He added that he promised to be a different prime minister, "and as a leader one has to strengthen the people and not get weakened by them."[130]

Representatives of the settlers tailed the Israeli delegation like a shadow to the summit, which was held at the Wye River Plantation in Maryland in October 1998. The prime minister was not insensitive to the voices of protest from Israel and outside the fence of the estate. He asked the hosts to allow the small delegation of settlers to spend the Sabbath with him. The Americans, who had brought the sides together at the estate in order to isolate them from external pressures, refused this request. The prime minister slipped away to a nearby wood, where his settler *"kashrut* supervisors" were waiting for him. The next day the Yesha Council published a picture of two settlers embracing Netanyahu. On Tuesday, October 20, the spies in Washington reported that "Bibi has folded to Clinton." Overnight, it was decided to bring the masses back out to the street intersections. The following morning the news broadcasts reported that Netanyahu had ordered the delegation to pack its bags. However, a source in Netanyahu's bureau leaked to the settlers that this was a maneuver and that Netanyahu had already agreed to hand over to the control of the Palestinian Authority another 13 percent of the territory of the West Bank. The Yesha Council called the Wye agreement a "treason agreement." A few days later the settler leaders apologized for the expression that was reminiscent of the incitement that had preceded Rabin's assassination. It was just a "surrender agreement," they gracefully agreed.[131]

But the demon of incitement returned. "Netanyahu has experienced an abject failure in the test of his loyalty to the security of Israel and the land of Israel," said Hannan Porat.[132] Another settler bigmouth, Zvi Hendel, a leader of the Gaza Strip settlers, declared that

"Netanyahu is about to sign the Declaration of Independence of the Palestinian state."[133] Extremist settlers called for insurrection. "If there is a resistance movement both within the government ranks and in the army, possibly the real alternative will arise," said Noam Arnon from the settlement in Hebron.[134] There were those who urged the immediate selection of an alternative premier to Benjamin Netanyahu.[135]

After the delegation returned from Wye, Foreign Minister Sharon, who had participated in the discussions there, called for settlers to take over the hills of the West Bank and occupy lands that were not theirs, contrary to the government's decision. He added with a wink to reporters that "in this way the Prime Minister's Bureau and the Defense Minister's Bureau are helping to keep the outposts on the ground."[136] The settlers needed no more encouragement than that. During the three weeks after the signing of the Wye agreement, eight new settlements were established.[137] In order to make it difficult to hand over an additional 13 percent of the West Bank to Palestinian Authority control, as stipulated in the Wye agreement, the settlers refused to cooperate with the army plans for the defense of isolated settlements. They argued that the government was trying to make them into a "second Lebanon."[138]

The race for more land was common to both the Israelis and the Palestinians. For their part, the Palestinians engaged in intensive construction in order to create facts prior to the Israeli withdrawal.[139] But their effort was a pale shadow compared with the settlers' endeavors. The general feeling that Netanyahu was about to lose the elections scheduled for May 1999 spurred the settlers to grab hilltop after hilltop. Just as they had behaved in the past before elections, this time too the settlers took full advantage of the twilight days of a crumbling government that did not have the ability to use force against them. This time, however, it was a decidedly right-wing

government, devoid of internal brakes. Within a few weeks, new settlements were established, one after another, unhindered. Netanyahu
was fighting for his political life and needed the settlers' votes. The
settlers scorned the Civil Administration officials who tried to
enforce the law. "You will not be able to stop us. We have help from
on high," they said.[140] In at least four cases, Netanyahu ordered that
Civil Administration inspectors who came to evacuate the settlements be stopped.

The settlers had not learned from the bitter experience of the
1992 elections. Seven years after they had dragged Prime Minister
Yitzhak Shamir into a conflict with the United States, and from there
into the opposition, they were now pushing Netanyahu into that same
crash trajectory. The blend of ideological fanaticism, local interests,
and power intoxication again served them ill. They demanded that a
leader who did not grant them everything must go. And perhaps their
rich experience taught them that there was no politician who would
dare to grapple with them. And yet, their belief that the concrete facts
that they were establishing day in and day out were resistant to any
government and would last longer than any political process proved
them right.

Deep Psychological Yearning

Ehud Barak was no stranger to the settlers. They became well
acquainted with him while he served as head of the Central Command and later as a chief of staff who did not conceal his reservations about the Oslo agreement. One spring night in 1994, ten weeks
after the massacre in Hebron, Barak was invited to a ceremony in celebration of Jerusalem Day at Rabbi Kook's historic yeshiva, Merkaz
HaRav, in Jerusalem. A throng of excited yeshiva students accompanied his entrance with loud singing and dancing. They tried to touch

his body and shake his hand, as though he were an esteemed rabbi. Near the Holy Ark, three rabbis, the yeshiva heads, rose to their feet and to the cheers of the crowd warmly shook the hand of "Israel's hero." Two months earlier those same rabbis had raised the flag of revolt and called upon soldiers to refuse to obey an order to evacuate settlements.

Two years later, when he was already a Knesset member, Barak poured out his heart to a *Ha'aretz* reporter: "When I see the hills to the east of my home, east of Kochav Yair, emotionally I have no doubt that I am looking at the hills of the Land of Israel. There is no meaning to our identity and everything that we are here for without the connection to Shiloh and Tekoa, Beit El and Efrata. These are the realms of our culture's childhood." Barak said that the settlers must not be put beyond the pale and that he felt affection for them. "In the context of a life of purpose, of mission, life in the service of something greater than oneself," said Barak, "I am closer to these people than to the people of the left."[141] His vision for a permanent solution to the conflict with the Palestinians included huge areas of the West Bank under Israeli sovereignty and control. But despite his great effort to placate the settlers, Barak, like his predecessors, was unable to reach their ideological hard core and satisfy them. In a last-ditch effort to rouse the settlers, about a week before the elections, one of the settler leaders, a public servant, sent out a letter to his colleagues. "If Ehud Barak comes into power he will lead to the *ethnic cleansing* of settlers from most of Judea and Samaria. To our regret, after weighing the matter, Barak has decided to create a rift in the nation and take an unambiguous line leftward. . . . We cannot remain unsullied outside of this struggle. The struggle is for our settlements and our region and therefore we must stand unanimously behind Netanyahu's candidacy."[142]

Barak's sweeping victory in the elections, and especially his winning of 18 percent of the votes in the settlements, created havoc in the settler community. The heads of the Yesha Council resigned from their positions. Israel Harel, however, attacked the Council for not having been more aggressive in its call to topple Netanyahu, and argued that Barak should not be seen as an enemy of "our project." In Harel's call to reach "strategic understandings" with Barak without adopting his "concession plan," one could see the usual attempt of the settlers belonging to the so-called "consensus" to enjoy the best of all worlds.[143] Yoel Bin-Nun called for reaching "national agreement on the issue of settlement" with the left.[144] A team on behalf of the Yesha Council that met with Prime Minister–elect Barak heard soothing words from him. "After all, you have known me for quite a while. I am a man of the center in my views, and I have a great deal of admiration for settlement."[145] Some of the settlers now expressed regret over their fight against Barak on the eve of the elections.[146]

The future plight of the new, "unauthorized" outposts from Netanyahu's day topped the agenda of the coalition talks with the right. "We will be flexible insofar as possible," said Barak, "but within the bounds of reason."[147] Leaders of the right reported that Barak had in effect promised them that no harm would come to the last-moment-outposts that had been snatched on the eve of the elections. What was concealed in the coalition created by the odd bedfellows from Meretz on the left, the National Religious Party and Shas in the middle, and Yisrael Beiteinu, the Russian far-right party, was greater than what was made public. Vague formulations and mechanisms for mediation enabled the continuation of the land grab. Barak's evident efforts to please their political representatives calmed the settlers. For a while he was considered a man whose word and deed are one.

It appeared as though the settlers' institutions were adopting a pragmatic mien. For the first time a secular settler, the mayor of

Ma'aleh Adumim, was elected chairman of the Yesha Council. He represented primarily the positions of the 100,000 secular Israelis who lived in the West Bank and who had come to terms with the Wye agreement and its implications. The familiar figure of the settler with the ritual fringes dangling from under his shirt, a large crochet skullcap on his head, and a submachine gun in his hand was replaced by a typical Israeli who aspired to a better quality of life and the exceptionally low mortgage rates available through government subsidy in the territories, and believed in the need for peace with the Arabs. "It is necessary to stop the fight for every hill and to 'settle in hearts,'" said the newly elected council head.[148]

Declaration of War

Five months went by before Barak began to deal with the issue of the forty-two newly established outposts during the term of his predecessor. A few of them received government authorization after the fact, some of them were established with various degrees of illegality, and no steps were taken in order to legalize the others. The security system determined their illegality and claimed that their establishment should be seen as a political act with far-reaching implications.[149] In a series of meetings with representatives of the settlers, Barak made it clear that he was determined to evacuate fifteen of the outposts.[150] Yet construction at the outposts slated for evacuation continued ceaselessly, as pressures were applied to prevent their evacuation.[151] At the end of negotiations with the prime minister, the settler heads agreed to the voluntary evacuation of ten outposts, four of them unmanned, and spoke about the rescue of twenty-three others. This was not the first time that the settlers sacrificed a goat or two, which had been intended from the outset to serve as bargaining chips, in order to legalize the whole flock. The contents of a newsletter that the Yesha Council distributed after the outposts agreement with Barak reveals this strategy. "The sites of the outposts that will be evacuated will continue to be effectively under the control of the settlements. We will be able to conduct agricultural and other activities at those locations, as the restriction applies only to residential use. Ever since Sebastia and Elon Moreh, the struggle for settlement has also relied on tactical moves of compromise. All of them, with no exception, only advanced and strengthened the settlement map. We have sanctified the building of the land and not our victory over the government."[152]

The extremists among the settlers were not satisfied. Refusal again proved itself effective against the feebleness of the republic's institutions. Rabbi Shlomo Aviner, the head of the Ateret Cohanim Yeshiva, published a rabbinical ruling that called for resisting the evacuation of the outposts.[153] From an emergency meeting at Havat Ma'on in the Hebron Hills, which was emerging as a bastion of the extremists, came a declaration of war on Barak.[154] The roads were blocked with boulders and tires. Signs cast the curse of *pulsa denura*— "lashes of fire"—on anyone who dared demolish a synagogue. Fliers called for soldiers to disobey the evacuation order. "The Yesha Council is not our representative. We come in the name of the Holy One, blessed be He," said the hilltop people.[155]

Barak was lured into another compromise. The settler leaders disclosed to the media that Barak had already retreated and had agreed that Havat Ma'on would remain in place for three more months, allowing its people to cultivate the land until an alternative site was found for them. After another series of barren compromise attempts, the prime minister ordered the chief of staff to evacuate the outpost. Young soldiers, men and women, had to drag the settlers away, to the sounds of protest from right-wing politicians.[156] Likud leader Ariel Sharon accused Barak of having "destroyed a Jewish locale."[157] Barak was pleased with the evacuation, which according to him combined determination and sense, and said that "the issue isn't the land of Israel but rather the supremacy of the rule of law."[158] Havat Ma'on, which was evacuated in 1999, was the only outpost uprooted while Barak was prime minister. Since then the settlers have tried to rehabilitate it, most recently in April 2007, in their attempts to expand the Jewish settlements around Hebron. Havat Ma'on was the exception to the rule; the dozens of other illegal outposts that have been established since then have become monuments to "the rule of law," which has been sacrificed to "the Land of Israel."

In the summer of 2000, in the midst of the Camp David summit negotiations between Israel and the Palestinians, the settlers began to position new mobile homes in a number of outposts, including some that had been "frozen" in the Sharm el-Sheikh interim agreement of September 1999. An ultimatum from Barak led to another agreement with the settlers, which was flouted by the settlers even before it was made public. The heads of the second generation of settlers declared that every single one of the outposts would be restored to its original site.[159] And this indeed happened: Barak's term saw the steepest growth of construction in the territories since the signing of the Oslo agreement. Housing Ministry figures show that during the first half of 2000 there was an increase of 96 percent in building starts in the settlements.[160] During the term of the Labor government headed by Barak, 2,830 new housing units were under construction, out of the 19,189 units that were built in the settlements since the signing of the Oslo agreement. About 1,800 of these housing units were public construction and the rest private construction. Altogether, during the course of 2000 there were more than 5,000 housing units in various stages of construction, and building permits were granted for 1,184 new apartments, of them 529 in the Jerusalem area. During that same period the settler population increased by nearly 12 percent, as compared to an increase of only 1.7 percent in natural growth in Israel.[161]

Just as they had acted during the Madrid conference in 1991 and the Wye summit in 1998, in July 2000 the settlers also sent their representatives to protest vigils at the Camp David summit. At the same time, "veterans of the settlements" in the territories embarked on a hunger strike under the prime minister's window, which had seen its share of demonstrations. The organization Forty Thousand Mothers, the answer by the women of the right to the Four Mothers organization that worked toward getting Israel out of Lebanon, cried out against what they considered to be the equivalent of the Munich pact between Chamberlain and Hitler.[162] The settlers made an effort to depict their struggle as the struggle of the entire Zionist settlement movement, throughout the generations, and obtained help from veteran kibbutz members.[163] The sweet talk and the quiet protest were but a thin cover to the fire of incitement that flared once again. This time too the settlers' incitement focused on the personality of the prime minister. The reports of possible concessions on the Temple Mount gave rise to the comparison between Barak and "the evil Titus."[164] The extremist circles were attracted to the fire and fanned it. The Jewish fanatics in Hebron threatened that if they were "pushed to the wall," they would fight to "the last drop of blood."[165]

Some 200,000 people demonstrated on July 17, 2000, in Rabin Square in Tel Aviv, against the negotiations that were going on at Camp David in an effort to achieve the unfinished peace project of the slain prime minister. The huge demonstration was aimed at validating the settlers' claim to a deep hold on the entire Israeli public. Israeli journalists who covered the rally did not get that impression. *Yedioth Aharonoth* correspondent Sima Kadmon wrote about the "homogeneity of the outcry." Daniel Ben Simon wrote in *Ha'aretz* that "apparently this is the only thing they are left with, to demonstrate, to protest, to cry, to make noise, to hunger strike, before the fate of the land is decided. They have embarked for nihilist realms. They spoke about the destruction of the state, about Auschwitz borders, civil war, the fall of the Third Temple, the Holocaust that was and the Holocaust to come."[166]

Ironically, the settlements and the settlers were the factor that dictated more than any other element the positions of the State of Israel in the first official negotiations with the Palestinians on permanent borders. In drawing up of the eastern border, Barak aspired to evacuate as few settlers as possible. He insisted on annexing to Israel the blocs of settlements where about 80 percent of the settlers live. The extent of the territories that the Palestinians were asked to cede amounted at the beginning of the negotiations to one-third of the West Bank. In the Stockholm talks of May 2000 it was reduced, until at Camp David 2000 the Israeli demands amounted to 10.5 percent of the territory. The Clinton proposals of December 2000, and the Taba understandings of the beginning of 2001, were based on Israeli annexation of only 4–6 percent of the territory of the West Bank. In exchange for the settlement blocs, Barak offered to relinquish the Palestinian neighborhoods of East Jerusalem and parts of the Old City. The fading-away prime minister even considered putting into the hands of the Muslim authorities partial sovereignty over the Temple Mount. Settlements, whose original purpose had been thwarting Palestinian contiguity and Israeli withdrawal from the territories, had become holy of holies to be defended at any price. However, the holy places for the Jewish people, and especially for the believers among the settlers, had now become an exchangeable, negotiable commodity.[167]

The reports that came from Camp David shattered the Palestinian territories. Demonstrators shouted, "There is no peace with the settlements!" Thousands of Palestinians from the territories and the Palestinian diaspora, among them Professor Edward Said, Palestinian Legislative Council member Rawiya al Shawa, Legislative Council political committee head Ziyad Abu Zayad, and Gazan leader Haider Abdel Shafi signed a petition stating that "all the existing Israeli settlements in the West Bank, the Gaza Strip and East Jerusalem are illegal, and any attempt to annex them and the land on which they are built is illegal." The petition demanded that any agreement that was achieved be subject to a referendum among the entire Palestinian nation, as an agreement that would not be approved in such a plebiscite "would not obligate the Palestinian people."[168]

The summit failed, and the negotiators returned home empty-handed. The diplomatic defeat was a political and psychological victory for the settlers. Barak's version—that the Palestinians' demand to exercise the right of return to Israel in response to his generous offers was what had broken the summit—brought the settlers back into the Israeli consensus and shattered the already worn-out peace camp in Israel. All the other interpretations of the failure of the summit had no chance to be heard amid the systematic, sophisticated media spin created by Barak's people and the bloody Palestinian uprising that swept the region. "We have had enough of the messages and the hints in the statements of Ehud Barak, who stresses his clinging to the settlements," wrote Hasan al Kashef, the director general of the Palestinian Authority Information Ministry, as far back as June 1999. Al Kashef called for a popular intifada against the settlements in order to cause Barak to follow a policy different from that of his predecessor. "There is no more room on our land for haggling or restraint, and there is no purpose to waiting or following new international advice. We know that we must begin the defense of our land in difficult circumstances, as the Israeli policy is gambling on our helplessness and [its ability] to hold us hostage to the option of negotiations. And this is at a time when the maximum that we will get from the American administration is an expression of concern. Five years of peace and of settlement that has not stopped for one day have been enough for us."[169]

Part Two

From Redemption
to Destruction

4

Soldiers of the Messiah

Gush Emunim stormed into the center of Israeli consciousness in the first week of December 1975, during Hanukkah. Like the ecstatic devotees of a crazed cult, masses of young men with unkempt hair topped by crochet skullcaps suddenly appeared and became at once part of the image of the time and place. On the backdrop of the hewn stones of the abandoned Oth'man railroad station at Sebastia in Samaria, a few miles northwest of Nablus, they swirled in circles of sweeping Hasidic dances, bearing their heroes on their shoulders and loudly singing *"Utzu eytza vetufar, dabru davar velo yaqum, ki 'imanu el"* ("Take counsel together, and it shall come to naught; speak the word and it shall not stand, for God is with us").[1] In one iconic photograph Hannan Porat is hoisted on the shoulders of his disciples and admirers, raised above the massed throng that is gazing at him devoutly. He is wearing a checkered shirt and a windbreaker with its zipper wide open, his arms are flung out to the sides, and his face is beaming. Porat is a totem, the idol of the tribe whom everyone worships: handsome distant, and intimate, unique and representative, distinct and similar at one and the same time. Leader, flock, and place meld in an event full of passion and eros that embodies a new beginning, a formative act of self-definition.

The event at Sebastia represented everything that was Gush Emunim: a group of radical youngsters, imbued with religious-messianic faith, shepherded by a charismatic leadership that trampled the law and the decisions of elected state institutions for the sake of their own absolute convictions. This group blended a mystical and irrational worldview with a modern, rational, and effective perception of the balance of forces and the possibilities of concrete action, employing elusive and two-pronged tactics of accelerating the coming of the Messiah on the one hand and on the other patiently and intelligently exploiting the damages of the day and the flaws of reality, all within a comprehensive ideology of illegalism.[2] Seven times the Elon Moreh group, the settlement spearhead of Gush Emunim, tried to settle at Sebastia, and each time Israeli soldiers evacuated its members in violent clashes. For a just man falleth seven times, and riseth up again. On the eighth time, which was planned like a military operation and carefully staged, thousands of enlisted devotees ascended the mountain, coming from all over the country with their families and their small children, religious and secular, representatives of the neo-Zionism of the settlers and of the old Laborite Zionist settlement movement. They came not only to protest an incumbent government's view of borders and of settling the land but also to offer a total, higher, state-overriding alternative to the democratic state and the rule of law, which are imperfect by definition. They did this by means of a sophisticated use of the contradictions inherent in the very structure of the State of Israel and its most sacred ideals, and by appropriating the state's means and resources to their ends.[3]

Judaism, Zionism, settlement, security, sacrifice, and redemption—the main pillars of the Zionist project in the Land of Israel and its ethos—were the motors that drove Gush Emunim. However, the Gush depicted itself from its inception as more Jewish, more

Zionist, more settlement-oriented, more security-minded, more devoted body and soul, and more active in bringing about full redemption. It was not by chance that the Gush people stressed that they were "the real Zionists," in the days of Zionism's slackness and disgrace throughout the world, the successors of Labor Zionism's settlement ideology and of the pioneering collective settlements such as the kibbutzim of Degania, Kinneret, or Merhavia. In a leaflet that was distributed on the eve of the operation, the Gush activists were told that they were "ascending in the rich-in-deed road of the fathers and the realizers of the Zionist movement, whose devotion, determination, and persistence had ignited the torch of settlement in the Land of Israel."[4]

The settlement in the Land of Israel, in the heart of the Arab-inhabited region of Samaria, was endowed with added value, beyond the realization of the divine right and the sacred work of cultivating the soil,[5] and beyond the expansion of the border and the distancing of the enemy. Settlement in the heart of Samaria was, according to the Gush's tenets, the only appropriate response to the spirit dwindling within Israel at that time; a response to its series of defeats in the international arena, from the UN resolution on the racist character of Zionism to the Harold Saunders document from November 1975, which called for recognition of the Palestinians' national aspirations and legitimate rights. The more distant trauma of the 1973 war, which propelled the establishment of the Gush, may have played its role too. In its deeds, Gush Emunim aimed also to compensate for the impotence and flaws of democracy, to cover for the government's failures, and to show the Jewish people the light. "We felt that apart from us there was no one who was able to display a proud Jewish presence on the map of the entire Land of Israel," wrote one of the heads of the Gush. A paid advertisement that Gush Emunim published in the newspapers on December 14, 1975, exhorted the government of Israel "to stop the withdrawal from Sinai . . . to stop immediately the entrance of the soldiers of Hitler's successor into Sinai . . . and to allow the Gush settlement cadres to establish themselves in Judea and Samaria, the Golan Heights and Sinai."[6]

"The zero hour has come! . . . Leave your home, postpone all your business, join the great move of the Jewish people's return home," Gush activists were urged in a special leaflet.[7] The leaders of the movement called on their followers to take an active part, in the form of direct action, in the divine plan, in the great redemptive move that was coalescing before their eyes. The immediate, ostensibly personal connection between the leadership and each and every one of the movement's activists is evident in this direct appeal. The perception of the absolute obligation and the personal responsibility of every member of the militant group to abandon the gray routine of life, to rise above the limitations of daily existence, and to perform himself, and not by means of mediated representatives, the redemptive collective and personal act were elements of Gush Emunim's practice at Sebastia and of the powerful messianic tension that prevailed among them. Every individual at the Sebastia event saw himself or herself as though they were bringing Redemption nearer, as though they were the very thresholds on which the Messiah would stride. The total sanctity of the time and the place applied to every clod of earth and every grain of dust upon which their feet trod, and to themselves.[8]

Gush Emunim had been officially established in February 1974, about two years before the event at Sebastia, but Sebastia was its November 29, its birth celebration, its founding myth.[9] The event at Sebastia also positioned the new organization in the heart of Israel's public sphere, expressed the breakthrough into Samaria and the great victory over the government of Israel, and all this in a well-constructed package that won extensive media coverage. Out of the pathetic slump in which Israel found itself, according to the Gush's claim, the force of Gush Emunim erupted like a primordial, ahistorical entity and defeated a temporary, ephemeral government locked into the conflicting positions and historical blindness of its members. The Rabin government's willingness, at the end of prolonged sparring, to allow the Elon Moreh nucleus of Gush Emunim to remain there, if only for a short time and in a military camp, was perceived by the Gush people as a formidable achievement and as a sign of the inevitable surrender of a state whose failed government was plotting against them. Sebastia was indeed the beginning of the agony of Rabin's first government. In its surrender to the settlers, wrote Shimon Peres's biographer, the government was fatally weakened. From that point, he said, the government went from bad to worse, until its final collapse.[10]

The singing of *"Utzu eytza vetufar,"* which became the anthem of Sebastia and Gush Emunim, was thus aimed not at an external enemy, the kings of Assyria in the prophet's verses, but rather at the government of Israel, as a message to anyone who would stand in the way of the envoys of the Messiah. For the settlers, the compromise with the government at Sebastia was confirmation of the guiding divine hand and a critical phase in the realization of the grand plan. "The Sebastia affair was a turning point in the life of Gush Emunim. . . . There are those who would call this a change in the direction of history. The believers will call this the realization of the divine will," wrote Gershon Shafat.[11] And thirty years later, still clinging to the stones of the abandoned railway station at Sebastia, Daniella Weiss, who in December 1975 was a young settler carrying her two small daughters in her arms, said that "there are some who speak about the consecrating of the tabernacle; I had the privilege of seeing the revival of a nation in the cradle of its birth. . . . These are the foundation stones on which a nation is forged."[12]

The Sharon's Fruits

In seeking the roots of the Gush Emunim phenomenon, some researchers have gone back as far as the 1950s, to the high school yeshiva at Kfar Haroeh, among the citrus groves of the Sharon coastal plain. The national-religious agricultural community, which was named after Abraham Isaac Hacohen Kook, the first Ashkenazi chief rabbi in Palestine, was located in the midst of Labor Zionist agricultural communities. It was there that Moshe Zvi Neriah, a student of the elder Rabbi Kook and one of the outstanding educators of the national religious movement, Hapoel Hamizrahi, established the model of a yeshiva that would eventually influence the system of higher yeshivas, religious Zionism, and Israeli society in its entirety. Out of the ghetto feeling and of the political and cultural marginality that the new secular state had imposed on religious Zionism in the first decades of statehood, this yeshiva enhanced the self-awareness of a national-religious and cultural-human mission and uniqueness. "Our problem," said Rabbi Neriah in 1952, is "how to relate to the state, which does not allow the Torah of Israel to determine its image. We do not want a ghetto, but others are forcing us into one."[13]

Other spokesmen of religious Zionism complained that the "state" was becoming sine qua non, and that it was bringing in and absorbing alien values and concepts while stealing from Jewish tradition only the concepts it needed, such as the sanctification of heroism and strength, and interpreting them in its own way. Jacob Bazak, of the younger generation of the National Religious Party and eventually, in the mid-1980s, the Jerusalem District Court judge who would deal leniently in the matter of the members of the Jewish terror organization, wrote: "Is this indeed the longed-for land? Was it for this that generations upon generations yearned in poverty and sorrow?

It was not for this that we fought, not of this that we dreamed. The Jewish People has not yet been redeemed."[14]

Facing the Ben-Gurionist nation-state and authoritarian etatism, with its monolithic symbols, ceremonies, memorial days, ethos, and discourse that were shaped in the early days of the state as part of the creation of a new civil religion, the people of the modernist stream in religious Zionism wanted to make accessible to all their own modernist, nationalist alternative. "The entire Torah must be translated into the reality and language of our generation in all the modern pipelines," declared Rabbi Neriah in 1952 in the words of Rabbi Kook. "With the approach of the Third Temple, we must proceed in the light of the revelation of Israeli thought. Inner ideas and the secrets of the Torah must become common property."[15]

In the early 1950s a group of yeshiva students, all of them sons of traditional Ashkenazi families of the urban middle class, adopted the mannerisms of an underground cult and the profile of a historic religious mission, calling itself Gahelet (Ember, a Hebrew acronym for an avant-garde nucleus learning the Torah). "We must constitute an ember for generations and be the seed of an entire nation that in the future will be observant of all the commandments and God's Torah," said the group's manifest.[16] Thirty years later most of the members of the Gahelet group were among the broad spiritual leadership of Gush Emunim and the settlers in general. In this group the basic structures of the Gush ethos, its guiding symbols and its practices, were shaped. Gahelet embodied the initial attempt to provide a religious answer to the Zionist challenge, and expressions of mystification of the Israeli national experience were evident. In this tiny group was also created a few years later the critical fusion between the elder Rabbi Kook's philosophy and the younger Rabbi Kook's personality, embodied in the Merkaz HaRav Yeshiva and the more radical national religious youth, who were already on the track of developing their self-perception as an elect and leading elite.[17]

The Gahelet youngsters sought inspiration and teachers of religious law, and they found them at the Merkaz HaRav Yeshiva in Jerusalem. It was not obvious that this fateful encounter would occur, although the Gush Emunim people later described it as inevitable, as if it were inscribed somewhere in higher spheres. The yeshiva was founded by Rabbi Abraham Isaac Hacohen Kook at the beginning of the 1920s. The elder Kook's philosophy and the yeshiva he established were not at the center of religious Zionism during his lifetime. The rabbi's renaissance personality was replete with contradictions, and his openness to general studies and secular phenomena—along with the profundity and opaqueness of his thinking and utterances, which were considered eccentric and too threatening or taboo—distanced his contemporaries from him. A man who wanted to serve as a bridge between contraries was in fact rejected, even though his genius and uniqueness were universally recognized, by foes and admirers alike.

After his death in 1936, the yeshiva was pushed even further to the margins of religious life. The yeshiva's scholarly authority, like the son's authority, was limited. Gideon Aran, a researcher of Gush Emunim, speaks in this context about the extinguishing of "lights"— *Orot* (Lights) was the title of a book of the elder Kook's writings— after the death of the awe-inspiring rabbi, who left a great void behind him, and of the familiar phenomenon of the inferiority of sons and heirs as compared to their extraordinary fathers.[18] Only years later, after the establishment of the state, which among Kook's disciples was perceived as the realization of the rabbi's messianic prophecy of redemption, did his philosophy begin to attract disciples and researchers.

In the Name of the Father and Son

Students and disciples of the two rabbis of the Kook dynasty have obsessively analyzed the philosophies and personalities of father and son. Many argue that the son could never liberate himself from the student's unbending admiration for his rabbi in his relationship with his admired father. Others say that between father and son a mutual, intimate, unique and hidden relationship existed where no one else could set foot. It was the elder Kook who decreed that his son Zvi Yehudah was his authorized commentator, who understood "the inner feelings of my heart." And indeed the younger Kook was considered until his death to be one of the main interpreters of his father's philosophy. He selectively edited parts of the elder Kook's writings, especially those that touched upon the Land of Israel, and published them in the collection *Orot* in 1949, the first year of statehood. This volume, which for years the younger Kook taught to selected students at his yeshiva, became a kind of sacred text for an entire generation of religious young men. Thus for many years Zvi Yehudah Kook influenced the way his father's words were perceived and understood and contributed to the expanding interest in his philosophy.[19]

In recent years, especially thanks to the ideologically biased use that Gush Emunim has made of the elder Kook's words, in academia and in the religious world there has been a struggle not only over the meaning of his thought and his statements, and their political applicability, but also over the very right to obtain access to his original writings. These have been kept for many years far from the eyes of researchers by order of the incumbent head of Merkaz HaRav, Avraham Shapira, formerly the Ashkenazi chief rabbi. However, following the murder of Eliahu Shlomo Ra'anan, the elder Kook's grandson, in Hebron in 1998, the family that holds the rights to the grandfather's writings published eight volumes of Kook's writings, unedited and uncensored. The publication created a sensation and was considered a historic event in the religious intellectual community and among Kook researchers. The thousand copies that were printed were snatched up overnight. Further editions have not been printed because of a ban by the head of the yeshiva. It was, however, impossible to undo what had been done. Like samizdat, thousands of privately duplicated copies of Kook's complete writings are in circulation from hand to hand.

It was not immediately clear upon Kook's death that his son would inherit his place. He was preceded by two yeshiva heads. Only when Zvi Yehudah remained the last senior person at the yeshiva did he become the head of Merkaz HaRav, and even then his stature as a Torah scholar was controversial. In this sense the encounter with the Gahelet youngsters served as the Big Bang for both sides. The rebellious youngsters conferred upon him spiritual authority, and thus "made themselves a rabbi." And the rabbi, who had grown up and had remained in the shadow of his revered father, found in these admiring students the suitable anvil for hammering out his rabbinical authority and forging unprecedented political influence.[20]

Thus, at a time when researchers were comparing the relationship between the father and the son to the relationship between Moses and Joshua, the son's influence increased and went much further than his father's had. Although he was not considered a great scholar or authority on religious law, and did not create a comprehensive philosophy of his own, Zvi Yehudah Kook, thanks to the combined powers of his radical and more simplistic messages and his zealous and practical students, achieved unprecedented educational and political power, which over the years went far beyond the realm of his yeshiva. Thanks to these students, and in historical perspective, the mark that Zvi Yehudah Kook left on Israeli society and the history of the state was and remains more comprehensive and profound than that of any other religious-spiritual figure.

The great figurehead for Zvi Yehudah Kook and his students was Kook the father, Rabbi Abraham Isaac Kook, who was considered by many one of the greatest religious and intellectual thinkers in Eretz Yisrael and the Jewish world of the first part of the twentieth century. The new reality of the sovereign state in all its concreteness was for Kook the son and his followers an inevitable and decisively messianic process, as Aviezer Ravitzky writes, a confirmation of the elder Kook's prophetic predictions. If the father wrote that "the End has already awoken, the third coming has begun," the son would write some fifty years later, when Gush Emunim was involved in its "divine" mission, that "the End is being revealed before our very eyes, and there can be no doubt or question that would detract from our joy and gratitude to the Redeemer of Israel. . . . The End is here."[21] In Zionism Kook the father saw a "heavenly matter" that paved the way for redemption, and the future state had a sacred basis. Long before the state was established, in an article from 1920 he had written that the future "State of Israel is a divine entity, our holy and exalted state!" The future state would be "ideal," at "its foundation . . . the pedestal of God's throne in this world," whose aim is that "the Lord be acknowledged as one and His name one, which is truly the highest happiness." This state was to be very different from any other, ordinary state.[22]

According to Kook the father, who immigrated to Palestine at the beginning of the twentieth century and established his yeshiva in Jerusalem, the return to Zion embodied "the roots of the coming of the Messiah," and the times were definitely "the generation of the Messiah." In the Chief Rabbinate that he founded in Jerusalem in 1921 he saw a step and a means toward the reestablishment of the

Great Sanhedrin, the supreme authority of the Oral Law in ancient times, and now a main tool in the national religious revival. As Ravitzky wrote, unlike other great Orthodox rabbis, Kook the father expressed an activist, worldly stance on the issue of the national rebirth. The Messiah, according to him, was not the driving force behind the historical process but its outcome, "since this return is the very root of the Coming of the Messiah, even though full redemption has not yet been attained."[23]

In his bold, somewhat iconoclastic worldview Zionism was to propel the nation not only to political but also to spiritual revival. He charged Zionism with the task of bringing about radical change in the life of the Jewish people, of sparking an all-encompassing renaissance of untold measures.[24] In a philosophical act that was Hegelian in its essence, Kook attempted to conceptualize the Zionist historical break with religion as a phase in the process of messianic redemption. The task he set for himself, writes Ravitzky, was to explain on religious grounds not only the historical crisis that was taking place but also the motivations of the antireligious rebels. In this attempt he eventually came to view the early Zionists and secular pioneers as unwitting *ba'alei teshuvah* (returnees to religious Judaism), who play a central role in the very process of salvation.[25] He believed that these freethinking rebels play an effective role in the sequence of events, helping to move matters along and even struggling toward a certain end, without grasping the inner logic of the occurrences, their true meaning, or real consequences. In the end, the elder Kook said, they will prove to have been actors in a cosmic drama quite different from what they personally aimed for, and it is they who unknowingly are laying the earthly foundations of spiritual rebirth and religious redemption. "When the time comes . . . the hidden meaning will be revealed," he said. "There are people who do not have the slightest idea what an important role they play in the scheme of Divine Providence. They are called but do not know who is calling them," one of the spiritual leaders of Gush Emunim would write, echoing the tenet of Kook the father.[26]

In the eulogy for Theodor Herzl that he delivered in Jaffa in 1904, Kook the elder depicted the founder of statist Zionism as a Messiah ben Joseph, the figure who is associated with "material" messianism, who embodies the inevitability of crisis and defeat, the final battle that is to take place on the eve of the age of redemption and the sufferings that come along with it.[27] Secularism and secular politics were tolerated by Kook the elder as long as they served the grand design of Providence. The moral and social pathos of the secular Zionists and their authentic search for freedom, wrote Ravitzky, were granted a positive, dialectical role in the national rebirth.[28] But political Zionism did not have an immanent value and status, and free-thinking Zionists' individual visions and aspirations were of no significance. Kook the father claimed that the motivations for the national rebirth and the return to the land were profoundly religious, even if their religious character was denied or repressed by secular Zionism.[29] He thus claimed that when the secularists achieved their earthly goals, they would realize that what they had really aspired for all along was something higher, a return to the Jewish soul and commandments.

The elder Kook did not have to grapple with the concrete reality of the events that were to determine the course of Jewish history during the second half of the twentieth century. Neither did he supply generations to come with effective religious or conceptual tools for bridging the gulf between his messianic utopia, the eschatological dimension with which he endowed the future messianic state, and the imperfect, partial political-historical entity, in the here and now, which was the concrete Israeli reality.[30] His disciples were thus plunged into the "messianic" reality, with all its imperfections and historical contradictions, and had to find their way on their own in this maze, for which Kook the father supplied a vision, not a map or a manual. Indeed, the Kookist utopian legacy could not help them to confront the reality of the modern revival of the Jewish people in concrete *halakhic* (religious) terms, "unless illumined by a prophetic, redeeming transformation," as Ravitzky put it.[31]

It was Kook the son who took it upon himself to bring utopia down to earth and transform a nonplace into a real one. The abstract, complex, dialectical writings of the father underwent a process of popularization and social application by the son. The broad, deep teachings of Kook the elder were translated into a "language of action," wrote Ya'akov Ariel, one of the younger Kook's leading students who was himself a rabbi and spiritual leader. What had been a messianic expectation had now become a political program. By removing the barriers between the theological and the political, the road was open for Kook the son and his followers to endow the existing state with messianic holiness, and to declare sacred all its concrete actions, phenomena, and symbols. By editing and publishing his father's writings, and with the help of his many students-agents, Zvi Yehudah Kook mobilized his life to bequeath his father's philosophy, transplant it into Israel's political reality, and transform it into a political tool that would realize his father's messianic vision. Zvi Yehudah and his school carried the elder Kook's notion of redemption to its logical extreme, wrote Ravitzky, himself a religious thinker. And this program did not allow its believers to continue to play secondary roles in the historical drama as mere passengers or accompaniers of the Zionist convoy, as their fathers had done. It demanded that, by virtue of their knowledge of the true meaning of the project of national revival, they take up the reins and lead the great endeavor to its proper place.

Between the Theological and the Political

The younger Kook, who shaped the language and terminology of Gush Emunim and molded its practices, employed every means to blur the difference between the theological and the political, creating a total overlap between the two. Any incongruity between the discourse or the model and the reality was resolved by a sophisticated dialectical mechanism. The necessity to hide the modern political discourse within the religious discourse—that is, to talk politics without politics—became an important element in Zvi Yehudah Kook's theological system. As against his father's, whose philosophy was descriptive in applying religious dimension to political events, the younger Kook's thought, which was influenced also by Zionist ideology, by Ben Gurion's and Western thinking, turned things upside down. The thinking structure moved from a descriptive status to an active language. In his intensive use of Hegelian concepts, such as the perception of history as having a dialectical and determinist course, and by applying the concept of the self-knowing spirit, the younger Kook molded a new, radical, and immediately applicable discourse.

Zvi Yehudah Kook's main debate on nationalism and the national body, for example, is based on his analysis of the concept of exile. Just as the Zionist movement had done, the younger Kook also negated the Diaspora, but its denial could not be absolute because of the Diaspora's closeness to religion and religion's commitment to the tradition of the past. Exile did indeed cause the "disfigurement," "disgrace," and "debasement" of the Jewish people;[32] it was a place of death, of "the scattering of bones," of rottenness and surrender.[33] However, in applying the dialectical mechanism, the younger Kook did not negate it completely but rather saw it as a crucial reality of evil, a necessary stage preceding the mending return to the Land of Israel. The elements of the dichotomy Land of Israel/Diaspora (life/death) were intertwined and enabled each other. The death of the Diaspora bore in "its depths" the opposite: national life, Zionism. The younger Kook understood the Holocaust within this same interpretive theological pattern. The State of Israel and the Holocaust were bound together, as life and death, light and darkness. While the elder Kook saw in World War I with all its horrors "birth pangs," shaking up, and a purification leading to rebirth (*tikkun*), in which the Messiah's power was evident, the younger Kook went even further and endowed World War II and the destruction of European Jewry with religious sense. He saw in them a "heavenly surgery," a "deep, hidden, divine therapy aimed at purging [us] of the impurity of exile," and "the angry blow of the Lord's hand [aimed at] removing us from the nations and their worthless culture."[34]

The return to a collective national life necessitated a single perspective, the national perspective: It is not the individual who is sacred; rather the entire place, with everything in it, is sacred in and of itself. Concepts of life and death were seen by Zvi Yehudah Kook only through the national perspective. The term "resurrection of the dead" was transferred from the realm of the individual to the national sphere. He perceived the return to the Land of Israel as "Resurrection" in the literal sense.[35] The national struggle for the land is a struggle for life, despite deaths of individuals. Kook, who maintained an interesting connection to the social studies of his time, did not negate the cultural and political, namely the non-natural dimension of nationalism, but he argued that unlike the gentiles, whose national struggle is a death struggle because their nationalism is a product of the *nomos*, an artificial product of social consciousness, the Jewish national struggle is the struggle of a living national organism, of an authentic *physis* fighting for its life and bringing about the salvation of the world.[36]

The "national body" was a masculine body, with phallic characteristics (as opposed to the Diaspora, which is "feminine" and
"devoid of qualities"), around which the society is coalescing and
organizing, and the living national organism is being created. National
strength, conquest, and heroism are not something new; however, they
are also not a replication or simple duplication of ancient times. They
were not lost during the years of the Diaspora but were hidden in
"the source" and "the inner truth" of the Jewish people, in the depths
of the nation. In Kook's teachings, only the nation's consciousness of
itself, and its "body," can reveal what is hidden in its depths.[37] Nationalism and the state underwent a process of mystification and sanctification. Jewish-Israeli nationalism was perceived as an entity beyond
time and place, based on a divine ideal. Hence, the state, the political
realization and embodiment of nationalism, was sanctified as was the
day of its birth, Independence Day, which had become a religious holiday at the Merkaz HaRav Yeshiva in the mid 1950s.

The nation's strength and success, Kook argued, depended only
on the nation itself and not on external circumstances, an argument
that eventually became a major pillar of the thought and political
practice of Gush Emunim. The nation's success and heroism are contingent upon national awareness, the nation's recognition of its "true"
essence, which can emerge only by means of the discourse and the
philosophy of the elder Kook and his son. According to the younger
Kook, his philosophy was not only the right interpretation of the
reality but also the power that creates reality.[38] This outlook of Zvi
Yehudah Kook's was strikingly evident at the time of the evacuation
of Sinai in 1982, when he thought that if he was totally convinced of
the improbability of returning Sinai to Egypt, and that if he kept
saying this, the peninsula would not be evacuated. And indeed, his
disciples and his followers continued to build their homes and pray

for the stopping of the withdrawal right up to the arrival of the Israeli soldiers to evacuate them, just as the settlers did in their struggle against the August 2005 disengagement from Gaza. The eventual defeat in northern Sinai in 1982 was explained, as was that from the Gaza Strip in 2005, in a typical dialectical move, to the effect that the sole purpose of the withdrawal was to perpetuate the settlement in Judea and Samaria, and that any victory needs to be preceded by a defeat that endows it with meaning. Kook's death on March 8, 1982, in the midst of the settlers' struggle for the settlements of the Yamit region in Sinai, was seen by his followers as a symbolic event of metaphysical import.

In his eulogy for his teacher, Haim Druckman, the head of the Or Etzion Yeshiva, said that Rabbi Zvi Yehudah Kook was "one of the few in his generation—I dare say the only one—to grasp fully the messianic revelation the State of Israel represents, to see the light of the Messiah shining forth from the State of Israel. . . . He was the only one who taught us how to embrace wholeheartedly the truth that this state, with all its problems, is a divine one."[39] The sanctity of the land thus applied to the state, ostensibly a modern, secular, and rational-legal entity. The State of Israel, according to the younger Kook, was "the embodiment of the vision of redemption," and from this also derived the absolute sanctity of the concrete statist reality.[40] Sanctified were all of Israel's endeavors, deeds, and failures. Israel's wars as well were to be perceived not merely in terms of national survival (Israel's claim since its foundation) but in theological terms, as mighty, sacred struggles to uproot evil, purify the land, and bring about universal *tikkun.* And every soldier who joins the army of Israel is another real spiritual step, another stage in the process of redemption.[41] The acts of the state are no longer concrete human deeds, which have a concrete and limited aim in a social and political context, but rather part of a divine plan, of a theological progression of repair and salvation. "The holiness of the divine service [*avodah*, literally "work"], the service of the Temple," wrote Zvi Yehudah Kook, "is extended to the work of the state as a whole, both practical and spiritual, both public and private."[42]

According to the younger Kook, the process of redemption was absolute and inevitable, an immanent course from which there is no return and which is not dependent on any external factor. "The divine historical imperative, clearly revealed to us, to put an end to the Exile," he wrote in the year of the establishment of the state, "cannot be changed or distorted, either by the wickedness and stubborn resistance of the nations or by our own mistakes and un-Jewish deviations. The brief delays all these can occasion do not have the power to reverse the movement, which proceeds onward and upward with utmost certainty."[43] In the midst of the 1948 war, he wrote that "it is this higher, inner life command that constitutes and clarifies the absolute certainty of the process of our return and recovery here, the building up of our people and our land, our culture and Torah, our military power and our sovereignty."[44]

The totalizing, simplified and ostensibly self-evident teleological progression that Zvi Yehudah Kook designed, his rhetoric of unconditional and undelayed redemption, the process of the deterministic and boundless sanctification, were like an intoxicating elixir for his followers. They adopted his words in their literal formulation and took them even further. "Our situation will lead us ineluctably to build the Third Temple," said Druckman. "There will be ups and downs, but there can be no reversing the process."[45] And at the beginning of the 1980s, Rabbi Eliyahu Avihail said that "we are living at the end of history," at a phase at which the "Redemption of Israel" no longer depends on Israel's deeds. "Divine Providence no longer operates, as a rule, according to Israel's actions but according to a cosmic plan."[46] Yet these views of the younger Kook and his diligent successors apparently posed a spiritual and practical dilemma. If indeed the trajectory and inevitability of the progression of redemption are foreknown and determined, what is the role of human will and action? The dialectical mechanism found an answer to this too. "No, it is not we who are forcing the End, but the End that is forcing us!" Kook told his students, who undertook the mission of bringing the End nearer.[47] They saw themselves as the elect, active, avant-garde force that would advance the divine redemptive course. Those who believe they know the future, said Ravitzky, want to be the first to announce it. They want to lead the march to the drumbeat of history. They want to be part of the flow and to help it toward its destined goal. "Whatever their social or numerical weight, they see themselves as playing a central role in the unfolding of events."[48]

The Holy Trinity

In these few lines of Ravitzky's lie the genetic code of Gush Emunim, the pillar of fire that illuminated its way from the day of its creation to the days of its renewed youth in the spring of 2004, thirty years after it was founded, as the sword began dangling over its formidable enterprises. This is because, like the phoenix, Gush Emunim comes to life again and shakes out its feathers precisely when it is threatened. Days of danger and anxiety have always been days of awakening and strengthening for Gush Emunim and its people, days of existential meaning, days in which the Messiah is in need of his messengers' most active help.[49]

It was not by chance that the Gush arose in the spring of 1974, when the plan for the withdrawal and the "separation of forces" in Sinai appeared on the horizon following the Yom Kippur War, threatening the wholeness of the land. This was and remains Gush Emunim's element: collective anxieties and the menace of losing parts of the land. Neither the great military victory of June 1967 nor the expansion of Jewish rule over the territories after 1967, which was perceived as an additional stage in the certain, absolute, bold messianic process, brought about the establishment of the Gush, nor did the blunders of the Yom Kippur War and the political crisis in its wake. Gush Emunim arose only when Israel was facing the threatening possibility of a change in the territorial conquests that the 1967 war had created, and in connection with the dangers of peace and its price in land.[50] Thus, at a time when demobilized reserve soldiers, who had returned from the killing fields of October 1973, were organizing all around the country for demonstrations protesting against a government that refused to recognize the toxicity of the fruit of the 1967 victory, a group of young religious people, disciples of Rabbi Kook, met quietly to stop with their own bodies any chance of liberation from the burden of this fruit. And whereas those protest groups have long since disappeared, leaving behind no trace, the Gush, parallel to the waning of the historical Labor movement, became the most influential political and cultural force in the history of the state.

The basic ideas of Gush Emunim—which were founded on the holy trinity of the Jewish people, the Land of Israel, and the Torah, and the essence of which was the commandment, breakable only on pain of death, of settlement in all the territories of the Land of Israel—were drawn, as noted, from the philosophies and utterances of the elder and the younger Kook. If the establishment of the state was a great and important step in the redemptive process, which began with the modern return to Zion, the conquest of the territories beyond the Green Line and the unification of Jerusalem in 1967 were an additional, earthshaking change in the messianic process. The Yom Kippur War, however, the destruction-that-was-averted and the thousands killed in its battles, posed a major challenge to the messianic interpretation of the history of the State of Israel. "What is the meaning of this war?" asked Yehuda Amital, a student of the younger Kook and a member of the group that founded Gush Emunim. For "our certain belief [is that] we are living in the age of the start of the Redemption. . . . On the backdrop of this belief, and on the backdrop of the Six-Day War, which taught us that indeed war has a real aim, and that is the conquest of the land, the question arises . . . as to whether there is not a regression here, heaven forbid? Does not the very fact of the outbreak of the war, with all its distressing phenomena, raise the possibility that there is apparently a move backward here in the divine progression of the beginning of the Redemption?"[51]

Precisely in order to avert the "move backward" in the "divine progression" of Redemption, Gush Emunim came into life. The name Emunim (faith) was first heard on Tu B'shvat (Jewish Arbor Day) in 1974, at a meeting of a group of young people in the prefabricated home of Yoel Bin-Nun at the settlement of Alon Shvut. The participants in that meeting were Zevulun Hammer, Moshe Levinger, Haim Druckman, Eliezer Waldman, Gershon Shafat, and Hannan Porat.[52] A year earlier, in 1973, the Elon Moreh settlement nucleus had been established when young religious ultra-Zionists, most of them settlers in Kiryat Arba, reckoned that settlement of the whole of the land had no father and mother, and that Samaria and Judea were empty of and crying out for Jews. Menachem Felix and his fellow yeshiva student Benny Katzover decided to "close their Gemaras" and go out into the field. In January 1974 and with no connection to the activities of Felix and Katzover, Gershon Shafat met Rabbi Haim Druckman at the funeral of the secretary general of the Bnei Akiva religious Zionist youth movement and complained that there was a "need to do something" in order "to get the wagon of the depressed that is stuck in the vale of tears up the mountain."[53]

The results of the elections that were held after the Yom Kippur War and the weakening of the Labor Party gave these young people the impression that Israel was ready for a new leadership, which resulted in a series of meetings that led to the founding and organizing of Gush Emunim. The same people from the original group were always present at these different meetings, in one configuration or another. They are the founding fathers. To this day they are considered the elders of the tribe, and their opinions are heard despite the changes in the profile of the Gush and in its functioning. Among them were Moshe Levinger, Hannan Porat, Gershon Shafat, Eliezer Waldman of Kiryat Arba, Yoel Bin-Nun, and the two young National Religious Party (NRP) Knesset members, Zevulun Hammer and Yehuda Ben-Meir. The method of recruitment was like that of classical elites: co-optation, using class, status, and family connections. People brought people—their relatives, friends, classmates, and the like. The network of the same worked in this case too.[54]

From its very first day the Gush saw itself as an avant-garde that would awaken and lead the entire nation, and was imbued with a sense of total confidence in the justice of its path. Its people endowed themselves with the role of a sort of collective prophet, and their excess privileges were derived in their eyes from this role and the obligation they imposed on themselves; hence they did not recognize any earthly obstacle that stood in their path, neither persons, be they Jewish or non-Jewish, nor one government or another, nor the law. Their goal was to shock the people awake and rescue Israel "from the despair that prevails in it, from the loss of the path, from nihilism."[55] Even though most of the leaders of the Gush and its activists came from religious Zionism, graduates of Bnei Akiva, and members of the NRP, they did not see themselves as part of the party system and refused to become a faction within the party. To them, party politics was base, a system of despicable compromises made by mediocre, dull people. To them, the NRP represented the old religious Zionist movement, which was marginal and contented itself with crumbs from the table of secular Zionism. The recoiling from party politics also derived from Rabbi Kook's view of the wholeness of their role, of their "pan-Israeliness." In every Jew, he said, "there is a spark of holiness, which even if it is hidden must be awakened, developed and brought close." The struggle for the wholeness of the land and its settlements, said Gush Emunim, has to be pan-national, with no connection to party affiliation.[56] And yet, from their very first days the founders of the new organization displayed a shrewd understanding of politics, zigzagging among rival political parties and positioning themselves among the branches of the noble family tree of the Labor movement, to endow their deeds with the aura of the pioneers who settled the land before statehood and in its first decades, and to partake of their unquestioned legitimacy.[57]

The identical sought for the distinctive among them, *primus inter pares*. In their search they came to the first, supreme settler, Hannan Porat of Gush Etzion, who was described as "a modern envoy, a kind of figure who has been reincarnated from the stories of the just men of ancient times."[58] Porat, a graduate of Kfar Haroeh and the Kerem Beyavneh yeshivas, was the ideal, natural leader, "a fine organizer, a manipulator, a fiery speaker and an excellent student of Jewish law, authoritative and charismatic."[59] Porat, who saw himself as a pragmatic leader and among whose spiritual ancestors he numbered Labor Zionist leaders Berl Katznelson, Manya Shochat, and Aharon David Gordon,[60] was prepared to enlist in the battle, but not at the price of leaving Kfar Etzion. At the other, extreme pole of the Gush leadership was the first settler in Hebron, Moshe Levinger, an admired yet controversial figure even among his colleagues. It was Levinger who argued that "the bulldozer named Theodor Herzl is no longer enough, and we need Rabbi Kook's bulldozer."[61] Porat and Levinger were joined by Yohanan Fried, a native of Jerusalem who was in charge of the research institute at the Merkaz HaRav Yeshiva, and who like his colleague Porat had been wounded on the banks of the Suez Canal in the Yom Kippur War. Thus came to life the triumvirate of Levinger, Porat, and Fried, who led the Gush in its first stages.[62]

The founders of the Gush were characterized by the journalist Danny Rubinstein as "members of the state generation, people with a higher [religious] education and people with a stable economic background; the sons of Ashkenazi, veteran and established families defined as religious."[63] This observation was supported by statistical findings. At the height of its activity, the people of the Gush were young (93 percent under the age of forty-five, as compared to 35 percent in the general population), most of them were native born (68 percent as compared to 53 percent in the general population), religious (92 percent as compared to less than one-third in the general population), educated (66 percent had post–high school education), and of Ashkenazi origin (82 percent).[64] The origins, the environment in which they grew up, and the spiritual-religious influences that the founders and leaders of Gush Emunim brought with them were similar if not absolutely identical: the same yeshivas, the same rabbis, the same scriptures, the same idioms. Their physical makeup—their scrupulously casual way of dressing and their body language, which combined the portrait of the Labor pioneer of the 1930s and '40s with the crochet skullcap and ritual fringes that, according to the move toward religious extremism, gradually began to peek out from under their shirts—was also characteristic and identifiable.[65]

The Gush people took pride in their being a voluntary nonparty, a nonestablished group. From the outset and over the years, until the creation of the Yesha Council in its stead in the early 1980s, there were never elections for manning the leadership positions of the movement. A group of "naturally" selected founders distributed the informal leadership roles among its members and met once a week to discuss the issues on the agenda, to plan Gush activities, and to initiate action among the masses. The sources of nonformal authority were multiple: veteranship, personal charisma, spiritual repute, networks of connections and support that each of them could draw from in time of mobilization, and the ability to deploy these connections upward, within the political system as well as the degree of sacrifice and devotion to the movement and talent at raising funds. The image of the Gush as an extra-political body was nurtured persistently by Gush people, both for outward and inward consumption, just as the direct and unmediated relationship was nurtured within the founding group, which developed for itself a mythological aura.

In contradistinction to the rigid and strict acceptance procedures for prospective settlers that were observed by Gush Emunim, those who joined the Gush activities never went through an official acceptance process. Apparently the founders made a point of being more selective about their neighbors at home in the territories than about their partners in street demonstrations and political campaigns. There was no formal membership procedure, and its members did not carry membership cards or pay dues but only donated what they could and in accordance with the needs of the Gush. The decision not to establish the movement formally was a calculated, formative move in the history of the Gush, and "very cunning," according to Ehud Sprinzak. In this way, apart from stalwart activists and members of Gush Emunim settlement groups, it was not possible to identify and quantify the membership, and the Gush could always claim a larger number of members without it being possible to contradict this. On the other hand, its fans and supporters could always join ad hoc, concrete activities without being totally committed to all its moves. Thus the Gush preserved an aura of vagueness around itself, which contributed to its mystique, and the lack of boundaries suited its universal claim and supposedly supra-political character. The power of the Gush derived in part from the establishment's inability to identify its real extent and power and from the intensive reciprocal relationships between the hard core and the soft periphery, which at any given moment could be jump-started and recruited for action. The recruitment was done by taking a dormant population and making it active and enthusiastic through the efforts of a charismatic and experienced leadership. In the context of this awakening, existing or suppressed sentiments of anxiety and distress were spurred into life.[66]

The interpretive grid that Sprinzak offered for the unprecedented strength of Gush Emunim and its social and cultural structure was "the model of the iceberg of political extremism." Sprinzak argued that the superstructure of the iceberg is the extremist movement, while the infrastructure (the part of the iceberg that is beneath the surface) is an entire social and cultural system, which is not extreme and functions in everyday life in a normal way. The extremist group is not cut off from the infrastructure and is able, in time of need, to put it into play and make use of all of its huge resources. Sprinzak also held that the Gush was not a small and fanatical group that had suddenly been "stricken" with a messianic vision, but that this was the tip of a large social and cultural body that struck roots and grew up quietly over many years within Israeli society. When specific historical circumstances developed, its extremist tip suddenly became evident.[67]

Earthly Politics

Politics for Gush Emunim was ostensibly the default option. The Gush people viewed themselves as a spiritual elite, a sanctified leadership, whom the circumstances of the hour—the poverty of political life, the absence of an alternative, and the knowledge or self-conviction that there is no one else who will do the holy work—compelled to descend to politics and involve themselves in the earthly practice. "We were aware that we were liable to join those who do things, and instead of being a spiritual elite become the fighters, the insurgent people at the gates," said Hannan Porat.[68] As the Gush leaders saw it, they were the emergency and rescue squads of the Jewish people and the Land of Israel. Faithful to the younger Kook's vision, the Gush leaders held that theirs was the movement of Redemption that was acting toward its realization, a movement of revival, trying to bestir both Judaism and Zionism, the first from its flabbiness and stagnation, the second from its straying and sins. The government of Israel, in their version, was a misleading and flawed government, devoid of inner vision and understanding, in which there was neither determination nor devotion nor the necessary self-awareness to catalyze the messianic process. Therefore, wrote one of the Gush ideologists who had been a member of the original Gahelet group of the 1950s, this government must be stopped by every possible means, and this will be done by those whose roots lie deep in the Jewish sources, who understand the politics of the higher sphere and are able to act.[69]

The view of the higher and the lower politics and the connection between them had its origins in the statements of Zvi Yehudah Kook. "The Master of the Universe has His own political agenda, according to which politics here below are conducted," Kook taught his students. "Part of this redemption is the conquest and settlement of the land. This is dictated by divine politics, and no earthly politics can supersede it."[70]

This connection between divine politics and human politics, the political action without politics that characterized the Gush, befitted its being a religious-political sect, as the sociology of religion defines it. In order to draw the entire nation into the "sacred process," argued sociologist Janet O'dea, and to convince others of the rightness of their ideas and their absolute truth, the members of the sect were to employ every means, including violence and harm to opponents and those perceived as standing in its way, and they were to do this "whether by persuasion or by physical force."[71]

Rabbi Kook was also a pioneer in his own personal engagement in politics and thus provided a convenient role model of the mixture of theology and politics for his students. He exchanged the venerated position of the head of a major yeshiva in Jerusalem, to which even secular people related with respect, for concrete political action. Kook justified his descent into "lowly" politics by the great crisis that Israel was in.[72] Employing modern techniques and tactics, Kook, served by his students and former students, disseminated his political theology widely. He invited government ministers for persuasive talks, met with Knesset members, military commanders, and members of the secular establishment, and even joined his students' settlement demonstrations. In the first attempt by the Elon Moreh group to settle at Hawara, at the beginning of the summer of 1974, the eighty-four-year-old rabbi stood face to face with the chief of the Central Command, Major General Yona Efrat and, to the consternation of his admirers, exhorted him: "Bring a machine gun and shoot me."[73] Even when the rabbi's and his disciples' strong connection to every clod of the land was manifested in political and settlement activism, their strangeness to the land they sanctified and their uncanniness in the landscape were evident.[74]

The greater Land of Israel, which was occupied in June 1967, was perceived by Kook and his students as a revelation, as a heralding of the Messiah, another giant step in the coming of Redemption. The war, the military victories, the blood that was spilled on this land and for the sake of this land, were interpreted, according to Uriel Tal, a scholar of totalitarianism and messianic politics, as evidence of cosmic dimensions of the metaphysical time in which the political reality was embroiled.[75] The preservation of the wholeness of the land and its settlement were the greatest, most important principle, in effect the sole principle, for which Gush Emunim organized and for the realization of which it acted during its peak years. For this principle the Gush pushed aside every other social-political issue. Its basic precept was that the Land of Israel was not a matter for choices and decisions by human beings, and was entirely in the realm of Heaven. "The State of Israel is divine," proclaimed the younger Kook. "Not only can/must there be no retreat from [a single] kilometer of the Land of Israel, God forbid, but on the contrary, we shall conquer and liberate more and more. . . . In our divine, world-encompassing undertaking, there is no room for retreat."[76]

About a month before Gush Emunim was established, in a kind of prelude to the founding act itself, Rabbi Kook came out with a public proclamation, in English, in *The Jerusalem Post.* Under the heading "That All Peoples of the Earth May Know," Kook wrote that "all this land is ours, absolutely, belonging to all of us; it is nontransferable to others even in part. 'It is an inheritance to us from our forefathers.'" Therefore, continued Kook, "once and for all, it is clear and absolute that there are no 'Arab territories' or 'Arab lands' here, but only the lands of Israel, the eternal heritage of our forefathers to which others have come and upon which they have built without our permission and in our absence."[77] A few months later, in the midst of Secretary of State Henry Kissinger's "shuttle diplomacy" among the countries of the Middle East, Kook declared that "the borders, these

kilometers, are ours, sanctified by divine holiness and we have no possibility, in any way in the world, of making concessions of them." He
added that the territories of the Land of Israel belong not only to the
3 million Jews who live in the land but rather to all the millions of
Jews who live in the entire world. Therefore "it is not at all permitted
to imagine—we have not received a power of attorney from them—
giving up these lands, in any way in the world! This is a divine commandment that must be carried out on pain of death—and no
political calculations, no government arrangements and no ministerial
statements will make a difference or avail in this."[78]

These declarations had already been said in the context of the
struggle against the plan for the separation of forces and the withdrawal in Sinai, which Kissinger had begun to promote at that time.
The huge demonstrations during Kissinger's visits to Jerusalem in
1974–1975 were in effect the launching of the Gush; in the course
of organizing, directing, and carrying out these demonstrations the
Gush formed itself as an influential political force, shaped its
unprecedented methods of action, and accumulated its first successes.
Each of Kissinger's visits was accompanied by protest actions of a
sort that had not been seen before—the blocking of roads in
Jerusalem to delay the secretary of state's convoy, mass demonstrations at Zion Square in the capital, violent confrontations with the
police, and noisemaking around Kissinger's hotel late at night. Ugly,
anti-Semitic epithets such as "*shiksa*'s husband" and "Jewboy" and
"Kissy" were hurled at Kissinger.[79] In a combined action of incitement, demonstrations, and massive paid campaigns in the press, Gush
Emunim shook the country and tried to harness the entire public to
its struggle. The Holocaust too was enlisted to describe the disasters
threatening Israel if it adopted Kissinger's plan.[80]

At the beginning of 1975 Major General (Res.) Ariel Sharon

joined Gush Emunim in its struggle against Kissinger and the arrangements he proposed, and against the government of Israel. In a secret consultation with the Gush leadership at an office in Jerusalem, Sharon called for interfering with Kissinger's visits and establishing new settlements every day and proving to the Americans that the Rabin government did not have the people's support.[81] Under the charismatic direction of Gush leader Hannan Porat, hundreds of activists and supporters were recruited, and new tactics were put into operation. Tractors, cotton wagons, cattle, and sheep were brought into demonstrations in urban areas; Gush people burst into government ministers' homes and danced and sang at all hours of the night under the windows of the prime minister's residence.[82] The modes of action, the recruitment methods, and the tactics that were honed at the displays of power against Kissinger and the government of Israel later served the Gush in all of its settlement projects. The actions against the secretary of state also served as a model for future protests against American political leaders who visited Israel, among them President Jimmy Carter; his secretary of state, Cyrus Vance; and his vice president, Walter Mondale. The Gush's actions made a dire impression in the United States, and the U.S. government learned that it was necessary to take the organization's power into account in every planned move in the Middle East.[83]

A Lone People by Choice

In the Gush ideology, the land is a realm of profound and primordial Jewish memory, and the land set in motion an entire aggregate of emotions of repressed anger and grudges. The prohibition on the presence of Jews in parts of the land conquered in the 1967 war was perceived as a continuation of the persecutions, uprootings, expulsions, pogroms—and the Holocaust—of which the Jews had been

victims throughout history. The silence of the world and parts of its Jewry had cost the Jews 6 million souls, and therefore it was forbidden to remain mute any longer and necessary to shake heaven and earth in order to obtain total Jewish existence, said Rabbi Kook.[84] Following his rabbi, one of them saw the Holocaust as a necessary preliminary stage of Redemption in the Land of Israel and the ingathering of the exiles there. "The Holocaust," argued Yohanan Fried after the Six-Day War, "was also a kind of gigantic broom that catalyzed the immigration to the land . . . as though the Holy One, blessed be He, had said to us, 'Enough, children. . . . You have played with what you wanted— Now I will forcibly move you to the land.' . . . The Holocaust was a very painful cutting of a branch . . . but an amputation that led to movement toward the land."[85] The utterly different reality of the Holocaust was transferred onto the inner Israeli conflict over the occupied territories, and not for the first time.[86] From this perspective any withdrawal, any threat of a withdrawal, could be perceived and depicted as a new holocaust, which legitimized any means in order to avert it. In this way the settlers enlisted the rabbis against the retreat from Gaza in 2005, so that, they claimed, the phenomenon of the rabbis' silence on the eve of and during the Holocaust would not repeat itself.[87] Expressions like *Judenrein* and "Auschwitz borders" were used extensively by the Gush people, even if they were not the first to have used them. "How is it possible to understand the pain and the insult that the Jewish People is now inflicting on the Land of Israel?" asked Hannan Porat upon the establishment of the Gush. "There are stretches of land about which there is general agreement that they are part of the space of the Land of Israel, and they are empty of Jews, they are *Judenrein*, by commands and ordinances."[88]

Gush Emunim's struggle for the land, for the territories, was experienced within the broader context of "a nation shall dwell alone," of the Jew against the whole world. The feeling of victimization and isolation, which sometimes became a political reality and had some real basis after the Yom Kippur War, aroused feelings of anger and self-righteousness among the Gush people and spurred them to act in accordance with the promptings of their hearts and with what they saw as an immanent, unchanging interest, divorced from historical circumstances. In a kind of replication of what political philosopher Hannah Arendt called "worldlessness," namely the Jews' seclusion from the world and from history—which was a characteristic of Jewish behavior in the diaspora until the late-eighteenth-century Jewish Enlightenment and, a century later, the rise of political Zionism—Gush Emunim called for intentional withdrawal from the world, nonconsideration of the "gentiles," and absolute loyalty to their own inner truth. Outside intervention of any sort in Israel's affairs was perceived as illegitimate and intolerable.

Thus Jews who maintained relationships with the non-Jewish world or with dubious Jews like Kissinger were perceived as flawed, errant Jews themselves who were betraying their people and its destiny, and who had no authority whatsoever over those faithful to the one authentic Jewish truth. Israel's image in the world, its shaky foreign relations, and the possibility of its international isolation not only did not worry the Gush people, they were like balm to their bones, the reason for their existence and action. This is the situation in which they—the redeemers—are called upon to fulfill their mission. Moreover, this was the correct situation worthy of the Chosen People, the people that is not like any other people. Its chosenness, its distinction with regard to all other peoples, is the source of the Jewish people's isolation. Balaam's prophecy that "the people shall dwell alone and not be reckoned among the nations" (Numbers 23:9) expressed the archetypal psychological, sociological, and theological stance at the heart of Gush Emunim. Isolation and glorious Redemption were the factors that made it possible to overcome the Israelis' basic existential anxiety and the complex reality of a life of constant tension in a modern Jewish state.[89]

Zionism's basic mistake, in the eyes of religious thinkers from whom the Gush drew inspiration and support, was precisely in its attempt to bring the Jewish people back into the community of nations, into history. "It [Zionism] failed because it tried to make the Jewish people into what it is not—that is, a normal people, one people among the peoples of the world, and thereby make the land of Israel into what it is not—i.e. what every state constitutes for the people that lives in it."[90] Israel's isolation, which political Zionism had worked so hard to thwart, is the natural and desirable condition of the Jewish people. This "glorious isolation" is essential in order to preserve the uniqueness of the people and the state. "Otherwise, the state is liable to lose the right and even the justification for its independent existence."[91] National isolation is the will of divine supervision. "The point in prohibiting the forming of a covenant of love and friendship with the gentiles is so that we will not connect with them excessively, so that we will not learn from their deeds. The Jewish people is currently in a situation in which formal peace with the Arabs will bring about the assimilation of parts of the nation into the Semitic expanse. . . . Therefore it is possible to perceive in the state of war between us and the Arabs the hand of divine supervision that is seeing to the preservation of the wholeness of the people."[92]

In a public call that was published by a group of religious professors in 1976, at the height of the settlers' struggle against the first Rabin government and against the withdrawal, international isolation was a yearned-for goal, the only proper reality for the Jewish people. "When we come to the core of these events," it said, "we necessarily reach a feeling of loneliness . . . from Abraham the Hebrew—'The entire world on one side and Abraham on the other'—to our own days, days of destruction and redemption, when our situation is like that of Israel standing before the Red Sea, surrounded on every side by enemies and haters, near and distant, who are about to destroy us. This faith, that 'the Lord alone' will lead us, is our savior and only guardian."[93]

In the formulation of Kook and his students, the Arabs therefore had a number of roles: to remind the Jewish people, which tends to forget and to adopt foreign culture, of its uniqueness and its chosenness, and to "preserve the unity of the people" by means of the constant war to eliminate them. The Arabs were functions of the Jewish existence and outlook, not sovereign human beings with identical and unalienable rights. Professor Uriel Tal, who tracked the sources of Gush Emunim's ideas, wrote that in the perception of the Gush there was no place at all for aliens in the Land of Israel. It was a matter, he wrote, "of a dogmatic method and consequent philosophy that inevitably leads to a policy that cannot tolerate the concept of human and civil rights." The very principle of civil rights is perceived as "an alien, democratic, European principle that alienates us existentially from the holy land." Tal argued that the Gush try to say little about the solution of expelling the Arabs, largely because these things are not acceptable to the public, but in principle they support the "purification of the land from its defilement."[94]

Statements by the Gush rabbis confirm this observation. Shlomo Aviner stated that the occupation of the land and settlement there are "above the moral-humane considerations of the national rights of the gentiles to our land."[95] Yaakov Medan wrote that "the Holy One, blessed be He, imposed the Six-Day War on us, to cleanse the domain of Abraham, Isaac and Jacob of the evil regime that ruled there."[96]

Dov Lior of Kiryat Arba wrote that the suitable situation for the Arabs is death, while Moshe Ben-Yosef (Hager) argued that "evacuating the land of its inhabitants is a Zionist goal of the first rank, no less and perhaps even more than settling the land with Jewish inhabitants." There cannot be a compromise because the land was never empty. Thus the slogan of "no rights for the Arabs to the Land of Israel" is the only possible slogan. Without it, "our right itself does not exist and we are all war criminals that are sentenced to death by a court for crimes against humanity."[97]

The equation between the Nazis and the Arabs became commonplace in the settlers' discourse,[98] and there were those who argued that the Arabs are even worse than the Germans in the Nazi period.[99] Peace is made with enemies, wrote the settler David Rosenzweig, but the Arabs are not enemies, they are deadly foes. The situation of a deadly foe, said Rosenzweig, one of the founders of Kedumim, is "a situation of struggle in which there are no compromises, for life and death. The aggressive side, that is the deadly foe, has as his aim to destroy, to kill and to exterminate."[100] The use of the term "deadly foe" was usually reserved for the Amalekites (a tribe that according to the Bible were an ancient foe of the Jews whom God commanded the Jews to annihilate utterly) and the Nazis. The allusion was self-evident.

However, a systematic scrutiny of the intense debate on the Arab question that has gone on over the years in the community of ideological settlers reveals a more complex picture. Among the leaders of the Gush there were and there are "transferists," but there were and there are pragmatists and even humanists. Professor Hillel Weiss, one of the most extreme and original of the settlers, wrote in 1980 that "we cannot expel the Arabs from Judea and Samaria, just as at this stage we cannot build the Temple. . . . It is not just that we cannot, we do not want to! An attitude of respect toward the Arab individual, his human liberties and his property, is an inseparable part of my world-view. Even an enemy is a human being, as long as he does not express in action his desire to harm me as a Jew in the Land of Israel." Weiss called for "relatively normal" neighborly relations as long as "they" do not fly their national flag.[101] A fervent disciple of Rabbi Kook and researcher of his thinking, Hagai Ben-Artzi of Beit El, stated that the Gush settlement project will be judged among other things by its moral attitude toward the Arabs. Ben-Artzi came out against collective punishment and against the confiscation of Arabs' privately owned lands but called at the same time for applying Israeli law in the West Bank. "Yes, we nationalist Jews believe in the right of the Jewish people to return to its homeland . . . but we are also Jews, whose heritage is replete with respect and love for every human being who was created in God's image," wrote Ben-Artzi.[102]

Hannan Porat was evasive in his explanation that "we do not need to scorn the Arab who has a feeling of connection to a house and a field, nor his work as a private person, as an individual. But when we come to examine the relation of Israel and Ishmael with respect to the connection, the tie, the right and the commitment to the land of Israel, there is an abyss between us and them. Not because Ishmael is lowlier than the nations—though there are also aspects of this point that we shall have to examine—but rather because Israel is special among the nations in its national relationship to the Land of Israel, more so than the French, the English, the Russians and the Chinese in relation to their own lands."[103]

Others, like Yoel Bin-Nun and Menachem Fruman, expressed recognition, throughout the years, of the Palestinians' rights to life, protection, and self-definition. "Any harm to Arabs who have not attacked us . . . stands in utter contradiction not only to morality and law but also to the principles of Gush Emunim," argued Bin-Nun.[104]

Fruman, who has maintained extensive relationships with Palestinian leaders and intellectuals, called upon Gush Emunim to be the pioneer in the creation of "a new human configuration," in the framework of which the Palestinians would have national symbols and a national leadership of their own in the greater Land of Israel.[105] However, both Bin-Nun and Fruman were considered oddballs to one extent or another among the settlers. Over the years, and especially in times of crisis and conflagration, trigger-happiness toward the Arabs predominated, and their rights were crushed. Levinger's exclamation as he brandished his pistol at the entrance to a court where he was accused of killing an Arab shoe merchant, "I didn't kill the Arab. If only I had killed him!"[106] was an expression of wishes of many among the settlers.

Media Wizards

The three years before the Likud came to power in 1977 were the peak years of Gush activity. Demonstrations, repeated settlement attempts in forbidden areas, mass marches in the territories, and violent struggles with the police and the military, designed and staged for the media's consumption, were the arena of Gush Emunim, its mode of action and its style. During those years the Gush was constantly on the move and expanding. Tranquillity was its enemy, anxiety and uproar its allies. Its hard core was joined, for purposes of the actions that were well covered in the media, by the youngsters of Bnei Akiva and the students of the Zionist nationalist yeshivas. They organized their demonstrations during school vacations in order to ensure the arrival of as many teenagers as possible, and to take advantage of the public equipment at the government-funded educational institutions.[107]

From their very first day, the Gush people knew how to make use of the media to serve their needs. They saw to coverage of their meetings, their assemblies, the demonstrations they held, and the actions they took. Here too they worked by the method of "direct action," without the mediation of politicians or parties, and formed close ties with journalists in the major media who served as mouthpieces for their ideas, "in order to create a change in the ideological climate."[108] And the Israeli media as a whole became a willing partner, as the Gush was such a good story. Every action by the Gush was accompanied by sympathetic journalists and cameramen who covered the organizers' intentions and events on the ground.

In many cases the media functioned as an arm of Gush Emunim. In the autumn of 1974 the Gush organized its "Circumambulation Campaign." It was first and foremost a well-executed media event. "Like all of our major 'underground' operations," wrote Shafat, "this operation too—of launching thousands of settlers at targets in Judea and Samaria—began on quite an innocent note: the invitation of a group of journalists to an apartment in Jerusalem, after they promised not to reveal the location, in order to receive a briefing from the Jericho settlement nucleus and its aims."[109] Yohanan Fried, one of the Gush leaders, explained that the activity of the Gush is legal and that settlement in all parts of the Land of Israel is done in accordance with the law and "out of faith" even when it is ostensibly against the law. He added that theirs was a political act that was aimed at putting the question of settlement in all parts of Israel on the agenda, to pressure the government and strengthen it in the difficult political bargaining it is conducting.[110]

The eighth attempt to settle at Sebastia, during Hanukkah 1975, which brought about the government's surrender and in a stroke transformed the Gush into a central and influential force in Israeli politics, was designed from the outset as a media event in which the media became a central element, influencing the sequence of events. "It was discreetly and fully coordinated with the media and news people," said

Shafat, who handled the press coverage of the event. "We saw to it that there would be a constant flow of reports so that a media vacuum would not be created. The dedication of the synagogue, the dedication of the kindergarten, the erection of the first prefab, everything was a reason to allocate space for an item in the newspapers, on the radio, on television. We fed them not only news of what had happened and what was happening, but also of what would happen in a few hours. There were reporters who helped us edit the reports we gave out. There were also quite a number of exaggerations, and these helped us later in creating the impression of impending fraternal strife, a civil war."[111]

The figures of the young settlers hurling their bodies onto the soil of the land and clutching at every clod of earth and boulder as though their lives depended on it, blending their personal anxieties and yearnings with a collective dream of Redemption that was coming true before their very eyes, became with the help of the sympathetic media heroes of the times, icons of Jewish spiritual elevation and bravery. The Gush events, as depicted in the media, had a formidable influence on the public. And the souls of poets, journalists, and military men, many of whom had come from the labor movement, went out to the Gush people, the real Jews, "the new pioneers" and the last of the Zionists, who cling to the soil of the land.[112] "They are not the gangsters from Sebastia. . . . They are the cream of the Jewish people, a fount of idealism, of devotion, of willingness for sacrifice and personal fulfillment. Anyone who speaks ill of them . . .spits into a wellspring of national inspiration from which all the germinations of lovers of this land have drunk," rhapsodized the mass-circulation afternoon paper *Yedioth Aharonoth.*[113]

Among those who were captivated by the Gush youngsters' determination and devotion was the leader of the left-wing Zionist Party Mapam, kibbutz member Yaakov Hazan, who roused a great deal of ire when he said that "they are not fascists but rather young religious people who have faith in the justice of their way . . . and they believe in their way of settlement just as the people of Hashomer Hatzair [the precursor and youth movement of Mapam] believed in their way in the 1920s."[114] Novelist Aharon Megged wrote in *Davar* what for many years characterized the ambivalent attitude that many Israelis, people of the Labor movement, developed toward Gush Emunim: "With all my intellectual opposition to the way of Gush Emunim, it is hard for me to find in my heart (or to enlist within myself) hatred towards them. . . . This is a problem. I am aware that something is wrong with me, and I must sort through my deeds. Moreover, I do not find the courage in my heart to scorn them, as many of my colleagues do. This is easy prey for the arrows of sarcasm, I know, but I think: perhaps too easy. . . . But perhaps this is some accursed legacy from the far-off days of the youth movement: not to scorn people who bodily fulfill the commandment of settling the land, even if their belief is different from yours. . . . It is worthwhile listening to what they have to say, without preconceptions. . . . Not all of them are 'forces of darkness.'"[115]

Godly State and Army

The political-theological conception that was constructed by Rabbi Kook enabled faith to turn night into day, defeat into victory.[116] Kook indeed bound together national life and nationalist phenomena in a package of mystification and poeticism. "The politics of the community of Israel is holy," he wrote; it is the "divine politics."[117] From this derived the obligation to honor and admire the state, its institutions, and especially its army, as representatives of the national organism, the living body of the people and manifestations of its profound truth. Even "non-Zionist" actions of the army required respect because they were deeds and an expression of the nation.[118] The army's weapons, destined to defend life, underwent a transformation in Kook's thinking and became holy vessels themselves, elements in the theology of Redemption. Things reached a point at which "the rabbi saw in the IDF tanks, artillery and aircraft—ritual articles, sacred objects, because they too serve the commandment of settling the Land of Israel."[119] And indeed in the discourse and praxis of Gush Emunim, the army was given cultic status. Enlistment in the army and service in elite combat units became Gush identity tags. Battle wounds added prestige and augmented the charisma. The ideal of the pioneering and pious settler was reinforced when it wore an IDF uniform. Combat duty was not only a means of legitimization, a social means of mobility into the heart of the consensus, but also became endowed with a spiritual aura and was bequeathed as an article of faith in the coming generations, who in this role replaced the sons of the kibbutzim. Thus, in a dialectical move, while conducting an uncompromising battle with the political establishment and its representatives, the Gush people sent tentacles into the system, very skillfully operated lobbying networks that embraced the entire state institutions, settled into the bureaus of ministers and that of the prime minister himself, and presented themselves for duty armed with their heavenly righteousness and their earthly demands.

The rabbi and his students also held that Israeli law was valid, not in the sense of its "secular" validity but rather by virtue of its theological significance. Because the nation is a single organism, whole and indivisible, the law too is an expression of this organism's will. Law and democracy were good, so long as they served the absolute aims of the Gush. Respect for the government's decisions and respect for the law, according to Kook, were derived from and a result of the fact that they represented the national will. However, Kook himself, his disciples, and his successors found sophisticated ways to desecrate the sanctity with which they had endowed the state, its institutions, and its laws. When the government ceased to represent the entire nation or what Kook and his people perceived as "the will of the people," its authority over its citizens ceased. No one has the right to give up even one kilometer of the sanctified land, even if this means war against a government that orders Israeli soldiers to oppose the settlers or to evacuate them, said Kook. "I will not enter into the terminological debate on the question of the idea of civil war," declared Kook. "War is liable to be necessary; our bodies, our limbs, our entire selves—are necessary," he said.[120]

The real and symbolic battlefield in this war was the Land of Israel. Anyone who takes pieces of the land away from Israel, and anyone who helps them, will be cursed by God, declared Kook. These people were called vulgar, petty, stupid, every possible name. "A bunch of fools" is the name Kook gave to the Rabin government at the demonstrations against Kissinger.[121] Of Rabin's remark that he "didn't mind" traveling to the territories with a visa, Kook wrote that "this is utter nonsense; the Jewish people minds, all of us, all the millions of Jews mind. Let the listener hear, and desist. *Desist! And desist!* Again and again I say: Desist! The Jewish people has no interest at all in anyone— be he a minister or not a minister—who says that he does not mind what the arrangements are for the plots of earth of the holiness of the land of our forefathers."[122] The political theology of this text and others was blatant. The Land of Israel was beyond political bargaining, beyond the decision of the citizens of the State of Israel and beyond the decisions of one government or another. The fate of the Land of Israel was the exclusive province of Rabbi Kook and his adherents as representatives of history and the millions of Jews from all over the world and all generations, past, present, and future. Thus, it was a good deed and a divine commandment to wage war on ministers who betrayed trust, who lost the way, and who defiled the name of God, and everything was permitted in this war, which ultimately also led to the assassination of a prime minister.

Indeed, the one elected political person whom the Gush Emunim people loved to hate above all others was the prime minister during their peak years, Yitzhak Rabin. Rabin and Gush Emunim ascended the political stage at more or less the same time, and they were each other's absolute nemesis, the punishment of mythological dimensions that tortured its object forever. From his very first day in office, Rabin, the beautiful, iconic son of the Zionist utopia and the biological son of "Rosa the Red," the feminist socialist Rosa Cohen, Rabin the professional soldier, the totally secular individual, the shy man of few words, who went through his political and diplomatic initiation rite in his role as ambassador to Washington, could not stand the messianic "blather" (he used a much cruder, American word for this: "bullshit") of the Gush people and scorned their "eye-rolling" toward heaven. Unlike his predecessors in the Prime Minister's Office, who came from the Diaspora and belonged to a previous generation, whose hearts melted in the presence of the "pioneering" envoys of the Gush and God, this taciturn man, the blunt, matter-of-fact sabra, scorned the Gush and found them repugnant. Instead of devoted and disinterested pioneers, who are willing "to give their souls" for their belief, he saw them as lawbreakers and extorters, and he never changed his mind. When he served as defense minister in the first unity government in the mid-1980s, he declared that "they have used themselves up. Now they are building apartment houses and we have to call up reserves to do guard duty at those apartments."[123]

And they repaid him in the same coin. As early as the 1970s and '80s, and more so after Rabin was elected prime minister in 1992, the settlers conducted a relentless, ruthless personal war against him and hit him at his weak points.[124] They called him almost every name imaginable, and compared him and his government to the *Judenräte*, implying that his goal was to leave Judea and Samaria *Judenrein*, as Hitler did in Europe.[125] The focused, merciless war that the Gush people conducted against Rabin after the Oslo agreement is extensively documented in Chapter 3 of this book. Just as an addendum here, one should notice that one of the chief inciters against the government and its ministers was Ariel Sharon, Rabin's aid in other times and "Gush Emunim's custodian."[126]

Disposables

The fall of the first Rabin government in 1977 was interpreted as suitable punishment for its primal sin, its fight against settlement in all parts of the Land of Israel. The Gush openly celebrated its enemy's fall. The heads of the movement nurtured the political manipulation and the politics of hatred into an art form. They knew how to exploit internal rivalries, especially in the top echelon of the Labor Party, but also in the parties closer to them, and pitted coalition partners, members of the same party, and partners to the same outlook against one another. In this way they weakened coalition governments that were in any case fragile and shaky, acquired public support and extorted decisions they desired. This was especially evident in the cunning role they played in the historical rivalry between Rabin and Shimon Peres and in fanning that mutual dislike. The great victory of the Gush in the eighth confrontation at Sebastia, with which we opened this chapter, and which marked the defeat of the first Rabin government and became the start of its decline, derived from the way its people knew how to extract the maximum from the deep hostility between the two leaders and their inability to cooperate.[127]

All in all, the attitude of Gush Emunim toward the government leaders with whom they had relationships, and to politicians from all parties, was cynical and instrumental. They used them and disposed of them from the moment these politicians could not or did not want to be of help to them. The Gush people had no difficulty in replacing admiration with scorn and loathing, and to make this emotional reversal overnight. Love of the Land of Israel permitted the symbolic elimination of anyone who was not a partner to it. In Rabin's case the act of elimination ultimately became concrete. Peres, Begin, Netanyahu, Barak, Sharon, and, more recently, Olmert—each of them in turn, left, right, and center, experienced the slap in the face by the heads of Gush Emunim, their utilitarian, purposeful attitude toward them and their unbridled manipulation.

Unlike Rabin, Peres, transportation minister and afterward defense minister in Rabin's first government, in fact expressed affection for the people of Gush Emunim in its first years, and his door was open to them. There is no way to trace all of the innumerable meetings that the settler heads held with Peres between 1974 and 1977 and in more recent years. It is also impossible to overstate the importance of the role Peres played in strengthening the course of settlement, the concrete help he extended to the heads of the Gush, and the symbolic support they got from him. Without him, presumably the fate of the settlers' flagship settlements, such as Ofra and Qadum, would have been different. It was for good reason that the Gush people saw Peres as "the darling" of their movement. "He saw with us, eye to eye, the obligation to settle along the mountain ridge in Samaria," they said. At the first of Benny Katzover's many meetings with Peres, back in the days of the Elon Moreh settlement nucleus, Peres expressed enthusiasm for the ideas and desires of the early settlers to strike roots in Samaria and promised to win support for their issue. "There is one thing I can promise you," said the minister of transportation at the time to Katzover and his friends, "when you first settle you will have a bus." When they settled at Qadum, Katzover reminded Peres of the promise. A few days later, the Number 81 bus line was inaugurated, connecting Qadum to the center of the country.[128]

When their paths diverged, the settlers' Good Samaritan became the villain of the day, a target of cold and calculated hatred. Examples could fill an ocean. During the Oslo period, Peres, together with Rabin, was the target of an organized, well-thought-out, and focused fight aimed at bringing about their elimination from Israeli politics and the national agenda. A few months after Rabin was assassinated, when for a moment it seemed as though the extreme settler right was reckoning and reviewing its conscience and taking upon itself the responsibility for the devastating incitement campaigns that had led to the assassination, it was written of Peres that he "is totally alienated from the Jewish people. . . . He has no loyalty and commitment to Jews, to Judaism, to his ancestors. . . . This insensitive Polish Jew dares to desecrate the memory of the millions who were murdered by the Nazis. Peres is a Jew who does not feel comfortable in the Land of Israel. He is a person without a homeland. With no God. . . ."[129]

The political upheaval of 1977 finally opened Peres's eyes, at least partially, and he began to see Gush Emunim and its activity as a real strategic threat to the existence of Israel. Apparently the world looks different from the opposition benches, to which he had been sent in part thanks to the votes of the Gush people, who did not credit him for having supported them in their battle for every hill of Samaria. In an article he published on October 19, 1979, under the heading "Emunim Why?" Peres gave a reckoning of historical accounts, too late and too little, with the Gush and its style of action, in the course of which he also revealed his anti-Palestinian outlook and his narrow, security-minded views, which he held for many more years. "The settlements," he wrote, "do not free us from any one of the factors that pose the threat, in combination, of the emergence of a Palestinian state." He argued that the settlements did not ensure Israeli sovereignty over Judea and Samaria. The activity of Gush Emunim, he wrote, with the dragging support of the Begin government, was causing serious damage to Israel. "It is weakening even further the feeble status of the government as the body that administers the State of Israel. . . . It is damaging one of the most consensual elements in Israel's life—an attitude of respect and admiration for the IDF." The barren demonstrations by the settlers in the territories, which compel Israeli soldiers to drag settlers by force and in front of the television cameras, seriously damage the army's image, interfere with its training, and create unnecessary national controversy, wrote Peres.

He also criticized the "threatening and violent" style of the Gush people, which cast "a chilling shadow on Israel's democratic strength." This style, argued Peres, depicted Israel in the eyes of the world as the extremist side in the Arab-Israeli conflict, whereas for many years Israel had been seen as seeking peace, not territories. The settlements, he added, depicted Zionism as a purely territorial movement, and not as a movement of liberation of a people. "To the credit of the Gush Emunim people, it should be said that they do not base themselves on the security argument, but rather on the historical argument. No one can alter the past: Our historical right applies to the entire Land of Israel. But in addition to our historical right there is also a historical obligation: to preserve the Jewish character of the state, and not just a formal deed of ownership."[130]

If Peres came to his senses, even in a partial twisted way, as he had to move from the coalition to the opposition, Menachem Begin needed a transition from his almost eternal opposition to the prime minister's chair in order suddenly to see the entire account of statesmanship, the picture of Israel's status in the world and its relations with the United States and the damage that the violent Gush Emunim settlements in the heart of areas inhabited by Arabs were causing. Years of mutual admiration did not grant Begin an insurance policy against the settlers' wrath. After he won the election for prime minister, in part because of the constant subversion of Rabin's government by Gush Emunim, a new account was opened with Begin. And from the moment he did not provide their entire vision they unsentimentally lashed out at him. Overnight he was transformed from an ally into a foe. "His love of the Land of Israel collapsed at the first test," wrote Uri Elitzur. "That was his Yom Kippur."[131] "The Begin of today is no longer a man of vision. . . . He is not evincing the leadership worthy of this hour. He no longer believes, as he believed yesterday, in the powers inherent in the Jewish people," wrote Israel Harel.[132] The settlers never regained trust in him.

In Straits

Ironically, it is with Begin's rise to power, and when the fleshpots were filled, that the slow decline of the Gush began. There was no longer a need for this extra-political body, which shook the system with its extreme and violent modes of action. The paradoxical need to stand up and fight "our" government was one of the main factors in the decline of the power of Gush Emunim.[133] The settlers' expectations of construction momentum and a new settlement on every hill, to the point of requesting a general ban on public building along the Coastal Plain, where most of Israel's population dwells, and the directing of all construction resources to Samaria and Judea, were swiftly disappointed.[134]

The ambiguous idyll that had existed between the government and Gush Emunim was terminated by Anwar Sadat, "the Hitler of the Nile," in the words of the settlers and their supporters.[135] Sadat's landing in Israel on November 19, 1977, relegated to oblivion "the existence of Gush Emunim," wrote Danny Rubinstein, perhaps with some exaggeration. The Gush people still tried to snap at the tail of the peace festival that had captivated the country by organizing protest rallies and demonstrations, but they got little response and were no longer, at least for the time being, the darlings of the media. The shock of the peace with Egypt and the rejoicing undermined the apocalyptic prophecies of Rabbi Kook's disciples and blurred the picture of the eternal Arab enemy that the Gush had skillfully painted. "The entire system of fears collapsed . . . Gush Emunim seemed to have disappeared; its adherents walked about in mourning because of what looked to them like the insanity that had gripped the people."[136] At a meeting of the Gush Emunim secretariat in May 1978, Hannan Porat acknowledged that "there is a feeling of weakness."[137] On another occasion he added that "ever since Sadat's visit there has been a kind of eclipse . . . the inner feeling that going toward Sadat is a disaster is the province of few. Most of the public is teetering in its faith and its mood. When a constellation changes there always remains the hard core, the granite rock, but the rest of the geological components begin to crumble."[138]

Although in 1978 and 1979, after years of struggle, a number of new settlements arose, this was one of the last settlement flurries by the Gush as such.[139] The direct political option once again engaged the heads of the organization. Various attitudes with regard to transforming the Gush into a political party and running for election had been bandied about in the movement since its inception. The religious-spiritual leaders of the organization knew that the strength of the Gush lay in the very fact that it was a supra-political movement that bore sacred values, absolute truths that are not subject to decision at a transient ballot box. However, the pragmatists in the group, who also aspired to seats in the Knesset for themselves, urged the establishment of a party like all other parties. And various existing parties also courted the Gush.[140] Yet its leaders did not see themselves as people who would lower themselves to "political haggling." Certain of their exaltedness and their superiority over any other organization, they rejected the proposals and the seductions that were cast at their doorstep.[141]

The establishment of the Tehiya (Revival) Party on a platform of opposition to the peace treaty with Egypt and its call for the acceleration of settlement construction in the territories compelled the Gush to decide. Those who only yesterday had opposed an entry into politics came to the conclusion that there was no alternative to embarking on political activity, in the hope of "rescuing what remains."[142] The Gush Emunim secretariat arrived at a compromise whereby it supported the establishment of a political framework and would help its members who devoted themselves to this activity. The explicit decision tore apart the Gush leadership. While Hannan Porat and Gershon Shafat moved away from the Gush activity and started to act in the framework of Tehiya, Moshe Levinger, who opposed the political move, stated that "our power was in that we have not been measured by the number of voters in elections, and by Knesset members." The two central, historical, and so very different icons of Gush Emunim who had been etched in the Israeli mind, Levinger and Porat, were now on opposite sides in the principled showdown that was also a personal and stylistic struggle for the image of the Gush.

The story of Tehiya is a story of a political failure. During the course of the 1980s the movement succeeded in putting a few members into the Knesset. In 1990, with Professor Yuval Ne'eman's resignation from its leadership, the party's positions and discourse became even more extreme and led to the toppling of Yitzhak

Shamir's government of the right, which it did not view as sufficiently faithful to the land of Israel.[143] And indeed, in the 1992 elections Tehiya did not make it past the electoral threshold and fell apart. The public of religious settlers did not support the party. Levinger, the traditional opponent of entering politics, who decided to run independently in the 1992 election in the belief that he would sweep tens of thousands of settlers after him, received only 6,000 votes. Those lost votes for the far right contributed crucially to Rabin's electoral victory.

Despite the decline of Tehiya and the failure of Levinger, the settlers' representation in the Knesset gradually increased. From the time that Porat served as the lone Knesset member who represented the settlements, the number of settlers among the legislators increased to eleven in the 16th Knesset (2003–2006), among them prominent spokesmen for the settler ethos. They embodied the whole range of the right-wing parties. The settlers no longer had a need for a party of their own. Their voice and their interests were and are heard in all of the parties of the Israeli right and in the important and relevant Knesset committees. The constant increase in the representation of the settlers in the Knesset testifies, or testified until recently, to the deepening of their hold on Israeli society and the Israeli mind.[144] The recent events of the retreat from Gaza Strip, and the rise of Kadima, the new party started by Ariel Sharon, may mark a change in course, although by the spring of 2007 this rather fata morgana party and its leader, Olmert, seemed to be in tatters.

The Perils of Peace

The peace treaty with Egypt and especially the uncovering of the Jewish terror organization in the mid-1980s were not good for Gush Emunim. The right's slogan "Peace kills" was correct first and foremost with respect to the Gush itself. The Gush, which arose and thrived on alarms and arms, and for which the raison d'être was the Jewish people's withdrawal by choice from the world and from historical reality, could not survive in a political environment where peace was possible. The transition from an exalted and all-engulfing ideology to the dull routine of everyday life in the settlements was also difficult. Hannan Porat resigned from activity in Gush Emunim and returned to his kibbutz, Kfar Etzion, to teach.[145] The other founders of the Gush also turned to new paths. Levinger worked at proofreading manuscripts at his home in Beit Hadassah in Hebron. "He is exhausted," said his friends.[146] "Professional" settlers Benny Katzover and Menachem Felix focused on building and expanding their home settlement, Elon Moreh. Gershon Shafat was one of the founders of Tehiya, which was established in the context of the withdrawal from Sinai.

"The protest movement Gush Emunim disappeared," wrote Danny Rubinstein in his book on the Gush, which was published in 1982. "There remains only the name and the symbol, which serve as no more than a heading for the activities of other organized groups."[147] The news of the death of Gush Emunim was perhaps premature, but it did contain a grain of truth. In June 1982, an attempt was made to renew the Gush activity in the territories. In view of the withdrawal from Sinai and the scenes of the evacuation of Yamit, the Gush held a gathering in Ofra with the participation of about one hundred of the group's founding leaders. The summation was that the movement would renew its activity to establish settlements. A new secretariat, in which there were younger, fresher members, was chosen.[148] But these steps toward revival and renewal were covered in the clouds of dust stirred up by the Israeli tanks that entered Lebanon on that very day. Once again the work of the just was done for them by others.

In the 1980s the Yesha Council and the Gush settlement movement,

Amana, replaced Gush Emunim as the central institutions of the settlers. It was in fact Amana that became the stronger and permanent body of the Gush, and the reins were later taken over by the more political Yesha Council.[149] "Gush Emunim lost its contents. Its people began to wonder about the nature of the body they had established," wrote Nadav Haetzni, the son of Elyakim Haetzni, one of the founders of the Gush.[150] The fact that some of the Gush people joined up with Rabbi Meir Kahane and his racist, violent Kach movement also did not help the unity of the Gush and its aspirations to legitimacy.[151] In the midst of the Jewish terror organization crisis, Daniella Weiss of Kedumim, who did not deny that "some of her views are identical to Kahane's,"[152] was chosen to head the movement. "Because this has already happened, and in the opinion of the security experts it had a positive influence on security issues . . . we have decided not to condemn and not to praise," said Weiss of the Jewish terror organization's deeds.[153]

The reduced secretariat of ten members, which was intended for running movement matters, ceased to meet. Yoel Bin-Nun, in whose home the Gush was founded, now came out publicly against the policy and heads of the Gush. He and Porat demanded that Weiss be deposed because of her extreme views, which were harmful to the Gush. Two camps were formed within the secretariat. One was the Levinger-Weiss group, which supported the Jewish terrorists and strongly opposed condemnation of Kahane and the democratization of the Gush. This was opposed by "the moderates' group," headed by Porat and Bin-Nun, which called for replacing the leadership and establishing democratic institutions.[154] "The current leadership of Gush Emunim is functioning like a committee for the underground detainees and has become an arm of the terror organization, and therefore it is disengaging from the majority in the settlements and in the nation," charged Bin-Nun.[155]

The private, nightly pogrom that Daniella Weiss conducted in the streets of Qalqilya, on May 5, 1987, the breaking of bottles and putting fire on the road in reaction to the killing of members of the Moses family, led in the end to her deposition from the leadership of the Gush.[156] Weiss had no remorse for her actions. She was involved again and again in violent riots and clashes with the army, with local inhabitants and with activists of human rights organizations in the territories.[157] During the first and second intifadas she refused to take measures to safeguard herself, her children, or her community because she saw this as a sign of the cowardice and weakness of diaspora Judaism.[158] But Weiss and her extremist friends were just the pawns. The accusations within the Gush were aimed higher, at Levinger. "Do not sacrifice a pawn or a rook when the king is hiding," exhorted the settlers' newspaper *Nekudah*.[159] Now, toward the end of the 1980s, many saw Levinger as the root of the problem, "the person mainly responsible for the decline of the movement."[160] The new secretary of the Gush, who came in after Weiss was deposed, held that "the Gush has to be taken out of the framework of a cult."[161] He supported the democratization of the Gush and the holding of elections to select leadership of the movement's institutions. Too independent, he was quickly deposed himself. It was Levinger who pulled the strings to get rid of him.

"Democracy" as a concept did not have a good reputation in Gush Emunim—neither democracy in general nor democracy within the camp. After the first elections for the secretariat, no new elections were held, and the members of the secretariat reappointed themselves to the various positions again and again.[162] Members indeed admitted that the debates in Gush Emunim were conducted by the *beit midrash* (traditional study house) method and spilled over into issues of Jewish law even when current political events were under discussion.[163]

The rank and file complained that the Gush leadership was "replete and spoiled," did not stand for democratic election, was appointed in a forum of few participants, did not give any accounting of its activities, and was not open to criticism. "The heads of Gush Emunim see themselves as defenders of their mystical philosophy against the evil spirits of nihilism and hedonism. And in this struggle they are not prepared to trust anyone—not even those who have answered their call and have come to settle in Samaria."[164] A veteran member, a woman activist of Amana, charged that it was not at all clear what the decision-making body in the Gush was, and who had determined that this was the body. "Rabbi Levinger has to confirm his mandate," she said. "It is definitely possible that he will win the public's trust—but this needs to be examined. Hannan Porat, for example, has been here and vanished. Has anyone come in his stead?"[165]

On the other side, Arieh Stav, the editor of the settler publication *Nativ* and one of the more extremist spokesmen of the settlement ethos, wrote that "against the structural defeatism of Israeli democracy, against the well-known Jewish inferiority, against the collapse of the pillars of the existential will and the crumbling of the Zionist left, Gush Emunim has posited Zionism in its purity." In ten years the Gush did what the entire kibbutz movement had done in seventy years, wrote Stav, and is irreplaceable. In view of "the Arabs' peace attack, more correctly [their] peace deception," it is the national obligation of the Gush to "solidify its lines and stand up against the Arab duplicity, which aims at destroying the national agreement on the Jewish 'iron wall.'"[166]

An Established Avant-Garde

Hagai Segal, freshly released in May 1986 from prison after serving part of the term to which he had been sentenced for his membership in the Jewish terror organization, wrote that "the Gush is dismantled, but they still have not announced this publicly. The Gush has achieved the primary aim—settlement in Judea and Samaria, and since the beginning of the 1980s, its people have not known what to do. . . . Gush Emunim has completed its role, and it no longer exists. Its historic role has ended."[167] Uri Elitzur, one of the heads of the Gush and eventually Prime Minister Benjamin Netanyahu's bureau chief, argued that a body like Gush Emunim can function in two ways, either as "a non-establishment underground, with personal leadership that exhorts 'follow me,'" the price of which will be a short life span, or as "an established body with rules and membership cards." In Elitzur's opinion, the Gush paid a high price in its choice not to establish itself formally. "Gush Emunim—the framework, not the idea—is functioning in a blind way now. There is a basic commonality of ideas, but the growing mass of tactical questions is weighing more and more heavily."[168]

And indeed, the disagreements about tactical questions grew deeper. There was no longer any possibility of bridging between Levinger and Fruman or Bin-Nun. Fruman of Tekoa supported dialogue with the Palestine Liberation Organization, at a time when this was prohibited by law, and Bin-Nun met frequently with Defense Minister Rabin during the first months of the first intifada. Other members of the leadership sent out probes to various groups, ideologically far from them, within Israeli society. They called for "stopping the incitement between the camps, preserving the sanctity of the human being and preventing bodily and other harm to innocent people."[169] Two decades after Levinger, armed with a refrigerator and his family, arrived at the Park Hotel in Hebron on Passover eve of 1968, he remained "a leader without a flock."[170] Out of respect for Levinger and his past deeds, the Gush continued to provide him with a salary and a small office, but his supporters had dwindled to just a handful of Kahanists. "For the majority of the public, the man has become a curiosity, a marginal person. A naïf wandering in the eternal fallow fields," it was written in *Nekudah*,[171] in a sort of symbolic beheading of the king.

Levinger's resounding failure in the 1992 general elections, which exposed his political and spiritual isolation, marked the termination of his public standing. On the eve of the elections, Yoel Bin-Nun daringly and brilliantly analyzed the successes and defeats of the Gush over the years. "The settlement activists, the professionals of construction and the builders of establishments all won splendid and unprecedented success, and their activity has been engraved on the map of the land," he said. However, "the intellectual leaders, the men of holiness, the rabbis, philosophers and public leaders have all failed, and I among them. . . . The entire settlement project has become a dazzling physical success, which is destroying itself in its unbalanced, violent, bullying, materialist tendencies, to the point of outrage. . . . The internal rift within us and the brutal enmity towards the 'left' half of the nation have become the main spiritual line." Bin-Nun complained that no one was listening to his charge because "a split in the people also leads to a split in the land."[172]

Bin-Nun's threnody was somewhat premature. The Labor Party's return to power two months after these lines were written, and more than that—the signing of the Oslo agreement in the autumn of 1993—revived the Gush. The threat of peace was, as always, the best elixir for the Gush, which returned to the days of its youth. Uri Ariel, the movement's general secretary, led the protest and incitement activity against the government. The common, sanctified aim of thwarting the peace moves bridged the gap between the different factions in the Gush and reassembled the veteran leadership. The strongman of the Gush at the time, Ze'ev Hever (Zambish), who had refrained from public appearances since his implication in the Jewish terror affair, now succeeded, if only from behind the scenes, in sweeping after him into action people who for years had retreated to their proper settlement life. Even a person like Menachem Felix, from the glorious founding generation, became active again after years of sequestration in his settlement, Elon Moreh.[173]

The Ghost of the Gush

Prime Minister Ariel Sharon's disengagement plan and the danger of withdrawal from the Gaza Strip were a new drug that breathed life, for the umpteenth time, into the sleeping beauty. In the midst of the uncompromising struggle against Sharon, in February 2004, the Gush reached its thirtieth anniversary, a date that was neither celebrated nor mentioned either in the Gush or outside it. This intentionally amorphous, borderless body, which was both a way of life and a state of mind, and which had forever changed the map, the profile, and the moral fabric of Israel, consciously refrained from marking the historic date. Presumably the heads of the movement, who had become older, fatter, and bourgeois, felt that their mature years in spacious villas in the flourishing settlements amid a devastated Palestinian population did a disservice to their pioneering youth. It is also possible that the graduates of the Gush were, in journalist Yair Sheleg's words, engaged in the urgent tasks of preserving the project they had established three decades earlier.[174] The work of the Gush was also being done by members of the second and third generations. The violent "hilltop youth," who are much more extreme than their predecessors, were doing the dirty work of physically establishing outposts on the rocky hills and fighting the security forces. However, the claim of the founders and heads of the Gush went even further. They said that the

Gush had ceased to exist two decades ago and that what remained of it was nothing but a "ghost." According to them, the Gush settlement action pushed aside the redemptive vision. The bodies that carried out the settlement—the Amana movement and the Yesha Council—were part of an establishment, rich in budgets, whereas the voluntary ideological body, which wished to mark the way as part of the great vision, had gradually withered. The tool that Gush Emunim had created for carrying out the settlement turned on its maker like the Golem. "And thus, while the brand Peace Now is alive and active, organizing demonstrations and 'watching the settlements,' the brand Gush Emunim has been nothing but a ghost for two decades now. It does not exist to such an extent, that no one remembers when exactly it disappeared," said the founders.[175]

In reading or hearing these words, one has to recall Benny Katzover's saying at one of those moments of waning and depression in the Gush, in 1980, when it looked as though the Gush had come to the end of its road. "The moment that something happens that will threaten the wholeness of the Land of Israel, they will hear about us," said Katzover then.[176] The ghostliness of the Gush, its evasiveness and slipperiness, its plural biographies, and its quality as an eternally living dead continue to serve it. These characteristics made it into a rival whose outline is hidden from the eye, neither here nor there—or here, there, and everywhere. They can also serve as a metaphor for the plurality of its identities and its historical attempt to enjoy the best of all worlds and settle in all hearts. Messianic and rational, revolutionary and anachronistic, political and apolitical, self-righteous and violent, sanctifying the state, the army, and its laws, and a serial lawbreaker, a faction of the extreme right that relies on the pioneering socialist heritage of the left—Gush Emunim is all these and more.

And it remains so. In a "time of Jacob's trouble," as Israel approached the Gaza disengagement, everyone was called again to the flag to protest and demonstrate and fight against a prime minister, against the law, against the State of Israel that went body and soul the whole way with them. For the "ghost" of Gush Emunim, about which its founders speak, has for more than thirty years also been Israeli society's demon, the Freudian *unheimlich* that emerges from time to time from the depths of its subconscious to reveal its own dark side and irrationality, and to torment it with the question of whether this blend of messianic belief with political astuteness and stunts, of bursts of irrationality with cutting-edge organizational and operational skill, of violence and lawbreaking with sweet talk and self-righteous discourse—which for many years characterized Gush Emunim—has defined Israeli society as a whole.

5

A Moveable Death

On August 23, 1929, an organized Arab insurrection broke out in Palestine, the first in a long series that continues to this day. A prolonged local dispute over worship arrangements at the Western Wall in Jerusalem, and in effect over control of the holy places, combined with the rising rhetoric of two emerging national movements to combust into an unprecedented conflagration. About ten days earlier, on the Jewish fast of the Ninth of Av, or Tisha B'Av, and right after the celebrations marking the establishment of the expanded Jewish Agency, members of the right-wing Betar youth movement had demonstrated in Jerusalem and at the Wall in defiance of the Zionist institutions' call for restraint and avoidance of provocations. They marched through the streets of Jerusalem under the watchful eyes of a heavy detail of British forces, flew the blue and white flag at the Wall, chanted "The Wall is ours!" and sang the national hymn, "Hatikvah."

The next day Palestinian youth held a counterdemonstration at the site. In the clash that erupted a young Jew was stabbed to death. His funeral turned into a violent mass gathering of Jews. On the following Friday, August 23, thousands of Palestinians from Jerusalem and the surrounding area flocked to the Al Aqsa Mosque compound.

Weeks of inflamed emotions and incitement by both sides had their effect, and despite attempts by the head of the Arab Committee for the Wall and by the Mufti of Jerusalem, Haj Amin al Husseini, to calm the worshipers, a horde of them spilled out of the mosques to attack Jews with sticks and knives. On August 24 riots broke out in Jerusalem. Arab inhabitants attacked the homes of Jews in Hebron, killing sixty-six people, among them women and children, and wounding fifty out of a community of about 600. The clashes continued for a week all over the country. In the northern city of Safed, local inhabitants killed forty-five Jews. The number of Jewish casualties came to 133 dead and 339 wounded. Among the Arabs there were 116 dead and 232 wounded.[1]

Although there had been clear signs of the rising tension and volatility between the two communities in Palestine, this outbreak of violence nevertheless shocked the small Jewish community. A sense of a fragile existence on the brink of "a volcano" replaced the relative security that in the 1920s had accompanied the impressive development of the Zionist Jewish settlement in the country.[2] The newspapers of the period used such terms as "pogrom," "massacre," "the city of slaughter," and "like sheep to the slaughter" to describe what had happened, especially in the mixed Arab and Jewish towns of Hebron and Safed.[3] In contrast to the armed self-defense by the people of new collective settlements, the Jews of these religious, non-Zionist communities were depicted as a disgrace to Zionism. They were condemned for allowing the Arabs to slaughter them, or for having fled without fighting back. "The martyrs of Hebron . . . died an utterly immoral death," wrote one commentator.[4] "We have taught our sons and our pupils . . . not to expose their necks to the slaughterers, not to die like the murdered Jews of Safed and the slaughtered Jews of Hebron," said the headmaster of the first Hebrew secondary school in

Tel Aviv, the Herzliya Gymnasium.[5] Yet the massacre served the strongman of the organized Zionist collective, David Ben-Gurion, as a lever for extensive political activity to bolster the Zionist project. He united the Labor movement in the country (in January 1930) under his leadership, establishing the Workers' Party of the Land of Israel, Mapai, and fortified the paramilitary organization, the Haganah, unifying it under a single command. "Our spilled blood cries out not for pity and succor, but rather to increase our strength and our work in the land," he declared.[6]

After forty years of historical slumber, the old story of the massacre in Hebron reawakened and became the most important political catalyst in the hands of the Jewish settlers in the territories that Israel occupied in 1967. The Zionist movement knew all too well how to transform historical disasters into heroic myths, cultivating them into tales of valor and sacrifice in order to forge through them national unity, social solidarity, and political action.[7] The massacre in Hebron was not one of these. It was alien to the hegemonic Zionist narrative and was not part of the active, pioneering settlement project of the Zionist "new man"; its victims, who belonged to the old, non-Zionist Jewish communities in Palestine (commonly called the Old Yishuv), did not enter the pantheon of sacrifice and memory that was established by the Jewish national movement to enlist its offspring in the Zionist project. But they dwelt in the marginal memory of the national-religious Zionist youth, to whom the territories conquered in 1967 afforded the platform of their life, the space and medium for the realization of their beliefs, and the conquest of the political sphere in Israel. The famous lament delivered by Rabbi Zvi Yehudah Kook on Independence Day, 1967, which his followers adopted immediately thereafter, while the June 1967 battles were still raging, endowing it with the awesome halo of a self-fulfilling prophecy, began with the words: "Where is our Hebron—are we forgetting it?" Only afterward came Shchem (Nablus), Jericho, and all of Trans-jordan, "Every clod of earth, every square cubit, every region and piece of land that belongs to the Lord's land—is it within our powers to relinquish even a single millimeter of them?"[8]

Eradicating the disgrace of the 1929 massacre and avenging those who were slaughtered was one element in the complex of motives for the settlement in Hebron by the first settlers there. The full range of memory, long-range and short-range, was both formative of their identity and a tool in the hands of the settlers for achieving their aims. More than other places, Hebron is a site where different registers of memory and motives of identity, culture, and politics converge. The sorts of sanctity that inhere there are also more varied and layered than elsewhere. To the Tomb of the Patriarchs were added the graves of the scorned and rejected Jews massacred in 1929, which have been joined by the graves of the dozens killed in the recent decades of conflict. "There is one justification for the return to Jerusalem, another justification of the return to the domain of the Ten Tribes and a unique and special justification for the beloved and also rejected, terrible and pitiable town of Hebron. The justification of the eradication of an ancient shame, the justification of the annulment of a decree and the removal of a curse, the justification of the implantation of life and the sowing of light in a place of darkness and the shadow of death, the justification of vengeance on the foes and the murderers—a Jewish vengeance of building, rebirth and return," wrote one of the first settlers in Hebron after 1967.[9]

The national-religious martyrology is sustained in Hebron in all its complexity: death as a creator of meaning, as a basis and a catalyst of the project of revival and renewal; the eradication of the shame of the slaughtered ancestors who did not know how to defend themselves;

revenge on murderers and enemies, whose names and faces change but who never die out. "The eradication of the shame" thus becomes a project of the perpetuation of the shame and a kind of intentional duplication of the deaths and their perpetuation. The site of the deaths is intended to be a place of life, in the words of Miriam Levinger, one of the first settlers, because "here, after the terrible bloodshed—they will not be forgotten! We thought that here we would redress the wrong, not out of reprisal and blood vengeance but from within rebuilding." However, the way the settlement is implemented inside Hebron, the location of the settlement and the settlers' aggression, ensured that the continuity of violent death would not in fact cease. Thus, in its replication of an ancient Jewish pattern of destruction and redemption, the cycle of catastrophe and revival, of wrongdoing and its redress, has revived and brought the dead victims into the community of their living redeemers. The living draw strength from the dead, and they have all become a single entity. On the eve of the first Sabbath of the settlers' stay at Beit Hadassah, after they left Kiryat Arba and settled again in the heart of Arab Hebron, related Levinger, the women there felt that as the yeshiva students danced under the windows of the building, the souls of the Jews who were murdered in 1929 joined her and her friends as though they had come "and crowded together with us at the window to watch what was happening, to rejoice with us at this sight of Jews dancing on the Sabbath eve in the streets of Hebron."[10] Less than a year later six yeshiva students were killed in an ambush under the window of Levinger's home.

The renewed Jewish settlement in Hebron thus became a replay of the tragedy of 1929, death-settlement, memorial site, a monument to the eternal Jewish martyrology in the land of Israel. More settlers from Kiryat Arba/Hebron have died violently than from any other settlement, and the carnage in the town has been going on now for a quarter of a century. It is as though the scores of new dead on the altar of the violent settlement in Hebron and the rest of the settlements, from the murder of the first yeshiva student in Hebron in 1980 to those killed in the recent intifada, draw the justification for their deaths from the original slaughter, affording it a continuing vitality and bearing eternal witness to it. In this way the dead and the living mingle in the Hebron of today, and the dead, like the living, are partners to the deed of Jewish settlement in Hebron, creating with their lives and their dead bodies the continuity of Jewish presence there. Conversation between the dead and the living is created by the very fact of the settlement and the significance that is given to it. The dead speak through the living and urge them on, issuing commands of "thou shalt" and "thou shalt not," and in this way they take an active part in the continuing political debate on Hebron. The living, as the Arab violence around the Jewish settlement escalates, look and act as though they are living on the brink of an abyss, like living-dead, as self-marked for a foretold death that is sanctified at every moment as a redemptive death.

The Hebron settlers' newspaper wrote of the soldier Elazar Leibowitz, who was killed in a car by Palestinian gunfire near the village of Yatta in July 2002, that he had always spoken about his desire to "die in the sanctification of the Holy Name and to be buried as befits a martyr . . . to shock the nation and impel it to act to eradicate the shame and restore confidence and security, pride and tranquillity to the Jewish people." Indeed, from the moment of his violent death Elazar Leibowitz's life and death were confiscated from him and in the hands of his friends became a symbol, a metaphor, and a tool of destruction and revenge. Leibowitz, stated the Hebron newspaper, was born on the seventeenth of Av, the date of the 1929 disturbances, and "was martyred on the eve of the holy Sabbath, the seventeenth of Av, the eve of his twenty-first birthday." He was laid to rest in the military plot adjacent to the "1929 martyrs' plot" in the old cemetery.[11] While Leibowitz's funeral was under way, settlers burst into Palestinians' homes, destroying and looting property and firing weapons in all directions. Nibeen Jimjum, a girl of fourteen, was killed, a boy of eight, Ahmad al Natsche, was stabbed, and another ten adult Palestinians were wounded.[12]

Death as a Way of Life

"There's a bullet out there for each one of us," replied Anat Cohen in answer to *The New Yorker* journalist Jeffrey Goldberg's question as to why she allows her little boy to play in a street that is exposed to sniper's bullets. "But you can always die. At least his death here would sanctify God's name."[13] Anat Cohen is a daughter of the prestigious Zar settler family. Her father, Moshe Zar, a wealthy land dealer who made his money mainly from trading in Palestinians' properties, was a member of the Jewish terrorist group in the 1980s. The Dome of the Rock, the "abomination" that the members of the group had planned to blow up, has vanished as though it had never existed from the picture of Jerusalem that hangs on the wall of his daughter Anat's home. One of her young sons is named after her brother, Gilad Zar, who was killed in a terror attack in May 2001. Gilad Zar lived in the settlement of Itamar and was the security officer of the Samaria regional council. On the day of his death he was driving his car to Kedumim and was ambushed and shot dead by Palestinians. Zar's car was not bullet-proofed and he himself did not wear a flak vest, out of choice. The soldiers of the Redemption do not need flak vests, and their "personal" death is of no importance, in the words of Zvi Yehudah Kook, relative to the grand messianic process of "mending" (*tikkun*).[14] Zar's funeral was one for a prince of the settlements, fraught with emotions, desire, and symbols. During the course of the ceremony, news came of another fatal shooting attack, near Neveh Daniel, in which women from the settlement of Efrat who had been on their way to Zar's funeral were killed. As the funeral procession was making its way to Karnei Shomron, the cortege was fired upon. "Gilad has ascended the steps to heaven, because he had a role as a commander of the platoon for the legal defense of the Jewish people. To bring about Redemption very sophisticated logistics are needed, and at this Gilad excelled," said his young widow, Hagar, at the graveside.[15]

Anat Cohen spoke at length about the sacrifice of Isaac with the American journalist, who attributed to her the "Mount Moriah complex." She was explaining her unbounded admiration for Abraham's devotion to God and for his willingness to satisfy His every whim, even at the price of sacrificing his son. She told the journalist the story from the Second Book of the Maccabees and in the Talmud about the mother and her seven sons who died in the sanctification of the Holy Name during the period of the occupation of the Land of Israel in ancient times. One after another the sons were ordered to appear before the emperor and eat swine. One after another the sons refused. The first said: "It is written in the Torah: 'I am the Lord thy God.'" The second said: "It is written in the Torah: 'Thou shalt have no other gods before me,'" and so on through all the brothers. One after another, the brothers were executed at the emperor's orders. But the emperor felt pity for the youngest brother and wanted to spare him. He threw down his seal so that the brother would pick it up as a sign of having accepted the royal decree. "Woe unto you, Caesar, woe unto you, Caesar," refused the youngest son. Before her son was executed, his mother said: "My sons, go and say to your father Abraham, 'Thou didst bind one son to the altar, but I have bound seven altars.'" Then she went up to the roof and leapt to her death. The Talmud says that upon the mother's death, a voice from heaven was heard singing: "A happy mother of children."[16]

Hebron does not permit normal life to its Jews. Life, like death, is magnified, deprived of its reality but rendered sublime, sanctified. "I, who grew up in the shadow of fear and horror whenever stories of the Hebronite murderers were mentioned at home, developed an allergy to the name Hebron," said one resident of Hebron. "You had only to say the word Hebron and I would tremble with fear. And today I find it hard to get used to the simple fact that I am living in the city of the Patriarchs. I am incapable of living even a single day of routine. The terrible fear has become a joyful delight."[17] In their perception of the past of the massacred community as their own personal and communal past, and of themselves as its heirs and its continuation by virtue of the command from above promulgated by the lives and deaths of the murdered, the inhabitants of Kiryat Arba and Hebron have branded themselves as victims or as potential victims of that same deterministic Jewish fate. The 1929 massacre is an absent present, not a past event of almost eighty years ago, and it is a motive that justifies everything. Yehuda Shaul, a religiously observant demobilized soldier who served in Hebron and organized the Breaking the Silence group, related that one of the events that shook him out of his moral stasis during his military service in Hebron occurred one day in Gross Square in the center of the town.[18] An elderly Palestinian woman laden with shopping baskets passed by. Settler children, girls, picked up stones, "as if automatically, and began to stone her." When he asked the girls why they were doing this, they replied: "How do you know what she did in 1929?"[19]

The 1929 massacre and violent Jewish death anywhere are the organizing principle of the Jewish settlers' existence in Hebron. This is instilled in the children born there, from the cradle on, as tantamount to the sacred injunction to know whence thou hast come and whither thou goest. The fact of the new Jewish settlement in the heart of an Arab town that is hostile by definition, a settlement that in the settlers' perception is interwoven into thousands of years of Jewish presence there, delineates for young and old alike the horizon of their lives and consciousness. The abandoned ancient cemetery, which more than any other site symbolized the hundreds of years of Jewish continuity in Hebron, was prohibited for Jewish burial in a decision by the government of Israel immediately following the start of the Jewish settlement there after it was occupied. A short time after the end of the war, Religious Affairs Minister Zerah Warhaftig ordered that the scattered bones be gathered and given a proper burial. As a rule, it was not customary to write the names of those interred on the tombstones in the cemetery in Hebron. An exception to this rule of posthumous anonymity was made for the 1929 martyrs. On their graves the names were engraved so that the slaughter and its sanctified victims would not vanish into oblivion and would have their names inscribed individually and forever, as ordained in a ruling by Chief Rabbi Kook.[20]

It is no accident that the renewal of Jewish life inside Hebron began through the old Jewish cemetery there. "The settlement of the Jewish living in Hebron was preceded by the settlement of the dead," acknowledged a woman settler from Hebron.[21] The body of a Jewish baby, who died of crib death, the son of a family from neighboring Kiryat Arba, was the one who paved the path later taken by the first settlers in Hebron itself. The body of the dead infant was the first in a long series of dead bodies that served the settlers' political claims. The funeral, which attained the dimensions of a founding, constitutive myth, is described in detail from the settlers' perspective on the

Jewish settlement's Internet site. The bereaved mother, Sarah Nachshon, who bearing her dead infant in her arms stood before the military commander there in protest against the prohibition on Jewish burials in the abandoned graveyard, is a new icon that replicates with just a few variations of detail the icon of the mother of sons who refused to accept royal decree and were executed. "The bereaved mother decided that as her son had been born in Kiryat Arba . . . and as her son, Avraham Yedidya, was the 'Nachshon' [the vanguard, after the first Israelite to enter the Red Sea], the first to have been circumcised at the Tomb of the Patriarchs after the liberation of Hebron, it was fitting that her son be the first to be buried in the cemetery in Hebron that had been desecrated in the 1929 riots. . . . Sarah descended from the truck, flung open its doors and said to the commander: 'Here lies the dead before you!' . . . The commander tried to dissuade Sarah. 'Hebron will be returned, and then what will you do?' 'I understand you, you have received an order and you are following it. But I too have received an order from on high, and I too am following it,' she said. At the crossroads she saw that they would not let her pass . . . and she, on her part, informed the commander that she would continue to Hebron on foot. And so she did. Sarah Nachshon began to walk, with the body of her son in her arms. The commander of the roadblock found it difficult to stop her in the situation that she had created, and passed the news along to the minister of defense. . . . After the child was buried, the need arose to post a regular guard at the cemetery for fear that the child's body would be exhumed and his grave desecrated."[22] On the heels of the first tenant, the dead baby, the living settlers moved in. The event included two fundamental, mythical elements in the settlers' discourse: death as the creator of life and as the expander of territory, and the establishment of "facts on the ground" that bring substantial developmental momentum in their

wake. Indeed, after the burial of the first child in the Hebron cemetery, the authorities caved in to the settlers and granted them general
permission for Jewish burial there.

A cemetery is not just a random collection of graves. It is a site
of organized mythic discourse, of a narrative that tells the drama of
death as construed into and as perceived immanent to the renewal of
Jewish settlement in the territories. Apart from the cemetery of the
first, senior settlement, Kfar Etzion, which was rededicated in 1973
with the military burial of a soldier who fell in the Yom Kippur War,
and the old Jewish cemetery in Hebron, there were no cemeteries in
the settlements until the mid-1980s. The settlements were young,
healthy communities that usually did not need final resting places.
Their few dead were buried in the mother locales from which the settlers had come inside the Green Line. The layers of meaning and
interpretation that would come later had not yet been associated with
the grave. The first intifada, which erupted at the end of 1987,
exacted its price in blood and exposed the fragile Jewish existence in
the territories and the vulnerability of the living. Death was political,
and it was formulated and interpreted as a life-giving elixir. New
graves were dug in the settlements, demonstrative graves intended to
give expression to the process of striking roots. The grave reinforced
the foundations of the home and extended the roots farther into the
ground. Life is mobile and can exist in many places. A house in which
there is life can, with regret, be abandoned, but a grave and a tombstone will never be forsaken, believe the settlers. The finality of the
grave, its being the terminal site, endows it with a numinous dimension that says touch me not. On the tombstone in memory of Yitzhak
Rofeh and Rachel Druck, who were killed in October 1991 as they
were on their way to participate in a settlers' demonstration against
the Madrid conference, these words are engraved: "This stone and

this monument bear witness / That in the rock of the mountain their blood has touched / We shall yet excavate foundations for their descendents' homes / Here in the bend of the road in the fold of the mountain / We swear that the covenant will never be broken."[23]

Rachel Druck's parents in fact had wanted to bury her in Jerusalem, for fear that her settlement in Samaria would be evacuated and their daughter's grave would be abandoned across the border. But from the instant of her death Rachel Druck ceased to be a private individual. The fact that she had been on her way to a political demonstration by the settlers against any possible peace step, and even more than that the fact that she was the mother of seven sons, the "mother of sons," imbued her death with utter sanctity and immediately transformed the place of her death into a site of memory and perpetuation, which eventually became a settlement that bears her name, Rachelim. The priestesses of her memory were women, all of them inhabitants of veteran, isolated, and lethal settlements in the West Bank such as Beit El, Elon Moreh, and Shiloh (Rachel Druck's settlement). Independent women with careers and mothers of many children, they were linked to one another by family, work, neighborhood, and social ties, and connected to the first of the settlers, the heads of Gush Emunim, the movement's elite. Various symbols were placed at the memorial site: A reversed military helmet that covered the memorial fire transformed Rachel Druck into a soldier woman committed to the battle for the land. Her photograph, which was duplicated in many forms suggesting the icons of Christian saints, was displayed in the memorial tent. While the women depicted their commemoration project as a spontaneous act into which they had been "drawn" by an uncontrollable power, there was a planning and organizing hand behind all the activities, wrote anthropologist Michael Feige.[24]

On the Path of the Dead

Death in the course of the struggle for a site transformed a nonplace into a place loaded with meaning. The poet and journalist Hava Pinhas-Cohen wrote of the settlements in Sinai, which left no graves behind when they were evacuated in early 1980s, that "this is the place where the myths connected to it are about a non-place, about wanderings without burial."[25] The building of cemeteries in the settlements was an ideological-political act. It was aimed at marking those lands as "Jewish lands." The grave and the cemetery deepened the foundations and were aimed at asserting the irreversibility of the Jewish settlement process.[26] The crisis of Oslo accelerated the settlement trend by adding a grave next to the home. Although not a word was said in the Oslo agreement about evacuating settlements, from the settlers' point of view the entire Oslo process was tantamount to a threat of the destruction of the Home, the undermining of foundations and the uprooting of life. Parallel to the organized political struggle they conducted against the agreement, the settlers also embarked on a campaign of striking roots by digging graves for their dead within the settlements. This was the settlers' new weapon; like the Palestinians' *sumud*—cleaving to the land. It was "Jewish *sumud*," as they said. "A burial plot near the home is in a certain respect the striking of roots and the perpetuation of the past, close to the present, in a way that the tie and the connection between the past and the future are clear and unambiguous," said Shiloh Gal, the head of the Gush Etzion local council, in 1995.[27]

After the victory of the opponents to the Gaza disengagement plan in the Likud referendum in May 2004, the spokesman of Gush Katif in the Gaza Strip said that "instead of victory celebrations we shall drive five more strong stakes into the land of the Gush, five more fresh graves that will be impossible to move."[28] He was referring to the graves of

Tali Hatuel and her four daughters, who were killed on the day of the referendum, as they were on their way to the polling places to encourage voters to cast their ballots against Sharon's plan.[29] Though the mother and her daughters were buried within the Green Line, in the town of Ashkelon—a "minor" detail that was blurred in the annexation of the five dead—their death, bodies, and funerals were appropriated for purposes of the settlers' political struggle, as advocates in the celestial court on behalf of Gush Katif in particular and the Greater Land of Israel in general. "Little girls, you are going way up high, to the place that only the supremely righteous can understand. Plead for the Gush, plead for our land, plead for Jerusalem the holy city," were the words spoken over the row of stretchers bearing the girls and their mother by Rabbi Mordecai Elon.[30] "Now all is well for them," said a woman from the settlement of Katif in an attempt to domesticate this terrible death and explain the children's death to her own daughters. "They are in Paradise, close to the Holy One, blessed be He, and anyone who is killed in a terror attack like that is a saint."[31]

The dead of the settlers' political struggle have been commemorated not only in the cemeteries. In many cases neighborhoods and outposts built in recent years, particularly since the outbreak of the second intifada, were planted in places where settlers had fallen victim, and for the most part they bear the names of people who were killed in terror attacks. Giv'at Assaf, Ginnot Aryeh, Tal Binyamin, Ma'oz Zvi, Ma'aleh Hagit, Mitspeh Danny, Mitzpeh Yair, Maahaz Gil'ad, and Ramat Gil'ad are all named after people slain for the sanctification of the settlements. Senior military people and career and reserve army officers who perished in various circumstances and whose views did not necessarily accord with those of the settlers have also been expropriated by the settlers and memorialized by having settlements in the territories named after them. "You have to understand that establishing outposts is like therapy for us," explained Yehoshua Mor-Yosef of the Settler Council. "It is the appropriate Zionist response, and it is the most popular action among the settlers. People almost go out of their minds when settlers are murdered, and the only way to vent the anger and distress is to build an outpost. For us, an outpost is a living memorial, and this is the only language the Arabs understand. They know that we cling to the land no less than they do. This is our best revenge. For every drop of our blood, they will pay in land."[32]

The discourse of death and the cult of the blood-soaked land are not solely the province of the extreme ideologists among the settlers. In recent years, as the human tragedies have magnified and with the increasing number of cases in which a number of members of a single family were killed in terror attacks, they have swept up settlements that used to display their "normality," as well as those settlers who had joined the settlement project out of considerations of comfort and "quality of life."[33] Geula Hershkowitz of Ofra was one of them. She and her husband, Aryeh, were not ideological settlers. "I was simply bored with life in the city and I was looking for quality of life, a house with a garden and a dog," Geula said. For family reasons Geula and Aryeh chose Ofra, and joined the settlement in the mid-1980s. Life was beautiful. "The people are charming, the weather is wonderful." The first intifada did not send them back to their previous home. The birth of their youngest son in their new settlement turned it into a home.[34] At the beginning of 2001, in a terror attack on the road between A-Ram junction and the settlement of Adam, Aryeh Hershkowitz was shot and killed. A few months later, another disaster struck Geula and her family. Her son Assaf was killed by Palestinians at the "T" junction near Beit El. Her neighbors in Ofra who came to console her spoke to her about death in the sanctification of the Holy Name. "They talked a lot about how Aryeh and Assaf are sitting by the throne," she said. She had brought different concepts from home, a different martyrology for the sanctification of the homeland. "In my eyes they are the Trumpeldors of 2001," she said. Drawing her strength from what happened to her mother, a Holocaust survivor ("What didn't they suffer in the Holocaust?"), Geula Hershkowiz invests her energy in public activity and in the defense of Givat Assaf and Givat Aryeh, the outposts named after her son and her husband. The deaths of Aryeh and Assaf Hershkowitz, the circumstances of their deaths, and the places where these occurred have also undergone a process of reification, ritualization, and fetishization. The private, personal work of mourning the specific, unique individuals who will no longer be among the living has taken on a cultish frenzy that sanctifies and anthropomorphizes objects. Geula Hershkowitz acknowledges that the way in which her husband and son died and the place of their death ease her sorrow and mourning. She draws power and status from them. She has an open line to heads of the government. "Had Aryeh been killed in a traffic accident it would have been harder for me," she admits. "In these circumstances I'm always in the headlines." She now promises "a war to the death," with no limits, against evacuation of the places where her husband and her son were killed. The war that she is waging will continue to empower and transcend her in a society that sanctifies death and will also ensure the continued vitality of the deaths of the members of her family. In the places where they are commemorated she is now able to see the continued life of her loved ones and the meaning of their death. "These are places where my blood is flowing. This is the holiest place for me, and I will not let them be evacuated in any circumstances. . . . My blood flows in the stones there. As the place flourishes, I feel that there is continuity for my son. He was not murdered and relegated to oblivion."[35]

The Cry of the Grave

Hebron is the most violent town in the territories and the place with the most victims. Violence has accompanied the renewed settlement almost from its inception. With the violence, death has become part of the family, a way of life. On January 30, 1980, soldier Yehoshua Saloma, a student at the paramilitary (*hesder*) yeshiva in Kiryat Arba, was killed in the market in central Hebron. Saloma was the first settler from anywhere in the West Bank to have been killed by Palestinians since the beginning of settlement in 1967. The incident set off a chain reaction that has steadily grown until the present. The day after the murder, and in reaction to it, a group of settlers from Kiryat Arba took over five empty buildings that in the past had been Jewish property in the old Jewish Quarter of Hebron. Prime Minister Begin publicly expressed his disapproval of the settlers' action but refrained from using force to evacuate the invaders. The historical owners of Beit Hadassah, Beit Romano, and other buildings opposed the settlers' break-in. "We missed the train," they said, meaning that it was too late to reclaim their old property.[36] Their words were blown with the wind in the violent riots. Settlers burst into Arab homes and beat up their inhabitants. A ten-day curfew was imposed on the Arab inhabitants of Hebron, a pattern of Israeli military response that would repeat itself in the following decades. A delegation of well-meaning Israelis from the left who tried to protest the renewal of the Jewish settlement and the settlers' violence was detained by the army at the entrance to the town.[37]

The killing of Yehoshua Saloma, the first in the renewed Jewish Hebron, gave substance to and made palpable the connection with the 1929 killing that is imprinted on the Jewish settlement. Blood had touched blood. Slaughter on slaughter made a loud outcry. "The outcry that began in the year 1929," said Rabbi Eliezer Waldman over the grave of his student Saloma, continues to reverberate in the present and its command is to act and to settle with no restraints. "The voice of our brethren's blood is crying out to us from the earth of the Land of Israel, from the earth of Hebron, a cry of innocent blood that has been spilled from 1929 until this day: This is the same flow of blood, the blood of life." In his eulogy the rabbi spoke about the guilt of the settlers who had not done more. "We will no longer be able to block our ears to this outcry; we will not be able to say that our own hands did not spill this blood. The blood is crying out for the removal of the restraints that are binding the Jewish settlement in Hebron, restraints that are preventing Jewish life at the site of the murder. Only a Jewish presence will prevent the insolence of evil," said Waldman over the grave that was dug not in Hebron but at Mount Herzl in Jerusalem. Drawing from Joshua 1:4, the rabbi said at the graveside that the command that the dead Yehoshua left behind was the divine command to settle in every place, from the wilderness to this Lebanon even unto the great river, the River Euphrates, the whole land of the Hittites and "unto the great sea toward the going down of the sun shall be your border."[38]

Saloma's death and funeral created a pattern for the funerals of settlers killed in the territories and for public reaction to the deaths. Saloma's spilled blood infused with additional sanctity a place that was already sacred in the eyes of the settlers. Stones sodden with the blood of the soldiers of God and the nation took on, it appeared, a life and propulsion of their own. Saloma's death did not lead to any reconsideration of the wisdom of the Jewish presence there but was rather the summons to strengthen the settlement in the heart of Arab Hebron. Even before the seven days of mourning for the murdered youth had ended, Agriculture Minister Ariel Sharon called for moving Jews into the five buildings in Hebron, thus increasing the Jewish presence in the town and giving "an appropriate Zionist response to the murder of the soldier yeshiva student." This move, said Sharon, would increase security, encourage the inhabitants of Kiryat Arba, and deter the Arabs from attempting attacks on Jewish inhabitants and visitors.[39] Moshe Dayan, who at that time was a Knesset member, argued that it would be a mistake to settle Jewish families in the town, where 60,000 Arabs were living, but said that Kiryat Arba, with its 3,800 Jews, should be strengthened. The Likud Defense Minister, Ezer Weizman, said that "we have come to the town of the Patriarchs not in order to take it over from its Arab inhabitants."[40] At a government meeting several weeks later he voted against the decision to establish a yeshiva inside the city.[41]

But by slim majority of eight to six, the government decided on March 23, 1980, to erect a building in the Jewish courtyard in Hebron and to put a yeshiva there, a branch of the yeshiva in Kiryat Arba. It also decided to add a third story to Beit Hadassah and locate a field school there. The Knesset Foreign Affairs and Security Committee gave its blessing to the government's decision.[42] This historic decision initiated a pattern of strengthening and accelerating Jewish settlement after every killing of settlers, and it was the first step in the "Judaization" of the town of Hebron and the routine, violent yet suppressed transfer of thousands of its Palestinian inhabitants, setting in motion a wave of unrest, protests, and rioting.[43]

Only three months after that first killing of a settler, on May 2, 1980, shortly after Jewish worshipers at the Tomb of the Patriarchs had read the supplication "May this hour be an hour of mercy,"[44] Palestinians who lay in ambush on the roofs of neighboring houses fired on them as they returned to Beit Hadassah, killing six in front of the house. The killing was planned and precise. The handwriting had been on the wall. The shots were fired from three or four different directions, said the commander of the Judea and Samaria region,

Binyamin Ben-Eliezer. This was the bloody "Palestinian answer" to Sharon's "Zionist response." In the new Hebron's tissue of tales of death, this conflict was analogous to the battle of Tel Hai, the site of Yosef Trumpeldor's legendary last stand in 1920, the defeat that was transformed into a victory in the chronicles of the community. It was from this event that the blessing of the renewal of the legal Jewish settlement in Hebron began, relates the settlers' book of legend, *Hebron Since Then and Forever.*[45]

The funeral of Eli Haze'ev, one of the six who were killed and a member of Meir Kahane's Kach movement, was held in Hebron and attended by thousands, among them leading figures such as Foreign Minister Yitzhak Shamir, Rabbi Ovadiah Yosef, Chief of Staff Rafael Eitan, and head of Central Command Moshe Levy. "We must not concede this blood,"[46] said Meir Kahane at the grave, which was next to those of the victims of 1929. "The Holy Name is the God of vengeance," he added. "Anyone who says that vengeance is not a Jewish virtue is simply wrong. There will be no atonement for the blood that has been spilled. . . . Henceforth we shall not pay with an eye for an eye, but rather with two eyes for an eye. . . ."[47] This was Jewish accounting of a new breed, and this accounting included doubled and tripled blood, and transfer on top of it. The rabbi of the paramilitary yeshiva in Kiryat Arba said over Haze'ev's grave that "at the side of your coffin we hope that we shall not be silent until a large and glorious Jewish settlement arises here in Kiryat Arba . . . that we may live to see the expulsion of all our enemies who surround us."[48] In his death in a remote and violent town in the Land of Israel, Eli Haze'ev, an American Christian and a member of a violent motorcycle gang who at the beginning of the 1970s had been convicted of murder and manslaughter, and who had converted to Judaism after his entanglement with the law in the United States,[49] became a surreal holy Jewish victim over whose grave unrestrained rabbis cry revenge and demand restitution.

Nourished by Yehoshua Saloma's funeral, the obsequies for the yeshiva students killed in Hebron further strengthened the model of the funerals for murder victims in the territories. These funerals became magnified, essentialized manifestations of the settlers' political struggle and its price. They were organized climaxes of the continuing process of self-constitution and of the creation of the identity of the settler as victim, a key pillar in the structure of the justifications for the settlements, a mixture of eulogies, demands from the government and from God, calls for vengeance and acts of violence. There were also those who took the calls for vengeance very seriously. At the funerals of the six slain in Hebron, the Jewish terrorist group's plans to attack Palestinians began to take shape. Similarly, the idea of assassinating Prime Minister Yitzhak Rabin was first conceived by Yigal Amir during Baruch Goldstein's funeral, which was held in Hebron-Kiryat Arba in April 1994. As a rule, the settlers have known unhesitatingly how to transmute the killings of Jews in the territories into the coin of practical, material demands from the authorities. In most cases the connection between the personal disaster of the individual and his family and the community's demands for recompense or revenge has been incidental and tenuous, but in the context of the settlers' struggle for the Land of Israel, death has never been private, mourning has never been personal, and the dead, like the living, are soldiers totally committed to a cause that is greater than their lives and their deaths.

The funeral of Tirtza Porat during Passover 1988, at the height of the first intifada, also became a milestone in the history of the settlements.[50] In this incident too there were all the elements of the model: repressed feelings of guilt compensated by self-righteous and extreme rhetoric of vengeance and redemption. Porat, daughter of one of the first venerated settler families, was the first victim from the second generation of the settler aristocracy. As her death was particularly unnecessary and tragic, the natural, spontaneous grief at her funeral was mingled with heated expressions of wrath at the authorities, at the state, at the law, and especially at the army. The bereaved father, Rabbi Yosef Porat, a pioneer among the ideological-religious settlers, consoled those who came to offer their solace to him. "In the end, this will be for the best," he said of his daughter's death. "My daughter was killed for the sake of the Jewish people; she gave up her life in sanctification of the Holy Name. But we shall be strengthened by this blow, just as we have always been strengthened in the past."[51]

A Just Man in Distress

It was not only around the murdered victims and their funerals that the settlers developed rites and cults, but also around a murderer. Particularly in Hebron, but also in less ideological and more moderate settlements, the man who carried out the massacre at the Tomb of the Patriarchs, Baruch Goldstein, was sanctified and became the savior of the Jewish people. The physician became a saint whose death embodied the sanctification of Hebron. If Hebron was perceived as atoning for the deeds and the sins of the entire Jewish people, Goldstein's massacre of Muslim worshipers was perceived by the Hebron settlers as "a supreme act of sacrifice that prevented a new Holocaust," a bodily and spiritual sacrifice for the salvation of the collective. It was as though Goldstein had brought with his act the 1929 massacre back to life, the memory of the murdered Jews hanging over the settlers of Kiryat Arba and Hebron as a threatening reminder of what might happen at any moment. "In a psychological process, many have reversed the order of events: They repress the fear of revenge for the incident at the Tomb of the Patriarchs. Instead, they speak about an event that was supposed to happen, which Goldstein, in his insane act, succeeded in preventing," wrote an Israeli journalist.[52]

Goldstein did not intervene in the political process, as his friend Moshe Feiglin said, "but rather in a clear and palpable danger to the lives of many of Hebron's Jews."[53] Thus the historical roles were reversed: The passive, frightened Jew who goes blindly to his death became a predatory and vengeful gentile. Goldstein not only redeemed the murdered Jews of 1929 but also liberated the entire Jewish people from passivity and from the traditional Jewish way of going like sheep to the slaughter. "Baruch Goldstein appeared and acted like a real gentile, with no inhibitions, during prayer time, from behind . . . shattering the house of cards in a single stroke, slaughtering the 'sheepish' image we had worked so hard to develop and upon which we relied. This basic element of the State of Israel, existential Zionism, was deeply undermined. It could not digest this, not to forget and not to forgive."[54]

According to the book about *Hebron Since the 1929 Pogrom to the 1994 Events*, published after Goldstein's mass killing, Goldstein himself is depicted as a descendant of the Schneorsohn family that was among the survivors of the 1929 massacre. Among the Jews there are still those who have not recovered from the trauma of 1929; while among those Muslims whom Goldstein killed, in the holy place of worship, there were also direct descendants of the murderers who participated in the 1929 massacre. Thus the immediate, material connection was made between the two acts of slaughter. The Brooklyn-born Jewish doctor's deed is perceived as the closing of a circle, as a great act of healing and the restoration of order, if only temporarily. In requital for the twenty-nine yeshiva students and rabbis who were slaughtered in 1929, Goldstein slaughtered the same number of

Muslim worshipers. The celestial hand and the terrestrial hand were able to balance the continuing bloody account.

The fact that he had been a doctor made it possible to endow him, after the death he brought upon himself, with attributes of mercy and salvation as a healer of the poor and a rehabilitator of the miserable. His story as told, after the mass murder he committed in a place of worship, was a story of redemption and rescue, not one of killing and destruction. "During his life the man had become a legend among his neighbors," Feiglin said, embroidering the legend. "His devotion to the inhabitants of the area knew no bounds. . . . The man brought the poor and the depressed close to him. . . . He regularly worked with retarded children. . . . Close to his pillow there was always a beeper that was never silent, day or night. . . . There was no one who had experienced the effects of the security wantonness [of the Oslo agreement] and the continuing bloodshed more than Dr. Goldstein. . . . Dr. Goldstein did not confine himself to treating Jews and he also contributed of his special medical talent to the Arabs of the area." The cries of *itbah al yahoud* (slaughter the Jews), which were growing louder and more frequent, went the sanctifying tale, were deeply felt by Dr. Goldstein, whose family had already experienced the murderous hand of Hebron Arabs and who interpreted these cries as a new holocaust threatening the Jews.[55]

In October 1994, about half a year after the massacre, the saint's admirers and devotees began to establish a grandiose site at his grave, at the northern exit from Kiryat Arba. The money for building the shrine came from private donations from Israel and abroad. On Goldstein's tomb they wrote that "he had sacrificed himself for the sake of Israel, his Torah and his land" and that he had been "murdered in the sanctification of the Holy Name." The graveside attained the dimensions of a mausoleum. The spot became a place of pilgrimage. Mass "midnight corrections"—all-night Torah study sessions—were held there. Barren women prostrated themselves on the grave to pray for offspring. A nucleus of worshipers came there every day. Throughout the country aid funds and charities were established in Goldstein's name. An extensive "souvenir" industry developed in memory of the murderer. His admirers distributed a prayer book dedicated to "the elevation of the sainted soul," T-shirts with his portrait, and key chains with Goldstein's picture on the backdrop of the Tomb of the Patriarchs. Kach activists market bottles of wine with a picture on the label of Goldstein wearing a yellow patch. A book drawing a portrait of the saint was published with the title *Barukh Hagever*—which in Hebrew carries the double meaning of "Baruch the Man" and "Blessed is the Man."[56] Only at the conclusion of prolonged parliamentary and legal struggles, and despite warnings by people from the Kach movement that they would take revenge on the graves of leaders of the left if the tombstone was removed, did bulldozers come to destroy the shrine at the end of December 1999. Only an ordinary marble tombstone remained, but the pilgrimage to the grave and the cult of the saint did not end. Kach members and others continue to hold gatherings there.[57] "There is one law, higher up there," said a woman who made it a practice to water the plants around the grave site.[58]

Over Their Dead Bodies

The battle over Goldstein's dead body, its burial, the tomb, and the location of the grave was but one episode in a series of such dramas. Like the living in the settlements, the bodies of the dead are enlisted in the struggle for the Land of Israel and serve as hostages to political propaganda needs and various demands from the authorities—as sacred ritual objects, in Rabbi Kook's terms, like the Israeli army's tanks, planes, and artillery.[59] The body of the infant Shalhevet Pas was used in this manner, as a tool in bitter negotiations with the government regarding the settlers' demands to retake control of Hebron's Arab Abu Snina neighborhood, which had been handed over to Palestinians by the Netanyahu government. On March 26, 2001, as Yitzhak and Oriya Pas were on their way with their baby daughter from their home to visit the mother's parents, a single bullet fired from the direction of Abu Snina fatally hit the baby's head, killing her instantly. Yitzhak was wounded in the leg. Inhabitants of the Jewish quarter swooped down on the traumatized family, grabbed the body of the baby, took control of it, and of the parents and prevented her burial until their demand to occupy the neighborhood from which the fatal shot came was met. Despite pleas from rabbis, including the chief rabbis of Israel, the parents and their friends refused to bury the baby. Instead of observing the seven days of mourning for the tiny victim, the Hebron settlers exploited the time for a campaign of revenge against the Arabs, looted Palestinians' shops, and burned down *waqf* (Muslim religious endowment) buildings.[60]

In Gross Square, which bears the name of yeshiva student Aharon Gross, who was killed in Hebron, a protest tent was erected "until the IDF occupies nearby Abu Snina." This time, too, the disaster served as a lever for expanding the settlement, another pillar in its justification. Settlement spokesman Noam Arnon declared that the new neighborhood that would be established would be called Giv'at Shalhevet, after the baby.[61] The most original explanation for the profanation of the dead infant and the injury to her human dignity was given by the settler essayist Emunah Elon. The postponement of the burial was in fact intended to rescue Israel and for the purpose of the Redemption of the people. "Oriya and Yitzhak Pas decided to delay the burial of their sweet infant because they wanted to donate her dear organs to save the sick body of the state of Israel. . . . As though there were anywhere to run, as though there were any safe place to hide children in this land, as though the settlements, and especially the one in Hebron, are not a reflection in miniature of the Jewish state: a tiny Jewish island surrounded by a huge and hostile Arab ocean that is threatening to sink it." An outsider would not understand this, wrote Elon, "but the injury to the dignity of this particular dead child would apparently have been much greater had the adults hastened to bury her body and cover her screaming and weeping blood."[62]

The Israeli Foreign Ministry went a step further. With the family's encouragement, the ministry distributed to international news agencies a picture of Shalhevet Pas taken after she was shot. The dead baby was not only a political tool in the hands of the settlers but also a propaganda tool in the hands of the State of Israel.[63] The nation gathered the tiny soldier to its bosom—just as it had gathered to its bosom its soldier sons who had died in the battlefields of its wars—expropriated and sanctified her, and promised her fifteen minutes of everlasting life and eternal glory in a media hungry for sensations and scenes of disaster. For but a fleeting hour Shalhevet Pas was an Israeli icon, the portrait of the State of Israel in the year 2001 in the figure of a baby with a smashed head, whose family preferred to endanger her life and live outside the recognized, sovereign borders of Israel, a Jewish minority in the heart of an alien and hostile population.

Revenge was not long in coming. A week after the killing of Gil'ad Zar and about two months after the death of Shalhevet Pas, two Palestinians were shot in their vehicle from a passing car. Three days later, three more Palestinians were wounded in a shooting attack near the settlement of Rimonim, in an action that followed a similar pattern. Two months after that, shots were fired from a car heading toward a Palestinian commercial vehicle on the Hizmeh-Ma'aleh Adumim road. In the vehicle were three Palestinians from Hebron, of whom one was killed and two wounded. An anonymous caller informed Israel Radio that a Jewish organization called the Shalhevet Gilad Brigades (after Shalhevet Pas and Gil'ad Zar) had carried out the deed and that it was a revenge attack. Three days later, at 10 P.M., near the Tarqumiya roadblock, shots were fired at a Palestinian vehicle from a passing car. In the vehicle were seven members of the Timzi family from the village of Idna on their way to a wedding celebration. Three of them were killed, including a six-month-old baby girl, and four were wounded. Responsibility for the attack was claimed by a Jewish organization called The Committee for the Defense of the Roads. The Pas family denied any connection to the deed. The mother, Oriya Pas, testified of her husband, who was among those arrested from the terrorist Bat Ayyin group, that "he would never hurt an Arab child and never in his life would he ask anyone to avenge Shalhevet's death. But we don't weep over an Arab child who is killed and it doesn't matter what the circumstances are. I have no sorrow about an Arab child who is killed. They are our enemies."[64]

In his death as in his life, Netanel (Nati) Ozeri would find no rest. His body would become a pawn in a political and personal game played by his family and friends and zealous rabbis, who refused to allow a quiet burial. Ozeri, a Kach activist and a disciple of Meir Kahane, was a charismatic young man who was considered a prince of the "hilltop youth"; many young people in the settlements followed him wherever he went.[65] Ozeri was also a lawbreaker. He lived in an illegal outpost in an area called Plot 26, about 400 meters from Giv'at Haharsina in Hebron, and for years defied government decisions and orders of the High Court of Justice. It was Ariel Sharon who, upon becoming prime minister at the beginning of 2001, allowed Ozeri and his friends to take over the hill once again, even though it had been defined as an illegal outpost. In April 2001 Ozeri got a mobile home and moved his family in. In defiance of decisions of the High

Court of Justice, he built a sheep pen for his flock and expanded his estate even further. Terror attacks postponed government vows to evacuate him again and again, for fear of setting tempers alight.[66] Like Gil'ad Zar and many others before him, Ozeri refused to fence and bullet-proof the mobile home and did not agree to accept the protection the army offered despite the illegality of his dwelling. Nonetheless, a military patrol regularly visited Ozeri's home several times a day to make sure that everything was all right.[67] One night in January 2003, as he was at dinner celebrating the Sabbath with his wife, his five-year-old daughter, and two friends who had come to guard the family, two armed Palestinians burst into the mobile home, shooting Ozeri dead and wounding his small daughter and the friends.

Livnat Ozeri, Netanel's widow, was a child in the mid-1980s when her father, the Jewish terrorist group member Shaul Nir, was sentenced to life imprisonment for his part in the killing of Arab students at the Islamic College in Hebron. Her uncle, Barak Nir, also served a prison term for his part in the group's activities. Livnat Ozeri grew up without her father, in an environment steeped in ideology and admiration for the members of the terrorist group and for Baruch Goldstein. The story of the baby Abraham Nachshon's burial in the cemetery of the 1929 victims; the bereaved mother's march on foot carrying her dead infant in her arms in defiance of the astonished military commanders; and her words—"Thousands of years ago Abraham buried Sarah in the Machpela Cave and thus purchased Hebron. Today, I, Sarah, am burying you, Abraham, in the cemetery in Hebron and thus Hebron is purchased in our own day"—were tantamount to a commandment of "thou shalt" in the minds of an entire generation that grew up in Hebron.[68] Along with the story of the terrorist group and Goldstein's story, the story of the bereaved mother shaped Livnat Ozeri's worldview and sketched the horizon of her conscience.

At first Livnat wanted to bury her dead husband next to Baruch Goldstein's grave, while Netanel's father wanted him buried in Jerusalem, near his own home. Then she decided to inter him in Plot 26, "to fulfill his will and testament" and to establish a "covenant of blood" with the land on which she and Netanel had built their home. During the course of the frenzied, hallucinatory funeral convoy, which was first delayed and then lasted for hours until the heads of the Kach movement were allowed to participate in it, Livnat received a rabbinical ruling from Dov Lior, the rabbi of Kiryat Arba, stating that Netanel Ozeri must be buried in the old cemetery in Hebron. Ozeri's friends, who wanted to bury him in the place where he had been shot, took his body out of the truck and ran around with it for hours, crushing Palestinians' grapevines and fields, breaking through military roadblocks and struggling violently with soldiers and police. "It was not the Arabs who killed him, but Yitzhak Rabin, may his name be eradicated, who gave them rifles," they screamed, and removed the winding cloths from Ozeri's face, contrary to Jewish law, on the grounds that he was "a martyr."[69]

Eight hundred soldiers and police secured the funeral of the terrorist Kach activist and tried to gain control of it.[70] Policemen and civilians were injured during the course of the funeral. Cries of "Nazis" were hurled at the police and the soldiers.[71] Only toward midnight, after twelve hours of running amok, trundling the corpse about and dishonoring it, was Ozeri's body returned to the Jewish cemetery in Hebron and interred there.[72] Two months after the funeral an army unit entered Plot 26 and dismantled the outpost there. On the subsequent nights the settlers returned and tried to recapture the plot, but each time the soldiers came back and dismantled the tents they had pitched and ejected them.[73] For one moment of glory, the idyll of the collaboration between the army and the settlers was broken.

6

Complicity

"Somewhere in the Valley, riflemen on horseback in the paths of the orchards ensure that all will bloom and thrive. . . . Somewhere in the Valley a settlement erupts that will guard the line. . . . There is no fear in hearts here but only great pride . . . because soldiers are singing and the Valley replies, safe through the night and the melody is fine."[1] At the beginning of the 1970s nobody saw anything wrong with the words "a settlement erupts that will guard the line" or "soldiers are singing and the Valley replies." The people was the army and the army was the people. The territories of the West Bank were considered a valuable security asset—a barrier between Israeli population centers and "the eastern front."

Government member Israel Galili, one of the heads of the Labor movement and a shaper of the policy in the territories in the first years of the occupation, used a more prosaic phrase to describe the symbiotic connection between the army and the settlements. A founder of Kibbutz Na'an, which settled in 1930 on land close to the Arab town of Ramle, he said that "the combination and the alliance between settlement and security is a source of strength and a reciprocal blessing for the future as well." He promised that "in case of a sudden attack," the new settlements would be "the main force stopping the enemy on the first line of defending the country."² And indeed, the view of Jewish settlements as a shield for larger population centers and as a way of laying claim to land within the context of the more comprehensive territorial feud was not a new invention. It was born during the Arab Revolt of 1936–1939, and was known as "stockade and tower." The method was the establishment of a tiny settlement within a single day, surrounded by a stockade of wood and gravel, and in its center a wooden tower topped by a searchlight. Dozens of Jewish settlements were thus established especially along the contours of Arab population centers and integrated into the improvised defense system.

The use of a military installation for purposes of civilian settlement also went hand in hand with the security doctrine of Yigal Allon, the mythic commander of the Palmach in the pre-statehood years, and now the leading supporter in the government of settlement beyond the Green Line. Allon argued that "the integration of civilian settlement in the defense plan, especially for outlying locales and the vulnerable regions, will provide the state with permanent advance lookouts that save mobilized manpower and are able not only to warn of the start of a surprise attack from the enemy side but also to try to stop it, or at least to delay the enemy's progress until the army takes control of the situation."³ The "enemy" that Galili and Allon had in mind was the Arab armies beyond the eastern border—the ground forces of the Jordanian Legion, and perhaps even the Iraqi army, equipped with tanks and artillery. They were blind to the potential danger for Israel in the very fact of its presence in other people's territories. Their statements and their decisions did not take into account that Jewish settlements in the West Bank and Gaza would give rise to a new enemy from among the local population. The Palestinians seemed invisible.

Prime Minister Golda Meir's famous statement from late 1969

that "there is no Palestinian people" succinctly expressed the state of mind of the country's leadership, which believed that the West Bank Arabs would quickly adapt to the new foreign regime, just as in the past they had adapted to consecutive Ottoman, British, and Jordanian rule. "Enlightened occupation" was the euphemistic term that Israeli society created for its own self-deception. The flush of victory on three fronts of "a small people surrounded by enemies" blinded the political leadership and the military from seeing the problems inherent in the daily friction between the army of one people and the population of another people that still harbored memories of expulsion and previous occupation. Despite its being the term on everybody's lips and in the zeitgeist, postcolonialism was foreign to Israeli society and far from its concerns. Other models of occupation of foreign territories that had ended in withdrawal and left both occupier and occupied traumatized did not serve Israel as warnings. Only five years earlier, the defeated French colonialists had withdrawn from Algeria after more than 100 years of rule that had relied on the spears of soldiers and the *pieds noirs* militias.[4] A bloody war in an occupied territory and a deep rift at home, which had been the lot of the French and the Algerians, and the very idea of occupying a foreign people and taking over its lands, had been largely denied and repressed. A country that had only just ended eighteen years of military government over its Arab citizens in the Galilee and the middle of its eastern border (the so-called Triangle) was swept almost distractedly into the swamp of military rule in the West Bank and Gaza Strip. Whereas the military government in Israel had been a mechanism for the control of citizens, military rule in the territories was a mechanism aimed at dominating another people.

To complicate the missions of the security system even further, its functionaries were ordered to protect Israeli civilians who settled in the territories. The army and other security services were given a mission for which they were not intended. An army that is called "Defense Forces" and nurtures an ethos of defense and "wars of no choice" is not supposed to train its soldiers to defend trespassers who settle outside of the sovereign territory, with or without the government's blessing. Military service in the territories suddenly hurled soldiers into the bottomless abyss that separates occupation from democracy.

The first ambiguous signal from the government to the security forces that they were to view the settlers as allies was given on the eve of Passover 1968, when Levinger and a group of his followers demanded that General Uzi Narkiss, head of the Central Command, allow them to hold the Passover service and spend the night in the Jewish quarter of Hebron. "I don't care," said Narkiss. "I don't know anything. Rent a hotel, put up tents, I don't know. I don't know."[5] In these words the army commander, the official sovereign in the West Bank, which had been declared a military zone, already expressed the vacillating position of the state's leadership, its unwillingness to see, to hear, to know, and to assume responsibility. Like the top government echelon, the military top brass was not inclined to disappoint such fine Jews, who only wanted to celebrate a first Passover in the town of the Patriarchs. To the question from Knesset Member Uri Avnery on the matter of Jewish settlement in Hebron, Defense Minister Moshe Dayan replied that the Levinger group "had acted and is acting in accordance with orders that were issued by the military administration." When Avnery inquired as to whether the group had deceived the army when it depicted its stay in Hebron as one that would last forty-eight hours, Dayan said that he "did not look into people's innards." The military administration, said Dayan, had approved their request to recognize them as permanent residents of Hebron, on the basis of a government decision.[6]

The official reaction to the settlers' deception was a blunt signal to the military. Instead of expelling Levinger and his friends from Hebron, Dayan ordered that the group be hosted in the building of the military government. To the Knesset he confirmed that the army had given the group weapons for self-defense and that an officer had given its members training in the use of weapons at the administration head-quarters. This was done without the settlers' having been officially recognized as soldiers.[7] Thus, the secured military installation served the settlers as a base from which they could usurp new sites and served the army as a training school for developing a special relationship between the state and the illegal settlers. An order from the Military Administration to dismantle stands that the settlers had set up adjacent to the Mosque/Tomb of the Patriarchs was rescinded by the government.[8] The military command thus learned that politicians prefer to collaborate with those who appear to be Jewish patriots.

While the invasion of Hebron on Passover 1968 was getting the government's blessing, Allon proposed the establishment of two Nahal (agricultural-military) outposts of units in the Gaza Strip in the area of Nuseirat (which eventually became the settlements of Kfar Darom and Netzarim). "These settlements are of supreme importance to the political future of the Gaza Strip, because they split up the Strip south of Gaza City," said Allon. "There is great security importance in a Jewish presence in the heart of Gaza."[9] The two tiny outposts, which were established in 1970 and 1972, respectively, in the midst of one of the most densely populated areas in the world, eventually became rich, covetous settlements that were evacuated in a huge uproar in August 2005.

The Coordinator of Government Activities in the territories at that time, Colonel Shlomo Gazit, was among the few officers who dared to warn of the security danger inherent in plunging civilian

Jewish settlements into the heart of a large Palestinian population. At a very early meeting of the ministerial committee on settlement matters, which met under Allon's chairmanship on February 24, 1970, Gazit said that from the security perspective, "it would be a catastrophe to bring two settlements into the heart of the Gaza Strip."[10] At a further discussion held by the committee on June 2, Gazit stressed that "the two outposts aren't going to solve any problem there, but will certainly create such a problem. The reason we are favoring the establishment of settlements is political and psychological, above all—political." However, Gazit remained in a minority. With a rival in the figure of the head of the Southern Command, General Ariel Sharon, who had acquired for himself a reputation as an expert on security in the Gaza Strip since his appointment to the position in 1969, and who pressed for the establishment of the settlements, Gazit's assessment stood no chance.[11]

About twenty years later, out of the accumulated experience of prolonged occupation and the violent struggle it entails, and now as a man of politics, Sharon wrote with impressive clarity that only increases his responsibility. At this point, he wrote in his autobiography, "Gaza is our southern security belt." But "what will we do once we withdraw from Gaza and find, as we will inevitably, that Arafat or his successors have stepped in and that squads of terrorists are again operating from there into Israel, murdering and destroying? What will we do when the Katyusha fire starts hitting Sderot . . . and Ashkelon . . . and Kiryat Gat? . . . Will the television pictures showing us shelling Gaza in return be more palatable than those that showed us in front of Beirut, or less upsetting than those of Israeli troops battling West Bank rioters? Or what shall we do if multinational forces are positioned around Gaza and there is still terrorism? Shall we hit the Italians, or the British, or the Americans? . . . These are the times when we will face the real dilemmas. And how will we react? After all those years and all the fighting and all the struggles, what will we do? Institute a modern version of the paratrooper operations of the 1950s and the 1960s? Will we go immediately to war? What will happen?"[12]

He had partners, both from the right and from the left. The head of the Youth and Nahal department at the Defense Ministry, Moshe Netzer, was a Palmach and 1948 war veteran and the scion of a family of Mapai functionaries. Netzer, who had been commander of the battalion that evacuated Kfar Darom in that war, saw the establishment of the outpost as "the closing of a circle." At the dedication ceremony for the settlement, on November 30, 1970, Netzer noted that there was "a two-fold meaning to the settlement Kfar Darom. This is both an outpost and the renewal of a community. Stubbornness and faith have won."[13] The ethos of security associated with the settlements was so robust and the politicians' awe of the military, especially after the 1967 victory, was so profound that even the youth groups from the left (not to mention the right) encouraged their people to settle in the Jordan Valley and the Gaza Strip. In September 1972 another Nahal outpost, called Morag, was established in the southern Gaza Strip, this one near Khan Yunis. Eventually Morag was the first Nahal outpost in Gaza to become a civilian settlement.

Sharon's response to all the questions he posed was, and for many years remained, more settlements, more outposts, and more force. About to be demobilized and already with one big foot in politics, Sharon conducted in 1970–1971 an extensive and ferocious operation to "cleanse" the Gaza Strip of terror. To this end, thousands of Bedouins who lived in tents and permanent structures in the Rafah Salient area in the northern Sinai were expelled from their land. In a most unexpected act, these wretched people petitioned the High Court of Justice, and the state needed the approval of senior military people to legitimize the deportation.[14] In his official testimony, Major General Yisrael Tal stated that security needs necessitated the isolation of access routes to the Gaza Strip and the creation of partition zones that would be an "area vacated of the routine life of humans and animals."[15] But very quickly, this empty area throbbed with the activity and daily movement of Jewish-Israelis and their animals. The lands were confiscated from the Arabs and a Jewish city, Yamit, was established there, which had already been on the drawing board at the very time when Major General Tal was promising the High Court of Justice that the place would be totally empty (for elaboration see Chapter 7).

Along with the settlements in Gaza, one after another Nahal outpost arose in the Jordan Valley, and in short order they were populated with civilians. Most of them bore the names of soldiers and commanders who had been killed in clashes with Palestinian insurgents in the area, evidence of the blood tie that bound the settlements and the army. Security and settlement became a single ethos, and the soldiers and the settlers, one flesh. All of these settlements still exist at the time of writing, although some are barely surviving. In 2000 there were 164 people living in Argaman; in Massua, 148; and about the same number in Ro'i. In that same year, there were 100 people living at Gittit.[16] "The army is here to serve you. This is the purpose after 2,000 years. Go forth to this land and inherit it," Palmach veteran Major General Rehavam Ze'evi promised the settlers in the Jordan Valley. He congratulated the first Nahal soldiers who had completed their military-civilian service and drove a permanent stake in the outpost. "You will establish a home and the IDF will protect you," he said. To the security myth the senior officer added the "historical Jewish mission" of the settlers. When the first baby daughter was born to Valley settlers, Ze'evi's helicopter landed next to the home of the new mother and the major general emerged bearing a large yellow teddy bear, which became his traditional gift to the newborns of the Valley. "Be fruitful and multiply, because this land is for your seed," Ze'evi exhorted the first settlers. He also took credit for the Hebrew names that were given to all the settlements that were established there in the 1970s.

While the ties with the army were becoming more binding and the security belt around the settlements was expanding, the settlers tried to free themselves of the army's patronage and live a full and routinely civilian life. In September 1977, four months after the political upheaval and the ascent to power of Menachem Begin and his party, the heads of Gush Emunim presented their plan for establishing twelve new settlements in the West Bank. The new prime minister and Agriculture Minister Ariel Sharon, who headed the ministerial committee for settlement matters, feared American disapproval and suggested that the settlements be disguised as military outposts and that the settlers from the Gush be inducted as soldiers. The Gush heads rejected the proposal "with a sense of burning insult" and called it "bad and demeaning, harmful to settlement and injurious to the honor of the government and the people." One of them ironically proposed "that the government see to the provision of suitable military uniforms for the group of pregnant women . . . and that the IDF be instructed to produce military diapers embroidered with the IDF tags, to clad the babies of the settler families."[17]

Sharon softened the settlers' opposition by promising that civilians willing to settle in military camps would be granted the status of "employees on behalf of the army." Attorney General Aharon Barak legally sealed this bizarre initiative and explained to the new ministers that the settlers who lived in military camp would be employed "in accordance with needs" on behalf of the army. The attorney general, a law professor who later became the president of the Supreme Court, promised that this would not break the Military Jurisdiction Law. The government approved the arrangement on October 2, 1977.[18] Six military camps were designated for hosting the settlers of Gush Emunim. It was further agreed that three new settlements would be established, which would be based on Gush Emunim settlement groups—Tapuah, Karnei Shomron, and Shiloh—and the establishment of the settlement of Yattir in the southern Hebron Hills was also approved.[19] "With great chagrin" the Gush people accepted the compromise, which they saw as "a humiliating arrangement."[20] It was not long before these camps, too, became legitimate civilian settlements.

Uniforms and Suits

The double role, of military commander and politician-to-be, that Major Generals Sharon and Ze'evi played in the matter of the settlements was a milestone in the blurring of the lines between the army, politics, and settlement in the occupied territories. This powerful combination was joined by the law, to which we shall turn in the next chapter. As in the case of the confiscation of Bedouin lands in the Rafah Salient, other senior officers mustered to grab (or "redeem," in the Zionist discourse) Arab lands in the West Bank. In response to a November 1978 petition filed by Palestinians, whose land was confiscated to erect on it the settlement of Beit El, Major General Avraham Orly, the coordinator of government activities in the territories, asserted in a sworn statement submitted to the High Court of Justice that the confiscation was "part of the government's security perception that bases the defense system *inter alia* on Jewish settlements."[21] As though nothing had changed since the "tower and stockade" days of the 1930s and '40s, the senior officer explained that the settlements were planted for purposes of presence, domination, and surveillance. As though it had not been just eleven years since Israel's formidable army had defeated the Jordanian legions in less than a week and pushed them back to the other side of the river, the major general declaimed that "the importance of these settlements is overwhelming especially in times of war, when the regular army forces are transferred from their bases, usually, for purposes of operational activity." Five years after the Yom Kippur War, when the false claim about the security settlements was exposed, when civilian settlements were evacuated under fire in the Golan Heights, the major general said that the settlements are "the main element of security presence and control in the areas where they are located."[22]

The public statements and opinions of military experts, which were presented as thoroughly professional and free of ideological leanings or political bias, played a decisive role in instilling the perception that the settlements were a strategic asset of the first order. They also led astray the Supreme Court, which was keen to accept them. The president of the bench, Justice Moshe Landau, ruled that the army's position was sincere and did not "camouflage other views."[23] When, half a year later, other Palestinians petitioned the High Court of Justice, against the intention to establish the settlement of Elon Moreh on their confiscated lands, the story developed differently.[24] Although the army chief of staff provided security justifications (contrary to the defense minister's opinions) and pulled the Zionist security doctrine of the 1930s out of the archive, this time military experts of equal reputation appeared on the other side and overturned the professional opinions of their predecessors, questioning the myth of "security needs."[25] Former chief of staff Haim Bar-Lev declared that the settlement at Elon Moreh, located in the heart of a dense Arab population, would only hinder security interests. Major General (res.) Matityahu Peled stated that the security argument was "made for one purpose only: to provide a justification for a takeover of land that could not be justified in any other way."[26] Yigal Yadin, a former chief of staff who was deputy prime minister, and Defense Minister Ezer Weizman gave ample hints to disperse doubts regarding their positions on the security necessity of the settlements in Samaria.[27]

The sparring of the generals, those in active service and those retired, in the guise of pure professionalism, was essentially political. The majority of them already held top positions in politics, or were on their way there. Their security views overlapped their political ones and their position on the political spectrum. The settlers, however, for whose sake this debate was taking place, did not remain idle. Just as they had already done in Hebron, they entered the interstices between the army and politics, detecting weak points in the political configuration, enlisting officers sympathetic to their cause as character witnesses while abusing commanders who dared to insist on their own views. Conversely, the military people observed the settlers' closeness to the politicians' ears and their capacity for contributing to their ascent in the army's hierarchy and beyond.[28] They came to know that sticking to the law and General Staff orders was not necessarily the key to a successful military career.

The politicization of the territories drew in the commanders in the field, who began to talk politics and act politically. The Central Command, the most "political" of the commands, which controlled the West Bank, was usually put into the hands of commanders who were considered "politicians," officers blessed with the ability to tiptoe between the raindrops.[29] Moreover, with the transformation of the settlement project into a decidedly political enterprise, the command acquired the reputation of an academy for military and civilian politics. Four of the six officers who became chiefs of staff between

1983 and 2002 passed through Central Command headquarters along the way.[30] Shaul Mofaz, who was appointed chief of staff in 1998, had previously commanded the Judea and Samaria Division and was noted as someone "who knew how to talk to settlers in the right language."[31] From there he went to the chief of staff's bureau, and shortly after he was demobilized, he was appointed defense minister, joined the leadership of the Likud Party, and later of Sharon's Kadima Party.

The list of generals of the Central Command and heads of the Civil Administration who came into political positions is even longer: Rehavam Ze'evi founded the Moledet (Homeland) Party and was a member of governments of the right; Ehud Barak reached the position of prime minister; Yitzhak Mordechai was appointed defense minister in Netanyahu's government in the late 1990s and was later elected head of the short-lived Center Party, and with Amnon Lipkin-Shahak was brought into the Barak government's cabinet; Amram Mitzna was elected mayor of Haifa and later chairman of the Labor Party and served in the Knesset on its behalf; Ori Orr, who was also the head of Central Command, was appointed defense minister on behalf of the Labor Party; Dani Yatom, who took up the position in March 1991, served as head of the Mossad, a decidedly political appointment, and served as Prime Minister Ehud Barak's bureau chief and as a Labor member of the Knesset; Binyamin Ben-Eliezer, who commanded military forces in the Judea and Samaria region, was elected chairman of the Labor Party, was a minister in various governments and defense minister in the unity government headed by Sharon; Ephraim Sneh, head of the Civil Administration, also attained a ministerial position in that same government and became a leader of the Labor Party.

From Defense to Attack

The first instance in which the army was entangled in a violent clash between settlers and the government occurred with the first settlement attempt by the Elon Moreh group on June 7, 1974, four days after Yitzhak Rabin put together a government on the ruins of Golda Meir's. Two days earlier a small group of people tried to settle at Hawara Hill, near Nablus, not far from an army training base. The settlers decided to test the determination of the new prime minister and Defense Minister Shimon Peres. The military received the evacuation order after Rabbi Zvi Yehudah Kook rejected a compromise along the lines of the Jewish Quarter in Hebron—to transfer the settlers temporarily to a nearby military camp. Army officers were surprised to encounter at the contested site the new Knesset Member Ariel Sharon. The lionized Yom Kippur War general, who had previously aligned himself with the settlers' cause, and who had now come to express his solidarity, argued with the senior officers. This is "a matter of higher politics," he said, in which the army has no authority to intervene. During the course of the evacuation, Sharon debated with soldiers, shoved them, and shouted at them. "Would you, as a commander in the IDF, have wanted your soldiers to refuse to obey an order?" a private asked the major general. "It is you who should be ashamed of yourselves. I would never have demanded the perpetration of such a deed," replied Sharon.[32]

The head of the command, Yona Efrat, still innocent concerning relations between the settlers and politics, contacted Prime Minister Rabin and reported on the problems that Sharon was causing at the scene. Less than ten years later, that same officer was a member of the Kahan Commission, which investigated the 1982 massacre at the Palestinian refugee camps of Sabra and Shatila in Beirut. The commission determined that Sharon bore both "indirect responsibility" and "personal responsibility" and was not fit to serve as defense minister. In August 1976, Efrat was also involved in another violent confrontation with settlers, this time in Hebron. In protest against the command's order prohibiting Jews from praying at the Tomb of the Patriarchs during the Muslim holiday of Id al Fitr, Moshe Levinger tore up the military order and together with other settlers shut himself into his home in Hebron. Other settlers surrounded the house, cursed the major general and poured water on him. Gush Emunim, of which Levinger was a founder and a leader, did condemn the act and placed the blame on the politicians,[33] but Levinger and his friends never desisted.

The Elon Moreh group did not give up, continuing its demonstrative attempts to settle its clashes with the army and the government. Not far from Hawara Hill, at the old railroad station at Sebastia, the military once again had to deal with illegal settlers. Chief of Staff Mordechai (Motta) Gur was not eager to carry out Prime Minister Rabin's instructions to evacuate the squatters. Rabin testified that Gur had said to him that it would take thousands of soldiers to evacuate the Sebastia demonstrators.[34] Gur also warned the government that Gush Emunim was not "just a body that breaks discipline, but rather a serious social and political movement," and that "against a thing like this, an army isn't deployed." According to one testimony, Gur said to Rabin: "How do you want to stop them, with battalions? By calling them names? . . . If you want to win, don't turn Nahal outposts into civilian settlements once every five years. Put up a settlement overnight and be done with it."[35]

The violent clash between soldiers and settlers, a nightmare for every politician, pushed Rabin into the famous Sebastia compromise. The chief of staff himself arrived at the site and tried to appeal to the settlers to leave voluntarily. "IDF soldiers, welcome to Elon Moreh. Follow orders but with sensitivity and a Jewish heart," a settler rabbi called out to Gur and the soldiers who were with him. "We hope to see you after you are demobilized from the IDF, on this side of the barrier." The chief of staff announced that "the evacuation will be implemented without the use of force. These were the orders I gave the soldiers."[36] After the chief of staff's pleas were rejected by the settlers, the soldiers picked them up and carried them away without violence. Thus the pattern of relations between settlers and soldiers was shaped in Sebastia: outflanking the army and disobeying its orders on the way to the destination, a prolonged struggle on the ground while negotiating with the authorities, and evacuation accompanied by passive resistance that sometimes degenerates into bodily harm.[37] These kinds of ceremonial, almost ritual, clashes, in which each side played its foreknown role, and which rendered service to both parties, characterized army-settler relations for more than thirty years, up to the most recent events in Gaza and Amona.

The settlers saw the territories as their domain and themselves as its lords. Officers who were unable to adapt to the settlers' lordship and did not see the nurturing of their sacred project as a key element in their military role were tagged as "leftists," as "defilers of Israel." The deterioration of the military situation in the territories, especially in the area of Hebron, and the violent clashes between the military and the rightist people who barricaded themselves at Yamit in 1982 appeared to erode the serene relations between the settlers and the army. The settlers' complaints about the military's "powerlessness" and their demands for a "free hand" in the struggle against "hostile" neighbors increased. In a letter to Prime Minister Begin, the settler heads called the Israeli soldiers "scarecrows in uniform" and "chocolate soldiers."[38] They did not confine themselves to condemnations but demanded that the government take steps against allegedly lax commanders, chief among them the head of Central Command, Ori

Orr. Orr, who eventually made his way into the Labor Party, was not indifferent to the settlers' attacks. In the wake of a series of incidents in which settlers opened fire on Palestinian civilians, he offered a defense brief for the settlers. "They are not bloodthirsty, and killing Arabs does not serve their interests," said Orr. He admitted that "there have been several unpleasant incidents" but noted that he met frequently with the settler heads and that "we are very strict about the briefings on the use of the IDF weapons in their possession." He also explained that "it is only natural that some of them [the settlers] are not very patient."[39] At the ceremony for the changing of commanders at the Central Command in May 1987, the outgoing major general, Ehud Barak, said that at the end of twenty years of Israeli rule the Palestinians are liable to "rise up" against the "occupation." The settler heads immediately cried out against the use of the word "occupation" and stalked out of the hall angrily. "Now that twenty years have gone by since the liberation of Jerusalem and the IDF takeover of Judea and Samaria," Barak corrected himself on the spot.[40]

A Palestinian uprising did indeed break out half a year later. The comprehensive civil insurrection of the Palestinians, which put an end to "the enlightened occupation," began a new chapter in the settlers' relations with the army. The settlers complained about the new chief of staff, Dan Shomron, who had distributed to the officers of the General Staff Alistair Horne's book *A Savage War of Peace: Algeria 1954–1972*, about the Algerians' fight to liberate their country from French occupation and about France's withdrawal. Ironically, it was the Defense Ministry publishing house that had seen to translating the book into Hebrew and publishing it.[41] The settlers charged that Shomron's statement to the effect that Israel could impose order and stability on the territories only at the price of starving and deporting the Palestinian population expressed "defeatism and politicization in the top echelons of the army." Knesset members from the Likud called for a thorough "purge" of the higher command of the army and other security branches.[42] In a Knesset debate in April 1989, army commanders were called "kapos."[43]

The first confrontation between Major General Amram Mitzna, head of the Central Command, and the settlers took place in 1987, after he took up the command following a rampage by settlers in the Deheishe refugee camp near Bethlehem. The commander of a reserve battalion who tried to block the rioting settlers was violently attacked. One of the settlers hit the officer and flung himself down on him to enable his armed friends to penetrate the camp. Another settler choked the battalion commander as his friends fired on camp houses and their inhabitants. The indictment against the settler-rioters stated that in their retreat they trampled one of the soldiers.[44] Mitzna came to the camp the following day to express his regret for the deed and to condemn it. "In Deheishe there has been a hideous, unparalleled deed," said Mitzna. The head of the Kiryat Arba council, Zvi Katzover, paid him back. "This leftist kibbutznik is a liar who makes false accusations." Levinger declared a boycott of the commander.[45] Even if only symbolic, this declaration damaged Mitzna's whole tenure. The Deheishe case was a formative event in Mitzna's period in the command, but it paled in comparison with what the settlers did later. And indeed, upon his retirement from military service, Mitzna noted that the rampage in the refugee camp was dwarfed by the settlers' actions against the Palestinians during the first intifada.[46] Every time they deemed that the army was sparing the rod from the insurgent Palestinians, the settlers took it up. At the beginning of 1989 the military prevented settlers from Ma'aleh Adumim from "imposing order" in the village of Azaria near Jerusalem. The settlers grabbed the area commander's firearm and tried to thrash him.[47]

While leftist circles attacked Mitzna for his strong-arm policy against the Palestinians, the settlers complained that his policy was too soft. The "leftist" label, which he had acquired after publicly demanding the resignation of Defense Minister Ariel Sharon in the wake of the Lebanon War in 1982, was not of great help to him among the settlers. At the funeral of Tirtza Porat, who was shot and killed on a Passover hike in 1988 by one of the settler guards who accompanied the youth, Mitzna was fiercely attacked. The introverted commander who came to pay his respects to the dead girl was blamed for her death and the army's alleged laxness. Despite the criticism and insults that were directed at him, Mitzna learned the hard way that if he wanted to survive and succeed in his task he would have to make an effort to appease the settler population. He claimed in a meeting with representatives of the kibbutz movement that there is "full cooperation and [mutual] satisfaction" between the security forces and the settlers.[48] Like all the senior commanders who experienced the "special relationship" with the settlers, Mitzna made an effort to emphasize the mutual respect and understanding and dismissed claims that his term in the command came to its end under pressure from the settlers and the right wing in the government.[49]

The next head of the Central Command, Yitzhak Mordechai, won enthusiastic praise with his retirement in March 1991. Benny Katzover congratulated the major general "on behalf of 100,000 inhabitants of Judea and Samaria, of them 20,000 who came during his period [as commander] and largely thanks to him."[50] The settlers were pleased with Mordechai's moves and with the prolonged curfew and tight closure he imposed on the Palestinians, and in return they complied to some extent with his request to act with restraint. The more social visits he made to the settlements, the fewer violent incursions by settlers into Palestinian areas. Public attacks on the army's "impotence" also decreased.[51] In a discussion with officers about securing the buses that took the children of Elon Moreh to school, the head of the command reprimanded the officers in the presence of settler Benny Katzover. "I am not prepared to hear any more about incidents of rioters beating children before your eyes," he said. "Every soldier who does not react will face trial." Within two days, said Katzover, "the whole situation changed."[52]

Relations with the military commanders were fluid and changed frequently, and it depended on settlers' satisfaction with the officers' obedience to their commands. Chief of Staff Ehud Barak's refusal to accede to Gush Emunim's demand to hold the traditional "Samaria march" sufficed to turn him into a target for attacks and crude threats. The chief of staff's explanation that protecting the marchers would compel the army to divert essential units from fighting the intifada brought upon him curses and assurances that the Gush would not rest until it "eliminated him [Barak]."[53] The Gush declared that "the chief of staff has finished his career. We have marked him and he will have such a long tail that he won't be able to move."[54] In response, left-wing Knesset member Yossi Sarid called the Gush "a mafia that has put out a contract on the chief of staff" and noted that this was not the first time that "the gangsters have threatened the IDF and its soldiers."[55] Three years later, thanks to his reservations about the Oslo agreement, Barak was the guest of honor at a ceremony in celebration of Jerusalem Liberation Day at the Merkaz HaRav Yeshiva in Jerusalem, and was greeted there with the respect reserved for admired rabbis or obedient leaders of the country.[56] Only ten weeks earlier, in the wake of reports of the intention to evacuate the Tel Rumeida settlement in Hebron in response to Baruch Goldstein's massacre of Palestinians while they were praying, the heads of the yeshiva had called upon Israeli soldiers to disobey the chief of staff's orders.

The symbiosis between the army and the settlers, which went awry in the days of Amram Mitzna and improved greatly in Yitzhak Mordechai's time, became in the days of his successor, Dani Yatom—the days of a government of the right—nearly perfect.[57] Yatom expanded the custom of courtesy visits to the settlers. His direct telephone number was listed in the Yesha Council heads' address books. He knew how to give them the feeling that he was there for them and how to shower them with gestures of intimacy and trust. Settlers' complaints about leniency toward the Palestinians were met by invitations of the commander to visit the command's special force unit. They were thrilled.[58] Yatom supported the establishment of a civil guard in the settlements. He increased the integrations of the settlers into the area defense units and helped them in civilian matters that are not in the jurisdiction of the command. In this way he successfully aimed at the opinion of the government level and of the minister to whom he was subordinate, Likud member Moshe Arens. On the eve of Independence Day 1992, Yatom was presented with a "Yesha faithful" award at a formal ceremony and in the presence of the defense minister and Prime Minister Yitzhak Shamir. Together with him, his colleague Major General Matan Vilnai, the head of the Southern Command, also received the award. Both men later became Knesset members on behalf of the Labor Party.

The Oslo Siege

With the Rabin government's signing of the Oslo agreement in September 1993, the head of the Kiryat Arba council, Zvi Katzover, hinted to Major General Ilan Biran, who had been given the Central Command during that stormy period, that he expected the army commanders to rebel against the government. "During the war in Lebanon two senior military people arose and said to the government, 'We are not prepared to participate in this game,'"[59] said the veteran settler, referring to Mitzna and Colonel Eli Geva, whose military career was consequently truncated. In a newspaper interview Katzover noted that during World War II, France's Marshal Philippe Pétain had also been an officer in uniform, a fact that did not prevent him from being tried for treason.[60] The analogy to collaborators with the Third Reich and the Nazi regime was reiterated by Elyakim Haetzni. "In Hitler's Germany there were officers who understood that their government was leading the German people to destruction and they rose up, set aside their emblems of rank and paid for this with their lives," he said to Major General Biran. "You are behaving like a defeated army that is on its way out. . . . In the Arabs' eyes, the lion is dead and they are now dancing on its grave. . . . There is a military echelon of senior officers that cannot deny responsibility. When political regimes are called to justice for their crimes, the generals who collaborated with them also bear responsibility."[61] Certainly Biran was not the settlers' dream incarnated, as he was not fulfilling all their demands. At a meeting of the Yesha Council he had to listen to a twenty-minute speech full of barbs from Moshe Levinger.[62] The tension with Biran reached its peak in the spring of 1995, in the midst of the Palestinian terror attacks and the protest actions at home against Rabin's government. It erupted during a meeting with the heads of the Yesha Council, this time in the wake of a terror attack at the Glass Junction near Hebron, in which two settlers were shot and killed. "You are in a trap, your hands are tied, you can't do anything," Ze'ev Hever, a member of the Jewish terror organization, said to the military commander. "There was a time when they let you punish, blow up houses, impose collective punishments. The soldiers' motivation is verging on zero and none of you is getting up and crying out the truth in the face of the government level."[63]

The settlers' protest came from various directions and levels. When the head of the Kiryat Arba council protested the head of the command's refusal to approve the holding of a rally and assemblies in Kiryat Arba and Hebron, as compared to his "lenience towards a Hamas rally," Biran was not deterred and fought back.[64] "Take a walk every night, before you go to sleep, to the expanses of 'Judea,' and look around at every soldier and patrol, and understand what they are doing. Get it into your head that it is thanks to them that you exist, and despite your behavior they will continue to fight with endless will of sacrifice. Return home from your outing, if you do this, and in the haven of your family remember that they are still awake and thanks to them you exist, and also sleep securely. And I too will continue, and even more concertedly, to protect Kiryat Arba and I will not settle accounts with you," Biran wrote.[65] The Hebron settlers gave Biran's letter to the media, accompanied by a message to the major general, "who should know that his military career will end here."[66]

A few months later, in response to Levinger's charges that the settlers had been abandoned at peril to their lives and were not getting any protection against terror attacks, the army's spokesperson made public the fact that because of death threats directed at Levinger, the Hebron rabbi had for years been assigned three soldiers in civilian clothing to serve as his bodyguards around the clock. It was also made public that the army had put a car and a driver at his disposal.[67] Yet these reports were transient creaks in the relations between the army and the settlers. For the most part the military establishment refrained from reacting to the scorn and insults heaped on its people by the settlers. The dispute with Biran ended, as usual, in a public reconciliation between the major general and the settlers, but the command was to be his last stop in his military service.[68]

The second Oslo agreement, which was signed in Washington on

September 28, 1995, and divided the West Bank into three areas, removed from the Israeli army the control of the urban areas but increased the burden of protecting the settlements. The military, which was not a partner to the secret negotiations, had reservations about the agreement's security provisions. The army demanded that the government add more and more territories for purposes of paving bypass roads and "corridors" that would separate the settlements from the Palestinian population. The comprehensive protection envelope for the settlements was called, in the best euphemistic tradition, "the line of security elements" and included, in addition to a fence, routes and lighting. Initially, at the instructions of Attorney General Michael Ben-Yair, the "security line" was drawn at a maximum distance of twenty-five meters (eighty-two feet) from the outermost house in a settlement. This decision was contrary to Major General Biran's demand that the line run at double that distance. Prime Minister and Defense Minister Rabin opposed the spread of the settlements in this way, at the expense of lands cultivated by Palestinians.[69] Gradually but quickly it stretched. Under Attorney General Elyakim Rubinstein, the "security line" was moved to a distance of fifty meters, and during the course of the second intifada, it was stretched to a distance of 400 meters (one-quarter of a mile) from the outermost house in a settlement. The meaning of this was the annexation "for security reasons" of thousands of dunams of Palestinian lands for purposes of expanding the area of the settlements.

Rabin believed that the bypass roads would reduce the friction between the settlers and the Palestinians and was willing to allocate huge resources to them. However, he instructed the people in the field to budget and pave roads that would connect the settlements to the Green Line only along the shortest and most economical route. He aimed at avoiding too many roads connecting settlements that, in his

view, were to be evacuated in a permanent-status agreement.[70] The settlers did not give up, however, and persuaded the prime minister to
visit the territory and see with his own eyes the meaning of his decision. Rabin did not change his mind. He resisted the settlers' demands
to enter Palestinian territory and refused to approve the paving of
other bypass roads.[71] Council head Pinchas Wallerstein also stood his
ground. Under the watchful eye of the army and with council
money—with state funds, that is—in broad daylight the settlers
paved a pirate asphalt road twelve kilometers (7.5 miles) long. It was
paved without the authorization of planning bodies and lacked minimal safety features. Some portions of the road traversed Area B,
which was under the civil authority of the Palestinians. The military
reported to Rabin about the paving of the wildcat road, defined it as
"unsafe for driving," and left it at that. As compensation for a fatal
attack on a settler vehicle that was traveling along this pirated and perilous road, some of the area of the Beit El military camp was transferred to the settlement itself for purposes of its expansion. At the
site a new neighborhood was established and named Maoz Tzur, a
memorial to those who were killed in the terror attack. Wallerstein,
who boasted of his "especially good" connections with the army
commanders in the region, related that during the period of the
1990s Labor government his personnel blazed at his instructions
dozens of dirt roads between settlements and that the military and
the Public Works Department later approved some of them,
anointing them with steamrollers and tar.[72]

Between reprimand and condemnation, the settlers requited the
officers for their good work. In the fall of 1998, a few months after
Moshe Ya'alon was appointed head of the Central Command, his
headquarters chief, in consultation with Wallerstein, who was chairman
of the Yesha Council at the time, decided to hold a "salute" to the

settlers. They saw the event as "an additional move by the new region commander to strengthen the trust between the settlers and the army."[73] Ya'alon said that he "definitely understands their [the settlers'] feelings; after all, in the existing situation they are the most threatened population in the region."[74] In order to clarify his own leanings, Ya'alon's successor, Moshe Kaplinsky, promised that even though he knew "that there is no precedent for this in the world," he would "prove that terror has a military and not a diplomatic solution."[75] But a single terror attack sufficed for the new commander to be transferred by the settlers from the friend's niche to the foe's niche. Following an attack in November 2002 by terrorists on the worshipers' route in Hebron, between Kiryat Arba and the Tomb/Mosque, in which twelve people were killed, among them the commander of the Hebron Brigade and three members of the Kiryat Arba alert squad, they hung placards beside Kaplinsky's home calling for his removal. The placards said, "Fire Major General Kaplinsky, the GOC of the extreme left, who exploits his authority in order to persecute Jews for their opinions instead of dealing with Arab terror."[76] Defense Minister Shaul Mofaz hastened to placate the settlers. He ordered that a military funeral be held for the civilians, members of the Kiryat Arba alert squad, and that a burial plot be allocated for them at the military cemetery at Mount Herzl in Jerusalem. After their death, these illegal settlers were "dressed" in reserve uniforms, and were granted all the rights accorded to soldiers who fall in battle.[77]

The heroism of the settlers—women and men who chose to settle in the heart of an occupied and hostile population outside the borders of the sovereign State of Israel, and in so doing to endanger their children's lives—was a central motif in the speeches of leaders of the military. Two months in his post gave Major General Kaplinsky enough evidence to declare the settlers "the real heroes of the current war." He said this to the settler leaders who accompanied him while he was touring the Binyamin area, which is known for its many pirate settlements established on privately owned Palestinian lands and for the harassment by settlers and brutal "hilltop youth" (the euphemistic term given in the Israeli discourse to the second generation of settlers) of local farmers, especially olive harvesters.[78]

In the spring of 2004, in the throes of the severe clash between Prime Minister Sharon and the Yesha Council over the prime minister's plan to evacuate the Gaza Strip settlements and a few in the northern West Bank, Chief of Staff Ya'alon participated in a large event under the heading "Yesha Settlers Say Thank You and Salute the IDF, the Security Forces and the Alert Squads." Alongside President Moshe Katsav sat the heads of the Central, Southern, and Home Front Commands. Government ministers mingled with Yesha Council heads and settlers rubbed shoulders with Knesset members. From the stage the chief of staff declared that the "mutual connection between the people and the army—one of the most important sources of our strength—is expressed here this evening in a way which there is none greater."[79]

The Settler Administration

One of the first decisions taken by Ariel Sharon upon becoming defense minister in 1981 was to erect a barrier between the classical mission of the Israeli army—defending the security and welfare of the citizens of the State of Israel—and its responsibility, in its capacity as the sovereign in the territories, to see to the needs of the Palestinian population under Israel's rule. For the latter he established the Civil Administration, a replacement for the Military Administration, which until that time had been delegated both tasks. The head of the administration was subordinated to the Coordinator of Activities in the Territories, a civilian security entity, which was headed by a senior officer who reported directly to the defense minister. In the job definition, the head of the Civil Administration was responsible for the military governors in the various districts and for the "desk officers" who represented the various government ministries. These officers were responsible for the departments of health, education, welfare, infrastructures, and the other needs of the population of the territories. Their decisions were a crucial influence on the Palestinians' daily lives. Since many settlers were part of the administration in charge of the territories, their constant pressures to expand their living space deep into the territories quickly pushed the Civil Administration into the heart of the conflict. Because of the situation in which they functioned, the commitment of the Civil Administration officers and their subordinates, like that of the Military Administration officers before them, was first and foremost to those who sent them and not to those who were under their responsibility. Both army officers and civilian bureaucrats discovered that in anything having to do with contentions between the settlers and the Palestinians about control of the area and competition over resources, Israeli politicians not only did not concern themselves with the needs of the local population but also worked hand in hand with those who infringed on Palestinians' rights. The security, property, welfare, and religious needs of the settlers always took priority over those of the Palestinians. The military command viewed the Civil Administration "with something of a squint . . . because what did military people have to do with matters like sewage, education or the transportation of cancer patients from the West Bank to hospitals in Israel," wrote journalist Amos Harel.[80]

The slackening and often the total evaporation of the political barrier to the settlers' takeover of more lands brought the most sensitive issue of Jewish construction in the territories into the hands of the Civil Administration. The physical planning authority in the West

Bank was delegated solely to one single planning commission—the Supreme Planning Commission, which was housed at the Civil Administration headquarters adjacent to the settlement of Beit El. This commission replaced the regional and local planning commissions that approve master plans and construction within Israel. Planning and construction activity in the territories is conducted under the Jordanian planning and building laws that had been applicable in the area in 1967. Military orders from the head of the Central Command adapted Jordanian law to the army's needs and the development needs of the settlements. The idiosyncratic procedures rendered omnipotent the members of the planning commission—officers and midlevel civilian employees of the army. The authority they had was greater than the interior minister's authority with respect to master plans inside the Green Line. The subcommittee on settlement at the Supreme Planning Commission was supposed to make certain that construction in the area was conducted in accordance with the accepted rules of planning and aesthetics. In fact, the commission focused on approving master plans and building permits for the settlements and did nothing to develop the area for the benefit of the Palestinian population.[81]

The settlers expected that the Civil Administration, in all its levels and branches, would complete the work of the government and the judiciary, which legitimized the seizure of lands for the settlements (see Chapter 7). In their view, this was never a question of confiscating Arab lands but rather the restoration of lost lands to their legal owners from the dawn of time. It was appropriate, then, in their opinion, and only too natural that Jewish officers and civil servants responsible for enforcing the law cooperate with them, or at least not obstruct them. They evaluated an Israeli public servant by criteria such as "Are you with us or against us?" An administration officer who acted like a balanced, businesslike, and law-abiding governor was branded as a hostile Israeli and a flawed Jew. The story of Brigadier General Ephraim Sneh, one of the first in the Civil Administration and one of the few who refused to enlist in the settlers' whims, served as a lesson to his successors. In the summer of 1985, a short time after he took up his position, Sneh said at a meeting with settlers at Kfar Etzion that he had come to talk with them about policy and not about one detail or another. Settler Benny Katzover accused the military commander of creating "utter alienation from the Israeli public while concentrating totally on the Arab public needs," and charged that he was "causing damage to the State of Israel."[82] The settlers also accused Sneh of expanding Arab towns at the expense of state lands.[83] In blaming Brigadier General Sneh for "the moral decline of the Civil Administration," they demanded his dismissal.[84] In September 1987, a few months before the outbreak of the first intifada, Sneh left the Civil Administration command in Beit El because of serious disagreements with Shmuel Goren, the coordinator of activities in the territories.[85] Ironically, Goren, who was considered a friend of the settlers, admitted when he completed his service in 1991 that there was a contradiction between occupation and enlightenment. "Is there such a thing [as enlightened occupation]? You cannot play with slogans like that and have a military occupation."[86]

The abetting of the "land grab," by commission or omission, as documented by various human rights organizations, did not cease in the wake of the signing of the Oslo agreement.[87] As the threat to the settlers' project seemed to increase, so did their greed, and along with it the collaboration of officials in the Civil Administration. More than one hundred settlements were established after the signing of the second Oslo agreement in 1995, which transferred to the Palestinian Authority security and civil responsibility for Areas A and left overall responsibility for Areas C in Israel's hands.[88] A special State Comptroller's Report reveals that between 1996 and 1999—the years of Netanyahu's government—illegal construction and squatting on "state lands" occurred at no less than 170 sites. This criminal activity included the positioning of mobile homes, the building of temporary structures, and the breaking through of roads. More than 500 cases were filed for building infractions during that period, and that was the end of the matter. No legal process whatsoever took place.

According to the State Comptroller, during that period the settlers carried out an unprecedented land grab right under the nose of army commanders and Civil Administration officials. Without authorization, they paved no less than 126 roads totaling 179 kilometers (111 miles) throughout the West Bank. This was in addition to the dozens of bypass roads, totaling hundreds of kilometers, that were paved by the government after the army issued orders for the confiscation of lands from Palestinian inhabitants. The State Comptroller's document shows that the settlers systematically transformed the "security elements," and particularly the security roads, into a means of territorial expansion.[89] The comptroller found documentary evidence that the Civil Administration itself had, during the years of the Netanyahu government, "detected many cases in which they built settlements and security elements that deviated from plans that were approved by the proper authorities."[90]

By law, three separate authorizations are required for the moving of a mobile home and its positioning on the ground: a building permit, in accordance with the planning and building ordinances; an authorization from the owner of the land to position the mobile home; and a permit for the transport of the mobile home. Building and authorization permits must be obtained before the third, and all of them are subject to the procedures of the Central Command and the Civil Administration. Only the head of the infrastructure department at the Civil Administration, who is the exclusive authority for the issuance or denial of permission to move mobile homes to existing settlements or to new sites, is authorized to issue the third permit.[91] Positioning a mobile home in the territories without a building permit and the other authorizations is a transgression of the law. The state comptroller found that in 2000 defense minister's aide Yossi Vardi had authorized local councils in the territories and other bodies to move and position mobile homes without regulation of the statutory status of the lands where they were positioned and without the approval of the head of the infrastructure department at the Civil Administration. Vardi claimed that he had acted in accordance with instructions from the defense minister at the time, Binyamin Ben-Eliezer (Labor). He claimed that the defense minister's policy was "to approve requests for public needs, such as the addition of classrooms to educational institutions and buildings for religious purposes as a result of natural growth in the settlements." Before approving each request, he said, he confirmed at the Civil Administration that it conformed to the statutory basis. The defense minister himself evaded responsibility and refused to give his version to the state comptroller on the grounds that he did not "deal specifically" with the cases in question. He said that his "general policy" was that "actions that are not according to procedure should not be approved."[92]

With his successor, Defense Minister Shaul Mofaz, things became much simpler. Mofaz's deputy, Ron Schechner, had no hesitation at all about taking upon himself the responsibility for establishing settlements and outposts, saying to the comptroller that because of the sensitivity of the matter "it has been determined that the defense minister's aide, being thoroughly familiar with the minister's policy, will be the one to give final approval for the movement of mobile homes."[93] Schechner, a colonel in the reserves, a resident of the settlement of Yattir in the Hebron Hills, the holder of a key position in the settlements' area defense and in the settlement leadership, and someone with a definite interest in taking over lands, took upon himself, with official consent, the key task of the enforcer of law on pirate settlement. The fox was put in charge of the henhouse. He was the perfect miscegenation of politics, army, law, and settlement. Together with Meir Dagan, a major general in the reserves and eventually head of the Mossad, and with his neighbor in the settlement Colonel Moshe Hager, deputy commander of a reserve division and head of the paramilitary training unit in his settlement, Schechner plotted openly to thwart Barak's peace initiatives in 1999. Immediately thereafter he lobbied Barak for the legitimization of the unauthorized outposts. In 2004, after Sharon had announced his plan to evacuate the settlements in Gaza, Hager threatened that he and his cadets would fight to prevent any withdrawal, just as the Russians had fought at Stalingrad.[94] Hager visited Shas mentor Rabbi Ovadiah Yosef that summer in order to extract a rabbinical ruling against the disengagement plan and thus prevent "the reoccurrence of the disastrous silence of the rabbis during the Holocaust."[95]

Schechner was appointed to the post of the defense minister's aide for settlement affairs at the end of 2002. He did not need a break-in period to familiarize himself with the laws for koshering Jewish settlement in the territories. From the days when he served as head of the Hebron Hills regional council, and before that as director general of the settlement department of the World Zionist Organization, he brought with him a wealth of experience in navigating through the Civil Administration corridors and the maze of its laws and regulations. When he was security officer of the Yesha Council, Schechner made the acquaintance of the senior officers, and thus his web of connections stretched over the entire system. Schechner did not mislead the men in uniform with regard to the direction the new wind was blowing. In February 2003 he ordered the ministry to budget for seven unauthorized outposts, which he called "independent settlements in every respect" and which were also given a "settlement designation."[96] The December 2003 decision concerning the evacuation of several of those settlements did not deter him. "I deal with construction, and even within the destruction of today there is construction. . . . I don't deal with matters of the evacuation, period. . . . There are many frustrated Jews in the State of Israel and I am one of them," said Schechner. "Our starting point all along has been that in every place where there are Jews—the government has to see to their welfare."[97]

The military and the Civil Administration people could not withstand the political pressures, and in many cases they did not want to risk conflict with those who controlled their personal careers and promotions. The comptroller found that the Civil Administration had located most of the illegal squatting and building operations in the territories, and had even issued instructions to cease work and demolition orders. However, he added in his dry language, "in fact the Civil Administration, the IDF, and the police have not taken steps to implement these orders." In a letter dated May 20, 1997, which is cited in the State Comptroller's Report, Attorney General Elyakim Rubinstein wrote to the judge advocate general—the highest legal authority in the army—and to the head of the Central Command that "the phenomenon of Israeli settlements squatting on land in the area, which is taking on the character of breaking through roads, positioning mobile homes and erecting buildings—is increasing." Nine months later the attorney general again wrote to the same addressees and stated that since his previous letter, "the phenomenon has only increased."[98]

Three months after that, the attorney general wrote to the head of the Central Command for a third time. He stated unambiguously that the situation that prevailed in the territories with respect to building was damaging to the rule of law and in no uncertain terms informed the high-ranking army officer of the urgent need to evacuate squatter settlers from Palestinian lands, since only when the squat is fresh is forced evacuation possible. The fact that nothing was being done with regard to illegal construction, added the attorney general, enables the transgressor to claim that the state authorities procrastinated in their action and that therefore the demolition of the structure should not be allowed.[99]

In June 2003 Attorney General Rubinstein ordered the government ministries not to transfer budgets for activity, particularly construction activity, in illegal outposts. He went on to issue an admonition about the illegality of government activity in the territories, but the Civil Administration and the government ministries continued to ignore his warnings. It must be noted that this particular attorney general was close in his opinions to the settlers' outlook and usually forgiving toward government transgressions of the law. The fact that Rubinstein saw fit to warn again and again of the illegality of the government's activities in the territories is a testament to the extent to which Israel deviated from legal legitimacy in its conduct in the territories. A few weeks after he took up the position, in April 2004, the new attorney general, Menachem Mazuz, ordered the Housing Ministry to freeze illegal activity in the settlements. The instruction was issued on the eve of the expected publication of an additional report from the state comptroller that cautioned about the transfer of tens of millions of shekels from the Housing Ministry to illegal activity in the territories. Mazuz demanded a freeze on any transfer of funds pending the establishment of a suitable mechanism for preventing the money from going to illegal destinations, and he threatened to take steps against anyone who ignored his instructions.[100]

A Mobile's Journey

After a mobile home is smuggled in on the back of a semitrailer by side roads and positioned on a high hill, a generator is hooked up to it. Not many days go by before the generator is exchanged for a proper electricity installation. The only official authorized to approve the connection of an outpost to the electricity grid is the electricity desk officer at the Civil Administration, who acts on behalf of the defense minister. At the Israel Electric Company there was an order prohibiting "in principle and in practice" the connection of illegal outposts in the territories to the electricity grid. However, despite this prohibition, the defense minister would issue "exceptional permits" or "an instruction to advance procedures" to transform an "illegal outpost" into an "approved outpost," a procedure that enabled its connection to the grid. All defense ministers, including those from the Labor Party, were very generous in granting such permits.[101] The building of a *mikveh* (ritual bath) follows the connection to the electricity grid. Over the years the *mikvehs* have become an important milestone in the process of transforming illegal mobile homes into legal settlements. The settlers made it a practice to apply to the Civil Administration officers and explain to them that electricity is essential for operating the *mikveh*, and without a *mikveh* they are prevented from conducting intimate intercourse, which is a commandment written in the Torah. The whole process is told with a smug, unpleasant wink. The settler society and the military and civil administrators charged with their welfare are like an extended family. Brothers. They visit one another and share their joys and their moments of sorrow. The settlers are champions at endearing themselves to officers who can do right by them.[102]

Years of experience and the development of a recurrent pattern taught the senior commanders that sooner or later the political class would approve the new outpost, so they cooperated.[103] Shaul Arieli, who was during the 1990s the liaison man between the Civil Administration and the defense minister's bureau, testified as to the method: "The head of the infrastructure department at the Civil Administration, and the person responsible for the inspection unit, both of them settlers, systematically saw to turning a blind eye to their friends' building violations. The reports on illegal outposts always arrived late at the defense minister's bureau. This was a tacit conspiracy that was convenient for all sides, cooperation with a wink. By the time clear orders to enforce the law were issued, the army would let them slide because it did not believe that the government level would stand by it when it came to the test."[104]

Another senior officer, who refused to be identified by name, described the process of "koshering" the settlements as it takes place on the ground: "The people from the inspection unit of the Civil Administration report to the head of the Civil Administration on an illegal outpost; the head of the Civil Administration sends the information to the commanding officer; this officer forwards the hot potato to the defense minister's bureau; the defense minister's bureau requests the opinion of the deputy chief of staff; the deputy chief of staff lobs the list of illegal outposts to the chief of staff; the two of them request instructions from the defense minister; the defense minister convenes a meeting of everyone involved and declares that illegal construction must not be permitted in the territories; the invitees depart and the minister remains in his bureau with the deputy for settlement matters and the chief of staff. While the commanding officer and the head of the Civil Administration wait for instructions from the minister, they, the settlers, do not wait for even one moment. They transfer in more and more mobile homes, hook up a generator, erect a synagogue, build a *mikveh* and break a road through."[105]

According to the internal official report issued in March 2000, the defense minister's aide for settlement during Netanyahu's government in the second half of the 1990s, Eli Cohen, himself a settler and eventually a Likud Knesset member and Israel's ambassador to Japan, "approved illegal activities in the area of land, planning and construction, delayed and prevented the implementation of enforcement measures at sites where illegal construction was carried out."[106] When Civil Administration inspectors reported on mobile homes that had been brought without authorization to Rahelim, the ardent aide worked out an agreement with the military on the establishment of a military-agricultural outpost that would protect the settlers at the new wildcat outpost. He also found funding for an access road, sewage pipes, and other infrastructure components. In this way, more and more wildcat settlements developed. The Civil Administration formulated a blacklist of illegal outposts, while the minister's aide was allocating funds to develop and "launder" them.[107]

More can be learned about the laundering method from the story of a new settlement in Samaria adjacent to the settlement of Kedumim, called Har Hemed, which was established in the spring of 1997. This occurred at a time when Prime Minister Netanyahu's commitment to transfer 13 percent of the territories of the West Bank to the Palestinian Authority was the word of the day. The Kedumim settlers, under the leadership of council head Daniella Weiss, stole out by night and occupied the top of Har Hemed, a high hill that overlooks the old settlement. "A road was paved to the mountain—Daniella Road. Mobile homes were brought in, Israeli flags hung, and an improvised synagogue opened. The army, which fought against the wildcat settlement, gave up and a short while later, stationed soldiers to guard the five families living on the hill. A few months ago, the electric company hooked up the mobile homes, thus completing the Zionist act."[108] The story of Har Hemed shows that the "Zionist act" was a blatantly criminal act, carried out with the active help of representatives of the government and the bodies charged with enforcing the law. Orders that were issued to cease the construction and demolish the houses were not implemented. The outpost is still standing at the time of this writing.

The Civil Administration failed in face of the settlers' endless claims and tricks, forfeiting its authority and in effect losing all control of what happened with respect to infrastructures in the territories. According to an official report never published before, at the end of the 1990s about one-third of the gas stations in the territories were operating without a permit; six gas stations were conducting their business without a contract having been signed with their proprietors. For many years, eighteen gas station owners did not pay fees for the franchise that was granted them. An examination by the staff of the State Comptroller's Office found that for purposes of paving roads, "enormous" quantities of stone and sand were extracted from quarries, some of them unauthorized quarries. The quantities were not at all proportionate to local needs. It is clear from the report that the materials mined from Palestinian lands were sold on the free market inside Israel. The intensive mining operations caused several roads in the territories to subside. This also caused a serious safety problem for travelers on these roads.[109] The comptroller did not mention that without the authorization of the ministers' aides for settlement matters over time, the franchises for a great many of the gas stations and quarries would not have been given to the settlers.

Most of the defense ministers' aides for settlement matters during the decade between 1996 and 2005 were themselves settlers who did not conceal that their commitment to fellow settlers took precedence over their commitment to the rule of law. Over the years, one after another, settlers filtered into key Civil Administration positions that deal with infrastructure, planning, construction laws, and enforcement. Some of the desk officers opened the gates of the Civil Administration to their friends in the regional councils and the settlement associations, supplied them with up-to-date information on available lands for purposes of settlement expansion, and warned them of intentions to evacuate illegal settlements.[110] Even officials who were not identified with the right have been captivated by the settlers' charms. Barak's aide for settlement matters, Yossi Vardi, who earned sharp criticism from the state comptroller, belongs to the third generation of the Mayflower Kibbutz Degania Aleph, the grandson of founders of the kibbutz and bearers of the collective commune idea. "I take my hat off to the leadership and inhabitants in Yesha, who face very difficult daily tests," said Vardi. "In Yesha today there are 200,000 citizens of the State of Israel, and the state is obligated to its citizens."[111] Barak himself did not hide his sympathy for the faithful, determined Zionists who settled on the hills of the occupied territories, and did his best to earn their sympathy and help their illegal project. Orders he gave to uproot illegal caravans were put into deep freeze in face of the settlers' protests.[112]

A People's Army and a Settlers' Army

The Palestinians' uprising against the occupation and the need to protect the settlements transformed the settlers from defenders of the homeland into a burden on its security. The second intifada, which broke out at the end of September 2000, forced the army to allocate regular divisions and also to call up reservists to protect the settlements. The Judea and Samaria Division, which controls the West Bank, includes five area brigades. Armored corps and helicopter units also participate in routine security. An army report revealed that in 2002–2003 about 600 soldiers were regularly engaged in protecting settlements and isolated outposts in the West Bank, which neutralizes them for other military tasks.[113] Senior officers in the military establishment cited sums of NIS (new Israeli shekels, about 4 shekels to the dollar at that time) 1.5 billion to 2.5 billion in direct expenditure destined for the protection of settlements. To this must be added another 100 million to 200 million shekels transferred annually to the settlements from the coffers of the Home Front Command and the defense minister's aide for settlement matters to fund about 200 job slots for security officers, fortifications, fences, lighting, and the like. The government's decision to build the separation wall along the longer, more tortuous route that bypasses from the east settlements in western Samaria, in the Jerusalem area, in Gush Etzion, and in the southern Hebron Hills has cost the controversial project many billions of shekels.[114]

The mission of protecting the settlers entails not only danger but also humiliation. Soldiers posted to protect settler Livnat Ozeri, the widow of Nati Ozeri, who was killed by a Palestinian on Hill 26, an illegal outpost in Hebron, were ordered to accompany the widow's flock of sheep to grazing land adjacent to Pottery Hill in Hebron. Other soldiers were sent to protect Menachem Livni, formerly a head of the Jewish terror organization, when he cultivated a field adjacent to a hostile Palestinian village until after nightfall.[115] Reserve soldiers reported that they spent their time chauffeuring settlers in army armor-plated vehicles. A soldier related that one night "one of the young settlers in Mevo Dotan felt like seeing his girlfriend, who lives inside the Green Line. At close to midnight he called and we took him in a military Jeep from Mevo Dotan to the Shaked roadblock. The previous day two settler women demanded that we drive them to do errands in the center of the country."[116] Innumerable soldiers were allocated to defend empty mobile homes or a lone family clinging to a bald hill and were sent to cater to settlers' whims, all under the umbrella of the false myth of "security needs."

Upon his appointment as chief of staff in 1978, Rafael Eitan decided to amalgamate the area defense department, which at that time was subordinate to the Operations Directorate at the General Staff, with the Civil Defense Command. Both of these were brought under one new roof, the chief force commander for civil defense and area defense.[117] Eitan hastened to transfer many reservists who lived in the settlements from their reserve units, among them combat units, to the area defense system, provide them with army equipment, and train them at military installations. From the semilegal children of Labor-led governments, who disguised themselves as Israeli soldiers and used army installations, the settlers became the darling soldiers whom Likud governments coddled openly and displayed with pride. From then on they were given the privileged status that previously had been reserved for the "confrontation settlements" and became an integral part of Israel's defense system.[118] The settlers were integrated into army policing activities throughout the territories and were considered devoted and conscientious soldiers. With the expansion of their project, they established cadres of their own and presented the army authorities with special military demands. "The result was that in the territories local, armed militias sprang up," wrote Yagil Levy, a scholar of Israel's army and society. "In this way a complex structure of relationships developed between the settlers and the army: The settlers are dependent on the army as the provider of weapons, the payer of salaries and the trainer of the local militias, but the army is dependent on the militias as those whose goodwill determines their behavior either in accordance with the army's directives or as a challenge against it."[119]

In May 1980, when the number of settlements reached more than fifty and their population more than 5,000, dozens of settler leaders convened in Elon Moreh and decided, "upon the recommendation of a senior IDF officer," to set up a security committee that would regularly present the settlements' security problems. A year later, upon his appointment to the position of defense minister, Ariel Sharon began inviting the committee to participate in operational discussions of the military command on a regular basis. Often they witnessed army commanders' confronting each other over issues that touched upon their interests.[120] The heads of the Central Command were ambivalent in their attitude toward armed civilians, and feared that they would become militias of a political hue. Amram Mitzna decided, in his day, to return the area defense units to the boundaries of the settlements themselves and to reduce their activity along transportation routes.[121] He preferred to deploy regular standing army or reserve units in the area. His successor, Yitzhak Mordechai, revoked the prohibition on this and later said that he had done so because it looked as though one was disqualifying a company of men from yeshivas or kibbutzim from serving in certain places.[122]

Following the events of the wall tunnel in Jerusalem in September 1996 (the so-called "tunnel intifada"), the army decided to establish an elite unit from among the settlers. High-level combat soldiers were posted to new area defense units. The warning time for calling up reservists in those units was reduced to six hours (as compared with thirty-six hours, which is the standard military norm). More important, this time the settler-soldiers were also assigned to mobile companies, the purpose of which was to secure the roads. The direct command of the new units was given to officers from the settler community.[123] The area defense doctrine was upgraded further while the second intifada was raging. In that period, under Sharon's government, the head of the command ruled that the boundary of the security envelope of every settlement ran adjacent to the outermost houses of the neighboring Arab villages. Until then it had been accepted that the security envelope spread from the fence of the settlement inward to the area of the settlement.[124] The military commander also set up units of ten or fifteen people from each settlement, under full military command, as was the case with every army unit, twenty-four hours a day. These were neither alert squads nor reserve units but rather soldiers who received training in combating terror and were supposed to reach a level in fighting terror close to that of fighters in the special forces.[125]

The dangerous side effects inherent in the complex ideological, political, and emotion-laden relations between the settlers and the army are not unique to the Israeli occupation. Historian Ian Lustick, who examined similarities between the conflict in Algeria and the conflicts in Ireland and in the territories of the West Bank and Gaza Strip, described the key role that was played by the French army in the opposition to Charles de Gaulle's decision to pull out of the French colony on the other shore of the Mediterranean. Nearly two years before the decision, on May 12, 1958, de Gaulle received a letter from the chief of the general staff, General Paul Ely, "informing him of the danger that the army would assume directly a political role by opposing the next government, which could lead to the secession of Algeria from France." Ely's appeal to de Gaulle was "to save the unity of the army and the nation."[126]

Army and politics were dangerously intertwined in the case of French occupation in Algeria. French officers developed an ideology and an emotional attitude and turned the army, in the name of the French nation, into the ultimate arbiter with regard to France's interests in Algeria. They saw Algeria as the supreme test of the army's glory, and pressed politicians to enable the army to pass this test. After the French cabinet's decision to pull out of Algeria, in February 1960, de Gaulle warned his ministers that the end of the war would be "an ugly business" and that "the ship is going to rock."[127] Months later, his prophecy came true. In April 1961 the generals led an attempted coup, which was planned by the "activist colonels" who had been transferred from Algeria after the Barricades Rebellion in January of that year. Their aim was to defeat the Algerian Front de Libération Nationale (FLN) by seizing control of the army in Algeria and then use their success to overthrow de Gaulle and establish a new regime dedicated to and capable of sustaining French sovereignty in Algeria.[128] Four times the French settlers (*colons*) tried to assassinate de Gaulle during his visit to Algeria. The 72 percent support that de Gaulle received in the referendum on his disengagement plan did not lead the opponents of the plan, settlers and army officers, to change their position.[129]

The putsch of April 1961 was purely a military affair. On April 23 de Gaulle addressed France on television in his general's uniform. He ordered the soldiers to "bar the route" to the rebellious generals and called on them to refuse to execute their orders. He then invoked Article 16 of the Constitution, declaring a state of emergency, which granted him dictatorial authority. Within a month after the collapse of the putsch, peace talks between France and the FLN began in Evian, but the Organization de l'Armée Secrète (OAS) continued its terror actions in both France and Algeria, with the support of the settlers. Fifteen generals and more than 200 other officers were imprisoned, and those who had gone underground were condemned to death in absentia.[130] In his conclusion Lustick wrote that an Israeli government that will decide one day to withdraw from the territories should not expect to encounter a similar measure of resistance on the part of the army senior command. He based his assertion on the fact that unlike the French army, with its paras and legionnaires, "the IDF does not contain elite units, or any units, with a particular political coloration." In fact, Lustick wrote, the segment of Israeli society that is significantly represented in the army's high command is the kibbutzim, which are inclined to vote for Labor and its leftist-dovish allies.[131]

The army's conduct during the August 2005 evacuation of the settlements from Gaza confirms Lustick's assessment. However, the army that Lustick knew and wrote about is vanishing. He apparently did not notice the changes that were already under way at the time of his writing. In any case, those substantial changes in the makeup of the army's officer cadre continued throughout the 1990s and afterward. Senior people in the military establishment note that in many units, among them units that serve in the territories most of the time, the number of kibbutz-born soldiers is negligible as compared to the number of religiously observant soldiers.[132] By 1995 the proportion of national religious soldiers in combat units stood at more than 30 percent, double their proportion in the general population.[133] The increase in the proportion of national religious soldiers and officers "accelerates with the increasing demand by the representatives of the 'crochet skullcaps' to shape the army in a manner that also takes their way into consideration," wrote Yagil Levy.[134] The impact of the August 2005 events on the settler youth and leadership attitude toward service in the army remains to be seen. The high number of national religious soldiers who were killed in the second Lebanon War (July–August 2006), twelve, upgraded their position in Israel's collective heart and symbolic pantheon, as was the case with kibbutz-born soldiers.

New winds among the national religious regarding service in the military could be detected as far back as the first decade of the state, with the shaping of a new image of the national religious sabra in the prestigious high school yeshivas. The 1967 war and the deepening of the hold on the occupied territories by virtue of their religious halo gave great impetus to the new phenomenon. After having fortified their communities against secularism, those in the national religious sector prepared to struggle for their place in the political system and the army.[135] Paramilitary yeshivas, which were established beginning in 1964 and were granted official status two years later, offered religious youth a cadre that combined study and military service. Conscription into the army filled a double goal for them: The first, which a decade later impelled Gush Emunim, was the rise in social standing of a group that had been marginalized for many years by the founding Labor elites of the country. The second goal was "partnership in the project that henceforth is donning religious-messianic garb, in the form of the liberation of the territories of the land of Israel and the defense of territories that have already been liberated."[136] These tasks took on an aura of heroism and sanctity, and the achievement of them was accompanied by a sense of superiority over secular society, which was in the process of Western normalization and separation from all-encompassing ideologies. The recognition of the combat abilities of religious youth was manifested especially after 1973, when the shattering of the myth of the omnipotent sabra soldier in the first days of the Yom Kippur War made a place for the new Israeli fighter, equipped with succor from higher spheres.

With the status of fighter came the resurrection of the status of "the pioneer," the national religious settler in the territories. Moreover, the ethos of masculine heroism that had won a central place in secular society also affected religious youth. From the 1990s there was a tendency among these young people to exchange the paramilitary yeshiva for elite units, which in the past had been considered secular bastions. One after another, premilitary preparatory courses sprang up, some of them in the territories, in the form of yeshivas whose graduates were destined for the officer cadre.[137] There they were given the privilege of bringing the three commandments to the highest level: the commandment to study Torah, the commandment to defend the homeland, and the commandment to redeem the Land of Israel. The quiet revolution fomented by the national religious sector in the army spread throughout the ranks, from the General Staff at the top to units at the company and platoon level. Though the military has been very cautious about what has been defined as "counting skullcaps," anyone with eyes in his head sees and knows that one-third of the graduates of the officers' training courses during the past decade have been from the national religious community. The main factor behind this revolution in the profile of the army is the premilitary preparatory program. A special report by the Personnel Directorate, the findings of which were published in *Ha'aretz*, detailed the huge influence that the graduates of the prep programs have on the army. Twenty-three such programs, thirteen of them religious, are recognized by the Defense and Education ministries. Each year approximately 1,100 students attend these programs, and receive a deferment of military service for a year to a year and a half. More than 70 percent of them are religious. Among the secular, more than one-third are girls, which means that fewer secular men are attending these programs. Nearly half of the programs are located in the territories. In the largest of the programs, Eli in Samaria and Atzmona (which was located in Gush Katif in Gaza and was transferred after the 2005 evacuation to another settlement), some 120 young people study in each class. The preparatory programs are notable for the proportion of their graduates who enter combat service in select units (about 85 percent). About a third of those who serve become officers (three times the average in the general population). The oldest preparatory program, at Eli, which was founded in 1988, has graduates who as of the time of writing were already serving as battalion commanders.[138] Graduates of the preparatory programs are considered to be more highly disciplined and motivated soldiers than average. However, army officers note that they lack "pluralistic thinking."[139]

Fraternal Strife

When the Sharon government decided to dismantle the Gaza outposts and was pondering the plan to evacuate Gush Katif, the leader of the National Religious Party, Knesset Member Effi Eitam, who had been the first religious division commander, suggested that the army be released from the mission on the grounds that "nearly 40 percent of the junior command people in the IDF, from the rank of lieutenant colonel down, wear skullcaps." Hinting at the major role Sharon had played in the evacuation of the Yamit region, Eitam said that "the IDF is not the IDF of the period when Yamit was evacuated . . . and Israeli society today is also completely different from what it was in that period."[140] The army's smooth functioning during the course of the withdrawal from Gaza gave Eitam the surprise of his life. The question is whether such obedience can be expected in the future. "Whom are they going to evacuate, my settlement, Yattir, where two colonels and two battalion commanders live?" demanded Colonel (res.) Moshe Hager, head of the premilitary prep course in his settlement, when the Barak government was considering a withdrawal from most of the territories. "Barak is coming to ceremonies at Training Camp I and sees the number of skullcaps." Hager too argued that it is not "the same IDF that evacuated Yamit."[141]

"Evacuating Jews" has never been considered an attractive task, even by secular commanders. As early as the mid-1970s, with the first settlement operations of Gush Emunim, Chief of Staff Mordechai Gur tried to avoid physical confrontation with the settlers.[142] The settler leaders, who have always been aware of the public's sensitivity to soldiers' well-being, also preferred at the last minute to avoid violent conflict with the army and adopted the method of "passive resistance," which worked well against a weak-kneed army. Hundreds of soldiers who were sent in June 2003 to evacuate the outpost of Yitzhar did not succeed in overcoming a few hundred young people who gathered at the site, or in blocking the way of the thousands who rushed to help them. There was a similar occurrence at the attempt to evacuate Givat Yitzhar a year later.[143] In the 2005 withdrawal operation from Gaza, the words of Major General (res.) Shlomo Gazit, the first coordinator of government activities in the territories, proved correct. He said that "there is no problem with evacuating settlers, on condition that we really want to," and that "it is the government that wants to create the impression that the Jewish people is going through a terrible trauma."[144] The army acted "with toughness and sensitivity," and the trauma was mainly the lot of the evacuees. Most Israelis relaxed en masse at the beach or on trips abroad. Like the trauma that did not happen in the evacuation of Yamit in 1982, the scenes of hysteria at the evacuation of Katif have long since faded from Israel's overburdened collective memory.

The orders to evacuate caravans that were put up by trespassers here and there, and more so the plan to leave Gush Katif and Gaza, again revealed the dilemma of the dual loyalties of settler soldiers. Ever since the Oslo agreement the dilemma of refusal, the wavering between the commander's order and the rabbi's order, has been an important part of the discourse of the national religious public in general and of the settlers in particular. The dilemma is frequently mentioned in connection with the soldiers who for reasons of conscience refuse to serve in the occupied territories on the grounds that a "black flag" of illegality and criminality flies over the entire occupation. In the announcement about a "reckoning of conscience" that was published shortly after Rabin's assassination, the national religious Bnei Akiva youth movement based itself on a precedent set by a military court after the massacre of Palestinian citizens of Israel at Kafr Kassem on October 29, 1956 (in that ruling it was stated that soldiers must refuse to obey a blatantly illegal order, one that, in the famous words of the court, has a "black flag" flying over it).[145] The religious Zionist youth movement expanded the applicability of the ruling, declaring that "orders that are contrary to traditional Jewish law are blatantly illegal," and therefore soldiers are not required to obey them. The heads of the movement placed the decision not in the hands of the military commander but rather in the hands of the religious authorities. "On every serious question, the soldier will consult his rabbi."[146]

From that time until the summer of 2005, various calls came from both within and outside the army to cancel the paramilitary yeshiva program.[147] A move of this sort, which would carry the potential of "fraternal strife"—the term usually given in Israeli discourse to civil war—and has thus been almost a taboo in the Israeli political discourse, has always frightened both the settler rabbis, on the one hand, and the defense establishment and the politicians, on the other.[148] This fear, which caused Rabin to retreat from his intention to evacuate the Elon Moreh group from Sebastia in 1975 and the Tel Rumeida settlers after the massacre in Hebron in 1994, enabled the rabbis to preach openly to soldiers to disobey orders to evacuate a settlement.

The former chief rabbi, Shlomo Goren, who had served as chief military rabbi during the Six-Day War and was a subordinate of Chief of Staff Rabin, published a rabbinical ruling back in 1993 to the effect that "an order to evacuate settlements has no obligatory validity, and soldiers must refuse to obey such an order. It is clear that according to Jewish law, a soldier who receives an order that is contrary to the laws of the Torah must observe the law of the Torah, and not the secular order. . . . And as there is a commandment to settle the land, and the uprooting of settlements is a violation of the commandment, the soldier must not carry out an order to uproot settlements."[149] Rabbi Avraham Shapira, one of the spiritual leaders of religious Zionism and also a former chief rabbi, issued a rabbinical ruling that "the evacuation of a Jewish settlement constitutes an illegal order and soldiers must refuse to carry it out."[150] He openly called for soldiers to refuse to evacuate army bases, as stipulated in the second Oslo agreement.[151] This call was joined by the Federation of Rabbis for the Land of Israel, in which the rabbis of the large settlements were members. In the evacuation of the camps there was a "violation of a commandment of commission, and also danger to lives and danger to the existence of the state," ruled the new security experts.[152]

The rabbis of the paramilitary yeshivas, whose salaries come from the state budget, rose up not against the damage to the law of the country but rather against the damage to the honor of rabbis and the attempts to deny them the right to make rulings in Jewish law. A group of rabbis who had been given the responsibility of educating thousands of young soldiers noted that "the Torah determines and decides in all areas of the life of the Jewish people and the State of Israel."[153] Knesset member Hannan Porat, the settler considered a moderate among the fanatics, was quick to declare his alignment with the rabbinical ruling and to assert that "the uprooting of IDF outposts is an act of national crime." According to Porat, "Fortunate are we to have rabbis strong as iron who utter words like spurs."[154] Only a very few rabbis, led by Rabbi Aharon Lichtenstein, head of the Har

Etzion paramilitary yeshiva in Gush Etzion, dared to condemn the rabbinical ruling. Lichtenstein said he was worried about the possibility that religious soldiers would disobey evacuation orders, but he was worried even more by the damage that expansion of the phenomenon of refusing orders could cause.[155] Attorney General Michael Ben-Yair ordered the police to open an investigation of the rabbis.[156]

At the end of 2002, following a commitment to US President George W. Bush, it was Prime Minister Ariel Sharon's turn to evacuate a number of illegal settlements in the West Bank. Sharon, who twenty years earlier had been the first to call on soldiers to disobey an order to evacuate settlers, now faced off with that same "Rabbis' Committee" that in its day had provided his fight against the Oslo agreement with a rabbinical seal of approval to disobey orders. This time the rabbis ruled that the army's concern is to vanquish the enemies of Israel. No one, they said—not even a minister in the Israeli government—is entitled to misuse his status by ordering the army to evacuate outposts and thereby drag it into the public debate.[157] When a paratroop brigade was sent in June 2003 to evacuate a wildcat outpost near a settlement adjacent to Ramallah, the commander, a resident of the settlement of Netzarim in the Gaza Strip, informed his superior officers that he was refusing to carry out a mission that is contrary to the spirit of the rabbis' rulings. His soldiers embarked on the mission without their commander. Later the commander refused to send his soldiers a Jeep carrying a load of drinking water. The brigade commander deposed him and sentenced him to twenty-eight days in military prison.[158]

Chief Education Officer Brigadier General Elazar Stern, himself a religiously observant officer, published a bulletin for soldiers in which he condemned refusal of all hues and defined it as "the provider of fuel" to the enemy's fighting spirit and "a blow to our own spirit and strength." The army must not be turned into a mechanism for political change, instructed the chief education officer; it is too dangerous to Israeli society. "The IDF does not choose whether or not to carry out a mission according to the degree of its congruence with its ideological or political worldview. . . . It is our obligation to carry out every mission that is given to us by the elected government, as long as it is not blatantly illegal."[159]

As the English edition of this book is going to press, Hebron has again caught the attention of the media. A new, wild Jewish settlement sprang one beautiful morning in the heart of the Arab town. Colonel Noam Tibon, commander of the Hebron Brigade during the second intifada and a son of Kibbutz Tzora, defined the people of the Jewish settlement in Hebron, the most fanatic and violent group of settlers in the territories, as "a democratic and responsible public that behaves in an exemplary manner under pressure that is not at all simple."[160] He revealed that he himself had "closed dozens of cases" that the police had opened against inhabitants of the Jewish Quarter in the town, "arbitrarily, without any particular reason," Tibon said. "There were Jews here against whom there were fifty or sixty cases and they didn't spend a single day in jail because there was nothing behind the cases." And he told Knesset members from the National Religious Party that he had "seen to distancing the police" from the Jewish area and also criticized its "unfair" attitude toward the Jewish inhabitants.[161] Dudu Schick, a senior army officer in the reserves, also from a kibbutz, who was the security officer of Kiryat Arba, complained that the settlers kept the army busy unnecessarily, spit on soldiers, and saw him as a collaborator with the army and a Shin Bet mole. This did not prevent him from seeing the Kiryat Arba-Hebron settlers as "a symbol of Jewish heroism," the antithesis of the "helplessness of the Jews in the Holocaust."[162]

Young Nahal soldiers who served in Hebron during the years of the second intifada saw different occurrences there, scenes of the settlers' daily harassment of the Arab inhabitants, streets empty of local inhabitants, a ruined, devastated town. "A small boy of 10 or 11, with a skullcap and earlocks, went into the courtyard of a house," testified one of the soldiers of the Breaking the Silence group.[163] "He picked a pomegranate off a tree in the yard, threw it at a window of the house and broke it. I tried to stop him, I asked him to move; maybe I put a hand on his shoulder. And then two adults come by. I was glad; I could tell them to take the child away because he was making trouble. Instead they shouted at me that I was another leftist soldier. Go deal with the Arabs and leave us alone." Another testimony: "An elderly Palestinian man, with a long white beard, all wrinkled, was walking with bags full of shopping. A little boy passes by, between 6 and 9 at most. He looks the Arab in the eye and says to him: 'You are a dirty Arab,' spits in his face and runs away. Then he goes up on a roof and throws stones at the old man. I was in shock. If by chance you manage to catch him, when you call his parents they say to you, in the child's presence, 'What do you want from my child?' As far as they're concerned, it's fine."[164]

And another Israeli soldier from Breaking the Silence, himself a young religious Jew, said that "after half a year in Hebron it has dawned on me that in fact our real task was to protect the Palestinians from being harmed by the Jews, and not to protect the Jews. . . . I am certain that some of them [the settlers] are from families of Holocaust survivors. If they are capable of writing on Arabs' doors 'Death to Arabs,' then somewhere for me the concept of Jew has changed."[165]

7

Everything Is Legal
in the Land of Israel

As the Israeli army advanced into the West Bank in June 1967, occupying Palestinian villages and towns, its soldiers posted notices in Arabic and Hebrew stating that "the Israel Defense Forces are entering the area today and taking over control and the maintenance of security and civil order."[1] A second proclamation distributed by the army in the coming days stated more explicitly that the law that had existed in the area before the entry of the army would remain in effect as long as it did not contradict the orders of the notice. It stressed that the authority to rule, pass laws, appoint, and administer with respect to the area and its inhabitants would be in the hands of the commander of the Israeli army or of such persons as he would appoint or as would act on his behalf.[2] An additional notice that dealt with the territories conquered in the war was a "general staff" ordinance that, *inter alia*, decreed that "a military court and the military court administration will observe the provisions of the Geneva Convention of August 12, 1949, that relate to a civilian population during wartime, while maintaining judicial procedure, and in case of a clash between the latter and the aforementioned convention, the provisions of the convention shall prevail."[3] This ordinance, which had been prepared prior to the outbreak of the war, was rescinded a short time later when senior members of the government and influential people in the ruling Labor Party, among them the minister of justice, began to talk about the "liberation" of the territories rather than their conquest and occupation. A few even played with the idea of imposing Israeli law on the occupied territories.[4]

Throughout the years of occupation, and under the auspices of the Israeli legal system, the steadily tightening Israeli rule had been in far-reaching breach of international conventions and particularly the Fourth Geneva Convention.[5] Israel has tried, successfully, to enjoy the best of several worlds that do not reconcile with one another legally. It has maintained a regime in the territories based on a military commander's authority and power in an occupied territory. However, it has not taken upon itself the limitations and prohibitions that obligate an occupying state, like the prohibition on transferring population from that state into the occupied territory, or the prohibition on confiscating private property. Nor has it fulfilled its obligation to serve as a trustee for the public property in the occupied territory, an obligation that the previous sovereign in the West Bank, Jordan, fulfilled properly. Thus, by various legal means and with the aid and even encouragement and support of the state and its institutions, immense territories, of which the local inhabitants could not prove ownership, have been taken from the Palestinians and given over for the settlement of Jews, which is prohibited by international law and custom.

The Jewish settlement, at God's command and at the government's will, has thus caused continuing and extensive damage to the basic human rights of the Palestinians who live in the territories, among them the rights to personal liberty, freedom of movement, and property; it has also thwarted any possibility for the realization of the collective rights of those who lived in the territory before the intrusion of the Israeli forces, such as the right to national self-determination, including statehood. The entrenchment of more than a quarter of a million Jews in the Palestinian territories (and close to twice that if one counts East Jerusalem), and the making of the well-being and security of the Jewish settlers Israel's top priority, created a situation of critical separation, persecution, and discrimination.[6] The state has given minimal protection and legal aid to the Palestinian inhabitants in the face of fanaticism and violence from Jewish settlers and the discriminatory attitudes of authorities such as the army and the police. A former senior attorney in a civil service position, Yehudit Karp, who at the request of the attorney general examined the law enforcement situation in the territories in the early 1980s, said years later that "we were like Sodom, we resembled Gomorrah."[7] This chapter deals with the various legal aspects of the Jewish settlement in the territories since 1967. It discusses the struggle over the legal definition of the territories, the mode of the confiscation of West Bank lands, the transfer of these lands to the Jewish people, and the process of the transformation of the territories into Sodom and Gomorrah.

New, revolutionary situations, especially those born in the storm of war, necessitate, when actual fighting has ended, legal arrangements to establish order, to acquire legitimacy, and to ensure the welfare and the rights of the vanquished. To this end, the Hague Regulations and Geneva Conventions were promulgated. These conventions deal mainly with the responsibilities incumbent on an occupying army in its relations with the occupied population. The 1967 military victory and acquisition of new territories, which many Israelis saw as the fulfillment of a divine promise, required adjustments in the legal system. The sweeping conquest of the West Bank and the Gaza Strip did not bring about an immediate change in the sovereignty over these territories. Instead, the state adopted a policy of ambiguity and vagueness.

Israel did not declare its sovereignty in the West Bank and the

Gaza Strip, nor did it recognize others'. The first, brief period was characterized by a general observance of accepted principles of international law regarding belligerent possession (or seizure) and belligerent occupation.[8] Gradually Israel began to change the discourse and influence consciousness in order to foster the historical, metaphysical connection of the territories to Israel and to undermine the idea that they were in fact occupied, and to obliterate the very term "occupation." In this area, too, the army was ahead of civilian institutions. On December 17, 1967, the army issued an order stating that "the term Judea and Samaria area will be identical for all purposes . . . to the term West Bank area."[9] This was a far-reaching move, in effect the conceptual, discursive annexation of the occupied territory to Israel, into its ancient history, and into the district of Israel's "historical rights," which by definition are in the realm of the "imagined," to use Benedict Anderson's term.[10] Starting in 1968, Jerusalemite law professor and eventual Israeli ambassador to the United Nations Yehudah Blum published articles in which he argued that because Jordan's annexation of these territories in 1950 did not receive broad international recognition, they were not the sovereign territories of another state when Israel seized them in 1967; he maintained that this meant the Geneva Convention regarding belligerent occupation did not apply to the West Bank.[11]

After the 1948 war the West Bank and East Jerusalem were controlled by Jordan, and the Gaza Strip by Egypt. While Egypt did not view the Strip as part of its own territory and handled it according to rules pertaining to a "belligerent seizure," Jordan had completed by April 1950 the annexation of the West Bank and East Jerusalem. It did this contrary to customary international law, which prohibits the annexation of territories occupied by force without the agreement of the sovereign.[12] This act of annexation collided with the position of the international community and even with that of the Arab League. Only two countries, Britain and Pakistan, recognized Jordan's unilateral annexation. From 1948 to 1967 the Jordanian regime treated lands that until 1948 had been Jewish property in accordance with the rules of the 1939 Mandatory Trading with the Enemy Ordinance.[13] Up until the Israeli occupation of the territories in 1967, the Jordanians did not pass any legislation concerning the territory.[14] The Jordanian minister of the interior, who took over the responsibilities of the mandatory high commissioner, was appointed the custodian of enemy property.[15] While the Jordanian authorities did seize properties that belonged to Jews in the West Bank, they preserved and managed them primarily in order to prevent local inhabitants from taking possession of these assets. They also did this in order to validate counterclaims by Palestinian refugees from the 1948 war concerning property they left behind in the State of Israel and in order to make use of the assets until an arrangement was obtained in the framework of a peace treaty.[16] The Jordanian custodian's efforts to preserve Jewish lands and properties for takeover by local inhabitants were impressive and generally successful, according to Israeli legal experts and scholars.[17]

"Administered" Territories

Under the influence of jurists like Meir Shamgar, who was the military advocate general at the time, Yehudah Blum, and others—and because many members of the government saw the territories as a legitimate, yearned-for expansion of Israel—the government began to refer to them as "administered" rather than "occupied." It refrained from officially recognizing the validity or applicability of the Fourth Geneva Convention on the protection of civilians during wartime despite Article 2, which stipulates that the convention shall "apply to all cases of partial or total occupation of the territory of a High Contracting Party, even if the said occupation meets with no armed resistance." The explanation that Israel gave for this stance, which was contrary to the opinion of experts on international law, including senior Israeli legal scholars, was that recognizing the applicability of the convention would be tantamount to an implicit acknowledgment that the territories belonged to Jordan and Egypt. Israel argued that these areas did not fit the definition that appears in Provision 2 of the convention, which states that the convention shall apply when it involves territory that had been under the sovereignty of a side to the convention before it was occupied; hence Israel had entered territories that lacked agreed sovereignty. This point was also made by the foreign minister in Menachem Begin's government, Moshe Dayan, in his speech to the 32nd Session of the UN General Assembly in September 1977.[18]

Yet in order to iterate Israel's membership in the community of civilized countries and to display its moral sensitivity, Israeli representatives declared in every international forum that Israel was taking upon itself voluntarily, but not out of any legal obligation, the humanitarian instructions of the Fourth Geneva Convention.[19] However, it was not explicitly stated which "humanitarian instructions" were meant and what they entailed. Shamgar thus wrote, when he was already the state's attorney general, that "in light of the *sui generis* status of Judea, Samaria and the Gaza Strip, the legal applicability of the Fourth Geneva Convention to these territories is in doubt. Israel prefers to set aside the legal question of the status of these territories, and has decided, since 1967, to act in a practical way in accordance with the humanitarian instructions of the convention."[20]

Israel also refused to recognize the applicability of the Hague Regulations of 1907, again for fear that the recognition of these conventions, which deal with military governance of the territory of an enemy state, would imply recognition of the sovereignty of others over the territories occupied in 1967. Addressing this issue, the Supreme Court ruled some twenty years after the 1967 conquest that the test for the applicability of "the laws of belligerent seizure" in customary international law is a factual test, related to exclusive military control over a territory outside the borders of the state. The meaning of this ruling was that the issue was not a legal matter, in the framework of which the legal linkage of the various claimants to sovereignty over a given territory is examined. Thus Israel's Supreme Court extracted the question of the sovereignty over the territories from the sphere of legal deliberations.[21]

Although the Jordanian annexation of the territories of the West Bank, which was finalized in April 1950, was contrary to international law and was not given international recognition, Israel recognized Jordanian law in the West Bank for its own political reasons and for reasons of convenience. Attempts by Jewish settlers to argue against the applicability of this law were rejected by the Supreme Court.[22] Thus, there existed three levels of law in the territories that Israel occupied. The first level was Ottoman law—the 1858 Land Law that established land rights—which was still in force in the territories. This law played a crucial role in the legal anchoring of the Israeli occupation and the seizure of vast Palestinian lands. The second level was British Mandatory law, which did not change the essential rules in the Ottoman law. The third level was Jordanian law. The Jordanian legislation concerning land was for the most part a rewriting of Ottoman law. Eventually this legal situation was exploited and became in Israel's hands a most sophisticated means of expropriation.

After June 1967 three more levels were added to this legal mix:

military security legislation, the rules of international law that deal with belligerent seizure, and Israeli administrative law. Article 43 of the Hague Regulations states that the occupant "shall take all the measures in his power to restore, and ensure, as far as possible, public order and safety, while respecting, unless absolutely prevented, the laws in force in the country." Israeli military legislation, however, made overwhelming changes in the legal status of the West Bank, both quantitatively and qualitatively. It was the routine of "prolonged" Israeli domination and what Israel defined as "immediate needs" that brought about these changes, which blatantly defied international law and custom. But more important was the political perception of most Israeli governments—at least until the 1990s—with respect to the linkage between the territories of the West Bank and the State of Israel, and as regards the question of the permanent status of the territories; that is, that these territories would one way or another become part of Israel.[23] As noted, the army formally abided by the rules of customary international law with respect to occupied territories as well as by the humanitarian articles in the Fourth Geneva Convention.[24] The Israeli Supreme Court ruled, as we will show later in detail, that the Fourth Geneva Convention is not purely declarative but does have a constitutive nature; that is, it is not automatically absorbed into the Israeli legislature but must be anchored in the local law by a formal legal act.[25]

In an extraordinary and controversial step, and in a demonstrative way as if it stemmed from humanist-liberal motives, the Supreme Court in its capacity as the High Court of Justice was authorized to review the administrative and legislative activities of the military government in the territories, to supposedly give the Palestinian inhabitants succor against the arbitrariness of the state institutions.[26] However, as we shall see further on, over the years the courts have evinced an impressive "judicial restraint" in judging the actions and deeds of the various Israeli authorities in the territories and have given considerable aid not to the injured Palestinian complainants but rather to the State of Israel and the settlers.[27]

Prepared and Willing

While statesmen and legal experts were splitting hairs over the question of the legal status of the territories and the matter of the proper terminology for them, the army was prepared and willing as always to fill the governing and administrative vacuum left by politicians. Simultaneous with its declaration of control of the territory and its responsibility for the rule of the law that prevailed there, the army began to shape Israeli politics in the territories. At least in the case of the military, it cannot be said that the territories it conquered "fell" on it out of a clear blue sky. On the contrary, inspired and instructed by an energetic and farsighted military advocate general like Meir Shamgar, who was appointed in 1961 to the highest position in the army's legal system, the military prosecution had prepared itself well in advance for "a theoretical possibility of the operation of the IDF in neighboring countries as a result of war." Expected coups in Jordan and the pending entry of the Syrian army into that country in the middle of the 1960s transformed theoretical possibility into a very likely eventuality, and the army even went on "supreme alert," ready to deal with any development on the eastern border.[28] In cooperation with the military government department in the army operations directorate, the military prosecution held courses to formulate a doctrine for military governance in occupied territories and to train its people for the occupation and administration. These preparations proved fruitful, both in the weeks before the outbreak of the war and after it was over.[29]

Moreover, military government was strange neither to the army nor to Israel's other security forces. After October 1948, Israel maintained full military government over its Arab citizens; hence the preparations that were taken for occupation and administration of territories were not made in a vacuum. These preparations were based on the experience that had been acquired over the years in the various security bodies. Furthermore, in a concatenation of circumstances and times, Israel's military rule over its Palestinian citizens ended in December 1966, not long before the outbreak of the war. "Everything was perverted, and the administration apparatus had been voided of any content, but it refused to leave the arena," said former head of the Mossad Isser Harel about the military government in its last years.[30] Thus, despite the differences in the nature of control in the two instances, Israel could transfer to the newly conquered territories the experience and know-how that had been accumulated during the eighteen years of military rule in Israel, including the large systems of control and intelligence that were shaped in its framework; but most important the culture and mentality of military occupation of a civilian population.[31] Scores of officers who had been trained by the military advocate general's office over the years in the laws of war and the "simulation games" in which they honed their skills created what Shamgar called "a trained reservoir of forces from within which it was possible to organize the units for action during time of war."[32] Specific officers were designated by name for key posts in the establishment of military occupation in the territories, and emergency boxes were prepared for the MAG units that included basic volumes on military occupation theory, among them Shamgar's own book, *The Military Guide for the Member of the Military Prosecution in Military Government*.[33] Major General Haim Herzog was slated "in time of need" to be military governor in the West Bank, a task he indeed was the first to fulfill in due time.

In one of the famous photographs from the war, Moshe Dayan, Yitzhak Rabin, and Uzi Narkiss stride together toward the Western Wall. A few meters behind them, but not visible in the picture, walked Military Advocate General Shamgar, who would become the éminence grise behind the legal occupation of the territories. When the command group entered the Old City of Jerusalem, Shamgar, according to his own testimony, saw the Israeli flag flying over the Dome of the Rock. He went over to Dayan and asked him to remove the flag. "You mustn't fly your own flag over a mosque. The mosque is a holy place, a place of prayer, which one doesn't occupy,"[34] he said. The senior military jurist's quiet and unseen pacing behind the occupying forces in order to ensure, on the one hand, the proper treatment of holy sites and the appropriate conduct of the rank and file, and at the same time to legitimize and legalize the military occupation, could serve as a metaphor for the activity of the entire legal system and for the crucial role played by Shamgar himself in formulating and shaping the legal envelope of the occupation. As Supreme Court President Aharon Barak said thirty-five years later, in words of praise made of both lace and strychnine for his predecessor: "President Shamgar was unique. As Military Advocate General he determined the pattern for this role. At the center of his work—the preparation of the infrastructure for the domination by the state and the army of the territories that came into our control after the Six Day War."[35]

As the battles of June 1967 raged, the fighting forces were closely accompanied by squads from the military prosecution. These teams set up courts; gave legal advice; and issued notices, orders, and announcements that had been prepared in advance to calm the conquered territory and take control of it. They also promised, as Shamgar put it, "legal activity with regard to the population of the administered territory and effective protection of its rights." How was the occupied, or "administered," population given effective protection of its rights? The army, at Shamgar's initiative, in effect subordinated the territories to the review of the High Court of Justice, the highest legal instance in the State of Israel. Even after thirty years of occupation, which brought upon the inhabitants of the territories confiscations, expulsions, house demolitions, closures, encirclements, arbitrary death, and various sorts of collective punishment, Shamgar saw this step, which was aimed at allowing inhabitants of the occupied territory to apply to the judiciary of the state and to its highest court, as an international innovation, which "even enlightened countries like the United States and Britain" did not follow.[36] This move of Shamgar's, even if it was originally intended to give legal succor to a population in distress, as he believed, had far-reaching effects that determined for many years the development and the nature of the occupation. In imposing Israeli judicial authority on the territories, and in thus expanding the authority of the Israeli courts beyond the boundaries of the State of Israel, the army in effect annexed the territories. Furthermore, it coerced the inhabitants, who had no other legal recourse, to appeal to these courts in their quest for justice, and thus to recognize, whether they wanted to or not, this legal annexation and the authority of the Israeli judiciary system over them. This single act also rendered the State of Israel and the territories a single judiciary-political entity, blurring the borders of June 4, 1967. Even if only for this formidable legal coup, Shamgar was indeed "unique," as his successor at the Supreme Court described him.

The Palestinians found themselves in a double trap; their application to Israel's highest court was tantamount to recognition of Israeli sovereignty. Even worse, only rarely did the Israeli court come down on their side. A systematic examination of the High Court of Justice rulings on petitions by Palestinians, and an examination of the

The wide empty paved road leading to the settlement of Naale near the Green Line, summer 2001. *Photo: Eyal Weizman.*

Settlements Yakir and Nofim on the hilltops, southwest of Nablus, in the heart of the Palestinian lands, May 2002. *Photo: Peace Now Archive.*

A settler demonstration against the newly elected Prime Minister Ariel Sharon during his official visit to Beit El, May 2, 2001. *Photo: Avi Ohayon, GPO.*

"Barak Is Losing the Land" and "Only Sharon Can" are placards borne by settlers demonstrating against Prime Minister Ehud Barak during the elections campaign, February 1, 2001. *Photo: Moshe Milner. GPO.*

Occupier's idyll: A settler and a Palestinian in Hebron after the heart of the city had been emptied of its Palestinian inhabitants, November 9, 1996. *Photo: Gregg Marinovitz, GPO.*

Prime Minister Sharon presents his condolences to the Shoham family from the settlement Shiloh, whose baby daughter was killed in a terrorist attack, June 17, 2001. *Photo: Avi Ohayon, GPO.*

Settlers attack a Palestinian in the street, in front of an idle Israeli soldier, during the second intifada, June 2001. *Photo: Naif Hashalmon, Reuters.*

Settlers physically attack and throw stones at Israeli soldiers in Hebron during the second intifada, July 2002. *Photo: Gil Cohen-Magen, GPO.*

Soldiers and police officers forcefully evacuate settlers from the outpost of Havat Maon, November 10, 1999. *Photo: GPO.*

A group of second-generation settlers dressed and acting as if they were the heirs of the early Zionists from the first years of the twentieth century, June 10, 2003. *Photo: Moshe Milner, GPO.*

Part of the separation wall erected in Abu Dis, East Jerusalem, January 25, 2004. *Photo: Moshe Milner, GPO.*

A wrecked bus, whose explosion in a Jerusalem street extracted many victims, is positioned by the wall, February 23, 2004.
Photo: Moshe Milner, GPO

Gush Katif settlers remove Torah Scrolls from a synagogue before evacuation, 21 August, 2005. All synagogues as well as every building in the evacuated settlements were destroyed by Israel. *Photo: Amos Ben Gershom, Government Press Office (GPO).*

Police forces and settlers clash during the evacuation of the West Bank outpost of Amona, February 1, 2006. *Photo: Avi Ohayon, GPO (Government Press Office).*

rulings by Justice Shamgar himself during his years in the Supreme Court, shows that the High Court rejected almost without exception petitions by inhabitants of the territories.[37] What Shamgar saw as a move aimed at imposing "essential legal reins" on actions of public administration and at imposing "on the military authorities not only the rules of international humanitarian law but also the norms of Israeli administrative law,"[38] eventually afforded the highest legal and moral seal of approval to Israel's ruthless occupation in the territories.

Shamgar's boldness, his centralism, his ability to handle and control large systems, and, above all, his formidable yet schematic legal-political vision in administering the occupied territories—all carried out with "more than a slight measure of correctness," as he said of his encounter with the territories, one that was full of "awe"—were the first building stones of the Shamgar myth in Israeli judiciary.[39] This was the myth of the supreme, unbiased, awe-inspiring authority. These characteristics accelerated his uninterrupted ascent in the hierarchy to the most elevated position in Israel's legal system. In September 1968, the justice minister appointed Shamgar to the position of attorney general. According to Shamgar, his proven success in preparing the military prosecution for the war and carrying it out during and after the war were at the base of the appointment, as well as the need "for an attorney general who had a centralist approach."[40]

A Precedent to Be Repeated

The process of the settlement of Jewish civilians in the territories in breach of the Geneva Convention, which does not permit the transfer of inhabitants from the occupier's territory to the occupied territory, was gradual and systematic, and was accomplished in ways that the Zionist movement had nurtured and sanctified from its inception. The methods that characterized the struggle before 1948 to obtain a

Jewish state, a combination of overt and clandestine acts carried out by underground or semiunderground organizations, were resurrected in the territories occupied in 1967. In their capacity as the custodians of the law, and as the dominant organized system on the ground, the army and its commanders were the settlers' main support in their illegal activities. In many cases they were also the settlers' resource for manpower and logistics, as demonstrated in Chapter 6. The first settlements were established for the most part on lands that the army had confiscated for what was defined as "a military security need," and were in fact intended from the outset for civil Jewish settlement.

The first instance in which local inhabitants were tempted into appealing to the High Court of Justice to request legal succor occurred in the early 1970s with regard to the Rafah Salient, the area where the Gaza Strip bordered on the Egyptian Sinai.[41] Already in this early deliberation, the question of the applicability of the Geneva Convention came up, in the matter of the prohibition of the transfer of the occupier's populations into the occupied territory. The petition by the complainants, Bedouins who had been ejected from their land for purposes of establishing a "buffer zone," on the grounds that they were abetting terrorists, ostensibly did not at all revolve around the settlement of Jews there, i.e., the entrance of the occupier's population into an occupied territory. This possibility, which was realized on the ground a short time later, was indeed mentioned vaguely in the statements, but the justices ignored it demonstratively. Yet in the answering statements to the Bedouins' petition, Major General Yisrael Tal, head of the Army General Headquarters, in fact revealed more than he should have from the state's point of view. He said that in a "buffer zone" it is possible either to close off the area and prevent the entry of local inhabitants by putting up fences and barriers or to settle the area with Jews, or to combine the populations.[42] However, the presiding judge on the bench, Justice Moshe Landau, stuck to the security argument and chose the first of these possibilities. He ruled that in transferring the petitioners from their location there was no violation of Article 49 of the Geneva Convention, which prohibits the forced transfer of "protected persons from occupied territory to the territory of the Occupying Power." The petitioners, he said, were transferred "within the territory of the Military Government and not from it to the territory of the state of Israel," and explained that they had to "come to terms" with their uprooting, because it had been done "for reasons of military necessity."[43] Another of the judges on the bench, Alfred Witkon, ruled that the Geneva Convention was not germane to the matter because both Geneva and the Hague Regulations belong to consensual international law and are not enforceable before an Israeli court. He added not only that the convention did not have validity in this case but also that this was a military matter that was not at all subject to judicial intervention. "It must be said that something that is not subject to judicial intervention cannot be rendered so even by agreement of the sides," Witkon ruled.[44]

What was not known at the time is that in the course of 1972, while the Rafah Salient Bedouins' petition was still being deliberated in the courts, "experts" headed by a team from the Defense Ministry were planning a large port city in the Rafah Salient, called Yamit. The plans were printed in a glossy twenty-two-page brochure in a large format, accompanied by detailed maps. The final aim was a city of 1 million. Leaked reports of Defense Minister Dayan's plan raised a storm in the Labor Party and led to the shelving of the brochure, the disposal of proofs of its existence, and the denial of the entire matter.[45] Yet the area that was supposed to have served as a security buffer zone, an "area vacated of the routine life of humans and animals," within a short time became a vibrant place full of activity by human beings (and their animals). There the Jewish settlers built themselves dream homes in place of the destroyed dwellings of the Bedouins and established splendid agricultural ventures with the help of the cheap labor of the expellees. And a city, too, was built not far from there. Its name: Yamit. The Rafah case was the beginning of the sweeping and prolonged sanction that was granted by the Supreme Court for depriving people of their land in the name of Israel's security needs.

One of the few Israeli jurists who had the courage to enter into conflict with the judicial system on the issue of the territories wrote about this first ruling by the High Court of Justice. "With respect to the High Court of Justice this [was] the beginning of a long career of approving actions by a military commander out of security justifications that proved to be false. . . . Was the Supreme Court naïve, was it the only one who did not know that the buffer area vacated of humans was prepared for the building of expansive settlements there, which enriched their owners with free land, cheap water and most importantly local workers who cultivated the beloved-hated land for the daily wage of a mere pita with oil?"[46]

Civilian Jewish Settlements

Another milestone in the relations of Israeli law and the settlements was the High Court of Justice's handling of the Beit El and Elon Moreh affairs toward the end of the 1970s. Within the space of a few months the court had to deal with two appeals by Palestinian inhabitants against the confiscation of their lands, and released two opposite rulings. The rulings dealt mainly with the question of the legality of the settlements from the point of view of Israeli law and international law. The court also had to address the question of whether a civilian settlement can be considered "a security installation," which is permissible under international law. The first plaint, which came before the High Court of Justice on November 23, 1978, involved the settlement at Beit El, and its story is the story of the way Israel robbed Palestinian lands for allegedly security purposes. In a swift reversal, these security "needs" took on a different form and became the needs of the Jewish settlement there. Twenty-five Palestinians, owners of lands in the area of El Bireh in the Ramallah district, adjacent to the Beit El military camp, and in the area of Tubas in the Nablus district, filed the plaints. The addressees of the plaints were Defense Minister Ezer Weizman and the military commanders in those areas. Because of the importance of the issues of principle these plaints presented, the court sat with an expanded bench of five justices, headed by Deputy Supreme Court President Moshe Landau.[47]

The Palestinians petitioned against the seizure of their lands by the army, against the denial of their right to enter their lands and make use of them, and against the intention to establish settlements there, which in the words of the justices themselves were "civilian Jewish settlements." Years earlier, on February 16, 1970, the area military commander issued an order to seize lands for "crucial and urgent military purposes." The landowners in the area were offered annual leasing fees. Some of them accepted this offer. For the most part, the seized lands were neither inhabited nor cultivated, because of their proximity to the Jordanian military camp, which came into the hands of the Israeli army in the wake of the war. At the beginning of 1975 the military commander in the Nablus area issued a land confiscation order in the area of Beqa'ot, which was also based on "security-military need." However, unlike in the previous case, the lands in the Beqa'ot area were cultivated. The landowners did not even know about the confiscation order. When they came to work their fields in the summer of 1978, they were ejected from the site by settlers who had taken control of their land and plowed it. In its reply to the High Court of Justice, the state argued that the owners of the land had known about the order. In both places, during the course of 1978 Jewish settlers established civilian settlements under the auspices of "security needs." The representatives of the state did not deny that a civilian settlement was being erected on the lands, but they argued that this settlement would be integrated into the defense system in the area, hence the military nature of the confiscation.

The owners of the lands presented to the High Court of Justice sworn statements and documents that testified to the robbing of their lands and the settlers' activities on those lands. For his part, the state prosecutor appended to his arguments a sworn statement from Major General Avraham Orly, the coordinator of activities in the territories. Paratroop officer Orly had an impressive past in the administration of territories in his capacity as commander of the Gaza Strip. The court accepted his statement without question as "an authorized expression of the government's position." The deliberations at the court took place during the peace negotiations between Israel and Egypt, and reverberations from these negotiations echoed in the court. It must also be recalled that for more than a year there had been a new government in Israel that was guided by an ideology, a historical-political outlook, and a map of Israel entirely different from those of the governments that had preceded it. "Every one of us knows, of course, about the recent political developments in our region," wrote Justice Alfred Witkon in his preamble, "about the peace negotiations, about the aspirations and hopes on the one hand and the concerns and objections on the other, but there is a need to understand that the judicial institution does not deal with things that pertain to the future. This we will leave to the politicians. We are deliberating on the rights of the parties before us in accordance with the existing situation between Israel and the Arab states. This is a situation of belligerency, and the status of the respondents with respect to the administered territory is the status of an occupying power."[48] The justice added that "the fighting is currently taking the form of acts of terror, and anyone who sees these acts (which harm tranquil civilians) as a form of guerrilla warfare will admit that the occupying power is entitled and indeed obliged to employ means necessary for their prevention."

The attorney for the plaintiffs, Elias Khoury, tried to distinguish the Beit El case from the precedent that the High Court of Justice had handed down in the Rafah Salient affair five years earlier. He added that the area of the Rafah Salient had been dangerous even before the land seizure order was issued, whereas the areas whose fates were under discussion at this time were quiet and serene. The court was not persuaded by this argument, and replied that "there is no better remedy for an illness than its prevention before it starts, and it is better to discover and thwart the act of terror before it is carried out."[49] And how was the link made between a military-security need, which requires and allows land seizure, and "a civilian Jewish settlement"? As if this were the most natural thing, Witkon wove the thread that tied the settlements to Israel's security system, thus mixing security needs and the needs of the "civilian" settlements. "There must be no doubt that the presence in the territory of settlements—even 'civilian' settlements—of citizens of the occupying power makes a serious contribution to the security situation in that territory and makes it easier for the army to fulfill its role. There is no need to be an expert on military and security matters to understand that terrorist elements are more easily active in a territory that is inhabited solely by a population that is indifferent or even sympathetic to the enemy than in a territory in which there are also people who are likely to keep them under surveillance and inform the authorities of any suspicious movement. In their midst terrorists will not find concealment, aid and equipment. It is simple and there is no need to elaborate."[50] Thus, with the stroke of a pen, Witkon "conscripted" the settlers into the army, transformed them into lookouts and alarm tools for the security services, a living shield against hostile elements. He had upgraded messianic settlement interests to the level of crucial "security needs."

Here too the Supreme Court addressed the key issue of Israel's domination of the territories, that is to say the question of whether the State of Israel is subject to international conventions regarding settlement. As noted, in its prior ruling in the matter of the Rafah Salient, the court had ruled that the Geneva Conventions and Hague Regulations are part of consensual international law, and as such must have special domestic legislation to make them applicable, which had not been done in Israel. In the wake of that ruling, Professor Yoram Dinstein, an expert on international law, published a critical article in which he said that the 1907 Hague Conventions must be seen as part of customary international law, a universal obligatory norm. He argued that the Geneva Convention gives expression to what in any case is accepted in the enlightened countries.[51] This article became a milestone. Justice Witkon, to cite one example, changed his mind after the article appeared and ruled that it is possible to sue under the Hague Regulations in a court in Israel. However, he continued to hold the opinion that the provisions in the Geneva Convention on the matter of the transfer of populations of the occupying power to the occupied territory had not automatically become part of Israel's domestic law.

This ruling by the High Court of Justice on the matter of the Geneva Convention left in the hands of the plaintiffs the possibility of basing themselves on the Hague Regulations only. Under these regulations it is prohibited to "destroy or seize the enemy's property, unless such destruction or seizure be imperatively demanded by the necessities of war." It was the occupier's duty according to these regulations to respect family honor and rights, human life, private property, and religious convictions and rites. The state prosecutor's argument that this was not a matter of land confiscation but rather of a demand to use it satisfied the justice, and with this the court eliminated in a stroke the obstacle of the Hague Regulations. When the attorney for the Palestinian landowners wondered how it was possible to establish a permanent settlement on land that had been seized only for temporary use, the presiding justice responded that this is "a weighty issue," and determined that the civilian settlement established on the plaintiffs' land could exist only as long as the army holds the land by virtue of a seizure order.

Justice Landau reinforced even further the deterministic connection between the settlements and the army's needs. He elaborated on the roles of the settlements in times of calm, yet argued for their special importance "in times of war, when the regular military forces are relocated from their bases in accordance with the needs of operational action and the aforementioned settlements constitute the main element of security presence and control in the areas where they are located." Accepting Major General Orly's sworn statement without question, the justice added a reflection of his own regarding the political dispute over the settlements, which was tearing Israeli society apart. "It is well known," wrote Landau," that in various circles of citizens there are different views of the importance of Jewish settlement in Judea and Samaria: There are those who negate it entirely and there are those who favor it as an expression of the political view that no part of the land of Israel will be closed to Jewish settlement; and there are those who put the emphasis on the military aspect of Israeli control in places of strategic importance in Judea and Samaria for the effective defense of the territory of the state and its inhabitants." The arguments in the major general's statement, wrote Landau, "testify to the last of these versions, and I have no reason to doubt that he represents this position faithfully and not in order to conceal any other view." Indeed, the moment the functionaries in uniform appeared in court, their words about "security reasons" and "military needs" were considered absolute, devoid of any political inclination, like holy writ that must not be questioned.

In view of the negotiations between Israel and Egypt that were under way at the time, Justice Landau supported the interpretation that the Geneva Convention did not apply in the territories. He argued that the court should refrain from deliberating on the matter of civilian settlement in an administered territory from the perspective of international law "because this problem is a matter of controversy between the government of Israel and other governments and it might be on the agenda in fateful international negotiations in which the government of Israel is involved." It is preferable, he added, to discuss what belongs to the realm of international policy only in that realm.[52] The court's decision to reject the Palestinians' plaint was unanimous. The justices accepted Major General Orly's sworn statement on the grounds that the plaintiffs had not succeeded in sowing doubt regarding the honesty of the statement and that there had not been a "misuse of security considerations," nor had the security considerations been "an excuse for other aims."[53]

The Likud government greeted the court's ruling with whoops of victory. Prime Minister Begin declared solemnly that "there are judges in Jerusalem." Civilian Jewish settlements on lands that had been occupied in war and had been "inducted" for the sake of appearances had received the seal of approval from the highest court in Israel, contrary to international law and custom. However, albeit in vague language and more for the sake of the record, the justices did not ignore the "temporariness" of the settlements. But this temporariness was relative and amorphous. An additional and perhaps even more important question arose from the court's ruling: In "conscripting" the settlers, had the court not provided them with actual weapons, thus validating the conditions for transforming them into militias to which the laws and limitations of a regular army do not apply? In so doing the court helped to turn the entire territory into a legal twilight zone, in which everything is permitted and where the demarcation line between enforcers of security and law and violators of security and law was irreparably blurred. Indeed, as was plain to see, the weapon that was legitimized in the first act would be fired in the subsequent acts.

Felix's Sworn Statement

Half a year later, the same bench of justices was required to hold another deliberation on the same question. This time it was the settlement at Elon Moreh, which had been established in the vicinity of the Palestinian town of Nablus, the center of Palestinian life and activity in the northern part of the West Bank. Seventeen Palestinian landowners in the area appealed to the High Court of Justice against the State of Israel, the defense minister, and the military commanders.[54] The plaintiffs were again represented by attorney Elias Khoury, and alongside him were two Israeli lawyers. After countless attempts to lay down a stake in Samaria, the Elon Moreh group had succeeded, with the government's help, in settling on the land of the village of Rujib, adjacent to Nablus. On June 5, 1979, the commander of the Judea and Samaria area signed the "Order on the Matter of the Seizure of Land, Number 16/79." The order "seized" 700 dunams (175 acres) in the areas that were required for "military needs." Two days later, in the early morning hours, the settlers of Elon

Moreh, aided by the army, embarked on a well-publicized settlement operation. Helicopters were mustered for the mission and heavy vehicles helped cut a route from the Jerusalem-Nablus road to the bare hill. By the evening, a tent had been erected and a flag raised.[55]

The Palestinian plaintiffs were landowners in the village, as attested by the Nablus registry. The total area of their lands was estimated at 125 dunams. On the morning of the day the settlers made their ascent up the hill, the land seizure order was handed to the village chiefs, the mukhtars. The landowners applied to the High Court of Justice in Jerusalem, which on June 20, 1979, issued an order nisi to the defense minister and the military commanders in the area requiring them to explain the reason for the seizure. It also handed down an interim order preventing additional work on the ground.[56]

By consent and support of the government, a Jewish settlement in the heart of a densely populated Palestinian area had aroused a political storm in Israel and abroad. The stabbing of "a knife into the heart of Palestinism," as the settlers put it, was also perceived as the stabbing of a knife into the heart of the fragile peace process.[57] Because of the public dispute, which split the government in two, the State Prosecutor's office turned to the highest military authority, Chief of Staff Rafael Eitan, whose opinion regarding the importance of settlements was known, as he had stated it at meetings of the ministerial committee on settlement matters in May. At those meetings, the chief of staff had expanded his vision and offered a historical interpretation attesting to the civilian settlements' contribution to the security of the Jewish community in the prestate period and claimed that it was impossible to answer to the current security needs in the area under question without establishing a civilian settlement. His view was contested by many. Defense Minister Ezer Weizman, himself a general of high repute, held the opposite opinion and did not at all keep it to himself. He also objected to the chief of staff giving a sworn statement on behalf of the security establishment. Eitan's attitude was thus not submitted as a sworn statement but rather as a general opinion, in which the particular settlement in question was not even mentioned.

The Palestinian plaintiffs, however, came armed with two impressive statements, one from former Chief of Staff Haim Bar-Lev, whose readiness to come down on the side of the Palestinians was a novelty. The other was from Major General (Res.) Matityahu Peled. Elon Moreh "does not contribute to Israel's security," asserted Bar-Lev. The existence of a Jewish settlement, he said, "on a desert island in the midst of Arab territory that is densely populated by Arab inhabitants is liable to make attempted terror attacks easier. The securing of movement to and from Elon Moreh and guarding the settlement will disengage security forces from essential missions."[58] Prophetic words. Peled was even more explicit. "The argument as to the security value intended for the settlement of Elon Moreh was not made in good faith, and for only one purpose: to give a justification for the seizure of the land that cannot be justified in any other way," he stated.[59]

The recent ruling on Beit El and the criticism of it by senior jurists was fresh in the minds of all concerned in the Elon Moreh affair, particularly the Supreme Court justices, who finally realized the significance of their earlier ruling, which had enabled a wave of civilian settlements on privately owned Palestinian lands. The state prosecutor also declared to the High Court of Justice that at government meetings he had explained to the ministers that the Beit El ruling did not constitute a priori legal permission for every seizure of private land for settlement purposes in the territories. In the initial stage, therefore, the court issued an interim order that froze construction of the settlement and the number of its inhabitants. The settlers responded with restraint combined with a threat. "We will obey the High Court of Justice order," they said, "and we are not alarmed, because even if we lose the entire case we will act to change the law so that the settlement will remain."[60] At this stage two members of the settlers' secretariat, Menachem Felix and Avraham Shvut, asked to join as respondents to the plaint, and the court agreed.

More than anything else, it was Felix's sworn statement that decided the fate of the case. One of the first settlers of Kiryat Arba and cofounder of Elon Moreh, an honest and above-board man admired by his peers, Felix declared that he and his friends had settled at Elon Moreh not "for security reasons" but rather because of the divine command to inherit the land of the patriarchs. He added that the act of settlement by the Jewish people in the Land of Israel is the most concrete, the most effective, and the truest act of security. The settlement, said Felix, does not derive from any physical needs but is an act of destiny and of realizing the command of Israel's return to its land. "Elon Moreh is the very heart of the Land of Israel," Felix said. "Not simply geographically and strategically, but above all this is the place where the land was promised for the first time to our first forefather, and it is the place where the first purchase was done by the father of the nation after whom this land is called— the Land of Israel." Felix claimed he had no doubt about the sincerity of the security argument, yet in his opinion it neither added nor detracted. "Whether or not the Elon Moreh settlers are integrated into the defense system in the area according to the IDF's planning, settlement in the Land of Israel, which is the destiny of the Jewish people and the State of Israel, is in any case the security, the peace and the well-being of the people and the state."[61]

The truth about the confiscation of the land thus burst through the impenetrable thicket of legal hairsplitting and the smokescreen of statements by military commanders about Israel's "security needs." Felix's sincere words exposed not only the false display of "professional" and "security" opinions from the military heads but also the submissiveness of the highest court to the magic word "security." Justice Landau, who since the Rafah Salient case had been presiding over the plaints of inhabitants whose lands had been stolen from them, very much disliked these deliberations that were forced upon the Supreme Court. At the depths of Landau's discourse was the fear that the High Court of Justice ruling would be perceived as the taking of a stance in the political debate that was ripping apart the Israeli collective, as if it could be otherwise in the first place. "As we sit in judgment, we must not involve our personal views as citizens of the country," said Landau. "There is great concern lest the court appear to have abandoned the place of which it is worthy and *descend* into the arena of public debate, and its decision be greeted by one part of the public with applause and by the other part with total and emotional rejection."

For Landau, as his words implied, the Supreme Court was positioned somewhere far above the public sphere, and it was thus within its powers to produce a sublime formula detached from the bustle of politics. In this he represented the view of many Supreme Court justices—certainly that of future president Meir Shamgar—that the very fact of their sitting in the most exalted public place in Jerusalem afforded them an all-encompassing gaze, the total objectivity and authority to interpret history, Zionism, the State of Israel, and its security needs, and to do this in absolute terms, without ideological or personal inclinations. This view is indeed a necessary, constitutive fiction of the law in general, but from the statements and rulings of the Supreme Court justices in that period it appears that they were identifying with this fiction without the proper self-awareness. Thus, for example, Shamgar said of himself, "In my positions in the army or in any other official role I never invoked political considerations . . . right, left or otherwise."[62] He said it in 2002, from the height of his years and experience and at the height of the second Palestinian uprising against Israel's long occupation, when one might have expected that he would apply to himself a somewhat more critical perspective. Justice Landau, for his part, complained that the court was compelled to rule on political issues and that any ruling would be interpreted as political. He asserted that the stature of the court, which is "above the disputes that split the public," was liable to be injured by this.[63] Yet at the same time, this justice, who perceived himself to be above politics, argued that Prime Minister Begin's argument to the state prosecutor—that it is necessary to stress in the trial the full right of Israel to settle in Judea and Samaria—is a view that "leaned on the very foundations of the thought of Zionism."[64]

The case of Elon Moreh was so blatant that even Landau, whose political views filtered like sunlight through the interstices of his legal formulations, concluded that in this affair the conditions of "military needs" were not fulfilled in accordance with the Hague Regulations. The main reason for his remarks was that the initiative for the settlement had come from the government level, which had requested that the chief of staff express his professional opinion on the matter. Landau saw the government's decision, which had been made in return for the cessation of Gush Emunim's illegal acts on the ground, as "clear proof that it was pressure from the Gush Emunim people that had stimulated the ministerial committee to have recourse at that meeting to the matter of a civilian settlement in the Nablus area." This process, he said, was in violation of Article 52 of the Hague Regulations. While noting the importance of "respecting the profound religious belief and the devotion" of the settlers, Landau made use of

Felix's admission that the security argument was an illusion in determining that the Elon Moreh settlement did not stand the test of the
Hague Regulations.[65]

What had happened to the justice between the Beit El ruling
and the Elon Moreh ruling? Why did he apply the Hague Regulations in the second case? Had it taken the bold, unvarnished truth
of the settler Felix for Landau to realize that it was not security
needs that drove the theft of land from the Palestinian inhabitants?
Had he and his colleagues on the Supreme Court bench been so out
of touch and naïve, finding it difficult to understand what every child
in Israel had long understood? Had they been affected by voices
coming from within the government itself, of generals and security
people like Yigal Yadin and Ezer Weizman, who opposed settlements
in the territories for security reasons? In any case, the court's ruling on
Elon Moreh was utterly at odds with the one handed down in the Beit
El case less than a year earlier. It revoked the military order to seize
the plaintiffs' land and ordered the government and the army to evacuate the settlers within thirty days.

Albek's Decade

Those who promptly understood the full import of the Elon Moreh
ruling were the settlers. On that same evening the Gush Emunim secretariat convened and decided to reject a priori any proposal that
involved the uprooting of the settlement. After twenty days of running around, threats, and attempts to circumvent the High Court of
Justice, the settler leaders declared a hunger strike. For his part, Agriculture Minister Ariel Sharon demanded that the government
"appoint a team of legal experts who will 'immunize' the settlements
against High Court of Justice intervention."[66] In a brilliantly formulated document, Gush Emunim elucidated, in a way that no political

body had done before, the legal status of the occupied territories and the status of the settlements. The document was intended of course to cry out against the disgrace and to undermine the legal state of affairs, but it revealed the truth that Israeli society had stubbornly refused to see and confront.

"Israel has constituted in Judea, Samaria, the Jordan Valley and the Gaza Shore a regime of *military occupation,*" the document began. "Under international law, a military administration is possible only when the occupying power has entered alien territory *that does not belong to it.* . . . The occupying power administers such a territory only temporarily, until peace. . . . In alien territory that is occupied the occupier is forbidden to create any permanent facts: It is forbidden to dig archeological excavations; it is forbidden to confiscate lands; it is permitted to do only what is necessary for the needs of the local population." In applying the law of military occupation in the heart of the Land of Israel, said the settlers, all of Israel's governments have determined that "for us Judea and Samaria are a foreign land that has been occupied . . . [and] our presence in Judea and Samaria is only temporary." The document also stated that the Labor-led governments built settlements in Judea, Samaria, and Gaza on land that had been seized *"for military needs."* They did this "so that they would be able to explain and offer the excuse that this settlement does not contradict the military occupation."

"The 'security' fiction," the settlers went on to say, "was kept as long as the Arabs—with American advice and encouragement—did not take up the weapon of the High Court of Justice. . . . In the Elon Moreh ruling [the High Court of Justice] determined that *the military needs are temporary and therefore no more permanent Hebrew settlement will be possible in the heart of the land of Israel."* Thus, asserted the settlers, "the ground has been stricken out from under any Jewish settlement project in the liberated territories. The fate of the new settlers, about 20,000 souls, the billions of Israeli pounds that have been invested, the security of the state of Israel that cannot be defended without Judea and Samaria, and the fate of the most intimate and beloved places in our home-land—all of these remain as though suspended in the air, like diaspora figures in a painting by Chagall. With no ground."[67]

It was not for very long that the Chagall-like figures remained with no ground beneath their feet, a picturesque but factually baseless bit of rhetoric. Following the Elon Moreh decision the Defense Ministry made public that since 1967, 61,000 dunams (15,250 acres) had been confiscated for "military needs." More than 40,000 dunams had been given to the settlements.[68] In their lands document, Gush Emunim raised the possibility of establishing settlements on "state lands," but lamented that on the hilly platform of Judea and Samaria *"there are no state lands."*[69] They knew what they were talking about, but they also knew that everything is relative and that lands, like other things—or even human beings, for that matter—can change their status with the sweep of a pen in the hands of the mighty and pow-erful. Indeed, from the crisis of Elon Moreh a tremendous settlement momentum surged, and from this defeat a victory was forged. Out of the strong came forth sweetness. Instead of the High Court of Jus-tice, which could no longer grant its legal seal of approval for stealing lands, after the truth about it was once and for all exposed in the full daylight, government stepped in by means of the attorney general and the State Prosecutor's Office. The government headed by Menachem Begin resolved that new settlements would be established only subject to the attorney general's decision with regard to the land rights.[70]

The next phase of the settlement project, the decade of the 1980s, was marked by the blanketing of the West Bank with dozens of Jewish settlements not only in fulfillment of the vision and ideology of

Greater Israel but also for the purpose of rendering the domination of the land and Jewish settlement on it irreversible. This period earned the name "the Albek decade," after the director of the Civil Department at the State Prosecutor's Office, Plia Albek, who effectively annexed by "legal means" more than half of the West Bank and legitimized the land for settlements. The revolution that Albek launched with regard to the settlements, and the status and influence she accumulated during those years, were so extensive that toward the end of the period, *Yedioth Aharonoth* wrote that Albek had become "a monument in the history of Israeli law." With her own hands, wrote the influential journalist Nachum Barnea, Albek created the legal structure that enabled the State of Israel to annex the territories de facto and to maintain massive settlements: "Thus she impressed an ineradicable stamp on the face of the state. . . . The history on the ground is being written by Plia Albek."[71]

Albek was a scion of the Jerusalem civil service nobility, from a family of German-Jewish extraction that had shaped the legal and civil service infrastructure of Israel. Her father was the venerated state comptroller Yitzhak Nebenzahl. At seventeen she had already begun to study law at the Hebrew University, and she began to work at the Justice Ministry before she turned twenty, by which time she had married Shalom Albek, who was later appointed professor of law at Bar-Ilan University. In 1969, at the age of thirty-one, Albek was given the post of director of the Civil Department at the State Prosecutor's Office, a position that she held for twenty-four years, until she was dismissed. From the end of the 1960s until her death in 2005, Albek lived with her family and other branches of the Nebenzahl clan in a large house her father had built in the Old City immediately after it was occupied by Israel in 1967, overlooking the Western Wall and East Jerusalem.

Her brother Avigdor Nebenzahl, the rabbi of the Old City who was considered a great Torah scholar, was suspected of having been one of the rabbis who issued the judgments of *din rodef* (permission to kill a person who persecutes Jews) and *din moser* (permission to kill an informer or one who turns a Jew over to non-Jews) against Yitzhak Rabin after the signing of the Oslo agreement and during the period before the assassination, but he denied this.[72] Eventually, during the settlers' struggle against the plan to withdraw from Gaza, in the summer of 2004, Rabbi Nebenzahl said openly, in front of television cameras, that according to the Jewish view, someone who hands territories of the Land of Israel to gentiles is subject to *din rodef*, and aroused a short-lived fuss, yet no legal measures.[73]

Slowly but surely, and under the cover of the legalistic professionalism that she radiated, Albek became responsible for one of the most sophisticated and virtuoso acts of annexation in recent generations. Albek came to the issue of lands in the West Bank almost by chance in 1977, when Attorney General Aharon Barak asked her—pursuant to a request from Defense Minister Ezer Weizman—to give her opinion on the question of whether the lands slated for the construction of the Ariel and Tapuah settlements were "state lands" or lands privately owned by Arabs. Barak asked her to go out in a helicopter and examine the status of the area. The main criterion was whether or not the land in question was cultivated. According to Albek, who told the story over and over again, the inexperienced religious woman lawyer toured the wild frontiers of the West Bank in an Air Force helicopter to glean lands for the sons of her people. Even though, she said, she did not know the first thing about navigation, maps, or aerial photographs, she came back after only forty-eight hours with a detailed report to the effect that they were indeed "state lands." From then on, this sequence of events became a regular mode of action: Albek, accompanied by military people, heads for the territories in a helicopter or Jeep, instructs officers and pilots on navigation there, and comes back with a detailed opinion.

During the period of Menachem Begin's government Albek gained a unique status that went well beyond her official position in the Justice Ministry. The prime minister personally invited her to sit in on regular meetings of the ministerial committee on settlement matters, which dealt mainly with the establishment of new settlements, and to serve as the committee's legal adviser. Begin's demonstrative admiration reinforced her considerable power, thus making Albek the most influential figure on settlement affairs. When she first embarked on the project, Albek confined herself to answering questions put to her regarding the availability of land intended for the establishment of a settlement and its legality. Later on she led the entire move. She would head for the territories regularly, and personally examine and approve the land even before it had been decided whether or not a settlement should be built there. At a subsequent stage, she would get ahead of the demand and at her own initiative would locate state lands even before she had been requested to do so and even before the maps for establishing new settlements had been drafted, in order to organize for the Jewish people a reserve of lands "for the next 100 years."

In a newspaper interview in 1986, Albek spoke about her pattern of action, which had attained tremendous dimensions. "When government ministries want to establish a settlement at a given site in Judea, Samaria or the Gaza region, they contact us with a request that we check the ownership of the land. First I examine the aerial photographs. If I see that it is a question of cultivated land, I do not go any further. I inform them that there is no possibility of establishing a settlement at that site. However, if it becomes clear to me in checking the aerial photographs that the territory is not cultivated, we examine the land registries in which there are listings of all the lands from back in the days of the British. The owners of lands from earlier periods usually have a title document (deed of purchase) that shows that the land belongs to them. Any lands that are not under private ownership are state lands and prima facie it is possible to build a settlement on them. At this stage I go out there, in a helicopter or a Jeep, to form a first-hand impression of whether the land is cultivated and whether the place is suitable for establishing a settlement in terms of its location, the quality of the soil and its size. Usually I try to keep the timing of the visit secret so as to enable an objective inspection. There have already been cases in which I arrived at the location and saw that they were unloading trucks full of seedlings and rushing to plant them in the ground to create the impression that the land was cultivated. When the land isn't cultivated and there is no registration of ownership, the administration people inform the mukhtar of the intention to put up a new settlement on the site. During a period of forty-five days anyone who claims ownership is entitled to apply to the administration appeals committee. In most cases appeals are submitted. Only afterward, at the end of all the examinations, which usually take a few months, do I submit a legal opinion and the ministerial committee discusses the approval of the establishment of a settlement and a permit is issued to begin work on the ground."[74]

In the Jordanian estate registries, more than half a million dunams of land, or 125,000 acres, in the West Bank are listed as "state lands." Another 160,000 dunams (40,000 acres) were also considered state lands, but not registered. And indeed, in 1973 official Israeli publications stated that the area of state lands in the West Bank amounted to approximately 700,000 dunams (175,000 acres).[75] As noted, the main criterion for defining the lands as state lands was whether or not they were cultivated. The legal structure that Albek erected to legitimize wholesale land confiscations was made possible by land laws that prevailed in the area prior to its occupation by Israel and because the effort to reorganize and regularize those laws in a way that would suit the twentieth century was just beginning on the eve of the Israeli occupation.

The means by which Albek provided the state authorities with the tools they needed to carry out settlement plans was an article she found in an 1858 Ottoman law. According to that article, "lands that were not in the possession of an individual, that is to say he cannot show a title deed, and have never been allocated to inhabitants of towns or villages, and are at a distance from a town or a village such that the sound of the voice of a man who is at the edge of the locality can be heard there . . . such as rocky hills, wild fields and oak forests (these lands) are *maout* (dead), and anyone who needs them may sow and cultivate this land on license from the authority, for no payment, and on condition that the right of ownership will remain in the hands of the sultan." After June 1967, the all-powerful sultan was the government of Israel. It was on this old text that Albek built her legal platform, which in effect robbed the Palestinian people of their land. Any plot for which there was not orderly registration, and which had not been cultivated for ten years, was transferred from the possession of the Palestinians to the Jewish people, which the Likud government at that time and large parts of Israeli society had seen from the outset as the legal historical owner of the territory.

Protection of Property Rights

Albek's colleagues at the State Prosecutor's Office knew that her main work during the 1980s was the creation of a system of justifications for stealing Palestinian land. They knew and they kept silent, or spoke anonymously, as did one prosecutor who appeared frequently in the courts in land cases. "Albek used every law, provision and regulation that was passed since the time of Napoleon. . . . She succeeded in harnessing to the theft chariot the entire many-layered and complicated structure of all of the laws prevailing in the territories: Ottoman law, mandatory law, Jordanian and Israeli, and the Emergency Regulations, with their whole complex system of regulations. Every dunam she could put a hand on, private lands, state lands, agricultural lands, areas that had been designated as archeological, she found the right trick and the legal cover."[76]

At the base of Albek's practice was the capitalist ideology of the Likud, which sanctifies private property. Whereas during the days of the Labor-led governments, settlements were established with no regard for the owners of the land and land confiscations were carried out under the cover of military purposes, the Begin government put a new policy into effect. New settlements were established only on state lands and not on private lands, and care was taken not to harm private ownership. "In this the government demonstrated much greater awareness of private property," said Albek. "As an attorney I am aware of the need to maintain the rule of law. I take fanatical care to ensure that the rights of the individual will not be harmed, but at the same time I must give the state authorities the possibility of carrying out their settlement plan."[77] Albek's approach was indeed that there was no need to settle against the law and in confrontation with it when it was possible to act within it and in cooperation with it. The question, of course, is which law and how it was interpreted. The act of confiscating Palestinian lands and transferring them to the possession of the Jewish people for purposes of moving Jewish civilians into those territories was, as noted, an utter violation of all the international conventions that relate both to the obligations of the occupying power and the rights of the occupied, including their private and collective property rights.

For while she was scrupulously overseeing every detail of the preservation of the West Bank inhabitants' private property, Albek was systematically striving to rob the Palestinian people of their collective assets and to pull the ground out from under their feet. In this way she confiscated the very basis of Palestinian common life and their political sphere. To paraphrase the French revolutionaries' formula concerning citizens of the Jewish faith—as individuals everything, as a nation, nothing—it could be said (with reservations, as after the French Revolution the Jews enjoyed civil equality, whereas the Palestinians live under prolonged military occupation) that Plia Albek recognized the Palestinians' individual property rights and protected them while dismantling their most basic national goods, the territorial basis of their nationality. "Nearly half of the West Bank lands were in this way declared to be state lands, which in the perception of the Likud government belong to the Jewish people and not to the inhabitants who have dwelt there for generations, as determined by international law," said historian and researcher of the territories Meron Benvenisti.[78]

Like many people in the legal system over the years, Albek argued vehemently that she was acting in an objective way, free of political bias. "My refraining from political activity," she said, "is what enables me to maintain objectivity. My role is to protect the rule of law." She admitted, however, that "someone who very much objects to the establishment of Jewish settlements in Judea and Samaria could not fill my position."[79] A decade after her retirement Albek boasted in a *Ha'aretz* interview that "there are more than 100 settlements that are built on my reports. Every time I came to visit them, I felt like they were my children."[80] Albek was dismissed from her position in the summer of 1993, not long after the Labor Party returned to power. Her clearly political worldview, her moral temperament, and the hubris that came with the enormous power she accumulated led to her downfall. In the face of a damages suit filed by a Palestinian after his wife's death from Border Police gunfire, the senior prosecutor gave the order to argue that "the plaintiff has only benefited from his wife's death, as during her lifetime he was obligated to support her and now he is not obligated." In the summer of 1992, Albek argued that an inhabitant of Hebron, whose arms had been amputated after he was forced to climb an electricity pole to take down a Palestinian flag, was not entitled to compensation from the state because "the handicap did not affect his livelihood as a seller of falafel since good prostheses were fitted on him in Germany." The new Labor justice minister decided to dismiss her.[81]

It must be said, however, that the religious attorney who was so fond of the settlements could not have played the role of "redeemer" of lands for the Jewish people with such great success without the full backing she received from the attorneys general to whom she was subordinate, Professor Aharon Barak, who eventually became president of the Supreme Court, and Professor Yitzhak Zamir, a Supreme Court Justice, both of them eminent liberal jurists who are considered champions of human and civil rights.

Legal No-Man's-Land

As soon as the Israeli army published Article I of the proclamation announcing its takeover of the West Bank, the military became responsible for enforcing law and order in the territories.[82] International law imposes on the occupying power the obligation to protect the lives, body, and property of the inhabitants of the territory under its control.[83] Thus it happened that the Israeli army officially bore the supreme responsibility for preserving the rights and welfare of the Palestinians. In the case of attacks on the local inhabitants by settlers or authorities' personnel, it was determined that the army would be responsible for carrying out the arrests—and that dealing with the investigation would be the responsibility of the police.[84] The authority of the police in the territories is anchored in an order issued by the military commander in the wake of the June 1967 war that gave the police all the authority that was given to soldiers, in addition to the authority they had assumed under the local law that applied in the territories.[85] In cases of unlawful acts attributed to settlers, the police were supposed to send the outcome of their investigations to the state prosecutor for possible indictment. Indictments were to be submitted to the Magistrate's Court of District Court (in accordance with the gravity of the alleged offense), and the court deliberations were to be held in accordance with Israeli penal law.

Since the end of the war the Palestinians in the West Bank and Gaza have been subject to two systems of criminal law. One is the local law (Jordanian law in the West Bank and Egyptian law in Gaza) as it was in effect before June 1967, subject to Israeli security legislation. This law included *inter alia* Britain's Defense (Emergency) Regulations, promulgated in 1945, which Israel had kept in its Law Book after statehood, and of which extensive use was made. The other system is defense legislation passed by the Israeli army as the governing power in the territories, and as determined by the Order in the Matter of Security Instructions.[86] Hence, two systems of courts have existed in the territories: the local courts, based only on local law, and the military courts, authorized to try criminal offenses under both local and military law. The military legal adviser in the territories was authorized to transfer criminal cases from a local court to a military court.

The settlers, too, have been subject to these two legal systems, and at the same time they have also been subject to Israeli criminal law, under an emergency regulation promulgated by the defense minister after the 1967 war.[87] The decision as to which system of laws would be applied to settlers was in the hands of the military commander in the area, the Israeli police, and the State Prosecutor's Office. In practice, it had been customary to try settlers before an Israeli court, under Israeli criminal law.[88] The Oslo agreements did not change the settlers' status because they left exclusive authority over settlers in Israel's hands[89] and did not grant the Palestinian Authority judicial authority over Israeli citizens, even when they commit offenses in an area controlled by the Authority.[90] Hence, a Palestinian who commits an offense is tried in the courts in the territories, mostly military courts, whereas a settler who commits an offense is tried in an Israeli court.[91] This separation has created a screaming inequality between the Palestinians and the settlers. For example, while it is possible, under local law, to hold a Palestinian under arrest for eight days before bringing him before a judge, it is not possible to hold a Jewish settler, who is subject to the arrangements of Israeli criminal law, for more than twenty-four hours before bringing him before a judge. Nor have the punishments been identical: A Palestinian convicted of manslaughter can expect life imprisonment, whereas a settler, for the same offense, can expect a maximum sentence of twenty years in prison. The inequalities do not end with this. While a settler who is sentenced to prison can be released after serving two-thirds of his sentence and even earlier, a Palestinian is not eligible for a similar break and has to serve out his entire sentence.[92]

The chain of law enforcement that eased the punishment of settler offenders in such a far-reaching way did not end with the laxity of the police or with the separate law that was applied to the settlers. The State Prosecutor's Office, which is the body that is supposed to formulate the indictments submitted to the courts, has collaborated with this legal discrimination between settlers and Palestinians. It has done this under the endless pressure that settler leaders have applied to the prosecution. For example, at the start of the trial of Rabbi Moshe Levinger in May 1989 for killing a Hebron Arab, the settlers organized a demonstration in front of the court against the very fact of putting him on trial. Levinger, who had been involved up to his neck in continued violence on the part of the Jewish inhabitants of the town, was now charged with causing the death of Qaid Salah during a disturbance in Hebron. However, his fellow settlers saw him as above the law.[93] The entire legal system was accused by the settlers of being "leftist."

The enforcement of the law on the Jewish settlers had been engaging the legal system since the beginning of the 1980s. As Jewish settlements in the territories expanded and grew in numbers, there were increasing cases of incidents in which settlers attacked Palestinians. During the years 1980–1984 there was a dramatic rise in the number of violent actions by settlers. The number of injuries doubled every two years. In 1980, thirty violent attacks on Palestinians were reported, with one killed and eleven injured; in 1981, there were forty-eight attacks by settlers, with two killed and thirty-five injured; in 1982 the number rose to sixty-nine, with seven deaths and forty wounded. In 1983, 119 attacks were recorded, with nine dead and eighty-three injured, while in 1984 there were 118 attacks, with four killed and twenty-two wounded. Altogether, during those five years twenty-three Palestinians were killed, of whom eleven were children, by shooting or other violent attacks by settlers. In two-thirds of the cases the deaths were caused by the use of firearms.[94] Presumably, the connection between the continuing rise in attacks by settlers and the strong-arm policy in the territories implemented by Ariel Sharon upon his appointment as defense minister in 1981, and his views on the future of the territories, was not random.

The Jewish settlers behaved as though the territories were their own, and the Israeli law and justice system collaborated, both actively and passively. The secretary of the settlement of Shiloh, who on May 17, 1982, opened fire on Palestinian youths who threw stones at his car near the village of Sinjel and killed one of them, went free after the court recommended reducing the charge from murder to manslaughter and after the police claimed that the fatal bullet had not been fired from his weapon. Two years later, with the exposure of the Jewish terror organization in the territories, that same settler was arrested with other Jewish terrorists. One week after the murder near Sinjel, the security coordinator of Kiryat Arba shot an eighteen-year-old from the village of Beit Na'im. The army prevented the police from arresting the shooter, and a delegation of Yesha Council members informed the police that it would not cooperate in the investigation of the incident. On January 31, 1984, that settler, along with five others, was convicted of setting the market in Hebron on fire and of sparking riots there during the course of July 1983.[95] On July 26, 1982, members of the Jewish terror group killed three Palestinians and wounded more than thirty at the Islamic College in Hebron (see Chapter 2). Another of the settlers' tactics was to block roads in the territories. The most extensive roadblock operation took place on February 3, 1985, with the participation of more than 1,000 settlers, who cut off twenty-eight main arteries that link Jerusalem to the towns and villages of the West Bank. For more than two hours traffic stopped entirely along these roads and the settlers conducted "inspections" of the Palestinian cars. No settlers were arrested in the wake of the incident.

Perpetrator Unknown

In November 1983 members of the Kiryat Arba Council met with the head of the Central Command, Amnon Lipkin-Shahak. The major general, who had a reputation as a moderate, in effect approved the militia actions of the lawless settlers. "Anyone who has stones thrown at him has to chase down the person who threw the stones and catch him," said Lipkin-Shahak.[96] It is no accident that the army senior officer met with the Kyriat Arba settlers. The town of Hebron and Jewish Kiryat Arba have been a focal point of violent disturbances and incidents between Jews and Palestinians since the late 1960s and early 1970s. Some of these came to the attention of the public and even to the courts. On May 19, 1981, the High Court of Justice expressed criticism of the police failure in dealing with an incident that had occurred at Beit Hadassah in Hebron, which was home to a number of Jewish families.[97] In response to the justices' criticism of the police, the state undertook to act sternly against disturbances of public order on the part of the settlers and to investigate every complaint thoroughly. A group of Israeli university law professors sent a letter of protest to the attorney general on the matter of the settlers' rampaging and the short arm of the law. In response to this, on April 29, 1981, Attorney General Yitzhak Zamir set up a commission headed by Deputy Attorney General Yehudit Karp. Karp was among the senior jurists in the civil service and was known for her integrity and professionalism. The commission was meant "to ensure insofar as possible that suspicions of offenses committed by Israelis against the Arab inhabitants of the region will be investigated swiftly, efficiently, and effectively." A team consisting of representatives on behalf of the attorney general, the police, the military advocate general, and the district attorney was delegated to coordinate among the various bodies responsible for law enforcement in the territories and to establish procedures and instructions for carrying out investigations, taking legal steps, and following up the implementation.[98]

Prime Minister Begin declared that the authorities would take stern action against all violations of public order and the law and that the government would be strict about this.[99] Karp's commission examined seventy incidents that had been reported during the period of its investigative work and previously, including murders, killings, threats with weapons, trespassing, assault, damage to property, and the way in which the police dealt with them. Of all these incidents, the police recommended filing an indictment in only fifteen of them. In all of the rest the investigations went nowhere and the cases were closed for various reasons and excuses. About a year after it was established, on May 23, 1982, the commission submitted its findings to Attorney General Zamir. For a number of reasons—among them the Lebanon War, which broke out two weeks after the findings were submitted— the official publication of the report was delayed until 1984. The commission's findings confirmed what everyone had already known, that the law in the territories was the law of the settlers and that the arm of the police was much too short in dealing with violent offenders. The commission found, among other things, that the police did not fulfill their obligation to prevent illegal acts, that the number of incidents in which the investigation was closed for reasons of "perpetrators unknown" was higher than usual, that the police evinced a forgiving and indulgent attitude toward the settlers, that in some cases no sincere effort was made to find the culprits, and that in some cases the witnesses were not questioned at all. The commission also found "a large incidence of injuries to the head or upper parts of the body" in cases of shooting injuries by settlers. Most of the reports in those cases "relied on questioning the soldiers only." In many cases the treatment took "an unreasonable amount of time with no attention to the sensitivity of the investigation."[100]

The Karp report stirred up a public storm, and the reactions to it split, predictably, in accordance with the cleavage between the political parties of the right and the left. The Labor group in the Knesset demanded that the commission continue to function in a permanent format, and MK Amnon Rubinstein, a legal scholar, expressed criticism of the representatives of the Justice Ministry, who in the face of the Karp commission's findings presented data about Arabs' actions against Jews.[101] From the other side, Knesset members from the Likud and other right-wing parties attacked Karp with unprecedented ferocity. "The Karp report is the expression of a political opinion in the guise of a legal report. Its political inclination is obvious in every line," declared the council of Jewish settlements in the territories. "Only self-hatred and the lack of elementary sensitivity could lead to such an utter distortion of the reality."[102] The Yesha Council went even further and demanded that disciplinary and public steps be taken against Karp. Jurists and public figures put out a counterdocument, arguing in it that the Karp report was full of lies and based in large part on the words of a police officer whose reliability was in doubt.[103]

The recommendations of the Karp report were never implemented. There was no need to shelve it officially—it was wiped out politically by those whose deeds were the subject of the report, the settlers and their lobbies within the political system. The extent of law enforcement in the territories not only failed to improve in the years after the report was submitted; it even degenerated and led to the creation of two totally different legal-judicial territories. "Apart from the public storm that the report provoked, it did not lead to any real change in the system," said Karp years later. "The storm was because the Israeli inhabitants of the territories refused to read what was in it and they insisted on claiming that the report constitutes an attack on them as settlers, whereas there was no connection at all between their claims and what was written in the report. . . . There is no follow-up commission that will investigate and there is no one who will give an accounting on issues of land disputes, and in the media they have stopped reporting on this as a topic of interest . . . . I cannot stop thinking about the connection between phenomena of dehumanization that occurred and are occurring in the territories and the violent face of our society and the scorn for the value of human dignity in it . . . . It is not possible to administer a system of law enforcement sporadically, and it is not possible to internalize norms with geographical variations. Failed law enforcement in the territories has direct implications for the quality of law enforcement in Israel."[104]

Some of the military officers directly responsible for the administration of the territories admitted as well that the area was lawless. The head of the Civil Administration in the territories, Brigadier General Yeshaiyahu Erez, said in 1988 that there was no law and no judge in the territories, that the police in effect did not exist and did not act on the ground, and that it was not within its ability to enforce the law and impose order.[105] A few years later, in his testimony before the Shamgar commission, which investigated the 1994 massacre carried out by Baruch Goldstein at the Tomb/Mosque in Hebron, Police Commissioner Rafi Peled acknowledged that "there really was a certain degree of superficial law-enforcement. Without a doubt . . . there are places where we are not even present. Therefore we do not know. Certainly there is no law enforcement there."[106] In the wake of the massacre, Prime Minister Yitzhak Rabin also harshly criticized the efficacy of law enforcement with regard to the settlers. In response, Attorney General Michael Ben-Yair proposed examining the possibility of transferring the deliberation of some of the settlers' security offenses to the military courts that operate in the territories. He argued that this move would bring about swifter and more effective execution of justice.[107] The heads of the army vehemently objected to the attorney general's view, arguing that military judges must not be put in the position of having to rule in cases that involve political-ideological controversies. This argument was in effect covering the military and judiciary systems' objection to equivalence between the Palestinians and the Jewish settlers by trying them in the same military courts. This situation would inevitably have exposed the inequality before the law that exists in the territories and would have obligated the military and legal systems to explain how, in the same court and for the same offense, one punishment was ruled for a settler and a far harsher punishment was imposed on a Palestinian.

The separate judiciary systems, whereby the settlers are tried in courts in Israel and the Palestinians in military courts in the territories, perpetuated the situation of juridical separation and inequality, and no one was willing to change this. Moreover, subjecting the settlers to the military courts would have also emphasized the status of military occupation, which both the settlers and the army took care to blur. In view of the army's objection, Prime Minister Rabin decided not to change the prevailing situation but instructed his justice minister to bring before the government a proposal to strengthen the prosecution and the courts so that the treatment of offenses perpetrated by settlers would be swifter and more efficacious.[108]

There Are no Judges in Jerusalem

Over the years the Israeli courts did indeed act extremely cautiously with respect to the punishment of settlers. Many of the verdicts on violent offenses constitute an impressive anthology of looking the other way, nonenforcement of justice, inequality before the law, and reversing the roles of villains and victims. The commander of the Hebron sector, Colonel Meir Khalifi, lamented to Prime Minister Rabin during the latter's visit there in December 1993 that "the army goes through all the procedures. We arrest a Jew. He goes to court and the judge releases him. . . . Justice is not exacted, and when justice is not exacted there is no deterrence."[109] Between 1988 and 1992 (that is, during the first intifada), forty-eight cases of violent deaths of Palestinians were recorded. Only twelve indictments, for one out of four of the cases, were filed against Israeli citizens who were charged with murder, manslaughter, or causing death of a Palestinian through negligence. Of these, only one case culminated in a murder conviction; another ended in a manslaughter conviction and six ended in a conviction of causing death through negligence. The defendant who was convicted of murder, for which the maximum punishment is twenty years in prison, was sentenced to only three years.[110] The minimal value placed on Palestinian lives repeatedly received legal confirmation at district courts in Israel. The light punishments that were imposed by these courts in cases of Palestinian deaths at the hands of settlers were based, *inter alia*, on the pioneering, pathbreaking ruling by Tel Aviv District Court Judge Uri Struzman in the matter of one Nissan Ishegoyev.

On October 26, 1982, Ishegoyev, a resident of the settlement of Hinanit, was driving a garbage truck in the town of Nablus. Two colleagues were with him in the truck. Ishegoyev was supposed to go through a narrow lane that leads to the Balata refugee camp in the town. Shortly before the garbage truck arrived there, Palestinian youths threw stones at the main road. The police advised Ishegoyev to take an alternate route. Young stone-throwers were along this route too, and the truck was hit lightly. The driver stopped his vehicle, got out, and opened fire with an Uzi submachine gun at the alley from which the stones were thrown. A Palestinian boy of thirteen was shot and killed.[111] Ishegoyev was tried for manslaughter.[112] Judge Struzman convicted the defendant of killing the Palestinian youth without malice aforethought. He recognized that the stone-throwing was not

endangering travelers in vehicles on the road. He also criticized the
police for having allowed the accused to enter a route along which
stones were being thrown. In his sentencing the judge continued to
blame the police, stating that the accused in his truck had encountered
trouble but the police and border police forces that were there "saw
him and did not come to his aid."[113] Although the maximum punishment is twenty years in prison, the judge sentenced Ishegoyev to three
months of public service work.

Ishegoyev killed the Palestinian youngster in an atmosphere of
state violence in the killing fields of Lebanon. Struzman handed
down his sentence, however, five and a half years later, on February
22, 1988, a short while after the first Palestinian intifada broke out.
Presumably the burning territories and the outbreak of Palestinian
violence were in the background of Struzman's sentence, and the act
committed by Ishegoyev, who, in a twisted time perspective, was perceived to be a victim of this popular uprising. "We regret," wrote
Struzman in the sentence, "that children and youths, and even adults,
fall victim in the struggle and the war between Israel and Arab world.
. . . As I come to pronounce sentence, as I consider the circumstance
of the accused and the fact that, to my regret, these circumstances were
caused by children and youths, who instead of being under their parents' and educators supervision in hectic times, were engaged in
throwing stones to the point of endangering the police and causing
them to withdraw from the area—I do not believe that it is just for the
accused to be punished stringently for the killing."[114] It would be
interesting to know whether Struzman was aware that the president of
the Supreme Court at the time, Meir Shamgar, had also, at the age of
fourteen, joined the ranks of a violent underground that fought to
liberate the land of Israel from British rule.[115]

Struzman's ruling stirred up a veritable storm among jurists and academics, at least in terms of the customary legal discourse that is usually rather courteous and vague. Prominent legal experts, both young and veteran, harshly attacked the moral position and the scrambling of the concepts that were reflected in the district court judge's sentence. Both sides appealed the sentence. The Supreme Court, which accepted the state's appeal, ruled that "forgiveness toward the appellant and the finding of 'contributory guilt' in the parents and teachers of the deceased . . . is not the appropriate approach for the court to adopt, in view of the outcome which there is none more serious of the killing of a person." The Supreme Court handed down a punishment of three years in prison and noted that it had decreased the number of years in light of the considerable amount of time that had elapsed between the incident and the sentencing, and because it is not customary to exact maximum punishment by the appeals courts. The justice made a point of stating that in this (lenient) Supreme Court sentence there was nothing to indicate the appropriate punishment that should have been passed by the district court.[116] However, most of the district courts ignored this firm statement and chose to relate only to the actual sentence that was handed down. From then on, a punishment of three years in prison for the killing of a Palestinian became the maximum price tag.

In another case, in which Pinchas Wallerstein was convicted of causing the death through negligence of Rabah Ghanem Hamed, District Court Judge Ezra Hadaiya sentenced him only to four months of public service work. Wallerstein was a prince of the settlers with a perfect biography, having been injured during his military service; he was seen as moderate and balanced among a group of hot-bloods, and was the incumbent of a key position in the settlement system. A month after the first intifada broke out, on January 11, 1988, Wallerstein, together with settler Shai Ben Yosef, was traveling along the road from

Psagot to Ofra. Near the village of Bitin he saw young Palestinians burning a tire on the road. He got out of the vehicle and went after the Arab youths, firing his weapon. In the course of the incident Wallerstein covered a distance of about 100 meters from the road and entered the village, firing rounds from his weapon the whole time. The result was one Arab youth killed and another wounded. The victims were shot in the back. In an initial reconstruction of the incident, on that same day, Wallerstein told police investigators that he fired at the youngsters "who fled." In his version, the distance between him and the fleeing youths was about fifty meters during the shooting (according to the police, the distance reached 100 meters). That is, there was no danger whatsoever to the shooter.[117]

Wallerstein's trial began ten months later, two weeks before the elections to the 12th Knesset. Before the trial there were disagreements between the army and the police as to the investigative authority and as to what had happened, as well as a campaign of intense pressures from the right, including the prime minister at the time, Yitzhak Shamir, to treat Wallerstein with kid gloves. A strange detail of this web was the comment made by the head of Central Command Amram Mitzna at the scene of the incident to a correspondent of Arabic television, to the effect that the shooting was justified "in a situation in which people found themselves in danger to their lives." The comment by Mitzna, who was considered by the settlers a "leftist" army commander and years later served for a short time as head of the Labor Party, sounded surrealistic in view of the circumstances of the shooting and Wallerstein's testimony.[118] The commander who had been relentlessly attacked by the settlers was apparently trying, in a moment of weakness, to gain some points to his credit from the settlers or perhaps to back a settler who was considered moderate. In effect, Mitzna was one of many military commanders who helped legitimize the armed settler militias that patrol the West Bank.[119]

"The case before us is with no doubt most regrettable, especially as a human life was lost," wrote Judge Ezra Hadaiya in his ruling. "However, at the same time, it must not be forgotten that the deceased and his friend Ziyad, who were apparently active in the 'Intifada,' were the 'attackers' whose crude and aggressive behavior threatened the well-being, the body and even the life of the accused.... Furthermore, I have taken into consideration the saying that one should not judge one's fellow until one is in his place."[120] Indeed, Hadaiya's ruling contributed a formidable innovation to jurisprudence by subverting it and altogether turning it upside down. The ruling by Hadaiya, who was about to retire, that a judge is entitled to judge an individual only when he, the judge, is positioned exactly in the same place as the defendant, removed the ground from under the entire judicial edifice and act. Yet anything was apparently possible with regard to sentencing Jewish settlers. And the accused himself, who performed public service tasks to which he was sentenced at Hadassah Hospital in Jerusalem, later revealed to the daily newspaper *Ha'aretz* the motives that pushed him and his settler colleagues to shoot at young Palestinians. It was not an act of self-defense but rather one of deterrence and punishment, a show of force. "We will not allow that stones and incendiary bombs be thrown at us, or a situation in which we are shot at and do not react," said Wallerstein. "If the judiciary system thinks that we are in Tel Aviv, and deliberates on our matters as though we are in Tel Aviv, then in the worst case, people will pay the price—but will remain alive. There is a law in Tel Aviv and there is a law in a state of war."[121]

The Gentle Hand and the Strong Arm

The small number of cases that have been discussed here shows that in a systematic way the courts did not exact justice from settlers who were convicted. And this despite the fact that from the outset many of the settlers in these cases were tried for "lesser" charges (manslaughter and not murder, causing death by negligence and not manslaughter, etc.). The Supreme Court did try to erect a dam, a final barrier, to the anarchy, terror, and ethnicization that the settlers and their lobbyists sowed in the judicial system, and against the sweeping devaluation of Palestinian lives, which the district courts repeatedly confirmed in their sentences. In some cases it increased the punishments handed down. However, all in all the Supreme Court was not able to establish an agreed-upon and obligatory precedent for practice in this matter. This is largely because the prosecution appealed to the Supreme Court in only a very restricted number of cases and because in accordance with the existing custom, maximum sentences are not exacted in appeals cases. Moreover, in order to exacerbate the inequality even further, alongside the "gentle hand" policy toward violent settlers, an especially "strong arm" policy was implemented against Palestinians who were suspected of harming settlers. "In Judea, Samaria and Gaza there are two legal systems, and two different kinds of people," MK Amnon Rubinstein, a thoughtful and measured jurist in his conduct and speech, told the Knesset. "There are Israeli citizens with full rights, and there are non-Israeli non-citizens with non-rights."[122]

During the years between the first intifada and the Oslo agreement, the settlers' acts of violence and lawbreaking multiplied. Abusing the "gentle hand" policy toward them that had been adopted by the courts, the settlers became a law unto themselves and changed the rules for opening fire. The prevailing instruction—that weapons should be used only when there is a real danger to life—was relegated to the junkyard. The settler leaders explicitly instructed their people to open fire "for purposes of deterrence," in every case of stone-throwing and even if the stone-thrower flees the scene.[123] At a meeting of the Matteh Binyamin Council, headed by Wallerstein, the settlers were instructed to "relate henceforth to stone-throwers as a life-threatening situation, with all that entails with respect to rules of engagement."[124] Furthermore, the settlers began to initiate and carry out actions against the Palestinians. Those self-initiated actions took various violent forms, among them the wild blocking of routes with the aim of interfering with the Palestinians' life routine, shooting at water tanks on the roofs in Arab villages, setting cars on fire, and destroying agricultural crops.[125]

At the beginning of 1989 Knesset members Yossi Sarid and Dedi Zucker sent a letter to Attorney General Yosef Harish sounding the alarm about the violent actions of the settler militias. Sarid and Zucker came out against the existence of the settler militias, a political army parallel to the Israel Defense Forces. They detailed the settlers' armed and organized patrolling activities and the punishments inflicted on Arab villages. "These activities," wrote Sarid and Zucker, "have not been a spontaneous reaction, but were and are part of an outlook based on a chain of command and an organizational structure that enables the implementation of the policy. . . . It is reasonable to assume that the settler militia has plans readied for possible developments in the territories, and it draws considerable encouragement for the continuation of its activities from the soft and forgiving attitude on the part of the military and legal authorities."[126] A manifesto signed by "community activists" that was distributed to the settlers of Beit El on December 12, 1991, was tantamount to a confirmation of Sarid and Zucker's well-founded accusations. The text reported on the establishment of a committee that would "initiate various actions in response to the Arab terror that is gaining momentum as we all hear, see and feel."[127]

On November 22, 1993, Police Minister Moshe Shahal reported to the Knesset Constitution, Law and Justice Committee on acts of violence toward Palestinians during the intifada that were attributed to Israelis. According to the police minister's data, in 1988, 106 cases were opened; in 1989, 200 cases were opened; in 1990, 189 cases were opened; in 1991, 134 cases were opened; in 1992, 184 cases were opened; and in 1993, 312 cases were opened. These figures reflected only part of the settlers' violent actions toward Palestinians, said the minister, since many of the victims of these violent attacks did not seek redress from the authorities because of the lack of trust they felt in them. In 1993 there was a significant rise in the number of violent actions, relative to the preceding years. The gravity of the settlers' violent acts also increased: During that year alone fourteen Palestinians were killed by Israelis, as compared to one Palestinian killed during the course of 1992.[128] In December 1993 the army distributed a brochure titled *Procedures for Enforcing the Law and Public Order with Respect to Israeli Inhabitants of the Territories.* The brochure, a cooperative effort of the attorney general, the military prosecution, and the police, was aimed at clarifying the legal situation in the territories. However, the instructions listed in it, like the authority of Israeli soldiers to arrest rampaging settlers, for the most part remained a dead letter. In an interview for Israel radio in January 1994, the commander of a select unit that was serving in the Hebron area related that soldiers were forbidden to use tear gas and other such standard crowd-control methods against Jewish disturbers of order.[129] In many cases soldiers just stood around without lifting a finger in the presence of settler violence against Palestinians.[130] Often the soldiers themselves harassed locals.[131] And the law enforcement system stood idly by in the face of the total blurring of borders in the territories: between army and civilians; between law enforcement and arbitrary killings by civilians;

between legitimate self-defense in case of imminent danger and acts of vengeance or "deterrence" committed by civilians immune to the law on civilians with no citizenship and no protecting law, living under military occupation.

Even during the relatively quiet Oslo years of 1993–2000, the settlers continued their violent activities. So much so that a slow and lenient attorney general like Elyakim Rubinstein, who was particularly forgiving toward Jewish lawbreakers, issued directives in 1998 for enforcing the law regarding settler actions such as shooting, stone-throwing, violent rampaging in Palestinian locales, blocking roads, and more.[132] According to these directives, the following division of labor was set: The police would be charged with the enforcement of law and order within the settlements, whereas the army would be responsible for the expanses between the settlements, called the "envelope." These directives "came to provide an answer to a continuing and grave situation of under-enforcement of the law on Israeli inhabitants of Judea and Samaria and Gaza," stated Rubinstein."[133] However, the attorney general's directives, like the Karp commission recommendations in their day, did not change the settlers' conduct in the slightest, nor did the "soft" attitude of the military commanders. What had been went on uninterrupted, with the legal system limping and stuttering in the face of the settlers' conduct.

Hilmi's Death

A dozen years after the question of "how much is the killing of a Palestinian worth" was raised, a precise answer was given. The price of killing a Palestinian child, ruled an Israeli court in coordination with the prosecution, is six months' public service work and NIS 70,000 (some $15,000). This punishment was meted out to settler Nahum Korman for killing the child Hilmi Shusha. The boy's killing was extricated from the mute, despairing statistics of foreknown and continuing death of Palestinians at the hands of settlers, and became a media-legal event not just because the child's killing was so cruel and arbitrary but because the incident exposed the Israeli legal system in all its weakness, vagueness, and moral failure in the face of the settlers and their political lobbyists.

The affair began on October 27, 1996, when Korman, in charge of the security in his settlement Hadar-Betar, chased Palestinian children from the neighboring village Hussan, who, according to his testimony, were throwing stones. Having caught the fleeing Hilmi Shusha, Korman beat him with his revolver and kicked him even after the child fell on the ground. Shusha stopped breathing. Resuscitation was performed on him *in situ;* he regained consciousness and was transferred in critical condition to an Israeli hospital. The best medical experts fought for his life, but two months later, on December 28, 1996, the child died. The affair refused to calm down, as if the whole tragedy of both peoples was embodied in the arbitrary death of this child. The American administration intervened and demanded an energetic investigation, even before the child succumbed.[134] The case moved back and forth from court to court; the Supreme Court reversed the ruling of the Jerusalem District Court, which had exculpated the settler, and in doing so exposed the settler's tissue of lies and double-talk and the destruction he and his comrades had for years sown in the Israeli judiciary. Some of the media, especially the daily newspaper *Ha'aretz*, turned the child into a symbol of the humiliation and suffering of Palestinians under Israeli occupation.[135] The issue was dragged up and down the legal hierarchy for nearly five years, until it reached its culmination at the beginning of 2001, in the midst of the second Palestinian uprising, with a ruling of "six months of imprisonment to be served in public work on behalf of the community."[136] The judge justified her sentence, among other reasons, by the clean record of the accused, a fact that was shown to be untrue.[137] All this did not prevent the banalization of death by the sentence, one more testimony to the special treatment the settlers won at the hands of the law or to the exhaustion and capitulation of the system in face of their lordly behavior.

Another murder case, which engaged Israel's legal system at the time, was that of the settler Yoram Shkolnick. Shkolnick, who in March 1993 heard over his communications equipment about the capture of a Palestinian who had tried to stab two settlers, arrived armed with an Uzi submachine gun and a pistol at the place where the assailant was lying on his stomach, tied up, and surrounded by settlers and soldiers. Without consulting anyone, Shkolnick fired at close range a round of bullets at the bound Palestinian, Moussa Abu Sabha. The man died on the spot. "He deserved it," said Shkolnick. "We must kill them, and this is a war." He added that it, "should serve as an example for the Arabs to see." Those present fell upon Shkolnick, took his weapons, and arrested him. In his interrogation he said that he wanted to "awaken the people. . . . I think that the people is asleep and not awake and I wanted to arouse it."[138]

The Jerusalem District Court, to which Shkolnick's legal defense had submitted a psychiatric opinion on his mental state at the time of the incident,[139] convicted him of murder, and on April 28, 1994, sentenced him to the mandatory punishment for murder—life imprisonment.[140] The Israeli right stood on its hind legs. The Shas faction, which represents the Orthodox Mizrahi and Sephardi community in the Knesset, said that the ruling was a result of "the witch hunt that the government is conducting against the settlers."[141] These were Oslo times, and the political atmosphere was highly flammable. "A situation in which there is one law for settlers and lawlessness for Arabs is untenable," said settler Elyakim Haetzni, who served as the defense attorney for Shkolnick in the first stages of the legal deliberations.[142]

On March 4, 1997, the Supreme Court unanimously rejected Shkolnick's appeal in sentencing him to life in prison.[143] The following lines sum up the reductions in Shkolnick's sentence that he received, one after the other, despite his grave crime: About half a year after his appeal was rejected, President Ezer Weizman mitigated his sentence to fifteen years from the day of his arrest. In January 1999 Weizman again reduced Shkolnick's punishment, to eleven years and three months. In this instance the reduction came in the context of the release of Palestinian prisoners as convened by the Oslo agreements.[144] Thus the end of Shkolnick's imprisonment was set for June 22, 2004. Two-thirds of the period of imprisonment was to end on September 22, 2000. On March 6, 2000, the release committee at the prison held a discussion on early release. The attorney general's representative stated that he objected to early release, "because of the risk inherent in it." The Shin Bet also objected. Nevertheless, the release committee decided to let Shkolnick go free at the end of two-thirds of his already twice-reduced sentence.

Once again the Supreme Court deliberated Shkolnick's case because of the decision on his early release.[145] This time the justices were vehement in their opposition to the reduction of the sentence. The president of the Supreme Court wondered whether this was not a political decision. Another justice wrote that "this is blatantly an act that has an ideological background. . . . Behind the commission of the murder there was a worldview. The respondent believed that he was acting on some sort of 'mission' to awaken the people." The murder, he said, "was committed on a backdrop of boundless hatred that has its basis in a nationalist-idealistic worldview. It is appropriate to speak at length about the danger that is inherent in this nationalist ideology, when it is manifested in the murder of a bound and defenseless individual."[146] Five of the justices joined their colleagues in the High Court of Justice.[147] Yet despite the Supreme Court ruling and the objections of the Shin Bet, the committee again decided to release Shkolnick from prison, although with certain restrictions. Once again an appeal was submitted to the High Court of Justice.[148] This time it was Supreme Court President Aharon Barak and other justices who spoke in several voices. Barak ruled that the reduction in Shkolnick's punishment did harm to the value of human dignity and encouraged scorn for human life, but added that the result of the early release is not "so mistaken" as to justify the court's intervention.[149] Three justices, however, stuck to their opinion and opposed Barak's ruling. Shkolnick's deed, they said, was so heinous that they could not come to terms with the early release. Justice Mishael Cheshin wrote that the abyss between the sentence that was passed on Shkolnick and the punishment he was supposed to serve "is so great, so deep, that it is difficult to understand how this has happened. . . . A person is sentenced to mandatory life imprisonment for murder, and now they are asking to set him free after about eight years of imprisonment. . . . Has human life become so cheap here?"[150] But the majority of the justices decided not to intervene in the release committee's decision. Yoram Shkolnick went free eight years after he murdered the shackled Abu Sabha.

The deep abyss, as Justice Cheshin wrote, between the suitable punishment and the imposed punishment was part of the routine devaluation of law in the territories and a result of the Supreme Court's erosion in its dealing with continued lawbreaking by the settlers and the delegitimization campaign that they waged against the law. The final chapter in the Shkolnick affair occurred in the midst of the second Palestinian uprising, in the shadow of the cruel deaths and sense of victimization on the Israeli side. As in the first intifada, the

Palestinians' street violence and later on the shocking terror attacks inside Israel, which exacted so many innocent victims, provided the settlers with a motive, a propitious hour, and a justification for increasing their own violent activities. In the first year of the second intifada, by October 30, 2001, eleven Palestinians had been killed at the hands of settlers. Shooting and rampaging in Palestinian areas, shooting and stoning of Palestinian vehicles, harassment of Palestinian farmers working in their fields, crop thefts, blocking of roads, and armed patrols by settlers became everyday activities.[151]

Many violent incidents during the course of the second intifada broke out in the wake of Palestinian attacks on settlers. For example, following the killing of Roni Salah, an inhabitant of the Gaza settlement of Gush Katif, on January 14, 2001, hundreds of settlers stormed into the Muasi area in the Strip, fired weapons, damaged property, ruined fields, and burned greenhouses.[152] Toward the end of July 2002, Palestinians opened fire on two Israeli vehicles in the southern Hebron Hills. Eliezer Leibowitz, a soldier from Hebron who was traveling in the first car, was killed. Also killed were three inhabitants of the settlement of Psagot who were traveling in the second car, Hannah and Yosef Dickstein and their little son Shuv-El. During the course of the weekend, from the time the death of the four settlers became known until after the funerals, while the Palestinians were under curfew, settlers embarked on a campaign of vengeance against the inhabitants of Hebron and its environs. A girl of fourteen was killed; two brothers of eight and nine and about ten Palestinian adults were injured. Houses were wrecked and looted. Settlers also attacked soldiers and police. A policeman who entered the cemetery during Leibowitz's funeral was stoned and driven out with curses by the settlers.[153] "Nearly every incident of a Palestinian attack brings in its wake a response on the part of the Jews," said a senior police officer.[154] The chief of staff admitted that the army, the sovereign in the territory, was impotent when it came to enforcing the law. "I too am not satisfied with the level of law enforcement over the years," Lieutenant General Moshe Ya'alon told the Knesset Foreign Affairs and Defense Committee in October 2002.[155]

Beyond the bloodshed and the thousands of innocent victims on both sides of the border who had been blurred in the more than three decades of occupation, during the course of the second intifada there was a marked increase in incidents of damage to Palestinian property and means of production. Olive groves, which cover 45 percent of the space cultivated by Palestinians and support thousands of households, and olive harvesters themselves were premeditated targets for attacks by violent settlers. Harvesters in olive groves close to the settlements of Itamar, Beracha, Yizhar, Shvut Rachel, Eli, Tekoa, and Pnei Hever were harmed on a daily basis. Many of the locals had to abandon their villages under threats and attacks on the part of the settlers. The settlers' deeds received backing and encouragement from political leaders and rabbis. All of the crops that grow in the Land of Israel belong to the Jewish people, ruled a former chief rabbi, Mordechai Eliyahu, because the land is the heritage of the Jewish people, and "if anyone . . . plants a tree on my place, both the tree and the fruit belong to me." The systematic attacks on olive harvesters and the trees themselves were not anything new, but now they earned worldwide coverage and a limp reprimand from Prime Minister Sharon.[156]

Ha'aretz journalist Amira Hass had reported as early as 1998 on the havoc caused by settlers to the olive economy and olive culture in the territories and on the chopping down of thousands of olive trees at night by unknown perpetrators who are never caught and never punished. "The famous immunity of the olive tree does not serve it in face of the settlers' attacks," wrote Hass. Not only is the living of hundreds of thousands of Palestinians harmed, but also centuries-old familial and social traditions of harvesting, a communal village event that happens every year regardless of changing regimes, have been irreparably damaged, so that the Palestinians have become strangers in their home, "trespassers on their own land."[157]

The Wall

Under the pressure of mounting terror attacks in Israeli cities in the spring of 2002, the Sharon government passed a decision to establish a "separation fence," which the prime minister had opposed for many years for fear that in the future its route would determine Israel's state border.[158] During the course of its construction, and in response to many petitions that were filed against the route of the fence, which in certain segments became a concrete wall more than eight meters high, the Supreme Court confined itself to issuing injunctions that stopped construction for only a few days at a time. In the deliberations on the case of the village of Beit Suriq, the court revealed the real rationale, tailored to fit the needs or whims of the settlements, that was at the basis of the route and was camouflaged in claims, once again, of "security needs." "I am not a great expert on military strategy, but I do understand proportionality," said Supreme Court President Barak, adding that military considerations also need to be applied in a proportional way.[159] Barak's "proportionality," which immediately became a worn coinage, still did not provide a probing account of the winding route of the fence/wall. The thirty-kilometer segment of the "Jerusalem envelope" between Maccabim and Giv'at Zeev, which was discussed in the court, was indeed resoundingly overruled by the High Court on June 30, 2004.[160] The objection that the court expressed in its ruling to the army's activity and the "security considerations" was indeed new, almost sensational. It was handed down at a time of relative quiet, but under the influence of the previous bloody years. "The bereavement and the pain inundate us," said the justices.[161]

As in the historic Elon Moreh ruling in 1979, the Supreme Court had recourse to "security" opinions counter to those that were submitted by the army, provided to it by the people of the Council for Peace and Security, all of them former senior army commanders. The opinions revealed that not only would the wall not increase security to Israel but it would reduce security by establishing hothouses of hatred and terror in the closed reserves created by its route and the "disproportional" harm done to the Palestinians locked into them. However, even on this occasion the High Court was cautious. It determined that the route chosen by the security establishment caused damage to Palestinians beyond "what is essential." "These damages are not proportional. They can be minimized in a significant way by an alternative route," said the justices, but no more than that.[162]

The High Court of Justice ruling was defined as bold and subversive, so very deviant was this rather minor intervention in the sacred area of "security considerations." However, at the end of a day of celebration after the ruling, it was necessary to interpret its long-term and double significance and ask whether, in overruling a tiny segment of the route of the wall, the High Court had not given an implicit seal of approval to its other segments. More important, it seems that the High Court justices did not have the courage to determine that this was a political wall no less than it was a security wall, and that "security considerations" can have a number of perspectives and interpretations, and that these things are inextricably intertwined with one another and will always be contingent on interpretation and political and moral attitudes. Nor did the justices take advantage of the opportunity to deal at long last with the argument that all of the settlements are violations of the Geneva Convention, which the State of Israel has ratified, and therefore the wall, the fence, and all the rest of the separation barriers that are being built in order to protect them are in and of themselves illegal when they are erected in Palestinian territories.

Facing the security establishment's insensitivity to all of these considerations, and especially in view of the basic illegality of all of the segments of the wall that have been built deep inside the occupied territory, the apologetic tone, in the words of President Barak, that "our role is difficult," and that "as we sit in judgment, we stand in judgment," was embarrassing. "As for the state's fight against the terror that has risen up against it, we are convinced that at the end of the day, its struggle in accordance with the law and in following its ordinances reinforces its power and its spirit. There is no security without law," added the president of the Supreme Court in a Delphic tone.[163] Even these humble remarks did not avail the court. This is "a black day for the State of Israel," declared Reserve Colonel Danny Tirza, a settler from Kfar Adumim and head of the barrier administration at the Defense Ministry; Tirza was responsible for building the wall.[164] The limp reprimands the settler officer received for his words from then–Prime Minister Ariel Sharon, the defense minister, and the attorney general made no impression on him. He continued to assert that the High Court ruling was "a critical mistake" and added with a threat that was also a kind of self-insurance policy, "because we will pay for it in human lives."[165]

Knesset and government members from the right proposed passing emergency legislation that would bypass the Supreme Court ruling.[166] Sharon, who twenty-five years earlier, after the Elon Moreh ruling, had been the one who called for passing a law that would remove matters of settlement in the territories from the jurisdiction of the court, this time stopped the initiative of his fellow party members, just as in his day Prime Minister Begin had done, and ordered that the orders of the High Court of Justice be implemented.[167] On July 9, 2004, only weeks after the Israeli High Court's ruling, the International Court of Justice in The Hague issued its own ruling on the wall. The World Court, as it's commonly known, recognized Israel's right to defend itself within its agreed-upon and recognized border of 1949–1967 but claimed that any construction of such a wall beyond the Green Line was a violation of international law—a stance that was accepted even by the American Jewish judge—and fatally injured the basic rights of the Palestinians. The ruling of the Hague court— a ruling that Prime Minister Sharon termed "pure evil"—gave the correct proportionality to the Israeli court's ruling.

Part Three

Epilogue

8

The Pace of Apocalypse

Prime Minister Ariel Sharon's mythological fading away, accompanied by his countrymen's unexpected love and the admiration of much of the world, was a denouement unsuited to his thunderous and controversial career and to his last great project, the uprooting of settlements in the Gaza Strip and northern West Bank. That late project, implemented with force, Sharon style, cannot, however, change the past, the long history of Jewish settlements on Palestinian land, and Sharon's crucial role in building them. Nor can it mitigate the recent years of violence and bloodshed, which have taken the lives of more than 1,200 Israelis and some 4,500 Palestinians, years that bear Sharon's indelible imprint. Indeed, everything that etched the portrait of Israel during the years 2000–2006—the continuing malignant occupation; the suffering and injustice entailed in it; the encircling of Israel by a gigantic barrier, in an era when walls of this sort are tumbling down, in a unilateral and illegal effort to draw the permanent border of a country that has lived for almost sixty years with blurred, unfixed boundaries; and the improbable attempt to dismantle some settlements while keeping, even expanding, most of the others—all of this bears Ariel Sharon's fingerprint and was carried out under his inspiration.

These were Sharon's years. The war that went on during these years, which continues to this day, was not endowed with a name by the Israelis, as if this could in some way undo it, or erase it from history or collective memory. The Palestinians call it the Al-Aqsa Intifada, but it could just as accurately be called the Settlements War, or Sharon's War. The Israel of those years was an Israel that was shaped by his bleak worldview and in his pessimistic and violent mold. The Palestinians' desperate terror war, which simmered beneath the surface during the years of occupation and flared up from the fire that Sharon ignited when he ascended the Temple Mount on September 28, 2000, incarnated on the ground, in intolerable ways, his perception of reality and afforded him both the justification of his views and the legitimacy of his solutions. The man who over the years had sown scores of settlements in order to thwart any possibility of a viable Palestinian state reaped in this war what he and many Israelis believed to be the very proof, in a kind of self-fulfilling wish, that Palestinians are not deserving of a state of their own because of their innate, murderous barbarity. The great victory, therefore, that Sharon succeeded in chalking up to his credit, before his withdrawal from Gaza, was the causal disconnection of the Palestinians' war against the forty-year Israeli occupation from any historical context, and from his own handiwork over many years. This victory is likely to prove to be short-lived, however. It will lead Israel along a sure path to more disputes, more hatred, and more bereavement. Hence, at the summation of this book it is appropriate to examine Sharon's part in all of this.

———

In this scrutiny, we could begin with Sharon's seemingly precipitate yet well-planned visit to the Temple Mount, where the third-holiest site in the Muslim world, the Haram al-Sharif, including the Al-Aqsa Mosque, is located. This ascent to the sacred and disputed site indeed brought Sharon the premiership, but it also plunged the two national ethnic communities that are struggling for the land into an insane tribal war. Even after Sharon's departure from the stage, his declarations before his fateful act of September 2000, about "the right of every Jew to ascend the Temple Mount," sound like the hollow verbiage of a politician in the throes of a struggle for survival.[1] For what was behind the move was the seemingly hopeless attempt to restore him to the leadership of the Likud Party. Before he set foot through the Dung Gate (also known as the Moghrabi Gate) into the Old City, all the signs indicated that Sharon was slipping away not only from his dream of becoming prime minister but also from his position of chairman of the party he had helped to found. The latest surveys commissioned by Sharon's advisers indicated that more than two-thirds of the party members wanted the return of Benjamin Netanyahu to the leadership.[2]

In one of those coincidences that later attain their full significance, on the day before Sharon's planned ascent of the Temple Mount Attorney General Elyakim Rubinstein announced that he had decided to close the criminal investigation of former prime minister Netanyahu, who had been accused of fraud and corruption while in office. Rubinstein's decision toppled the last barrier, if there was one, on the way to the Temple Mount. It put Sharon in a frenetic state, wrote *Yedioth Aharonoth* analyst Nahum Barnea, "and he felt an irresistible urge to prove that he could do it too. The events of Rosh Hashanah were his 'tunnel.'"[3] A close strategic adviser at the time later testified that the ascent of the Temple Mount was carefully planned by Sharon's aides. The thinking was that "the fact of the ascent of the Temple Mount will restore the rightist camp's enthusiasm for him and this would also have added value in face of [Ehud] Barak's [peace] maneuvers," he said. "It was clear that action had to be taken. The feeling was that if in this situation we were going for elections, Bibi [Netanyahu] would return."[4]

Sharon's visit to the Temple Mount was aimed not only for internal party manipulation but also at achieving a larger and ostensibly more legitimate political goal, like the torpedoing of negotiations with the Palestinians that were going on at that time and approaching a delicate climax.[5] "A spirit of sanctity rested on the shoulders of the leader of the opposition," wrote Shlomo Ben-Ami, who was then foreign minister and minister of public security. In Sharon's provocative ascent of the Temple Mount, he was not trying to harm the Palestinians or Arafat but rather the government of Israel, which was in the process of "relinquishing what Israel holds most sacred," wrote Ben-Ami, criticizing Sharon's abuse of what is considered untouchable for many Israelis.[6]

Days before Sharon's fateful visit, Prime Minister Barak hosted the top Palestinian leadership at his home in Kochav Yair, and a rare meeting was held between Arafat and the Israeli prime minister, who had not seen each other since the failure of the talks at Camp David.[7] The meeting was aimed at preparing the atmosphere for yet another, crucial round of talks in Washington. Also present in Barak's living room were the heads of the negotiating teams. The meeting was full of pathos and genuine emotion. Arafat announced that he had given his representatives to the talks "a full mandate," while Barak declared optimistically that "we are on the verge of arriving at a formula on all the issues. . . . All of us here have fought together, cumulatively, for perhaps 200 years. This is an effort that the coming generations deserve."[8] To the members of the Israeli delegation, Barak said that they were "embarking on a historic mission," and he shook their hands warmly.[9]

Sharon's planned visit to the Temple Mount did not put a damper on the good cheer at the Barak residence. The visit was not mentioned at all in the living-room conversation. Only in the dialogue between Arafat and Barak out in the garden did Arafat urge Barak to do everything possible to stop Sharon. "Why now?" asked Arafat. "Why didn't Sharon visit the Temple Mount when he was defense minister or foreign minister?" Barak replied in the worn coin of "our democracy." I can't, he told his interlocutor, prevent the leader of the opposition from going there. He offered a similar reply to President Hosni Mubarak of Egypt two weeks after the riots erupted and well after everybody knew about the dozens of victims the disturbances had exacted.[10] "No one was happy with the visit, but no one had expected the conflagration or had warned of it," wrote Ben-Ami later.[11] The optimism continued through the second half of that week. Two days after the Palestinians' visit to his home, Barak received a report from Washington that the members of the American peace team were describing a "new atmosphere" in the Palestinian delegation and that its people were repeatedly saying that Arafat wanted an agreement.[12] For their part, the Americans had put the finishing touches on the outline that President Clinton was going to present to Barak and Arafat immediately after Yom Kippur, on October 9. On the afternoon of Thursday, September 28, the Israeli delegation set out from Washington on its way back to Israel in order to brief Barak for perhaps the most critical encounter with Arafat. The fate of the Temple Mount was among the sensitive issues that necessitated a bold political decision, a choice that threatened to cause an earthquake. The following day, with the outbreak of the riots, the negotiations between the Palestinians and the Israelis and the hopes that they embodied already belonged to the distant past.

Warnings from the field about harsh reactions to Sharon's

planned visit were not comprehended in their full severity in the places where they should have been. Previous visits to the Temple Mount by Israeli dignitaries had usually proceeded without serious incident. Sharon was a different story. His long history of bloodshed had made him Enemy Number 1 for the Palestinian people, their mythological nemesis: It extended from the slaughter of sixty-nine civilians at Qibya in 1953 and a series of other reprisal raids throughout the 1950s to his unrestrained fight against terrorist activities in Gaza in the early 1970s and the 1982 invasion of Lebanon, which he masterminded as defense minister and which was intended to wipe out the Palestinians and their leadership there and establish a "new order" in the Middle East. This war culminated in the slaughter of 1,000–3,000 Palestinian civilians in Sabra and Shatila by Lebanese Phalangists who were overseen by the Israeli army. The man who had compared Arafat to Hitler and the Palestine Liberation Organization to the Third Reich, and who had determined that the Palestinian organization and its leader were disqualified forever as interlocutors,[13] was also the man who for years had not recognized the Palestinians' right to self-definition and a state of their own, and who held the opinion that Jordan is the Palestinian state.[14]

"God preserve us if the visit takes place," said Arafat at a meeting of the Palestinian leadership at the Muqata (the Palestinian government offices in Ramallah) six days before the planned visit. At the end of the meeting an official call went out from the Palestinian leadership to the government of Israel to prevent the visit, which would be "the end of the diplomatic negotiations and the start of negotiations of another sort."[15] The Palestinian leaders begged their interlocutors in Israel, their partners in the negotiations, to prevent the visit in any way possible. They warned explicitly of "tragedy" and "bloodshed."[16] The heads of the Waqf, the Islamic trust that administers the holy sites in the Old City, met with the commander of the Jerusalem Police District, Yair Yitzhaki, and warned him about "violent confrontation."[17] The Israeli commander of the police unit responsible for the holy places in Jerusalem, Nisso Shaham, who in his official capacity maintained relations with the Palestinian worshipers and their leadership and understood the implications of the visit, also tried through every possible channel to prevent Sharon's visit, warning of a "bloodbath." When the senior ranks of the police rejected his warnings, in his desperation he requested permission to make a personal visit to Sharon's home, Sycamore Ranch, to persuade him to cancel the visit or postpone it to a less tense period and to a time that would not be so close to the Muslims' Friday prayers. This permission, too, was not granted.[18] The head of the research department in Military Intelligence, Amos Gilad, also issued a warning of riots if Sharon went ahead with the visit.[19]

While calling upon the Palestinian Authority "to evince toughness in the face of terror" following a series of terror attacks that week, Prime Minister Barak sealed himself off from the ill omens coming from the field and preferred the more idly positive assessments of the army, the Shin Bet, and the police affirming the absence of clear evidence of ferment against the visit.[20] All of these Israeli systems once again proved their persistent imperviousness and lack of alertness to the hardships of the Palestinians and the frustration of their leadership in the face of the political dead end, the expansion of the settlements after the Oslo agreements, and the degenerating situation on the ground, as well as to the special sensitivity inherent in the sacred site itself. To this were added the political weakness of Prime Minister Barak and his disintegrating government and the faint-heartedness of Attorney General Rubinstein, who held that it was impossible to legally prevent the visit. The Palestinians could not believe that a government led by the Labor Party, while conducting crucial negotiations, was not preventing such a fateful, provocative act, whereas its predecessors from the right had prevented similar showy political demonstrations in the explosive compound.[21] Only after the conflagration did senior military commanders, who did not identify themselves by name, dare to whisper cautiously that "it was clear to everyone in advance that the visit was a recipe for disaster and this was said at all the assessments of the situation this week." When they were asked why they had not spoken out in time, these deep throats replied that "it is a political matter. We were all afraid to get implicated in that."[22]

Barak, who that week was also serving as acting public security minister (Shlomo Ben-Ami was in Washington at the time negotiating with the Palestinians in his capacity as foreign minister), handed the authorization to Sharon. And the leader of the opposition strode forward, accompanied by six of his most faithful followers from the Likud faction in the Knesset and hundreds of police and bodyguards in a typically brutal scene in which there was nothing of the reverence and respect appropriate to a site precious to millions of believers. At the site, members of the Arab Knesset factions and some young Palestinians were already waiting to protest. The visit itself went by in the blink of an eye—a blink of an eye that cast the entire region into a prolonged, bloody tragedy. A few seconds before Sharon's departure, several demonstrators tried to break through the police phalanx by force, and right after it the Palestinian demonstrators stormed toward the mosque, throwing stones and other objects at the police. The police fired rubber bullets and wounded a number of the demonstrators. The riots spread rapidly to other parts of East Jerusalem. The results of that first day: thirty police and about ten Palestinians wounded.[23]

The next day, Friday, September 29, the prayers at the Al-Aqsa

Mosque culminated in violent disturbances and a hasty response by the police. Seven Palestinians were killed and hundreds were wounded by Israeli police fire. Dozens of police were lightly wounded by stones. The reports of the dead fanned the conflagration and led to exchanges of fire between the Israeli army and the Palestinian police. On Sunday, the second day of the Jewish New Year, thirteen Arab Israeli citizens were killed by Israeli police bullets in an unprecedented wave of protest that spread through the Arab locales within the borders of the state in the Galilee and the Triangle region.[24] In a predictable and mutually destructive interrelationship in which it is difficult to distinguish between the active forces and the affected forces, the uprising of Israel's Palestinian citizens, on the one hand, and the Palestinian uprising in the territories, on the other, fed into one another and ignited the territories under Israeli domination. Dozens of talks with the leadership of the Arabs of Israel, panicked calls to Arafat's bureau, and requests for intervention aimed at colleagues in Egypt, Jordan, and the European countries were to no avail.[25] The events had spun completely out of control.

The aggregate of incidents that unroll in a chain of action and reaction, a consequent or random continuum of cause and effect that accumulates into a significant historical event, is infinite, and there is hardly any way to trace its beginning or all of its causes.[26] Sharon's visit to the Temple Mount on September 28, 2000, was not the sole cause of the Palestinian uprising. But the story told by both Barak's and Sharon's governments—that Arafat was just waiting for a spark to ignite a violent uprising that he had planned in advance—relieves the two leaders of any responsibility for the uprising and detaches the events from Israeli actions.[27] It is both irresponsible and ahistorical.[28]

The territories were indeed at the boiling point before Sharon's visit. September 13, 2000, the seventh anniversary of the Oslo accords, had passed without a permanent-status agreement and without declaration of a Palestinian state, the economic situation in the territories was getting worse, Palestinian prisoners had not been released, the settlements were growing unhindered, and Israel was refusing to implement "the third phase" of redeployments in accordance with earlier commitments. A violent outburst was in the air, and it was discussed at every meeting between Israelis and Palestinians.[29] Thus, the handwriting was on the wall. But all of this would not have led inevitably to the conflagration had it not been for the irritant of Sharon's visit to the holy site. The ground was indeed soaked with flammable materials, but it was Sharon, and not for the first time, who played the role of the pyromaniac. In contrast to their traditional stance of not blaming any side or of almost automatically backing Israel, even the Americans declared that it was Sharon's visit that detonated the explosion.[30] And in sparking the uprising, Sharon brought the Palestinian people to its feet to form a rare, united front, bringing all the members of the Palestinian leadership, Hamas (the Islamic Resistance Movement) and other radical elements included, into Arafat's coalition in support of a sharp response to the visit. Any reaction other than violent protest would have been interpreted as yet another capitulation to the Israelis, said the Palestinian leaders.[31] And even if the uprising subsided after several years, there is no doubt that the landslide victory of Hamas in the January 2006 parliamentary elections in the West Bank and Gaza is a political incarnation of it, i.e., a continuation of the violent uprising by other means.

Total War
The overreaction by the Israeli army, headed by chief of staff Shaul Mofaz and his deputy Moshe Ya'alon, contributed to the escalation of the cruel war that replaced the limping peace process. Despite

Prime Minister Barak's order at the first stage of the clashes to "contain" the hostility and lower the flames, the heads of the army followed an unprecedented and disproportionate military reaction, with the help of tanks, antitank missiles, helicopters, and air force jets.[32] The use of massive firepower exacted a price in victims on the Palestinian side beyond anything that had been known in the past, as compared to nearly zero losses on the Israeli side. The ratio of victims during the first two weeks of the conflagration stood at twenty to one. Senior military people were said to have spoken about the army's violence in terms of "a bullet for every child" (Palestinian child, of course). *Ma'ariv* journalist Ben Caspit argued in a series of articles in his rather mainstream newspaper that no one disputed that the army's destructive resort to lethal force at the start of the intifada exacerbated the conflict in a way that no one had imagined.[33] Amnon Lipkin-Shahak, a former chief of staff who on Barak's behalf was coordinating the effort to achieve a cease-fire, charged angrily that the army was "waging a war on the ground different from the one the government had instructed it to conduct." In protest against the fanning of the flames on the part of the army and the large number of victims as a result of this policy, Lipkin-Shahak resigned.[34] Ephraim Sneh, to whom Barak had delegated the responsibility for easing conditions for the Palestinians, wrote to the prime minister that "from the chief of staff to the last of the sergeants at the roadblocks, no one is implementing your policy."[35]

Backed by Mofaz's spirit of "victory at any price" and Ya'alon's vision of "searing deep [total defeat] into the consciousness of the Palestinians,"[36] the commanders in the field conducted a vengeful and cruel war of their own, indiscriminately shooting, crushing, uprooting, and harming civilians. The army acted not as a means in service of the defense of the State of Israel and the protection of its citizens but rather as an agent of a terrible lesson, as an educator, as an organization that waged its own campaign of etching into the minds and souls of the Palestinians, once and for all, who has the power and who is "in charge." Again and again the heads of the army thwarted probes toward negotiations by the Barak government, opposing a cease-fire and a decrease in the violence.

At a meeting between Shimon Peres and Yasser Arafat in Gaza, at the height of the violence in late 2000, a meeting in which Peres said to Arafat that Israel cannot allow itself another holocaust, and which aimed at bringing about a cease-fire, it was agreed that Israel would open a main route (the Tanzer axis) and not slice the Gaza Strip in two. The instruction was passed along to the army. The route remained closed, despite repeated instructions. "We nearly broke them, but all of the wiles and sweet talk about a truce spoiled it for us," a senior officer was quoted as saying.[37] Ya'alon stated that there is no point in talking when there is shooting. "Talk about a truce during the course of shooting is harmful and superfluous," he said. The settlers waged a political war of their own, demanding the political echelon "to let the army win." To instill their views, both top senior army officers, Mofaz and Ya'alon, spoke directly to "the people of Israel" over the heads of the government to whom the military were supposed to be subordinate. "We owe a report to the people of Israel," said Mofaz, using the term "*Am Yisrael*," which is commonly used to refer to the Jewish people. "I am the chief of staff of all of *Am Yisrael*," said Ya'alon after he was appointed chief of staff during the course of the fighting. And with Sharon's rise to power in February 2001, very much with the aid of the popular despair engendered by the spiraling violence, the last restraints were removed from the army in its goal of crushing the uprising.

Ya'alon did not stop there. He wanted to silence the media and gag anyone who took a critical view of his war on the Palestinian "cancer."[38] Speaking in his new capacity, in the midst of the disaster that he himself helped generate, he was giving a lesson in democracy to the people of Israel. He spoke threateningly of the "price" that "Israel would pay" because of the media's criticism of the army and of the way the war was being waged. "People are coming from all sides, and really undermining you. Sometimes this drives you crazy," said Ya'alon.[39] The war that Mofaz and Ya'alon were fanning was not the war of the "entire Jewish people" but rather, most explicitly, the war of the settlers, and of the army's command, a relentless war for the preservation of the occupation, the containment of the Palestinian civil uprising against it, and the eradication of the rebellious Palestinian elites. During the course of this frenzy, the war increased the despair on the Palestinian side, which led to suicide terror attacks in Israel starting in 2001 and to the collapse of personal security in the civilian hinterland, the likes of which Israel's citizens had not experienced since the establishment of the state.

The accumulation of the suicide terror attacks in buses, cafés, markets, on the street—the horror scenes they created and the intrusion of meaningless, wholesale death into Israelis' daily lives— brought plans for a separation barrier out of the minutes of the committees and into belated but hasty reality. From the outset of its implementation, in June 2002, the barrier was a typical Israeli project—desperate, hasty, greedy, unilateral, a patchwork job, brutal and devoid of long-term, coolheaded strategy. The story of the separation wall or fence or barrier also has long and tangled roots. It derives mainly from the deliberate vagueness that Israel has cultivated since 1967 with respect to its national border and from its intentional and continuing refusal to establish such a border. This refusal is borne of denial, repression, and the illusion that the world will come to terms with a Greater Israel, that the Palestinians will surrender, and that the entire land will be forever Jewish. Even the cumulative experience of the futile and undignified fights that Israel has waged in negotiations on its southern border with Egypt, its northern border with Lebanon, and, to a lesser extent, its eastern border in the Arava with Jordan—at the end of each of which it was shamefacedly forced to withdraw from every last centimeter—never led any of Israel's governments to acknowledge that, in the end, Israel would return to the Green Line or very close to it. And the sooner the better and at its own initiative, which would bring international diplomatic and moral gains, rather than later and in disgrace. The taboo of the permanent and mutually agreed-upon border and the Palestinian state that would arise on the other side, a historical inevitability, brought upon all Israeli governments a cognitive and moral paralysis, and caused their prolonged submissiveness to the settlers, which, as an added dividend, left Israel's borders porous and Israeli citizens less secure.[40]

When Yitzhak Rabin, under the impact of the 1994 terror attacks, spoke about the necessity of separation, claiming in January 1995, in a speech to the nation after the horrifying slaughter at the Beit Lid junction that took the lives of twenty-one young soldiers, women and men, and wounded dozens more, the necessity of "creating separation between Israel and the Palestinians" while conducting the war on terror and with the aim of ending the control over the Palestinians,[41] he was accused even by close friends of bringing about the Palestinian state with his words.[42] The day after his speech Rabin established a committee to formulate a "separation plan."[43] In order to circumvent the psychological pitfall of the term "border" or even "line," the word laundry of the military establishment coined the term "seamline zone," and the idea ostensibly took off. At the head of the planning committee for the seamline zone along Israel's eastern border was Police Minister Moshe Shahal, a prominent member of the Labor Party. This "zone" was supposed, according to Rabin's instructions, to be congruent to the Green Line or to pass close to it in order to avoid annexation of territories. However, even in Rabin's government there were those like Shimon Peres and Avraham (Beiga) Shochat who opposed the idea of the separation itself and the seamline zone, as well as its route, its efficacy in preventing terror attacks, and the potential for a permanent border that it embodied. Finance Minister Shochat ridiculed the police minister's plan and the measures that were included in it, as "Shahal's helicopters, dogs and camels."[44]

The army also dragged its feet and saw in the convergence and barricading behind a fence or a wall a return to the obsolete defensive methods of the period that preceded statehood and as damaging to its fighting spirit.[45] Taking up the post of prime minister after Rabin's assassination, Shimon Peres hastened in that very month (November 1995) to establish a multi-ministerial committee headed by the deputy chief of staff that had the task of finding alternatives to the slain Rabin's plan for a seamline zone. Swift at its task, the committee had by January 1996 already submitted its recommendations, which were immediately swept away by the harsh wave of terror attacks in February and March of that year. The explosion on bus Number 18 in Jerusalem on March 3, 1996, in which nineteen were killed, led to the government decision on a new separation plan. In the background, the discussions of interim agreements in the Oslo framework continued, as well as the preparations for the talks on a final-status agreement, which were supposed to begin in May of that year. The fear that the separation line would serve as a basis for drawing up the permanent border cast its shadow on all the attempts to erect any sort of physical barrier between Israel and the Palestinians, whatever its definition and outline might be. One of Peres's closest colleagues, Yossi Beilin, claimed that Peres in fact opposed any such barrier because he believed that it would thwart the Israeli-Palestinian cooperation toward which he aimed. And thus nothing was done. Peres's defeat by Netanyahu in the May 1996 elections imposed a coma not only on the vision of Israeli-Palestinian cooperation but also on the seamline zone or any other term behind which a political border lurked.[46]

In the State Comptroller's Report Number 48, which was published in April 1998, the comptroller wrote that "the governments of Israel have passed decisions concerning the seamline, in which importance was attributed to the control and supervision of the people and merchandise that pass between the territories and Israel, but dealing with the seamline zone has boiled down to taking decisions on the establishment of committees that were required to recommend action plans, usually in the wake of terror attacks. Since January, 1995, there have been a number of committees that have prepared plans in order to afford a systemic solution for the seamline zone, but as of the end of this review not a single plan has been implemented." The absence of thorough systemic measures afforded freedom of action to hostile and criminal elements to carry out their activities in both Israel and the occupied territories, the comptroller added.[47]

Only in the wake of the failure of the Camp David summit in July 2000 did Prime Minister Barak return to the idea of building a "barrier" along the Green Line in order to prevent the infiltration of terrorists and unauthorized laborers from the territories.[48] In November 2000, the second month of the uprising, Barak approved the building of a barrier against vehicles stretching from Mei Ami in Wadi Ara, at the northern edge of the West Bank, south to the Latrun junction on the main road to Jerusalem. For the implementation of the plan, NIS 100 million (about $22 million) was budgeted, but it was only in May 2001, when Barak was already outside of politics and securing his own financial status, that the Finance Ministry allocated NIS 15 million for the plan (close to $4 million). According to this scheme, the Council for Public Works began to erect safety rails to prevent the passage of vehicles at various places along the line. The army also woke up from its stagnation and accelerated the construction of various barriers at sensitive points.[49]

In July 2001 the ministerial committee on security matters decided to approve in principle a plan for the seamline zone that was presented to it by the minister of defense on Sharon's government, Binyamin Ben-Eliezer of the Labor Party. From the perspective of Sharon—the man who had done more than anyone else to delegitimize and blur the Green Line and who had for many years opposed the establishment of any barrier at all along this line lest it be interpreted as the demarcation of a border, or develop de facto into a permanent border—this was a revolution, a total change in his mind-set. In retrospect, it is possible to see this plan as a stage on the way to his idea of the disengagement, in which some portions of the territories would be relinquished. The building of the barrier did not begin at once, but only a year and hundreds of victims later. The source of the postponement, in addition to Sharon's initial deep resistance, was the settlers' inveterate pressure against any such physical barrier, arising from their understanding of its potential political meaning. During this interim phase hundreds of mobile barriers were erected as well as more than fifty roadblocks manned by soldiers on the roads of the West Bank and the connection between it and Israel. These roadblocks embittered even further the lives of the Palestinians, turned their movement in their land into a relentless, continual nightmare, and exposed in an unprecedented way the ugliness of the occupation and its moral degradation.

"This was the world's atrocity. I felt like a mean human being. . . .

I was a bad person who was embittering other people's lives," admitted a soldier, a staff sergeant in the regular army who manned one of the roadblocks, in August 2003.[50] Even people from the mainstream, who are not among the traditional protesters against the occupation, were disgusted by the roadblocks and the moral collapse they represented.[51] The chief of staff himself, one of the begetters of the roadblock system, expressed concern that "even if we win the war, in the end we won't be able to look at ourselves in the mirror. . . . A soldier who is required to stand at a roadblock, and the accessibility and the temptations that lead people to loot, don't add to our moral strength."[52] Adding insult to injury, these roadblocks succeeded in preventing only a small number of suicide terror attacks. The State Comptroller's Report of July 2002 cited internal army documents in which it was stated that "the roadblocks are not fulfilling their function of preventing the passage of attackers or materiel from Judea and Samaria to Israel," and that the army is not doing what it could have been able to do, and what it knows how to do in many areas, "in order to prevent the infiltration of terrorists through the roadblocks."[53]

During the course of a single month, March 2002, ninety-nine Israelis lost their lives in seventeen suicide terror attacks within the State of Israel. Black March was a turning point in the building of the barrier. Parallel to the reoccupation of the West Bank towns that ensued (Operation Defensive Shield), the seamline-zone project finally went into gear, this time with Sharon at the wheel. Sharon's homing in on the fence project and the acceleration of construction exacerbated the relations between the settlers and the prime minister. It was the beginning of the end of a wonderful friendship. Devoid of sentiments even toward the man who had settled them on the land, they embarked on a fierce struggle both against the fence and against Sharon himself. And their protest was, as usual, systematic and focused, multichanneled yet well coordinated. They argued that the barrier would bring Israel back to the ghetto, that it is a "bluff," that it leaves them "outside," turns Israel into a "protectorate state," and testifies to fear and weakness. "A nationalist government can give a different answer to terror," said Yehuda Lieberman, one of the first settlers at Karnei Shomron.[54]

Commentator Israel Harel, a settler of Ofra, compared the "Sharon line" to the disastrous Bar-Lev line along the Suez Canal, which collapsed instantly at the start of the Yom Kippur War and exacted many casualties. It was not by chance that Harel made this comparison. Sharon, who in 1973 was a brigadier general in the career army, was one of the staunchest and most vociferous opponents of the Bar-Lev line and the military doctrine behind it. "Now, when one can argue against Sharon's line in nearly every word that Sharon uttered against the Bar-Lev line—is the prime minister intending to visit Haim Bar-Lev's grave and ask his forgiveness for all the bad things he said about him before, but especially after, the Yom Kippur War concerning the disasters caused by that line, and justify its erection in retrospect?"[55]

However, from the moment the settlers realized that the Israeli public, distraught with panic because of the suicide bombings, was clinging desperately to the idea of a separating "Great Wall of China" ("we are here and they are there," as Ehud Barak had put it in his 1999 campaign for prime minister), they took a different tack. They came on board and started to navigate the ship, that is—to concentrate their efforts on shaping the route of the barrier. From total negation of the fence, the settlers switched, though with considerable internal disagreement, to focusing their efforts on pushing the wall eastward so that the large settlement blocs, including the Ariel bloc, Emmanuel, the Etzion Bloc, the "Jerusalem envelope," Givat Ze'ev, and Beit Arieh would be on its western side.[56] "If this is really going to be a security fence, there is no reason why we should not benefit from it too," the settlers explained. They saw no problem in bringing more and more settlements into the area bounded by the fence and expelling the Arab villages located to the west of it from their age-old sites.[57] Arieh Haskin, one of the founders of the isolated Tekoa settlement and director of the education branch of the Zionist Council, divulged the whole new strategy. At the beginning of 2004 he wrote that "it appears that it is not possible to fight against the construction [of the fence]. It is thus necessary to put up a fight so that the side that will remain under Israeli rule will include maximum portions of the Land of Israel, maximum settlements, maximum settlers and maximum strategic depth, in order to prevent the danger of their abandonment. . . . It is necessary to concentrate forces for a public and vocal battle for the route of the eastern fence. . . . At a difficult hour of surgery, sometimes it is necessary to harm one organ in order to save another organ, as long as it is possible to do this, as long as it is not too late."[58]

The settlers' efforts were by and large successful. Sharon adopted most of their demands. The route that they proposed drew up a map that almost exactly overlapped his bantustan cantons, from which he would never disengage, even though he refrained from saying so in public. However, there were quite a number of people who did hear directly from him about his plan for cantons and saw it taking form on maps. One of the people closest to Sharon during that period, Knesset Speaker Reuven (Ruby) Rivlin told journalist Ari Shavit in an interview in June 2003 that Sharon had already decided to evacuate seventeen settlements "located on the point of connection between one Arik Sharonic canton and another."[59] Several more Israelis learned at that time about Sharon's cantons, which he called "a Palestinian state." In his book in German, *Terror als Vorwand* ("Terror as Pretext"),

Ambassador Avi Primor reconstructed a dinner that was held in the spring of 2003 at the King David Hotel in Jerusalem in honor of Massimo D'Alema, who had been prime minister of Italy at the end of the 1990s. One of the guests, a supporter of Sharon's, tried to convince the Italian guest that Sharon was sparing no effort to find a true solution to the Palestinian problem and that he was prepared to recognize a Palestinian state and help establish it. D'Alema responded with a smile, and related that three years earlier in Rome, when he was prime minister, he received the person who was leader of the Israeli opposition at the time, Sharon. "Even then he declared to me that he supported the establishment of a Palestinian state," related the Italian statesman. "On maps that he had brought with him he showed me exactly where that state should arise and how it should look. It was a chopped-up bit of land in part of the occupied territories with no continuity between the various bits. Sharon declared that 'the only possibility for a solution for the Palestinians would be the establishment of bantustans.'" In response to his interlocutor's claim that the Italian was giving his own interpretation of Sharon's remarks, D'Alema replied: "No interpretation. I am quoting exactly. The term bantustan doesn't come from me, but rather from Sharon."[60] At that time Sharon's disengagement plan was still a distant horizon.

Sharon's plan also had a clear translation on the ground. A senior American official noticed that the route of the barrier followed the plan Sharon had presented back at the end of the 1970s, the purpose of which, he said, was to take hold of as much West Bank territory as possible and block the establishment of a viable Palestinian state.[61] The map of Israel's takeover of the West Bank by means of declaring large areas to be state lands, which journalist Aluf Benn published in *Ha'aretz* at the end of September 2004, is almost exactly congruent with the map of Sharon's cantons.[62]

The Bad Fence

The sophisticated electronic fences, on both sides of which security roads were paved and barbed wire was stretched—a complex barrier between fifty and 100 meters wide—as well as the gigantic stretches of concrete wall that started to soar above the ground as early as the summer of 2002, were constructed with no reckoning and no logic other than the purpose of enclosing as many settlements as possible on the western, Israeli side and dividing up and seizing Palestinian lands. The point was to implement the bantustan idea. The route of the barrier along the128 kilometers (eighty miles) between the village of Salem and the settlement of Elkanah, for example, which was completed in August 2003, represented the many and contradictory purposes and implications of the project. Not only did it twist and turn and penetrate deep into the territory in order to provide security and protection to small settlements like Salit and Zufin; the route was also aimed at ensuring the settlers huge reserves of land stolen from the Palestinian owners. This particular sector of fence separated the inhabitants of the villages of Faroun (3,000 inhabitants), Al Ras (500), Kafr Sur (1,100), Kafr Jamal (2,300), Falamiya (500), and Jayyous (2,800), which are to the east of the fence, from 23,000 dunams (roughly 6,000 acres) of their lands and grazing grounds for their flocks, which were locked out to the west of it.[63] At the time of writing, the inhabitants of these villages need about ten different kinds of documents and permits in order to move around in the area and get to their fields. Moreover, the route of the fence obviously does not derive from security considerations. In several segments it passes through wadis and suffers from considerable topographical inferiority, whereas the purely military, security consideration would have called for locating the barrier on high ground. The belated willingness of the barrier administration—following the international criticism and under pressure from the High Court of Justice—to make significant changes in the route, and even to dismantle segments that were already built, undermined the government's claims that less-harmful alternatives didn't exist.[64]

The example of the fence near Salit contains an interesting and less predictable, yet not less shameful, part of the story. Salit was established during Sharon's thriving years as agriculture minister, in the late 1970s. On outrageously cheap land, at a convenient distance from the Green Line and the center of Israel, a settlement of villas went up. Most of the inhabitants were former officials of the security forces, and some of them were born in kibbutzim, voters for Labor and Meretz, the salt of the earth. According to the original design of the fence, in accordance with security considerations, this real estate extravagance was to have remained to the east of the fence. After the well-connected inhabitants put up a fuss, applying pressure in the right places, the fence made a big loop, growing longer by many kilometers, stealing more Palestinian land and cutting more and more inhabitants off from their fields.[65] Toward the completion of the segment between the settlement of Elkanah and Salem, which among other places protects Salit, the Defense Ministry planned to hold a festive dedication ceremony. Only an international uproar cast a pall on the rejoicing and brought about its cancellation.[66]

The barrier system demonstrated Israelis' existential anxiety, on the one hand, and the arrogance of the government bureaucracy, on the other. Like a blind monster it penetrated, along improbable routes, into the depths of the West Bank and East Jerusalem, enveloping even the tiniest settlements, splitting Palestinian villages, chopping up neighborhoods, uprooting olive trees, separating children from their schools, cutting people off from their fields and other sources of income, from hospitals and public institutions, and violating basic human rights.[67]

The brutal land grab, the penning in of entire towns and villages, and the harassment of hundreds of thousands of Palestinians, supposedly in the name of security, was carried out in the spirit of Sharon. That spirit overwhelmed everyone, from the uppermost echelons of government to the head of the barrier administration, himself a settler, through the legal apparatus that out of idleness or cowardice or even political orientation approved a route that mocks international law, Israel's critical political interests, and, above all, basic moral considerations.

This megalomaniacal project, which competes in its extent and cost only with the settlement project itself, which it is intended to protect, quickly became a gigantic boomerang. The barrier that was supposed to prevent attacks by suicide terrorists inside Israel restored to Palestinians the legitimacy they had lost because of those murderous attacks. The route of the fence demonstrates that it is intended to perpetuate the occupation, and with it the settlements, and not necessarily to provide security for Israelis within their recognized borders. With the help of the barrier the Palestinians succeeded, at least for a while, in establishing an international anti-Israeli front. The army's brutal reaction to nonviolent demonstrations along the route of the fence, which brought together Palestinian villagers, international volunteers, "anarchists against fences," and groups of Israelis including former military people, added fuel to the flames.[68] These injuries to peaceful civilian demonstrators, Israeli, Palestinian, and international alike, were in stark contrast to the measured and "sensitive" treatment the army afforded to Israelis violently protesting evacuation from Gaza in August 2005. It revealed that the Israel Defense Forces are in fact made up of two different armies: the army for dealing with Jewish settlers and the army for dealing with Palestinians, Arab citizens of Israel, and the minority on the Israeli left that has not yet despaired of demonstrating against the occupation.

The fence/wall/barrier has engendered hallucinatory scenes. The gigantic concrete wall, which soars to the height of eight meters (more than twenty-five feet) in the stretch between Azariya and Abu Dis east of Jerusalem, slicing through lives and neighborhoods, has become one of the most documented sites in the world, a place of pilgrimage for journalists, demonstrators, peace activists, tourists, fashion shows, and graffiti artists. Above all, it has become a black joke, a symbol of the stupidity of a mighty military empire that is being gnawed at by the occupied territories it insists upon holding. The expanding opposition to the barrier, which has brought about strange momentary coalitions between the left and the settlers, also comes from within the Israeli consensus.[69] Protests, demonstrations, critical articles, insupportable sights provided by the barriers and gates, and the temporary restraining orders issued by the High Court of Justice all came together into an increasing civil, social uproar that began a movement toward change. "The hijacking of the separation fence by the settlers, with the government's help, and its transformation from a fence intended for protection into a political fence, is liable to contribute to the deepening of the occupation," wrote the senior military analyst for *Ha'aretz*, Ze'ev Schiff.[70] Sharon's unexpected volte-face, namely his 2005 disengagement project, gave him yet another hour of grace, enabling him to accelerate construction of the barrier. The 2006 Hamas electoral victory and the international ban on aid to and relations with its government, along with the short memory and fatigue of everybody concerned, gave Israel the protective umbrella it needed to erect this monster.[71]

Even before the dramatic court rulings regarding the barrier, the first by Israel's High Court of Justice on June 30, 2004, and the second by the International Court of Justice (the World Court) in The Hague on July 9 of that year, those responsible for the project understood that they had gone too far. The zigzags and greedy improvisations they had carried out, the result of maneuvering between the contradictory pressures of Sharon's plans, the settlers' desires, signals from Washington, and the army's demands, as well as Palestinian protests, did not stand the test of reality and ultimately led to the toppling of parts of the wall. By the beginning of February 2004, the government informed the High Court of Justice that the route would be moved closer to the Green Line and that a small number of fence segments that had been erected would be dismantled and rebuilt.[72]

When the High Court of Justice handed down the June 2004 ruling regarding the route of the fence in the area of Beit Suriq, the justices proved that they dwelt among their own people, and that their people were not necessarily identical to the settlers or the military establishment. The ruling, which called for major changes in the barrier route, was reinforced by the International Court of Justice, which recognized Israel's right to defend its borders, even with the help of a physical barrier, but rejected its right to build a wall deep inside Palestinian territory. Though the Hague ruling was greeted in Israel with predictably vituperative and clichéd reactions, it did, as noted, bring about changes in the Israeli legal system.[73] The instruction from Attorney General Menachem Mazuz to Prime Minister Ariel Sharon to the effect that the government must "examine in depth" the applicability of the Geneva Convention to the territories would not have been possible were it not for the World Court ruling.[74] This revolutionary admonition is also tantamount to a belated admission that Israel has ignored the convention for almost forty years.

However, Sharon's decision to extricate the army from Gaza, uproot the settlements there, and return the settlers to Israel proper (or to settlements in the West Bank, as some have indeed done), which was carried out with great drama, together with the relative reduction in violence and the fragile cessation of Palestinian terror attacks within Israel, to a large extent diverted attention both in Israel and abroad from the separation barrier. From the summer of 2005 to the time of the writing of these lines for the American edition, construction of the wall has continued, generally out of sight and out of mind. Although from time to time its route is brought to the attention of the High Court of Justice, it is not within the powers of the court to determine it entirely, even if it wanted to do so. The wall continues to butcher Palestinian territory, increase the Palestinians' distress, and steal from them not only fields, houses, and private and public spaces but also their future state. Both in Sharon's day and now in the days of his successors, the wall is seen as the outline of Israel's permanent border.[75]

The wall, together with the road blockades and the permanent and temporary barriers, has already in effect divided the Palestinian territories into enclaves, or cantons, and has left the inhabitants with less than two-thirds of the territory for a future state.[76] According to a World Bank report released in May 2007, Israel has restricted Palestinian access to more than 50 percent of the West Bank. This fragmentation not only does not allow the inhabitants to lead normal lives with respect to their economy, education, health, and culture but also prevents them from shaping the institutions of an active and cohesive democratic society. Israel's lofty demands that Palestinians strengthen their democracy and impose control on extremist organizations is thus nothing but deceptive talk covering its own deeds, which are aimed at achieving exactly the opposite—of eroding Palestinian society.

On a Collision Course

The horizon viewed from the Prime Minister's Bureau modifies the worldview of the person who sits there, or at least moderates it. This is what happened to Sharon immediately upon taking the oath of office in 2001, and it put him on the road to his crucial confrontation with the settlers. The man who had systematically refused to take political constraints into account as long as the settlement of the entire land was at stake was finally forced to recognize that there is a world out there, with its different views and opposing interests. The demand of his partners in the government, the Labor Party, to cease the construction of new settlements was also a factor, even if marginal, in reshaping his mind-set, and set him on the path of renewing some semblance of a peace process. The head of the right-wing nationalist camp in Israel, who together with the settlers had scorned anyone who voiced concerns about the disaster of the occupation and the demographic threat, started to talk about the need for "painful concessions."

The loss of settlers' lives during the Palestinian uprising denied the prime minister even a single hour of respite in his new position. Thus, even before his 100 days of grace had elapsed, Sharon could look out the window of his official residence in Jerusalem at the view the previous tenants had already seen so often. The pavement that had known many demonstrators, among them people on the left who had blamed Menachem Begin and Sharon for the blood of the victims of the Lebanon War, was now overflowing with settlers blaming him for the blood of the victims of the conflict with the Palestinians. Those because of whom the war of 2000 had erupted were the first to raise an outcry over the victims and warn about "the Jewish blood."[77] They were also the first citizens to demand special treatment and round-the-clock special protection. "We are second-class citizens," complained the secretary of the settlement of Beit Hagai in the Hebron Hills.[78] Every new victim in the settlements and on the roads of the West Bank increased the settlers' demonstrations. Settlers' threats of taking the law into their own hands became a daily routine.

The fear that after he reached the summit on their shoulders Sharon would turn his back on them had already begun to dispirit the settlers during the 2000–2001 election campaign. Sharon presented himself as a grandfather figure, spoke in a number of voices and succeeded in soothing worried voters of the center with the promise that if he was elected prime minister he would offer the Palestinians "painful concessions" in return for peace and security. The settlers saw this as a sign of things to come. The report that the prime minister was prepared to discuss the evacuation of three settlements in Gaza—Netzarim, Morag, and Kfar Darom—in the context of "ongoing interim agreements," and in return for a cessation of violence, gave the signal to the settler camp for mobilization against Sharon.[79] In his efforts to conciliate the Gush Katif settlers, Sharon invited five of their leaders for talks and promised them that his position was as firm as ever. "As far as I am concerned, Netzarim is like Tel Aviv. You can be certain of this," he said. But as he spoke to them and about them, Sharon revealed his deep feeling of being the rejected leader-victim. "The figures who led the Jewish people throughout the years were always lonely. I am bothered by the fact that you do not serve as a model for emulation and esteem," Sharon said to the settlers, even as he was speaking about himself.[80]

The joint path of Sharon and the settlers was about to split. His many efforts over the years to shed responsibility for the 1982 Yamit withdrawal were unsuccessful.[81] Victims or those who perceive themselves as victims always have a longer memory, which tends to cling to disasters rather than happy events. As far back as 1997, after Sharon, in his capacity as minister of infrastructures in Netanyahu's government, met with Yasser Arafat's deputy Abu Mazen in a meeting the press reported as having been particularly hearty, the Hebron settler Elyakim Haetzni wrote that a kind of "sealed fount of traumatic memories" had sprung up in him, "surrounded by the clouds of dust of the city of Yamit in its final moments, when the defense minister at the time, Sharon, was destroying the city." Haetzni called Sharon "the ideal executor for the expulsion of Jews" and added that he "is ideal because Begin knew that psychologically it would be difficult for the settlers, who admired Sharon and had been close to him, to pose real resistance to him. . . . Between him and the settlers there is close-ness and great esteem. Every effort must be made to convince Sharon and dissuade him from actions he is likely to regret, as happened in Sinai."[82] Rabbi Yaakov Madan of Elon Shvut, one of the heads of the Har Etzion Yeshiva and a spiritual leader, who wished to warn of Sharon's plan to withdraw from the Gaza Strip, also returned to Yamit: "When we muster for the struggle we will be accompanied by a sense of the injustice that has been done here to three generations of settlers. . . . Some of them have already been uprooted in the past from the Yamit Region, and now they are slated again to become root-less refugees. . . . Who will guarantee us that this will not also pave the way to the uprooting of settlements in Judea and Samaria, and after them also the neighborhoods of Jerusalem?"[83]

The role of prime minister and the noblesse oblige that derives from it did not wean Sharon from his characteristic duplicity of speech and action. While he was handing out glass beads to the Labor Party and his partner-rival Shimon Peres in the form of a provision in the unity government guidelines stipulating that "during the period of the government's term new settlements will not be established," he circum-vented the phrase with a vague ending, which stressed that "the govern-ment will provide an answer and see to the steady needs of the development of the settlements." In this way Sharon, while speaking about "painful concessions," could expand settlement construction in the territories, deepen the advance of the canton plan, and transfer huge resources to existing and new settlements that took on the guise of "new neighborhoods."[84] At a ceremony to mark the twentieth anniversary of Jewish settlement in the Hebron Hills, which was held in July 2001, the prime minister declared, "It is clear to me that the settlers who live here, they and their descendants, will also celebrate the jubilee of fifty years of settlement in this area, which will be a part of the State of Israel for all eternity. The best answer for security is settlement." To back up his intentions and declarations, he formulated a government decision to increase aid to the settlements in the West Bank and Gaza by a total sum of NIS 1.5 billion (close to $350 million).[85]

During the first six months of Sharon's unity government, from March to August 2001, settlers established approximately thirty new outposts in the territories. Among them were permanent outposts adjacent to mother settlements, along with temporary settlements, most of which were established in response to shooting attacks and some of which were evacuated before they became permanent.[86] All of these settlement operations were carried out under the watchful eye of the defense minister from the Labor Party, Binyamin Ben-Eliezer, and in effect with his agreement. Thus the statement by Foreign Minister Peres, at a meeting of the Labor faction in the Knesset, to the effect that the government had ceased to confiscate lands in the territories and had suspended building in the settlements apart from construction in built-up areas, was entirely baseless.[87] Not for the first time in his long career, Peres succeeded in not seeing, not hearing, or not knowing what was going on around him.

It was only rivalry within the Labor Party and the internecine struggle for party leadership that forced its heads to respond to the scandal of the expanding settlements. At the Council for Peace and Security, Peres said that "the map of the settlements, the way it is today, does not enable peace. Anyone who wants annexation should say so openly, and the result is clear: Israel will become an Arab state." Peres added that it would be a big mistake to make the settlements and not the fight against terror the top priority. "In that way we will lose in advance," he said, "and we will create international harmonization [*sic*] against us."[88] The prolonged deceit concerning the outposts was not simply a matter of the empty demonstrative character of many of them, which were established not as actual places to live but as gestures of defiance, or as bargaining chips to be shut down later at little psychological or physical cost. Nor was it the grotesque, half-hearted efforts at evacuating them. Its essence was in the very definition of the outposts as "illegal," a definition that legitimized by default all the other settlements, at least in the Israeli discourse and consciousness.

The establishment of the "illegality" of the outposts and the well-publicized evacuation games that were enacted around them on the hills not only did not harm the settlers but also played into their hands. In discussions between the settlers and the heads of the security systems, from the minister down to the brigadier general on the ground, a kind of agreement was achieved for the evacuation of isolated outposts here and there, which in many cases were nothing more than a lone container, an improvised guard post, a water tank, and a ragged flag. At a few outposts that were defined as "problematic," in order ostensibly to differentiate them from all the other, supposedly consensual outposts, soldiers were stationed so that they would be depicted as "a military outpost without civilians."[89] Every pseudo-evacuation of this sort, staged and ritualized according to a fore-known script, added another pillar to the legitimization of the rest of the settlements and undermined Israeli democracy and institutions. The rules of the game had not changed since Sharon's ascent to Hawara, together with the people of Gush Emunim, twenty-five years earlier. Everyone continued to play their preassigned roles in this ritual. While the army was busy evacuating an outpost or two, settlers were setting up two or three new ones somewhere else. The settlers squatted, the heads of the Labor Party protested, Sharon winked, the army officers mediated, and the settlers—they took down one container here and set up two there.

When Ben-Eliezer was struggling again for the leadership of his party, this theater came back and became the best show in town. In July 2002 Ben-Eliezer came to an agreement with the Yesha Council concerning the evacuation of twenty outposts, most of them uninhabited. The heads of the organization openly ridiculed their own "understanding" with the defense minister and claimed that most of the outposts that were evacuated were "decoy outposts" that had been put up as bait in order to distance the minister from the real, inhabited outposts.[90] "The state of Israel is a law-abiding country," was Prime Minister Sharon's contribution to the show in his remarks to the Likud faction in the Knesset. "If in certain places people break the law, this has to be dealt with,"[91] he said, and approved the removal of several containers, mobile homes, and old guard towers.[92]

Ghost Report

In October 2002, during the last days of the unity government and amid the hope that Labor would remain in his government and continue to hold up his toppling pavilion, Sharon approved the evacuation of twenty-four outposts. This time too most of them were uninhabited, and had been intended only as bargaining chips. Exceptions were the outposts of Havat Gilad and Giv'at Assaf. The two outposts were named after sons of settler families who had lost their lives in terror attacks on the roads of the West Bank (see Chapter 5). The settlers' rabbinical establishment, the Yesha Rabbis Council, among them rabbis who had issued *din moser* and *din rodef* rulings against Yitzhak Rabin in 1994–1995, renewed the rabbinical ruling that forbids soldiers to evacuate settlements. Two former chief rabbis, Mordechai Eliyahu and Avraham Shapira, expressed opposition to any compromise concerning the outposts. On October 19, 2002, army units arrived at Havat Gilad. More than a thousand settlers were waiting at the site. Most of them confined themselves to passive resistance and allowed the security people to drag them away. Scores of young people who had assembled in many places in the country, especially at brother-outposts, went further. They lashed out at the police with iron rods, threw stones at them, heckled them, and punctured the tires of police vehicles and the buses that had brought the soldiers. The violent spectacle was renewed the following day, when an attempt was made to complete the job of evacuation.[93]

The settlers' organized, violent resistance and the direct physical harm to representatives of the law who had come to evacuate them at the government's orders only served the interests of Sharon, the father of the outpost system. Indeed, one has to admit that all of Israel's prime ministers and defense ministers at the beginning of the second millennium either failed in their dealing with the outposts or did not want to deal with them at all. The first to have surrendered was Prime Minister Ehud Barak, who in 2000 signed the "Yesha-Barak settlements agreement," which legalized dozens of outposts in return for the evacuation of a few empty mobile homes from scattered places. The amoebic chain that stretched across many kilometers of satellite outposts of the settlement of Itamar was born and legitimized in the agreement that Barak signed.[94] And this is but one of many examples. The settler leaders wrung another agreement out of the defense minister in the unity government, Ben-Eliezer, who in effect approved many additional outposts, which were established with the formal approval or under the blind eye of the security system.[95] Yet the visionary and planner of the whole project was Ariel Sharon. It was he who invented the method of breaking through the fences of the settlements and sending tentacles out in order to create chains of Jewish settlement and take control of strategic areas and the aquifer of the West Bank. No obstacle hindered him in the course of carrying out his plan—neither distance, nor topography, nor logistical difficulty, nor price, and certainly not the rights of the Palestinian inhabitants.

The outposts are not a caprice of lawless settlers or a fantasy of the "hilltop youth," as official Israel would like to depict them. They are the realization of Sharon's big plan to thwart the establishment of a Palestinian state and thus thwart a peace agreement. The continued nonevacuation of the outposts is not a result of anarchy or laxity or the government's loss of control over the settlers, as senior military commentator Ze'ev Schiff of *Ha'aretz* wrote, but rather a calculated and well-targeted policy, for which the display of confusion and embarrassment was perfect cover.[96] "This is a matter of precise planning, of the takeover of strategic locations, [coordinated] with the prime minister," said the man who was the secretary general of the Yesha Council, Adi Mintz.[97] "Everything is done with consent and approval. Every road that is paved here, every mobile home that arrives, everything is done under the protection of the army and with state funds, and with everyone's knowledge," a young settler told us in a soft, mellifluous voice near the locked gate of the outpost of Migron, on a warm autumn day in 2004.[98] It must be recalled that the Migron outpost began its life in April 2002, in the form of a ghost antenna that was erected on private Palestinian land. The head of the regional council in the jurisdiction of which Migron was established, Pinchas Wallerstein, a public servant on the state payroll, promised in writing that this antenna would not become an illegal outpost. Four years later, in the spring of 2006, it was a flourishing outpost where 150 families lived, with public buildings, electricity, and all the rest. And all of this was done with the tacit blessing of the government.

Ha'aretz's Schiff reported in June 2004 on an authorization issued by the defense minister to bring hundreds of new mobile homes to "marked places" on the ground. Nearly half of them were brought to unmarked places, places where the settlers wanted them. While Sharon had sworn fealty to the American president's road map, which calls for a halt to new settlement construction, his government continued to allocate generous budgets to their development and expansion.[99] His explicit written commitment to President George W. Bush, upon acceptance of the process, to take down all of the outposts that had been established after March 2001 was, therefore, another one of those countless times when he did not speak the truth or did not mean what he said. Another instance of this was at the 2003 Aqaba summit, in the presence of Palestinian Prime Minister Mahmoud Abbas (Abu Mazen), in which Sharon reiterated his promise to dismantle the outposts. In his speech at the Herzliya Conference in December 2003, which attracted attention in Israel and worldwide, Sharon again repeated that "the government under my leadership will not compromise on the implementation of the road map in all of its phases. . . . The illegal outposts will be dismantled. Period. Israel will stand by all its commitments also in the matter of construction in the settlements. There will be no construction beyond the existing building line, there are no confiscations of lands for construction, there are no special economic incentives, and there is no construction of new settlements."[100] Yet while the prime minister and his defense minister were repeatedly professing the dismantling of the outposts, new ones were springing up on the hills, while outposts that had been marked for evacuation deepened their grip on the land. Sharon's evident scorn for President Bush's road map and his promises to take down dozens of outposts was interpreted by the United States as "technical difficulties." In June 2004 American Ambassador Dan Kurtzer deviated a bit from vague diplomatic speech and said that "until now Sharon has not kept his commitment."[101]

Sharon's most brilliant, virtuoso maneuver in the matter of the outposts was, however, his appointment toward the end of 2004—when he was already formulating details of his evacuation plan for Gaza and as the settlers were beginning their fight against it—of attorney Talia Sasson to investigate the policy and conduct of various government bodies with regard to the settlements. Sasson, who formerly held a senior position at the State Prosecutor's Office, is an independent, fair, and unbiased attorney of impeccable repute. Her appointment to this role from the outset, by the person who was considered the father of the idea of illegal outposts as a way to circumvent the government decision not to establish new settlements, is thus a typical Sharonic appointment in its innocent-looking perversity. Thus the decision to launch this investigation was both generally welcomed and greeted with raised eyebrows, as observers attempted to understand Sharon's motives in making the appointment.

Here a full disclosure is appropriate. During the course of the work on this book we met with Sasson in Jerusalem several times for long conversations. Her testimony and her analyses are evident in the passages on enforcement of the law in the territories. Although she appears on the list of people who were interviewed for the book, because of the sensitivity of the issues and at her demand we have not quoted her directly, and we have blurred her identity when writing things that are based on her testimony. In her capacity as the appointee to investigate the question of the outposts, Sasson did serious and fair research, as is her way. During the course of her work she confirmed what she had already known, what we had known for quite a while, and what everyone who has dealt with the subject of the settlements—researchers, peace activists, journalists, jurists, people from human rights organizations who are active in the territories, and government officials in all the systems—has known, namely the phenomenal involvement of the State of Israel and all its institutions in the "illegal activity" concerning the outposts and the settlements in general, and the culture of deceit, concealment, and evasion of responsibility that has characterized this involvement. The shameful way in which many public servants—from members of the government, headed by Defense Minister Shaul Mofaz, through directors general of government ministries to minor officials—responded to the attorney's request for files or replied to her questions could fill a separate volume. Some of this appears in the report itself.

Talia Sasson's report to Prime Minister Sharon was submitted on March 8, 2005, at a ceremony that was documented and publicized worldwide.[102] Large parts of the report were published in the Israeli and foreign press. This was a brilliant public relations coup, which attracted formidable coverage and added wall-to-wall support for the prime minister, who was already in the midst of his political battle over the Gaza disengagement plan. For a number of days the local and international media were abuzz with the Sasson report. Talia Sasson was invited for television interviews, took part in conferences, and became the heroine of the fight against the settlements. However, this bang did not move a single one of the houses in the outposts or a single antenna. The government established a ministerial committee to follow the implementation of the recommendations in the report, which met a few times and then faded away. The fate of the Sasson report was very much like the fate of the Karp report from the beginning of the 1980s on the issue of law enforcement in the territories (see Chapter 7): It was nullified with indifference, a wink, or scorn for its findings by the government ministries. Two years after the publication of the report, construction in the outposts has not stopped, and most of them are deepening their hold on the hills of the West Bank. The main weakness of the report and Sharon's main achievement, which was unmentioned by the media at the time of publication, are inherent in the single fact that the father of the outposts, Sharon himself, does not appear at all in the report. The principal responsible for the whole enterprise is just not there; he has evaporated. As in other cases, in this case too Sharon did not explain to the public his intention in commissioning Talia Sasson to prepare the report, nor his motives for selecting Sasson.

The Strong Stony Land

In the fussy attempts to evacuate the outposts, a new generation and a new kind of settler came to life, and they have earned the nickname "hilltop youth."[103] Groups of youngsters, some of them younger than eighteen, who have disengaged from the educational system and in most cases also from their families, have settled on the hills on the margins of Jewish settlements and have created for themselves a closed, alternative subculture of violence, harassment of Palestinian neighbors, and confrontation with representatives of the state, which they perceive as "foreign rule." Some of them have also nurtured a lifestyle of simplicity and intimacy with nature, together with organic agriculture, and have tried to emulate the lifestyle of both the ancient Hebrews and the pioneers of early, communal, kibbutz settlement during the first decades of the twentieth century. These young people see the state and its institutions as a nuisance at best and in many cases as an enemy. Although they are hoarding weapons and explosives in order to wage their militia war when the day of struggle and evacuation comes, as they did during the evacuation of the Gaza Strip in the summer of 2005 or in the struggle over the nine houses in Amona on February 1, 2006, many of them do not serve in the Israeli army, service that the veteran, classical settlers considered to be a sacred obligation, or at least thought so before the 2005 Gaza crisis.

A few days after the violent 2002 confrontation at Havat Gilad, a number of the teenaged boys and girls who participated in it sat together in their outpost near the settlement of Yitzhar and read the poem that Natan Alterman wrote in 1945, "The Land at Biria."[104] Three times the British soldiers uprooted the fences the Zionist settlers had set up at Biria, and three times they were replanted. The settlers at the site, and the hundreds of people who had come to their aid, lay down on the ground and clung to it, grappling tooth and nail with the British soldiers. Alterman published these lines in their honor in the Labor movement daily *Davar:*

> *Full length in the field his body he flung*
> *and his eyes gleamed like a knife*
> *and the stony, wild and ancient land*
> *grasped him, clasped him, clung.*
> *The army was ordered: "Take him away. Despite him, we'll pull him*
> *upright!"*
> *But the strong stony land, the Devil's daughter, held him with all her*
> *might.*
> *Face up and face down he was rolled to and fro.*
> *They tugged him,*
> *they dragged at his limb.*
> *But the stony land on that day*
> *did not want to let*

his body be torn from it.
Thrice was he ripped away
and thrown back
and pulled up and flung prone once more—
for the gray daughter of wraiths, the stony land,
pursued him with force and roared . . .
Three times the fence was taken down
and thrice the fence was restored. [105]

Small wonder, then, that the young lawbreakers of the years 2000–2006 see the national poet of Israel's independence, the chronicler of the Jewish revival in the Land of Israel, as someone who represents them in his words more than all their rabbis and mentors. Just like them, sixty years earlier Alterman saw the rocky earth of the Land of Israel as a primordial and absolute creditor that is not subordinate to any political decision, a living and breathing entity with a will and a vision of its own, clasping its settlers and its builders even more than they clasp it. Within a mythological, static, and eternal present, these hilltop youth perceive themselves as soldiers in the unending struggle that bends every other value not only to another dunam and another hill but to the establishment of their own state, which as far as they are concerned has not yet arisen. And who can plead their case better than the hallowed poet Alterman?

The hilltop youth created an uproar in the settlers' discourse and ethical code. These youngsters see the veteran settler activists, often including their own parents, as collaborators with an illegitimate regime and with the country's debased politics. They also openly scorn the rabbis' rulings when they do not suit them. However, the veteran settlers' attitude toward them is a complex mix of anxiety and admiration. Yehoshua Mor Yosef, formerly the Yesha Council spokesman, was a victim of the hill settlers' violence and threats because he defined them in a radio broadcast as "criminal elements and all kinds of educational mutants that have wandered from public square to public square and in the end stuck in the margins." The rabbi of the settlement of Itamar, which is considered a fanatical settlement, Avi Ronsky, who has since been appointed chief rabbi of the Israeli army, was beaten up by these youths during the course of a funeral because of his "moderation." The secretary general of the Yesha Council, Adi Mintz, called the youths "criminals who need police treatment" but expressed the fear that they are liable to sweep after them also "part of the more tender circles."[106] The tires of his vehicle were punctured. This is the same Mintz who a few days earlier had warned the government that the evacuation of Havat Gilad was tantamount to "crossing a red line."[107] He and his "moderate" colleagues could see how their own hasty words and acts of violence toward representatives of democracy and the law were now turned against them by the uninhibited successor generation. They also learned that the crossing of lines is never in one direction.

In contrast, others in the settler leadership see in the hilltop youngsters the future leadership of the settlements.[108] They believe that those youths are doing the real work, the "dirty work" of settlement in the Land of Israel, and that they are carrying on the war for it, which the political leadership has abandoned in trying to present an appearance of legitimacy and shared interests with the regime. Daniella Weiss declared that these young people are "our children, flesh of our flesh." Moshe Levinger, who was present at Havat Gilad at the time of the evacuation, defined the youths' violence as "a lesson in devotion." For educating the youth, he said, "one day here is better than ten lessons on love of the land in an air-conditioned classroom."[109] And settler journalist Hagai Huberman, a reporter for the

National Religious Party organ *Hatzofeh*, alluded to ancient Roman tormentors of the Jews in describing the people of the outposts as the victims of an alien tyrant. "Were they to have arisen yesterday from their dust, Titus and Adrianus [Hadrian] would certainly smile at each other in satisfaction," wrote Huberman. "Once again a ruler of the Land of Israel has arisen who is commanding the razing of Jewish homes to the ground and is carrying this out . . . and is furthermore publicly trampling the Jewish Sabbath to this end."[110] The prophecies of senior Shin Bet officials and government officials about another assassination of a prime minister[111] have not come true thus far, but the possibility of an assassination in the context of withdrawal from territories and evacuation of settlements has become a household nightmare in Israel's culture.

An Eye That Weeps and an Eye That Winks

From the moment Sharon made public his disengagement plan,[112] the settlers and the prime minister headed toward a crucial, emblematic battle over their future. For what was on the agenda seemed so momentous not only because it could shape the fate of the settlements but also because it could determine the future of Israel and the entire region. This formidable, dramatic struggle sometimes took on a Shakespearean dimension. And because the settlers, who represent the disaster of the occupation and in the long term also the loss of Israel if they continue to maintain their project, remained faithful to themselves, and honest in their own fanatical way, whereas the prime minister, who for the first time had presented an alternative that offered hope, hobbled so clumsily toward the implementation of his plan within the web of contradictions he had woven and the deceptive maneuvers he had concocted over the years, the choice between them, ostensibly obvious, was not simple.

Few, if any, knew what really put Sharon on the road to the disengagement. He was not a person who easily invited others into the byways of his thinking. However, his manipulative conduct in the matter of the disengagement showed that he remained as he had always been and that it was neither a probing reckoning of conscience about a whole way of life nor the taking of responsibility for his deeds over the years that channeled him into this route. Again, as in the past, Sharon acted out of a survival instinct and in reaction to external pressures. This time these were various political plans that were sawing away in the air, but especially the so-called Geneva Accord, which had gathered momentum in Israel and abroad, and the movement of refusal to serve in the continuing occupation that had spread even among elite units of the Israeli army and air force.[113]

On May 26, 2003, Sharon uttered the word that his predecessors had been very careful not to mention. He declared at a meeting of the Likud Knesset faction that "the occupation cannot continue forever." He added that it was impossible "to continue to hold 3.5 million Palestinians under occupation" and that it was necessary to put an end to this situation.[114] However, it was neither in order to end the occupation nor to bring permanent peace to his people that Sharon planned the disengagement. On the contrary, the plan was aimed at deepening the occupation in the West Bank and perpetuating the domination over the Palestinians. All that is necessary to do is to follow his public statements attentively. Although he spoke about "maximum security" and "minimum friction between the Israelis and the Palestinians," and about "an incomparably difficult measure of change in the spread of the settlements," because "under a future agreement Israel will not remain in all the places where we are today," in almost the same breath he promised that "in the framework of the 'disengagement plan' Israel would strengthen its control of those parts of the land that will constitute an inalienable part of the state of Israel in any future agreement."[115] And while the disengagement plan was presented as a first step in the implementation of the road map, which referred to the establishment of a Palestinian state in the near future, Sharon admitted that the road map no longer existed for him. "The disengagement plan releases Israel from adopting a diplomatic plan that is dangerous," Sharon told Nachum Barnea and Shimon Schiffer on the eve of Rosh Hashanah, 2004. "Even now we are not going for the road map," declared Sharon.[116] However, no one could have said these things in a blunter and more arrogant way than Sharon's confidant and close adviser Dov Weisglass. "The disengagement plan is . . . the bottle of formaldehyde within which you place the president's [President Bush's] formula so that it will be preserved for a very lengthy period," said Weisglass. "The disengagement . . . supplies the amount of formaldehyde that's necessary so that there will not be a political process with the Palestinians." Weisglass acknowledged that the withdrawal from Gaza was aimed at diverting international attention from Israel and to preserve Israel's hold on the West Bank, and that the uprooting of a few thousand settlers from one place would perpetuate the hundreds of thousands in the other place.[117]

Because the settlers had not learned to give an inch and keep hold of a mile, and because they had, however, learned to know Sharon and his destructive power and his tendency to get into complex situations without an exit strategy, they mustered unanimously to thwart his plan. Those who had worked with him shoulder to shoulder to establish the settlements made him their mortal enemy, who threatened their project down to the least, smallest, and remotest of the settlements.[118] "This is not about Gush Katif and this is not about Ariel Sharon," wrote Uri Elitzur, but rather a process that is liable to end in the uprooting of all the settlements. "And the more settlements are uprooted, the more the international pressure to uproot more will wax, and thus the public support for the settlements inside Israel will wane."[119] The settlers' old pattern of action, which had already proven successful, reasserted itself: sophisticated political lobbying, huge demonstrations, enlistment of the entire community, including women, children, babies, and the comparison of the evacuation of even one single settler to the persecution of the Jews during the Holocaust period. Sharon's deeds were defined by the settlers as crimes against humanity, and Sharon himself was put on par with the heads of the Nazi regime, the leaders of the left in Israel, Mussolini, and the pied piper of Hamlin, all put together in one sticky, hallucinatory amalgam. Those who did Sharon's bidding were declared *Judenrat and kapos*.[120] Sharon's old methods of action against his political rivals were now turned against him.

God, too, was enlisted to play a role in the national survival showdown. "In this war against the Holy One, blessed be He, about the return to Zion, no one will prevail. Not even Arik Sharon," declared the prime minister's friend Yaakov Katz (Katzeleh), one of the settler leaders.[121] The evil spirits of incitement that were reminiscent of the days before the assassination of Rabin came back to perform their act in the Israeli political space. The settlers' rabbis again proclaimed *din rodef* and *din moser*, and eulogized secular Zionism, which "has come to the end of its road," as a self-fulfilling wish.[122] Other settler leaders called upon settler soldiers to refuse to obey their commanders' orders during the disengagement. The lines between center and periphery and between moderates and marginal crazies were blurred in settler society, and the cries of refusal and despair swept up the community.[123]

Toward the end of 2004, while Israeli army forces were crushing refugee camps in the Gaza Strip yet again and demolishing dozens of

Palestinian homes with their inhabitants in another one of the army's overreactions in the war of Israel against the Palestinians, a war in which the Israeli army had "defeated" terror so many times, the outposts remained in place and the method flourished.[124] But for one impressive moment, the shaky Israeli democracy stood on its feet and mustered the country's institutions to defend itself, its authority to decide, and its representatives, and erected a dam against the powerful antidemocratic forces it had nurtured. The Disengagement Law passed in the Knesset by a large majority. And less than a year later, in the summer of 2005, this democracy, by means of its institutions, such as the army and the police, which for years had sunk deeper and deeper into the mire of the occupation, carried out the withdrawal in a way that gave the lie to all the prophecies of disaster.

The writing and publication of this book in its original Hebrew version were completed more than two years ago, before the implementation of Sharon's withdrawal. The book ended with this concluding paragraph: The Middle East teaches its inhabitants that it is best not to foresee what a day will bring, or to do this with the utmost caution. Therefore, it must be said at the conclusion of this book that perhaps the move of Sharon's disengagement will bring Israel to a historical exit from Gaza, and perhaps not; and it is possible that the exit from Gaza will perpetuate the settlements in the West Bank, and perhaps not; and it is possible that the exit from Gaza will indeed be a first step in Israel's journey of liberating itself from the enslavement to the territories that it occupied in 1967, and which have occupied it since then and have brought it to the verge of destruction, and perhaps not. But it is possible that the thrilling moment of the mustering of Israeli democracy to defend itself and to have its say testified that this democracy is still capable of saving itself, even if at the price of a civil war. But on further reflection, perhaps this too will not happen.

And Sharon himself, "the unexpected dove," as *The Economist* put it, who is now conducting in his hawkish way the battle of his life against the settlers, who have embarked on the battle of their lives, has won his moment of eternity in his speech at the Knesset, as if he were saying, while weeping with one eye for the settlements and with one eye for himself, in Antony's words over the slain body of Julius Caesar: "My heart is in the coffin there with Caesar, and I must pause till it come back to me. . . . I rather choose to wrong the dead, to wrong myself and you."[125]

Two years have passed since the Hebrew edition was completed. Israel's departure from Gaza, which was followed with great excitement in the world media, has long sunk into the abyss of forgetting. In Gaza Israel left behind scorched earth, devastated services, and people with neither a present nor a future. The settlements were destroyed in an ungenerous move by an unenlightened occupier, which in fact continues to control the territory and kill and harass its inhabitants by means of its formidable military might. But the trauma that was promised to the Israelis passed them by without leaving a mark. The tragedy remains the exclusive province of the evacuated settlers themselves, not of the Israelis as a whole. The great victor of the withdrawal and the destruction of the settlements, Ariel Sharon himself, was able to cause a political uproar in Israel and to undermine from within age-old political structures that had seemed eternal.

Sharon is no longer on the scene. He disappeared from the arena at his peak, enveloped in admiration he had never won before, in part thanks to the disengagement. With him ended the age of the dinosaurs, who fought for the establishment of the State of Israel and saw, even if unconsciously, in the fact of its existence, its way of conduct and its practices, a nearly miraculous, mythical occurrence, immune from rational and critical debate. Sharon's successors, and in fact the heads of most political parties in Israel today, already belong to another era. All of them were born with the state or after it, and take it for granted. They are no longer historic, charismatic leaders, who never retire but only fade away in one way or another, but rather are pragmatic, all too human, flawed politicians in the age of globalization, the Internet, and relentless media. The time of grayer, duller days is here. On the whole this is good news for Israel, because even if Sharon's successors declare that they will follow in his footsteps and cherish his legacy, their vision and their discourse have already departed from his, and so have their deeds. The words that were written here at the end of 2004, about the future of the territories and the future of the settlements, even with the new protagonists on the stage, remain as valid as they were then. Everything is possible; everything is hidden in the unknown. History happens every day, right before our eyes. It is open, like the ending of this book.

Acknowledgments

This book owes its existence to a long list of people and organizations. Special thanks are due to the Marc Rich Foundation for Education, Culture and Welfare in Lucerne, Switzerland, and to its director, Avner Azulay, for his unflagging encouragement and generous help with the research and writing. Philip Wilcox and the Foundation for Middle East Peace in Washington were most generous in their support for our research. The Heinrich Böll Foundation and its representative in Israel at the time of our work on the book, Julia Scherf, and the Friedrich Ebert Foundation and its representative Herman Buenz, were very helpful. Some Israelis, including Dan Ofer, Yaakov Borak, Nehama Karpol, and Raffi Rosenstein, as well as a small foundation that chose to remain anonymous, were generous and helpful in their own way.

We met with dozens of Israelis: settlers, politicians, people from the legal system, officials from the security establishment, human rights organizations, and members of academia. Our conversations with them were always enlightening, and they enriched our knowledge and under-standing. We appreciate the long talks we had with settlers Israel Harel, Ron Nachman, Pinhas Wallerstein, and all the others who wished anonymity, who offered hospitality in their respective settlements and spoke candidly with us. We owe special thanks to Dror Etkes, Shaul Arieli, Michael Ben-Yair, Avigdor Feldman, Yagil Levy and Haim Yavin, who gave us advice and commented on parts of the manuscript. Without their knowledgeable help, this book would have been poorer.

Many archives served our work. The archive of the Israeli daily *Ma'ariv* proved to be a mine of journalistic material of all kinds. The archive of *Ha'aretz* was an endless source of information. The Press

Archive at the Ariella Central Library in Tel Aviv, the archive at the Rabin Center for Israel Study, the Labor Party Archive in Beit Berl, and the State Archive and the Knesset Archive, both in Jerusalem, were gracefully helpful, and we thank them all.

Because *Lords of the Land* addresses an immensely intricate phenomenon of contemporary history over a period of forty years, which from the outset has enjoyed remarkable press coverage, the documentary record is immense, indeed endless. Without the help of research assistants, we would never have been able to master this ocean of documents and other material. Most prominent among them was Hagai Vered, whose rare intelligence and diligence made him a real partner. Our sincere gratitude is extended to him. We are indebted also to Nimrod Goren, Dana Winkler, Michal Aharoni, Shlomit Gur, Matan Gringer, Reut Paz, and Moti Basok for their help at various stages of the work.

We extend our thanks to our Israeli publishing house, Dvir, which made possible the publication of the original, Hebrew edition. We are grateful to Eva Koralnik from Liepman Literary Agency in Zurich, who accompanies our book worldwide with her special grace. Nation Books chief editor Carl Bromley had enthusiastic faith in *Lords of the Land*, for which we are grateful. We extend our profound thanks to Vivian Eden, who is responsible for the imaginative and diligent translation of this voluminous and sometimes quite idiosyncratic text into English. Special gratitude goes to the American editor of the manuscript, Roane Carey, whose knowledge and grace were a source of pleasure. All the above-mentioned people contributed their part to this book, yet the sole responsibility for what is written in it is ours.

Idith Zertal, Tel Aviv-Zurich
Akiva Eldar, Netanya
June 2007

Notes

Introduction

1. See Lillian Hellman, *Pentimento* (Boston, Toronto: 1973), p. 3. "Old paint on canvas, as it ages, sometimes becomes transparent. . . . When that happens, it is possible, in some pictures, to see the original lines. . . . Perhaps it would be as well to say that the old conception, replaced by a later choice, is a way of seeing and then seeing again."

2. Article 49 of the Fourth Geneva Convention stipulates: "The Occupying Power shall not deport or transfer parts of its own civilian population into the territory it occupies." Israel ratified the Geneva Conventions in July 1951, and thus became committed to them.

3. The common name for the 1949 armistice line, which formed Israel's de facto borders from 1949 to 1967.

4. Gershom Gorenberg's book *The Accidental Empire: Israel and the Birth of the Settlements, 1967–1977* (New York: 2006) covers only the first decade.

5. Amnon Rubinstein, *Knesset Proceedings*, Vol. 98, Session of January 2, 1984, p. 923.

6. For example, a recent Tel Aviv University study found that local councils in the territories receive from the state equalizing grants that are three or four times larger than those given to local councils in southern Israel: In 2003 the Hebron Hills settlements received additional funding of NIS 6,110 per inhabitant (approximately $1,360), as compared to only NIS 1,751 (approximately $390) per inhabitant in the Negev town of Sderot. The researchers state that in 2002 the extent of budgetary discrimination on the basis of geographic location and nationality came to NIS 1 billion and in 2003 to NIS 844 million. See Tamar Trabelsi-Haddad, "In Sderot They Get Less Than the Settlers," *Yedioth Aharonoth*, October 20, 2005.

7. Even a powerful and respected finance minister in three governments, Avraham (Beiga) Shochat of the Labor Party, who tried to dam the multidirectional torrent of resources to the settlements, has admitted his partial failure. Conversation with Shochat, May 5, 2003.

Chapter One: Blindness

1. It is not clear when exactly the convoy went to Gush Etzion. According to the book *Gush Etzion from Its Inception to 1948* [Hebrew], "On September 27, 1967, the settlement at Kfar Etzion was renewed." (Unless otherwise noted, all translations from Hebrew publications are the authors' own.) Reuven Pedatzur, however, wrote that the move to Gush Etzion took place the day after Government Decision 839 on September 24, 1967—that is, on September 25, 1967. See Reuven Pedatzur, *The Victory of Embarrassment: The Eshkol Government's Policy in the Territories after the Six Day War* [Hebrew] (Tel Aviv: 1996), 190, 193.

2. Yigal Sarna and Yuval Karni, "At the Age of Three He Had Already Asked: So Many Arabs and We Are All Alone?" *Yedioth Aharonoth*, October 10, 1999.

3. The mythical, poetic story of Palestinians wearing around their necks the keys to their lost homes in Palestine became a major component of the Palestinian national identity, based on the ethos of the right of return. Israeli society and identity were also built on the concept of return to the land of the ancestors.

4. Yigal Sama and Yuval Kami, "At the Age of Three," Ibid.

5. Ibid.

6. Ibid.

7. Zvi Reich, "Hannan Porat Is Alive," *Yedioth Aharonoth*, April 1, 1988.

8. Shlomo Gazit, *Fools in a Trap: 30 Years of Israeli Presence in the Territories* [Hebrew] (Tel Aviv: 1999), 217–224.

9. Yehiel Admoni, *A Decade of Consideration* [Hebrew] (Tel Aviv: 1992), 20–21.

10. David Kimche (on behalf of Yitzhak Oron, Alouph Hareven, and Dan Bavli), "Proposal for a Solution to the Palestinian Problem" (top secret), unnumbered, June 14, 1967. Kimche has informed the authors that the paper came to Prime Minister Levi Eshkol's attention very close to the time of its writing.

11. Pedatzur, *Victory*, 46.

12. Ibid., 189–203.

13. Yosef Shavit, "Hannan Porat—Politician in the Role of Messiah," *Yedioth Aharonoth*, November 2, 1979.

14. Ibid.

15. The Prime Minister's Meeting with Gush Etzion People, State Archive, Hativa I-1, 153.8/Container 7920, File 7.

16. Pedatzur, *Victory*, 190.

17. Ibid., 191–192.

18. Admoni, *Decade of Consideration*, 51.

19. Delegation of People from Gush Etzion Meet the Prime Minister, September 22, 1967, State Archive, Division I-19/153.8/Container 7920, File 7; Pedatzur, *Victory*, 192–193.

20. Admoni, *Decade of Consideration*, 53–54.

21. Ibid., 53.

22. Tamar Meroz, "The Establishment of Kiryat Arba, No-Man's-Land," *Ha'aretz*, April 4, 1988.

23. Labor Party Archive, 4-04-1965-15; see also Yossi Beilin, *The Price of Unity* [Hebrew] (Tel Aviv: 1988), 43.

24. Beilin, *Price of Unity*, 42–43.

25. Yosef Heller (ed.), *In the Struggle for the Land, 1936–1948* [Hebrew] (Jerusalem: 1985), 436.

26. Yitzhak Tabenkin, "The Factors in the Establishment of the State," in *Settlement, Essence and Way* [Hebrew] (Ramat Efal: 1983), 28.

27. Tabenkin, "The Wholeness of the Land or Its Partition?" in *Settlement, Essence*, 69.

28. Tabenkin, June 1966, Hakibbutz Hameuhad Archive, cited in Aryeh Naor, *Greater Israel: Ideology and Policy* [Hebrew] (Haifa and Lod: 2001), 122.

29. Minutes of the Government Meeting, June 19, 1967, Israel Galili Archive, Yad Tabenkin, quoted by Pedatzur, *Victory*, 49–50.

30. Ibid., 51.

31. Admoni, *Decade of Consideration*, 36–37.

32. Moshe Ozeri, *Kiryat Aarba Is Hebron, Passover 5728-Passover 5738* [Hebrew] (Kiryat Arba: 1977), 15.

33. Amnon Barzilai, "A Brief History of the Missed Opportunity," *Ha'aretz*, June 5, 2002.

34. Hagai Segal, *Dear Brothers, the History of the Jewish Underground* [Hebrew] (Jerusalem: 1987), 20.

35. Ibid., 22. In their various remarks and publications, the first settlers in Hebron deny the charge that they had deceived the army and the government. For example, Rabbi Levinger said: "We never told anyone that we were going only to celebrate Passover. The government authorities knew that we wanted to settle. . . . We didn't want to play tricks. . . . [Had they] followed us closely they would have seen that anyone going to Hebron with Frigidaires and washing machines wasn't intending a pleasure trip. . . . I don't think that it is respectful of the truth, respectful of the Jewish people or respectful of Hebron to say that if there are Jews in Hebron it is because we rebelled and went against the will of the government of Israel." Geula Cohen, "Tête-à-tête with the Hebron Settlers," *Ma'ariv*, June 8, 1973.

36. Pedatzur, *Victory*, 233.

37. Ibid., p. 232. On their participation in the Passover night and the renting of the hotel rooms, see Segal, *Dear Brothers*, 20–23.

38. Aryeh Bar-On, *Personal Imprint, Moshe Dayan in the Six Days War* [Hebrew] (Tel Aviv: 1997), 135.

39. Pedatzur, *Victory*, 234.

40. Gazit, *Fools in a Trap*, 225–226.

41. *Davar* reporter in Jerusalem, "The Group of Settlers from Hebron Moves to the Military Government Building," *Davar*, May 20, 1968.

42. Dayan's reply to Uri Avnery's Parliamentary Question, Knesset Protocols, Vol. 29, Session on June 12, 1968, 2,230–2,231.

43. *Davar* reporter in Jerusalem, "The Group of Settlers."

44. Ibid.

45. Ozeri, *Kiryat Aarba Is Hebron*, 18.
46. Admoni, *Decade of Consideration*, 58–60; Pedatzur, *Victory*, 241.
47. Admoni, *Decade of Consideration*, 58.
48. Hagai Huberman, "Kiryat Arba-Hebron: The Pioneers of the Urban Jewish Settlement in Judea and Samaria Are Eradicating the Shame of 1929," in Avraham Shvut, ed., *The Road to the Mount: The Renewed Jewish Settlement in Judea and Samaria* [Hebrew] (Jerusalem: 2002), 41.
49. Gazit, *Fools in a Trap*, 176; Huberman, "Kiryat Arba-Hebron," 44.
50. Admoni, *Decade of Consideration*, 58–59.
51. Ibid., 59.
52. Cited in Pedatzur, *Victory*, 164.
53. Ibid., 130.
54. Admoni, *Decade of Consideration*, 60–61.
55. Segal, *Dear Brothers*, 24–25.
56. Aryeh Dayan, "Gazit: Kiryat Arba Arose Because Dayan Was in the Hospital," *Koteret Rashit*, May 29, 1985; Gazit, *Fools in a Trap*, 177.
57. Uzi Narkiss, *A Soldier for Jerusalem* [Hebrew] (Tel Aviv: 1991), 357.
58. Elyakim Haetzni, "Open Letter to Lieutenant General (res.) Haim Bar-Lev," *Ma'ariv*, June 28, 1969.
59. Yehoshua Bitzur, "Team to Manage Kiryat Arba," *Ma'ariv*, December 23, 1971.
60. Segal, *Dear Brothers*, 25.
61. Zvi Lavie, "The Interior Ministry Is Seeking a Way to Grant Hebron Municipal Status," *Ma'ariv*, November 11, 1971.
62. Danny Rubinstein, "Who Will Control the Settlement in Hebron," *Davar*, November 16, 1971; Zvi Lavie, "Two Grasp Kiryat Arba," *Ma'ariv*, November 12, 1971.
63. Bitzur, "Team to Manage Kiryat Arba."
64. Itim News Agency correspondents, "The Status of Kiryat Arba," *Ma'ariv*, January 31, 1972.
65. Lavie, "Interior Ministry."
66. Yaakov Erez, "230 Dunams Expropriated Near Kiryat Arba in Hebron," *Ma'ariv*, October 6, 1971.
67. Quoted by Yehuda Litani, "Kiryat Arba Has Too Many Fathers," *Ha'aretz*, March 14, 1973.
68. Yehuda Litani, "There Is a Need for a Town of 100,000 Inhabitants," *Ha'aretz*, November 26, 1972.
69. Dan Margalit, "Volcano in Hebron," *Ha'aretz*, December 12, 1977.
70. Dov Goldstein, "Interview of the Week" with Israel Galili, *Ma'ariv*, May 14, 1976. Galili also said, "The government will not stand for any ultimatum from the Qadum people and it has the authority and the means to evict them from their current location."
71. Yehdua Litani, "Jewish Projects—Arab Workers," *Ha'aretz*, March 11, 1973.
72. Margalit, "Volcano in Hebron."

73. Cohen, "Tête-à-tête."

74. Hava Pinhas-Cohen, "Gush Emunim: The First Days," *Nekudah*, No. 69, February 3, 1984, 5.

75. Ibid.

76. Ibid., 7.

77. Ibid.

78. Ibid., 10.

79. Danny Rubinstein, *On the Lord's Side* [Hebrew] (Tel Aviv: 1982), 64–67.

80. Admoni, *Decade of Consideration*, 150.

81. David Newman, *The Role of Gush Emunim and the Yishuv Kehillati in the West Bank* (PhD diss., Durham University, 1981), 295–296.

82. Michael Feige, *Two Maps for the West Bank: Gush Emunim, Shalom Akhshav* [Hebrew] (Jerusalem: 2002), 132.

83. For an extensive sociological discussion of the two settlements see Feige, ibid.

84. Shlomo Tzazana, "Ofra Is 25, Celebrating and Pondering," *Ma'ariv*, July 7, 2000.

85. Gemer, "Ofra: Deceit," *Al Hamishmar*, February 23, 1976.

86. Ibid.

87. Segal, *Dear Brothers*, 34–35.

88. Peter Demant, *Plowshares into Swords: Israeli Settlement Policy in the Occupied Territories, 1967–1977* (Amsterdam: 1988), 362–363.

89. Rubinstein, *On the Lord's Side*, 72–73.

90. Gemer, "Ofra: Deceit."

91. Ibid.

92. Ran Kislev, "An Emunim Settlement Was Established East of Ramallah—A Month and a Half Ago," *Ha'aretz*, June 6, 1975.

93. Gemer, "Ofra: Deceit."

94. Political party correspondent, "Settlements in the Guise of Work Camps in Ofarim, Qadum and Ma'aleh Adumim," *Al Hamishmar*, February 19, 1976.

95. Demant, *Plowshares into Swords*, 365–367.

96. Yehuda Litani, "Ofra from a Dormitory," *Ha'aretz*, December 29, 1976. In a series of addresses to the Knesset on the Ofra issue, Peres acknowledged his support for security reasons. In later interviews he explained that because of manpower shortage there was a need for the settlers to man and maintain military installations. The head of the Jewish Agency Settlement Department, Yehiel Admoni, argued that there was no need for civilian services at the camp and that Ofra was not part of the plan for reinforcing Jerusalem. Peres also claimed that the government had approved the employment of the Ofra people on security projects. Eventually, when it turned out that Ofra was located in the heart of an area slated for the establishment of a Palestinian state, Peres took upon himself the full responsibility for its establishment, and admitted that he had not foreseen the long-range consequences of such a settlement.

97. Litani, "Ofra from a Dormitory"; Demant, *Plowshares into Swords*, 363.

98. Aharon Dolev, "Get Yourself a Settlement through Trickery," *Ma'ariv*, April 15, 1975.

99.   Ibid.

100. Avner Avrahami and Relly Avrahami, "The Baruchi Family," *Ha'aretz*, June 6, 2004.

101. "This Is How the General Assembly Voted," *Ha'aretz*, November 12, 1975.

102. The first organized pogrom the Nazis waged against Jews in Germany and Austria, in November 1938. More than a hundred Jews were killed, dozens of synagogues and Jewish stores were burned and desecrated, and windows all over the land were smashed, hence the name *Kristallnacht.*

103. Chaim Herzog, Address by Israeli Ambassador to the United Nations Chaim Herzog to the General Assembly of the United Nations, November 10, 1975.

104. Yitzhak Rabin, *Service Bloc-Note*, Vol. 2 [Hebrew] (Tel Aviv: 1979), 550.

105. *Ha'aretz* correspondent, "Settlers Accompanied by Thousands of Supporters Tried to Settle in Samaria Yesterday," *Ha'aretz*, December 1, 1975.

106. Gershon Shafat, *Gush Emunim: The Story behind the Curtain* [Hebrew] (Beit El: 1995), 180–181.

107. Meir Harnoy, *The Settlers* [Hebrew] (Or Yehuda: 1994), 46.

108. Ibid., 48.

109. Ibid., 43–48.

110. Rabin, *Service Bloc-Note*, 550.

111. Ibid.

112. Shafat, *Gush Emunim*, 180–201.

113. Ibid., 188.

114. Rabin, *Service Bloc-Note*, 550.

115. Shafat, *Gush Emunim*, 188.

116. Matti Golan, *Shimon Peres: A Biography* (London: 1982), 173.

117. Shlomo Nakdimon and Arieh Zimuki, "The Protocols of the Qadum Mediators," *Yedioth Aharonoth*, April 30, 1976.

118. Haim Gouri, "Back to Sebastia," *Ha'aretz*, September 30, 2003.

119. Shimon Peres, *Tomorrow Is Now* [Hebrew] (Jerusalem: 1978), 47–48. White Papers were Britain's official policy documents during the Mandate period (1920–48) concerning immigration, settlement, and security in Palestine.

120. Gouri, "Back to Sebastia."

121. *Ha'aretz* correspondent in Jerusalem, "Sharon Has Postponed His Intention to Resign as Advisor," *Ha'aretz*, December 12, 1975.

122. Rabin, *Service Bloc-Note*, 551.

123. Harnoy, *The Settlers*, 51.

124. Nakdimon and Zimuki, "The Protocols of the Qadum Mediators."

125. Yosef Walter, "Harsh Statements in the Government," *Ma'ariv*, January 8, 1976.

126. Nakdimon and Zimuki, "The Protocols of the Qadum Mediators" (emphasis added).

127. Ibid.

128. Admoni, *Decade of Consideration*, 165.

129. Ibid., 163–167.

130. Aviezer Golan, "Qadum Is a Fact on the Ground," *Yedioth Aharonoth*, March 19, 1976.

131. Admoni, *Decade of Consideration*, 167–168.
132. Goldstein, "Interview of the Week."
133. Harnoy, *The Settlers*, 51.
134. Nakdimon and Zimuki, "The Protocols of the Qadum Mediators."
135. Cited in Segal, *Dear Brothers*, 35.

Chapter Two: Bad Faith

1. Meir Harnoy, *The Settlers* [Hebrew] (Or Yehuda: 1994), 87–91.
2. Aharon Dolev, "Gush Emunim Prepared for Settlement Momentum," *Ma'ariv*, July 1, 1977; Aharon Dolev, "'Ready and Willing to Accept This File from Your Hands'—Said Menachem Begin When the Settlement Plan was Submitted to Him," *Ma'ariv*, July 27, 1977.
3. Dolev, "Gush Emunim Prepared."
4. Arye Naor, *Begin in Power, Personal Testimony* [Hebrew] (Tel Aviv: 1993), 123–125; Naor, lecture at Tel Aviv University, June 2, 2003.
5. Harnoy, *The Settlers*, 104–105; see also Hagai Segal, *Dear Brothers* (Jerusalem: 1987), 37.
6. Aharon Dolev, "Let the Government See to Providing Uniforms for Pregnant Women and Let the General Staff Issue Military Diapers for the Babies," *Ma'ariv*, September 30, 1977; recorded by Uri Elitzur, "'Settle in a Partisan Way,' Said the Prime Minister, and Then He Says: 'My Sons Have Vanquished Me,'" *Nekudah*, No. 51, December 12, 1982, 6–7; Segal, *Dear Brothers*, 37–38.
7. State Comptroller, *Annual Report 34 for the Year 1983 and the Accounts of Fiscal Year 1982* (Jerusalem: 1984), 81.
8. Uzi Benziman, *Sharon: An Israeli Caesar* [Hebrew] (Tel Aviv: 1985), 203.
9. Naor, lecture at Tel Aviv University, June 2, 2003.
10. Ibid.; Shlomo Gazit, *Trapped* [Hebrew] (Tel Aviv: 1999), 238; Ariel Sharon with David Chanoff, *Warrior: The Autobiography of Ariel Sharon* (New York: 1989), 356–360; Benziman, *Sharon*, 203; Robert Friedman, *Zealots for Zion: Inside Israel's West Bank Settlement Movement* (New York: 1992), xxvi.
11. Knesset Protocols, Vol. 81, Session on November 9, 1977, 360.
12. Sharon with Chanoff, *Warrior*, 360–361.
13. Knesset Protocols, Vol. 81, Session on October 26, 1977, 135.
14. Utta Wallisch, "The Jewish National Fund Sows—The Hebrew Nation Reaps," a JNF poster from the 1930s, reproduced in Batya Donner, *To Live with the Dream* [Hebrew] (Tel Aviv: 1989), 21.
15. Dan Soen and Michael Sheffer (eds.), "The List of the Settlements in Judea and Samaria, Their Populations and Their Symbols," in *The Central Statistical Yearbook, Judea and Samaria, 2000*, 5–7.
16. Sharon with Chanoff, *Warrior*, 238.
17. Dolev, "Let the Government See."
18. Aliza Weisman, *The Evacuation: The Story of the Uprooting of Yamit's Settlements* [Hebrew] (Beit El: 1990), 30–31.

19. Gershon Shafat, *Gush Emunim* [Hebrew] (Beit El: 1995), 343; Uzi Benziman, *Prime Minister under Siege* [Hebrew] (Jerusalem: 1981), 198–199.

20. Israel Harel, "Gush Emunim's Peace Plan," *Yedioth Aharonoth*, September 8, 1978.

21. Ibid.

22. Ma'ariv Service, "Rabbi Kook's 'Order of the Day': all of Our Forces Will Hasten to Seize the Essential Positions," *Ma'ariv*, September 21, 1978.

23. Yosef Walter, "Ezer Weizman Landed at the Settlers' Encampment Near Nablus and Said: We Are Prepared to Start to Augment the Existing Settlements," *Ma'ariv*, September 21, 1978; Yosef Walter, "'I Didn't Promise Many Elon Morehs'—Said Weizman and Ordered the Evacuation of the Settlers by Force," *Ma'ariv*, September 22, 1978; Gil Kesari, "The Sixty Hours of Confrontation on the Top of Mount Shchem," *Ma'ariv*, September 22, 1978.

24. Dan Margalit, "Begin Calls upon the Settlers to Disperse and the Likud Faction Abstained at His Request from the Decision," *Ha'aretz*, January 5, 1979.

25. Unoffical document "given," apparently by Sharon, to the Elon Moreh nucleus. Quoted in Shafat, *Gush Emunim*, unnumbered page.

26. Ibid., 349–350.

27. Amnon Barzilai, "Weizman Fears Problems with the United States over Questions of the Autonomy," *Ha'aretz*, June 6, 1979.

28. *Ma'ariv* correspondent, "By the Stockade and Tower Method," *Ma'ariv*, June 8, 1979.

29. Moshe Simon, meeting of the expanded Gush Emunim secretariat, May 15, 1978, appendix in Danny Rubinstein, *At the Lord's Side* (Tel Aviv: 1982).

30. *Ma'ariv* correspondent, "By the Stockade and Tower Method."

31. High Court of Justice 79/390, *Izzat Muhammad Mustafa Dueiqat v. the State of Israel*, Decision 34 (1); see also chap. 7.

32. Herzl Rosenblum, editorial, *Yedioth Aharonoth*, October 23, 1979.

33. See, for example, Moshe Negbi, *Chains of Justice, High Court of Justice v. the Israeli Government in the Territories* [Hebrew] (Jerusalem: 1981), 70.

34. Naor, *Begin in Power*, 183.

35. Hagai Segal, *Yamit's End: The Struggle against the Withdrawal from Sinai* [Hebrew] (Beit El: 1999), 141.

36. Ibid., 243, 244. "War between brothers" means struggle between Jewish Israeli citizens; the term "civil war" is rarely used in the Israeli political discourse, as the idea of citizenship apart from ethnic or religious identity is tenuous.

37. Ibid., 333.

38. Ibid.

39. Elyakim Haetzni, "Sinai Shall Not Arise a Fourth Time," in *Nekudah*, No. 42, April 7, 1982, 10–11; Segal, *Yamit*, 59.

40. Weisman, *The Evacuation*, 46–47, 136, 216.

41. David Oren, "Evacuation and Temptation," *Ha'aretz*, October 23, 1981.

42. Segal, *Yamit*, 235.

43. Harnoy, *The Settlers*, 172.

44. Yehuda Litani, "The Yesha mass," *Ha'aretz*, December 26, 1980.

45. Harnoy, *The Settlers*, 174–175.

46. Pinchas Wallerstein, "Settlement Is Not Enough," *Nekudah*, No. 44, June 11, 1982; Segal, *Yamit*, pp. 288–289.

47. Haetzni, "Sinai Shall Not Arise" (emphasis added).

48. "The alternative to this [the war] is Treblinka, and we have decided that there will never be another Treblinka," said Begin at the government meeting of June 5, 1982. Cited in Arye Naor, *Government at War: The Government's Functioning in the Lebanon War* [Hebrew] (Tel Aviv: 1986), 47.

49. Elyakim Haetzni, "Three Gifts to the Nations of the World and One to the Jewish People," *Nekudah*, No. 45, July 1, 1982, 8–9. The *Judenrat* (Jewish Councils) were the bodies, composed of senior and elderly Jewish leaders, created and imposed by the Nazis on Jewish communities and in the ghettos in order to organize and control the implementation of Nazi extermination policies during the Final Solution.

50. Eli Sadan, "To Re-establish the Jewish State," *Nekudah*, No. 35, October 30, 1981, 11; quoted in Segal, *Dear Brothers*, 42.

51. Segal, *Dear Brothers*, 43.

52. Menachem Livni's statement to the police, which was submitted in evidence during the course of the trial at the Jerusalem District Court, marked Tet/138 Alef.

53. Nadav Shragai, "Menachem Livni and Pragmatic Terror," *Ha'aretz*, May 8, 1985.

54. Nadav Shragai, "Waldman Conducts a Polemic with the Shin Bet Interrogators," *Ha'aretz*, May 5, 1985.

55. Nadav Shragai, "Nir Said: Rabbis Getz and Lieberman Are in Favor of Actions against the Arabs," *Ha'aretz*, May 6, 1985.

56. Ibid.

57. Ibid.

58. Segal, *Dear Brothers*, 16.

59. From the District Court ruling in the Underground affair. See Criminal File (Jerusalem) 203/84, *The State of Israel v. Menachem Livni and Others*, District Decisions, 1990 (3), 330, 398. (Henceforth, Underground Court Ruling.)

60. "It was my intention to shoot him in a way that would prevent him from his continued activity as prime minister," said Amir at his trial. Also: "I have nothing against Rabin himself." See the decision by the Tel Aviv District Court, Severe Criminal File 498/95 (Tel Aviv), *The State of Israel v. Yigal Ben Shlomo Amir*, 3, 17–18.

61. Segal, *Dear Brothers*, 53–54.

62. The portrait of Ben Shushan is based on Segal, *Dear Brothers*, 52–53.

63. Ibid., 29. The portrait of Etzion is also based on Segal.

64. Ibid., 55.

65. Shabtai Ben-Dov, *Prophecy and Tradition in Redemption* [Hebrew] (Tel Aviv: 1988), 159–160, cited in Segal, *Dear Brothers*, 43–46.

66. Segal, *Dear Brothers*, 51 (emphasis added).

67. Ibid., 56.

68. Nadav Shragai, "I Have Cut Short Murderers' Legs . . ." *Ha'aretz*, May 13, 1985.

69. Segal, *Dear Brothers*, 77. Segal relates that when Etzion approached him, he said

immediately that he agreed to participate in "any response action that he would propose." Ibid., 78.

70. Segal writes that the establishment of the Palestinians' Commission for National Direction "threatened by the very fact of its existence the life of every Jew in Yesha." He explains how, in his opinion, "participation in such a grave violation of the law became more of a technical and less of a moral problem." Ibid., 83.

71. Ehud Sprinzak, *Every Man Whatsoever Is Right in His Own Eyes—Illegalism in Israeli Society* [Hebrew] (Tel Aviv: 1987), 135.

72. Ibid., 102.

73. Uriel Ben Ami, "Hannan and the Pardon," *Davar*, November 13, 1986.

74. Ibid.

75. Ibid., 61–62.

76. Ibid., 117–118.

77. Ibid., 114.

78. Ibid., 137.

79. Menachem Livni's testimony to the police, which was submitted in evidence at his trial at the District Court and marked T/138D.

80. Segal, *Dear Brothers*, 165.

81. Nadav Shragai, "It Is Not Possible to Initiate Criminal Proceedings against Levinger and Waldman on the Basis of the Testimony of the Accused," *Ha'aretz*, May 3, 1985.

82. Segal, *Dear Brothers*, 184–185.

83. Shragai, "Menachem Livni and Pragmatic Terror."

84. Underground Court Ruling.

85. Segal, *Dear Brothers*, 244.

86. The defendants with whom the plea bargain was signed were: Ze'ev Friedman ("Zambish") Hever, Dan Beeri, Uri Meir, Gil'ad Peli, Menachem Neuberger, Yosef Zruya, Avinoam Katrieli, Yehuda Cohen, Noam Yinon, and Yossi Edri.

87. Quoted in Segal, *Dear Brothers*, 263–266.

88. Underground Court Ruling, 380.

89. Ibid., 391.

90. Ibid.

91. Ibid., 400.

92. Ibid., 445–446.

93. Ibid., 446–447.

94. Ibid., 437–438.

95. Ibid., 440.

96. Ibid., 442.

97. Ibid., 447.

98. Ibid., 450.

99. Akiva Eldar, "They Were Certain That the Government Wanted This," *Ha'aretz*, July 23, 1985.

100. Ibid.

101. Gideon Alon, "An Appeal Has Been Filed Against the Leniency of the Sentences of 5 of the Jewish Terror People," *Ha'aretz*, August 29, 1985.

102. Nadav Shragai, "The Supreme Court Left Standing the Sentences of the Five Members of the Terror Organization," *Ha'aretz*, April 15, 1986.

103. Gideon Alon, "Uri Meir of the Terror Organization Convicts Received Amnesty from the President," *Ha'aretz*, September 10, 1985; Avinoam bar-Yosef and Talma Freud, "Natan Natanson: 'I've Been Waiting for This Moment for a Long Time, Let Me Enjoy It to the Full,'" *Ma'ariv*, May 5, 1986; Talma Freud and Baruch Meiri, "I'm Sad, Said Gilad Peli as He Emerged from His Prison," *Ma'ariv*, May 15, 1986.

104. Freud and Meiri, "I'm Sad, Said Gilad Peli."

105. For the president's attitude toward the Underground convicts, see Naomi Gal-Or, *The Jewish Underground, Our Terrorism* [Hebrew] (Tel Aviv: 1990), 154–156.

106. Reuven Shapira, "Two of the Underground Prisoners Have Been Taken Out of Prison and Are Learning at a 'Rehabilitation Yeshiva,'" *Ha'aretz*, August 16, 1987.

107. David Halevy, "(Obstructed) Probe Spurs Resignation," *Washington Star*, August 8, 1980, cited in Ian Lustick, *Unsettled States, Disputed Lands: Britain and Ireland, France and Algeria, Israel and the West Bank/Gaza* (Ithaca: 1993), 367; see also Segal, *Dear Brothers*, 105.

108. Dan Margalit, Akiva Eldar, and Ilan Shechori, "Trend in the Likud and the Alignment: Amnesty for the Accused of the Underground after the Trial," *Ha'aretz*, May 30, 1985.

109. Gideon Alon, "Haim Zadok: We Are on the Brink of Sinking into Rule by the Street and the Destruction of the Legal System," *Ha'aretz*, May 30, 1985.

110. Ibid.

111. Gideon Alon, "Zamir: The Trial Proceedings of Three of the Jewish Underground Prisoners Must Not Be Delayed," *Ha'aretz*, June 4, 1985.

112. Gideon Alon, "For the Third Time the President Has Reduced the Sentence for 3 of the Jewish Underground Prisoners," *Ha'aretz*, June 6, 1989.

113. Conversation with Yuval Ne'eman, May 14, 2003; State Comptroller, *Annual Report 34*, 81–82.

114. Yuval Ne'eman, "The Settling of Eretz Israel," *Midstream*, January 30, 1984, 7–11.

115. State Comptroller, *Annual Report 34*, 81–104.

116. Knesset Protocols, Vol. 98, meeting on January 18, 1984, 1,205–1,215.

117. Conversation with Yuval Ne'eman, May 14, 2003.

118. Gazit, *Trapped*, 239.

119. Friedman, *Zealots for Zion*, 74–75.

120. Central Bureau of Statistics, *Statistical Yearbook for Israel*, Jerusalem, various years.

121. Ibid., No. 53, Jerusalem, 2002.

122. Tzali Reshef, *Peace Now: From the Officers' Letter to Peace Now* [Hebrew], (Jerusalem: 1996), 59.

123. Ibid.

124. Conversation with Shimon Sheves, March 10, 2003.

125. Ibid.

126. Knesset Protocols, Vol. 100, meeting of September 13, 1984, 116–118.

127. Shahar Ilan, ed., "The Price of the Settlements," September 26, 2003, based on

Interior Ministry and Central Bureau of Statistics data. In 1990, the first year of the government of the right, the number of settlers increased by 9,000, almost twice that of the previous year; and in subsequent years the number was already increasing by 10,000 a year and more.

128. Knesset Protocols, Vol. 100, meeting of December 17, 1984, 805; Geoffrey Aronson, *Israel, Palestinians and the Intifada: Creating Facts on the West Bank* (New York: 1990), 310.

129. Ori Nir, "The Settlers in Face of the Disturbances," *Ha'aretz*, April 7, 1988.

130. Ibid.

131. Shahar Ilan and Avi Pozen, "A Proper Intifada According to Jewish Law," *Kol Ha'ir*, August 11, 1989; Nadav Shragai, "Debate between Rabbis and Gush Emunim People Who Met to Discuss Matters of the Settlers," *Ha'aretz*, June 28, 1989.

132. Nadav Shragai, "An Eye for an Eye, a Bullet for a Bullet," *Ha'aretz*, May 26, 1989.

133. Ibid.

134. Ibid.

135. Avinoam Bar-Yosef, Yosef Walter, Gideon Meron, and Ehud Rabinowitz, "Mother and Daughter Arrested in the Village of Beita: Suspected of Murdering of Porat as Revenge," *Ma'ariv*, April 7, 1988.

136. Aryeh Bender and Adar Avissar, "Merom Aldovi Suffered Brain Injuries and Breathing with the Help of Apparatus," *Ma'ariv*, April 7, 1988 (the misspelling of Aldovi's name is in the original).

137. Ben Caspit, "It Was Horrible: Huge Stones Few at Us, We Lay in Puddles of Blood," *Ma'ariv*, April 7, 1988.

138. Ben Caspit, "Thanks to Two Good Arabs We Are Here," *Ma'ariv*, April 7, 1988.

139. Ori Nir, "The Bloody Hike: Girl of 15 Killed by a Stone to Her Head; the IDF: the Route Was Not Coordinated with Us," *Ha'aretz*, April 7, 1988.

140. Tali Zellinger, Danny Rubinstein, and Uriel Ben-Ami, "Efforts to Prevent Acts of Revenge Following the Murder of Tirtza Porat," *Davar*, April 7, 1988.

141. Dan Sagir, "What Shall We Hold First, the Funeral or the Circumcision?" *Ha'aretz*, April 7, 1988.

142. Ibid.

143. Ori Nir and Dan Sagir, "Tirtza Porat Was Shot in the Head by Romem Aldovi, Who Opened Fire Indiscriminately," *Ha'aretz*, April 10, 1988.

144. Ze'ev Schiff, "A Settlers' Hike Like This Invites Trouble: Like Crossing the Street on a Red Light," *Ha'aretz*, April 10, 1988; Eitan Levine, "The Village of Beita 20 Hours Later: Only the Blowing-up of Houses Disturbs the Silence," *Ma'ariv*, April 10, 1988.

145. Ori Nir, "'The Village of Beita Must Be Wiped Out, Revenge,' Cried Mourners at the Funeral of Tirtza Porat," *Ha'aretz*, April 4, 1988.

146. Akiva Eldar, "Rabin Rejects Attempts to Besmirch the IDF and the Chief of Staff," *Ha'aretz*, April 11, 1988.

147. Benny Katzover, "The Report Burst the Calumny," *Nekudah*, No. 120, May 15, 1988, 26.

148. Alex Fishman, "Mitzna Is Now Getting Dastardly Acts in an Organized Way," *Hadashot*, February 10, 1989.

149. Ibid.

150. Ron Ben-Yishai, "The Fanatics Want a Blow-up," *Yedioth Aharonoth*, June 2, 1989.

151. Ronny Shaked, "The Army Is Interfering with Our Attempts to Impose Order in Hebron," *Yedioth Aharonoth*, May 3, 1989.

152. Nadav Shragai, "The Settlers' Actions against Their Neighbors," *Ha'aretz*, June 21, 1989.

153. "*Yedioth Aharonoth* Survey: The Majority Objects to the Settlers' Disorderliness," *Yedioth Aharonoth*, June 8, 1989.

154. Haim Shibi, "The Settlers' Punishment Activity Will Increase the Violence—And Perhaps Also the Terror," *Yedioth Aharonoth*, May 31, 1989.

155. Nadav Shragai, "Settlers Now," *Ha'aretz*, June 8, 1989.

156. Uriel Ben-Ami, "Katzover, Levinger and Ariel Are Autistic in His Opinion," *Yerushalayim*, February 17, 1989.

157. Ori Nir, "The Settlers Vis-à-vis the Riots," *Ha'aretz*, April 7, 1988.

158. Aronson, *Israel, Palestinians and the Intifada*, 311–312; Yehezkel Lein, *Land Grab: Israel's Settlement Policy in the West Bank* (Jerusalem: 2002), 15.

159. Knesset Protocols, Vol. 112, appendices to the meeting of December 22, 1988, 252–254.

160. Friedman, *Zealots for Zion*, 79, 238–239.

161. On Levi, "Secret Government Decision: Land in Yesha for Free," *Davar*, July 26, 1991; Friedman, *Zealots for Zion*, 79–80, 238–239.

162. *State Comptroller, Annual Report 42 for the Year 1991 and the Accounts of Fiscal Year 1990*, Part I (Jerusalem: 1992), 162–295; Friedman, *Zealots for Zion*, 79–80, 90, 238–239.

163. Conversation with Yuval Ne'eman, May 14, 2003.

164. James Baker, *The Politics of Diplomacy: Revolution, War and Peace, 1989–1992* (New York: 1995), 122–123.

165. Ibid., 130–132.

166. Ibid., 555; Gideon Doron, *A Strategy for Elections* [Hebrew] (Rehovot: 1996), 32, 38, 117.

167. Ariella Ringel-Hoffman, "What Arik Has Built, Even Sharon Will Not Be Able to Dismantle," *Yedioth Aharonoth*, July 7, 2003.

168. Baker, *The Politics of Diplomacy*, 557. It should be noted that the terms were very loose; not only would Israel be allowed to complete construction already begun, but also the terms allowed for "natural growth" of existing settlements and construction was permitted without restriction in places deemed by Israel to be "security areas."

169. Ministry of Finance, *State Budget 19903* (Jerusalem: 1992); *State Budget 1994* (Jerusalem: 1993); Sarah Ossetzky-Lazar and Assad Ghanem, *Between Peace and Equality: The Arabs in Israel during the Labor-Meretz Government* [Hebrew] (Givat Haviva: 1995), 19.

Chapter Three: Fire on the Hilltops

1. Ronny Shaked and Zvi Singer, "The Blood Prayers," *Yedioth Aharonoth*, February 27, 1994.
2. Conversation with Michael Ben-Yair, April 25, 2004.
3. Shimon Schiffer, "Rabin: This Is a Grave Mistake, but the Argument Is Super-fluous," *Yedioth Aharonoth*, February 28, 1994. On the futility of the commission of inquiry on Rabin's assassination less than two years later, which was also headed by Supreme Court President Shamgar, see Idith Zertal, *Israel's Holocaust and the Politics of Nationhood* (Cambridge: 2005), chap. 5.
4. Knesset Protocols, February 28, 1994, Vol. 136, 4,906.
5. For elaboration see Michael Karpin and Ina Friedman, *Murder in the Name of God* (New York: 1998); Zertal, *Israel's Holocaust*, chap. 5.
6. Conversation with Mati Steinberg, April 14, 2004.
7. Conversation with Yossi Beilin, April 17, 2003.
8. Conversation with Ahaz Ben Ari, March 6, 2003; conversation with Ben-Yair.
9. Ben Ari.
10. Testimony of former Chief of Staff Amnon Lipkin-Shahak, March 7, 2003.
11. Thierry Arad, *The Rabbis: March 1994–February 1996* [Hebrew], undated, Archive of the Yitzhak Rabin Center for Israel Studies, Sprinzak Collection, Container 2, File 14, 2–3.
12. Nadav Shragai, "'Defy with All Your Might the Criminal Initiative to Evacuate Hebron,' Rules Rabbi Goren," *Ha'aretz*, March 7, 1994.
13. Conversation with Noah Kinarti, February 2, 2003.
14. Nadav Shragai, "The Nissan Force," *Ha'aretz*, December 16, 1994.
15. Arad, *The Rabbis*, 4.
16. Sprinzak's lecture at the Jerusalem Institute for the Study of Israel, May 1993.
17. Conversation with Ehud Sprinzak, 1994.
18. Conversations with Israeli reporters at Blair House shortly after the meeting with President Clinton.
19. Dennis Ross, *The Missing Peace: The Inside Story of the Fight for Middle East Peace* (New York: 2004), 127.
20. Investigation Commission on the Matter of the Massacre at the Tomb of the Patriarchs, *Report* [Hebrew] (Jerusalem: 1994), 222, 246–252; Dalia Shehori and Eitan Rabin, "Rabin at the Labor Faction Meeting: The Shamgar Report Contains Criticism That Must Not Be Ignored," *Ha'aretz*, June 28, 1994.
21. For more on Rabin's attitude toward the settlers, see Karpin and Friedman, *Murder in the Name of God*.
22. Ibid.
23. Yitzhak Rabin, *Service Bloc-Note*, 551.
24. State Comptroller, *Annual Report 42 for the Year 1991 and the Accounts of Fiscal Year 1990*" (Jerusalem: 1992), 162–295.
25. Shlomo Aviner, "Our Government and Our Land," *Yesha Rabbis Newsletter 2*, September 7, 1992.

26. "In Lieu of an Editorial," *Nekudah*, No. 162, September 1992, 10.

27. Aryeh Stav, "The Mission: To Topple Rabin," *Nekudah*, No. 165, November 1992, 30–31, 50.

28. Elyakim Haetzni, "Crossing the Red Lines," *Nekudah*, No. 165, November 1992.

29. Hagai Segal, "My Brother Settlers," *Hadashot*, June 26, 1992.

30. Ibid.

31. Appendix to the coalition agreement between the Labor Party and Meretz from the Knesset Protocols Vol. 126, July 13, 1992, 64.

32. Conversation with Ahaz Ben-Ari, legal adviser to the Prime Minister's Office, March 6, 2003.

33. Knesset Protocols Vol. 126.

34. The state comptroller criticized in detail certain aspects of this method in one case: the establishment of the settlement of Tel-Zion in 1998 in the guise of a "neighborhood" of the settlement of Kokhav Yaakov. See State Comptroller, *Annual Report 51B* (Jerusalem: April 2001), 398–405.

35. Yair Fidel, "Why Uri Ariel Is Behaving Politely," *Hadashot*, October 29, 1993.

36. Ibid.

37. Ibid.

38. Late at night he personally phoned *Yedioth Aharonoth* editor Moshe Vardi and dictated the formulation of the resolution to him. Conversation with Ahaz Ben-Ari, March 6, 2003.

39. Government Resolution 360, November 22, 1992.

40. Conversation with Mossi Raz, May 5, 2003.

41. Aviner, "Our Government."

42. Zalman Melamed, "Settlement and the Establishment of New Settlements," *Yesha Rabbis Newsletter*, 2, September 7, 1992.

43. "In Lieu of an Editorial," *Nekudah*, No. 162, September 1992, 12.

44. Conversation with Shimon Sheves, March 10, 2004.

45. Conversation with Shimon Peres, April 10, 2004.

46. Mahmoud Abbas, *Through Secret Channels* (Reading: 1995), 121–123.

47. Ibid., 128.

48. Yair Hirschfeld, *Oslo: A Recipe for Peace* [Hebrew] (Tel Aviv: 2000), 133–137.

49. Conversation with Yoel Singer, June 17, 2003.

50. Conversation with Yossi Beilin, April 17, 2003.

51. Yossi Beilin, *Touching Peace* [Hebrew] (Tel Aviv: 1997), 84, 110, 152.

52. Abbas, *Through Secret Channels*, 157.

53. Ibid., 81.

54. Conversation with Philip Wilcox, March 10, 2004.

55. Hanan Ashrawi, *This Side of Peace* (New York: 1995), 260–261, 283–287.

56. Conversation with Uri Savir, February 5, 2004.

57. Knesset Protocols, June 22, 1994, Vol. 138, 8,591–8,592.

58. Ze'ev Schiff, "Settler Leaders Are Holding Secret Talks with Senior People from the Palestinian Authority," *Ha'aretz*, April 7, 1996.

59. Ibid.

60. Yossi Alpher, *And the Wolf Shall Dwell with the Wolf: The Settlers and the Palestinians* [Hebrew] (Tel Aviv: 2001), 15.

61. Ze'ev Schiff, "Yes to Settlers, No to Settlements," *Ha'aretz*, April 30, 1996.

62. Ze'ev Schiff, "The Sides Discussed the Establishment of a 'Hotline' to Deal with Emergency Situations in the Territories," *Ha'aretz*, April 7, 1996.

63. Quoted in Alpher, *Wolf Shall Dwell*, 81–94.

64. Ibid., 91–100.

65. Ibid., 99–101.

66. *Newsletter from the Heads of the Local and Regional Councils in Yesha*, undated, Archive of the Rabin Center for Israel Studies, Sprinzak Collection. Container 1, File 3.

67. Ibid.

68. Zvi Singer, "Secret Yesha Council Campaign Revealed for Lightning Establishment of 130 Settlements," *Yedioth Aharonoth*, December 1, 1993; Zvi Gillat, "Operation Wool-over-the-Eyes," *Yedioth Aharonoth Friday Supplement*, February 4, 1994.

69. Moshe Feiglin, *Where There Are No Men: The Struggle of the Zo Artzeinu Movement against the Post-Zionist Collapse* [Hebrew] (Jerusalem: 1997), 54–55.

70. Ibid., 60–63; Singer, "Secret Yesha Council Campaign Revealed"; see also Zvi Singer and Haim Broide, "Warming the Gun Barrel," *Yedioth Aharonoth*, December 26, 1993.

71. Nadav Shragai, "For a Viewer of CNN in Atlanta, 5 People, a Tent and a High Flag Are a Settlement Like Ariel," *Ha'aretz*, December 12, 1993.

72. A public opinion survey in February 1993 showed that 7.2 percent of all radio listeners listened to Channel Seven.

73. Karpin and Friedman, *Murder in the Name of God*, 120.

74. Hannah Kim, "Rabin and Porat, from Sebastia to Efrat," *Ha'aretz*, January 6, 1995.

75. Karpin and Friedman, *Murder in the Name of God*, 96–97.

76. Israel Radio, August 4, 1995; Israel Radio, August 6, 1995.

77. Conversations with Shaul Arieli, 2003–2004.

78. Ibid.

79. *The Israeli Palestinian Agreement on the West Bank and the Gaza Strip* (Oslo II), chap. 5, Article 31(7).

80. Geoffrey Aronson, *Settlements & Israel Palestinian Negotiations* (Washington: 1996) 50–51.

81. Nadav Shragai, Aluf Benn, Gideon Alon, Reuven Shapira, and Eitan Rabin, "Ben Yair Will Examine the Legality of the Rabbinical Ruling by the Rabbis of the Right That Prohibits Evacuation of Bases," *Ha'aretz*, July 13, 1995.

82. Thierry Arad, *The Rabbis*, Container 2, File 14, 21.

83. Shragai, Benn, et. al., "Ben Yair Will Examine the Legality of the Rabbinical Ruling."

84. Elyakim Haetzni, "And If the 'People's Decision' Will Be Giving Away the Land of Israel," *Nekudah*, No. 188, September 1995, 60–61.

85. Yesha Council, "A Mourning Declaration and Call for National Reconciliation," November 5, 1995.

86. Letter from Uri Ariel, director general of the Yesha Council, to Yossi Beilin, minister of the economy and planning, November 7, 1995.

87. "Document: The Reckoning of Conscience Conference," *Nekudah*, No. 190, December 1995, 60–61.

88. Ibid., 63–64.

89. Itim reporters, "Mourning Descended Again: Rabbi Nachum Rabinowitz Is Indirectly Responsible for the Assassination," *Yedioth Aharonoth*, November 15, 1995.

90. Aryeh Bender, "We Will Not Be Able to Say That Our Hands Did Not Spill This Blood," *Ma'ariv*, November 12, 1995; Arad, *The Rabbis*, 41–42.

91. Shlomo Tzasana and Yael Carmi Danieli, "Yesha Rabbis: We Warned Rabin," *Ma'ariv*, November 14, 1995; Shahar Ilan and Nadav Shragai, "Rabbi Bin Nun: Para-Military Yeshiva Heads Dov Lior and Nachum Rabinowitz Are the Ones Who Issued the *Din Rodef* Judgment against Rabin," *Ha'aretz*, November 13, 1995; Shlomo Tzasana, "Rabbi Bin Nun Gave the Names," *Ma'ariv*, November 13, 1995.

92. Nadav Shragai, "Bin Nun Accuses Rabbi Rabinowitz of 'Indirect Responsibility' for Rabin's Assassination," *Ha'aretz*, November 15, 1995.

93. For elaboration see Zertal, *Israel's Holocaust*, especially chap. 5.

94. Nadav Shragai, "Next Week the Prime Minister Will Meet with Council Heads from the Territories," *Ha'aretz*, February 13, 1996.

95. Guy Bechor, Nadav Shragai, Gideon Alon, and Yerach Tal, "Contacts between Labor and the Settlers on an Agreement Whereby No Settlement Will Be Evacuated," *Ha'aretz*, April 3, 1996.

96. Avirama Golan, "The Yesha Council Has Decided to Recruit Forces for the Rightist Bloc and Support Netanyahu," *Ha'aretz*, January 26, 1996.

97. Menahem Felix and Yossi Peli, "Another Spirit," *Nekudah*, No. 196, June 1996, 14–17.

98. Nadav Shragai, "Wallerstein Will Watch the Baby," *Ha'aretz*, August 9, 1996.

99. Central Bureau of Statistics, *Statistical Yearbook for Israel*, several years.

100. Nadav Shragai, "Yoel Bin Nun: If Indeed Netanyahu's Victory Proves to Be a Fait Accompli," *Ha'aretz*, May 31, 1996.

101. Nadav Shragai, "Wallerstein Will Watch the Baby," *Ha'aretz*, August 9 1996; Nadav Shragai, "Someone Has Reversed the Prime Minister's Shoes," *Ha'aretz*, September 6, 1996.

102. Shragai, "Wallerstein Will Watch the Baby"; Nadav Shragai, "A Moment before the Protest," *Ha'aretz*, October 18, 1996 (authors' emphasis). It is noteworthy that Wallerstein is using the term "beyond the fences," which was formulated in the 1930s by the Labor movement's activist circles of the prestate Yishuv, and became the basis of the offensive doctrine of the Haganah and subsequently the IDF.

103. Yitzhak Deutsch, "A New Wind in Judea and Samaria," *Hatzofeh*, September 26, 1996.

104. Nadav Shragai, "The Yesha Council Meets This Morning for an Emergency Discussion," *Ha'aretz*, October 11, 1996.

105. Nadav Shragai, "Someone Has Reversed," *Ha'aretz*, September 6, 1996.

106. Ibid.
107. Nadav Shragai, "The Yesha Council Will Release Land for Construction," *Ha'aretz*, November 6, 1996.
108. Nadav Shragai, "A Moment before the Protest," *Ha'aretz*, October 18, 1996.
109. Nadav Shragai, "Yesha Council Meets This Morning," *Ha'aretz*, October 11, 1996.
110. Nadav Shragai, "Agreement in Principle between Netanyahu and the Settlers to Reduce Mordecai's Involvement in Building Permits," *Ha'aretz*, November 6, 1996.
111. Shaul Arieli, personal notes on the land grab after Oslo, March 2003.
112. Nadav Shragai, "A Moment before the Protest," *Ha'aretz*, October 18, 1996.
113. Arieli's notes.
114. Official document written at the State Comptroller's Office and distributed to the Civil Administration in the territories.
115. Ibid.
116. Nadav Shragai, "The Prime Minister to Arafat: The Extent of the First Phase Will Increase if the Building of Har Homa Goes by Peacefully," *Ha'aretz*, February 27, 1997.
117. Nadav Shragai, "Olmert's Har Homa Test," *Ha'aretz*, January 2, 1997.
118. Yerach Tal, "Arafat Calls upon the United States to Establish Embassies in Jerusalem to Two Countries," *Ha'aretz*, March 5, 1997.
119. Sami Sokol, "Husseini—Without Diplomatic Movement—Building at Har Homa Will Lead to an Explosion," *Ha'aretz*, October 15, 1996.
120. Guy Bechor and Amira Hass, "Arafat Threatens: I Will Declare a Palestinian State in Protest against the Construction at Har Homa," *Ha'aretz*, March 2, 1997.
121. Akiva Eldar, "Thanks from Arafat to Benjamin Netanyahu," *Ha'aretz*, March 5, 1997.
122. Conversation with Ed Abington, October 19, 2003.
123. Ibid.
124. Dalia Shehori and Amira Hass, "Netanyahu Rejects Hussein's Request to Postpone the Construction at Har Homa; Is Considering Gestures toward Arafat," *Ha'aretz*, March 17, 1997.
125. Yossi Beilin, *A Guide for a Wounded Dove* [Hebrew] (Tel Aviv: 2001), 28.
126. Sami Sokol and Eitan Rabin, "Palestinian Demonstrators Rebuffed by Security Forces," *Ha'aretz*, March 19, 1997.
127. Beilin, *Guide for a Wounded Dove*, 29.
128. Nadav Shragai, "Simulation Games," *Ha'aretz*, October 23, 1998.
129. Ibid.
130. Ibid.
131. Hagai Huberman, "Yesha Settlers Increasing the Struggle," *Hatzofeh*, October 25, 1998.
132. Yehoshua Mor Yosef, "Minister Levy: Netanyahu Failed to Achieve the Three Goals Decided on by the Government," *Hatzofeh*, October 16, 1998.
133. *Hatzofeh* Knesset correspondent, "The National Religious Party to Meet This Morning to Discuss Advancing the Elections," *Hatzofeh*, October 25, 1998.

134. *Hatzofeh* correspondent, "Noam Arnon Calls upon Army Officers to Thwart the Agreement," *Hatzofeh*, October 26, 1998.

135. Nadav Shragai, "Domb Is Considering Resignation from the Yesha Council; Harel: The Council Has Put the Public to Sleep," *Ha'aretz*, October 26, 1998.

136. Amos Harel and Nadav Shragai, "Sharp Criticism in the IDF of Sharon's Call to Take over Hilltops," *Ha'aretz*, November 17, 1998.

137. Shlomo Tzasana, "The Settlers Have Established 8 New Outposts since the Signing of the Wye Agreement," *Ma'ariv*, November 18, 1998.

138. Shlomo Tzasana and Felix Frisch, "Barricading the Settlements—Yesha Heads Reject the Plan for Defending the Isolated Settlements," *Ma'ariv*, November 23, 1998.

139. Amos Harel, "Netanyahu Is Preventing the Evacuation of Illegal Outposts in the West Bank," *Ha'aretz*, May 9, 1999.

140. Ibid.

141. Ari Shavit, "I Don't Want to Draw Up a Precise Map," *Ha'aretz*, October 4, 1996.

142. Zvi Singer, "Yesha Council Chair: 'Barak Will Carry Out Ethnic Cleansing of the Settlers,'" *Yedioth Aharonoth*, May 10, 1999 (Authors' emphasis).

143. Yair Sheleg, "The Right's Left Hands," *Ha'aretz*, May 19, 1999.

144. Nadav Shragai, "Wallerstein and Domb Resign from the Council," *Ha'aretz*, May 19, 1999; Zvi Singer, "Yesha Council Chairman Resigns," *Yedioth Aharonoth*, May 19, 1999; Sheleg, "The Right's Left Hands."

145. Nadav Shragai, "The Government Has Changed; the Construction Will Apparently Continue," *Ha'aretz*, June 29, 1999.

146. Ron Levine, Menachem Rahat, and Aryeh Bender, "The Right Has Fallen in Love with Barak," *Ma'ariv*, May 27, 1999.

147. Shragai, "The Government Has Changed."

148. Shlomo Tzasana, "A Secular and Moderate Chairman Will Try to Change the Settlers' Image," *Ma'ariv Weekend Supplement*, July 6, 1999.

149. Elisha Efrat, *A Geography of Occupation* [Hebrew] (Jerusalem: 2002), 68–69.

150. Aluf Benn, Nadav Shragai, and Amos Harel, "Barak Has Informed the Yesha Council: 15 Outposts Will Be Evacuated," *Ha'aretz*, October 13, 1999.

151. Ibid.

152. Amos Harel, "The Yesha Council Will Evacuate the First Outpost Today; by the End of the Week Four More Will Be Dismantled," *Ha'aretz*, October 19, 1999.

153. Zvi Singer, "Rabbinical Ruling Calls for Resisting Evacuation," *Yedioth Aharonoth*, October 14, 1999.

154. Shimon Schiffer, Zvi Singer, and Yuval Karni, "The Yesha Council Has Agreed to Evacuate 10 Outposts," *Yedioth Aharonoth*, October 14, 1999.

155. Yuval Karni and Alex Fishman, "Evacuation Order Has Already Been Transmitted to IDF Forces," *Yedioth Aharonoth*, November 9, 1999; Yuval Karni, "Pulsa Denura Curse on Anyone Who Participates in Evacuation," *Yedioth Aharonoth*, November 9, 1999; Uri Bender and Shlomo Tzasana, "We Are Here in the Name of the Holy One, Blessed Be He," *Ma'ariv*, November 11, 1999.

156. Nadav Shragai, "The Settlers Clutched Their Children to Make the Evacuation Difficult; 'We Shall Return,' They Promised," *Ha'aretz*, November 11, 1999.

157. Gideon Alon, "Sharon: 'The Prime Minister Had Destroyed a Jewish Settlement,'" *Ha'aretz*, November 11, 1999.

158. Eli Kamir and Aryeh Bender, "Barak: 'This Is a Test of Democracy and a Red Light on the Road to Anarchy,'" *Ma'ariv*, November 11, 1999.

159. Nadav Shragai, "The Settlers Have Returned to Man the Settlements That Were Evacuated a Year Ago," *Ha'aretz*, August 14, 2000.

160. "A State Captive to Extremists: Groups That Are Dangerous to Democracy in Israel—Trends and Processes," *Keshev* (online), October 2000; Nadav Shragai, "96 Percent Increase in Building Starts in the Settlements," *Ha'aretz*, September 12, 2000.

161. Menachem Klein, *Shattering a Taboo: The Contacts toward a Permanent Status Agreement in Jerusalem, 1994–2001* [Hebrew] (Jerusalem: 2001), 11–13; according to B'Tselem report, during Barak's tenure as prime minister, construction of some 4,800 new housing units started. Yehezkel Lein, *Land Robbery* [Hebrew] (Jerusalem: 2002), 42.

162. Nadav Shragai, "Residents of the Jordan Valley Will Demonstrate Near Camp David," *Ha'aretz*, July 11, 2000.

163. Lily Galili, "The Scarred General, the Bereaved Father and the Settler in the Protest Tent," *Ha'aretz*, August 14, 2000.

164. Nadav Shragai, "If, Heaven Forbid, Some Nut Succeeds in Harming the Mosques," *Ha'aretz*, July 25, 2000.

165. Daniel Ben Simon, "It Was Alright All Night," *Ha'aretz*, July 21, 2000.

166. Sima Kadmon, "No to Concessions," *Yedioth Aharonoth*, July 17, 2000; Ben Simon, "It Was Alright."

167. For more, see Shlomo Ben-Ami, *A Front without a Rearguard: A Voyage to the Boundaries of the Peace Process* [Hebrew] (Tel Aviv: 2004); *Scars of War, Wounds of Peace* (New York: 2005); Menachem Klein, *Shattering a Taboo*; Gilad Sher, *Just Beyond Reach: The Israeli-Palestinian Peace Negotiations 1999–2001* [Hebrew] (Tel Aviv: 2001). See also the blow-by-blow, different account of the Camp David talks in Clayton E. Swisher, *The Truth about Camp David: The Untold Story about the Collapse of the Middle East Peace Process* (New York: 2004).

168. Amira Hass, "Two Percent That Are a Lot More," *Ha'aretz*, July 20, 2000.

169. Hasan al Kashef, "Not [Just] for One Day," *Al Ayyam*, June 1, 1999 in "Exacerbation of the Struggle against the Settlements," http://memri.org.il.

Chapter Four: Soldiers of the Messiah

1. Isaiah 8:10.

2. Ehud Sprinzak talks about "the practice and ideology of illegalism developed by Gush Emunim." See Sprinzak, *Every Man Whatsoever Is Right in His Own Eyes—Illegalism in Israeli Society* [Hebrew] (Tel Aviv: 1987), 124.

3. See the discussion on Gush Emunim in Boaz Evron, *A National Reckoning* [Hebrew] (Tel Aviv: 1988), 353–380. See also Zvi Raanan, *Gush Emunim* [Hebrew] (Tel Aviv: 1980).

4. Cited by Gershon Shafat, *Gush Emunim, the Story behind the Curtains,* [Hebrew] (Beit El: 1995), 177–178, 180.

5. Uriel Tal, "The Bases of Political Messianism in Israel," in *Myth and Rationalism in Contemporary Judaism* [Hebrew] (Tel Aviv: 1986), 119–120.

6. Shafat, *Gush Emunim,* 177.

7. Ibid., 180–181.

8. Tal, *Myth and Rationalism,* 9–20.

9. "There was a feeling of a further move, a continuation of the day the state was born," wrote settler Meir Harnoy. "Now I could understand the unmediated experience of the dancers who took to the streets on November 29 [the day of the 1947 Partition Plan Decision at the UN, which approved the creation of Israel]." Meir Harnoy, *The Settlers* [Hebrew] (Or Yehuda: 1994), 51.

10. Matti Golan, *Road to Peace: A Biography of Shimon Peres* (New York: 1989).

11. Shafat, *Gush Emunim,* 220.

12. Daniella Weiss in a filmed interview with Haim Yavin, *In the Land of the Settlers* [Hebrew], March 27, 2003.

13. Moshe Zvi Neriah, *Religious Judaism and the State* [Hebrew] (Tel Aviv: 1952), quoted by Gideon Aran, "From Religious Zionism to Zionist Religion: The Roots of Gush Emunim and Its Culture," PhD diss., Hebrew University of Jerusalem, 1987, 78–79; Yohai Rudick, *Land of Redemption* [Hebrew] (Jerusalem: 1989), 31.

14. Jacob Bazak, *Almavet* (Jerusalem: 1950), quoted in Moshe Samet, *Religion and State* [Hebrew] (Jerusalem: 1972), 45.

15. Neriah, *Religious Judaism,* quoted by Aran.

16. Aran, "Religious Zionism," 1.

17. Ibid., 2–3.

18. Ibid., 213.

19. Ibid., 218.

20. Ibid., 214.

21. Abraham Isaac Hacohen Kook, *Lights* [Hebrew] (Jerusalem: 1963), 73; Zvi Yehudah Kook, *Hatzofeh,* January 16, 1975, quoted in Aran, *Religious Zionism,* 445; both quotes are cited in Aviezer Ravitzky, *Messianism, Zionism and Jewish Religious Radicalism* (Chicago: 1996), 82.

22. Abraham I. Kook, *Lights of Holiness* (Jerusalem: 1964), Vol. 3, 194; *Lights,* 160, quoted in Ravitzky, *Messianism, Zionism,* 5–6, 82.

23. Abraham I. Kook, "On Zionism," 30, quoted in Ravitzky, *Messianism, Zionism,* 87–89.

24. Ravitzky, *Messianism, Zionism,* 88.

25. Ibid., 101.

26. Abraham I. Kook, *The Vision of Redemption* [Hebrew], 201; Shlomo Avineri, *The Making of Modern Zionism: The Intellectual Origins of the Jewish State* (New York: 1981), 192–194. Both quoted in Ravitzky, *Messianism, Zionism,* 111.

27. Abraham I. Kook, "The Eulogy in Jerusalem," *Ha-Reiyah's Sayings* [Hebrew]; see also Maurice Kriegel, "Nation et religion: Aux origines des 'neo-messianismes' dans l'Israël d'aujourd'hui," in *Annales,* janvier–février 1999, No. 1, 3–28.

28. Ravitzky, *Messianism, Zionism*, 118.

29. Dov Schwartz, *The Theology of the Religious Zionist Movement* [Hebrew] (Tel Aviv: 1996), 216–218.

30. Ravitzky, *Messianism, Zionism*, 82–83, 118.

31. Ibid., 120.

32. Zvi Yehudah Kook, *Israel's Paths* (1st ed.), Article 21 [Hebrew] (Beit El: 2002), 148–149. The first edition of this collection of articles was published in 1967, and about ten years later a second volume of articles was published.

33. Ibid., Articles 8, 14, 21, and *passim*.

34. Shlomo Aviner, ed., *Conversations with Rabbi Zvi Yehudah* [Hebrew] (Keshet: 1980), 11; Kook, *Israel's Paths*, 82. According to this same logic, Rabbi Yehuda Amital saw the Yom Kippur War as a war of purification from the defilement of Western culture. See Tal, *Myth and Rationalism*, 118–119.

35. Kook, *Israel's Paths*, Article 26, 152.

36. Ibid., Article 1, 1–11; Article 2, 19–25.

37. Ibid., Article 2, 17; Article 14, 102; Article 18, 116–117.

38. Ibid, Article 18, 103, 138.

39. Haim Druckman, "Our Rabbi," *Rabbenu ztz"l* [Hebrew] (Jerusalem: 1982), 47, quoted in Ravitzky, *Messianism, Zionism*, 83.

40. Aran, "Religious Zionism," 224.

41. Zvi Yehudah Kook in an interview with *Ma'ariv*, April 8, 1963. The term "the armies of Israel" was perceived in its two senses: the Jewish people and its concrete army. Druckman said that Kook accepted his father's claim that "the armies of Israel are the armies of God" to the extent "that he saw even in the tanks of the IDF, its cannons and planes, objects of mitzvah and of holiness, as they served the commandment of settling the Land of Israel. Ravitzky writes that the boundaries between the spiritual and the military were consciously blurred by Kook and his followers, and that this constituted an especially acute expression of their political messianism. Ravitzky, *Messianism, Zionism*, 83, 254.

42. Kook, *Israel's Paths*, 183; Ravitzky, *Messianism, Zionism*, 83.

43. Kook, *Israel's Paths*, 125; Ravitzky, *Messianism, Zionism*, 124.

44. Kook, *Israel's Paths*, 188–195; Ravitzky, *Messianism, Zionism*, 125.

45. Druckman, quoted in Ravitzky, *Messianism, Zionism*, 129.

46. Eliyahu Avihail, *By the Dawn's Light* [Hebrew] (Jerusalem: 1982), 107 and *passim*, quoted in Ravitzky, *Messianism, Zionism*, 128.

47. Yosef Bramson, *Days of World: The Forcing End*, Jerusalem, 1980, 7 [Hebrew], quoted in Ravitzky, *Messianism, Zionism*, 80.

48. Ravitzky, *Messianism, Zionism*, 129–130.

49. Regarding this characteristic of Gush Emunim, see Danny Rubinstein, *On the Lord's Side: Gush Emunim*, [Hebrew] (Tel Aviv: 1982).

50. Janet O'dea [Aviad], "Gush Emunim: Roots and Ambiguities," in *Betfutzot Hagola*, No. 79/80, Winter 1977, 95–96.

51. Yehuda Amital, *Ascending from the Depths* [Hebrew] (Jerusalem: 1974), 12. See also Tal, *Myth and Rationalism* [Hebrew], 118–119.

52. Amiram Cohen, "Waiting for Redemption," *Al Hamishmar*, November 6, 1987.

53. Shafat, *Gush Emunim*, 12.

54. Nissan Slomiansky, a scientist at the outset of his career, a key person in the Gush, and eventually a Knesset member on behalf of the National Religious Party, recalled his recruitment. "One day, at the beginning of 1974, three crazies came to me: Gershon Shafat, Hannan Porat and Rabbi Moshe Levinger, and they say to me: We need you. Leave everything and come establish a movement with us. They didn't sound serious to me. . . . We intend to found a large movement that will prevent the handing over of Judea and Samaria to the Arabs, they explained. This sounded a bit too big to me. I said to them: I am a man of the book, I'm not a man of praxis or organization. . . . After long conversations into the night they succeeded in persuading me that if I wanted to help the Jewish people through physics and mathematics, that would be a good idea if I were Einstein. But as I was not Einstein, I was persuaded that it would not be felt if I weren't there." Shafat, *Gush Emunim*, 121.

55. Yair Kotler, "The Fanatics," *Ha'aretz*, September 5, 1975.

56. Israel Harel, "Gush Emunim: National and Religious, Not Party Political and Not Rightist," *Ma'ariv*, August 24, 1975.

57. Aharon Bachar and Yeshayahu Ben-Porat, "Discussion with Gush Emunim," *Yedioth Aharonoth*, October 3, 1976.

58. Ronit Matalon, "Letters to the Secular Stereotype," *Ha'aretz*, August 12, 1988.

59. Eli Tavor, "Time Out," *Yedioth Aharonoth*, December 5, 1980.

60. Naomi Guttkind, "The book of Long Roots," *Hatzofeh*, June 24, 1988.

61. Dan Margalit, "Signs of an Internal Crisis," *Ha'aretz*, Decemebr 9, 1977.

62. Kotler, "The Fanatics."

63. Rubinstein, *On the Lord's Side*, 12.

64. David Weisburd, *Jewish Settler Violence: Deviance as Social Reaction* (Pennsylvania and London: 1989), 20–21.

65. Zvi Raanan had already sketched the figure of the Gush Emunim man along similar lines in 1980. See Raanan, *Gush Emunim*, 50–55.

66. Muli Peleg, *To Spread the Wrath of God: From Gush Emunim to Rabin Square* [Hebrew] (Tel Aviv: 1997), 79–80.

67. Ehud Sprinzak, "Gush Emunim: The 'Iceberg Model' of Political Extremism," in *Medina, Mimshal Veyahasim Beynleumiim*, spring 1981, 36, 37.

68. Hannan Porat, "The Meeting of Shdemot and the Gush Emunim People," in *Shdemot*, 58 (Tel Aviv: 1976), 46, 47.

69. Zephaniah Drori, quoted in O'dea, "Gush Emunim."

70. Zvi Yehudah Kook, *In the Public Debate*, 112, quoted in Ravitzky, *Messianism, Zionism*, 131–132.

71. O'dea, "Gush Emunim," 99.

72. Ibid., 98.

73. Assaf Inbari, "100 Years of Solitude," *Ma'ariv*, September 15, 2002.

74. Aran, "Religious Zionism," 250.

75. Tal, *Myth and Rationalism*, 117–118.

76. Yosef Bramson, ed., *In Public Debate*, 244–246, quoted in Ravitzky, *Messianism, Zionism*, 132.

77. Zvi Yehudah Kook, "That All the Peoples of the Earth May Know," *The Jerusalem Post*, January 4, 1974; See also O'dea, "Gush Emunim," 96–97.

78. Kook, "Arise and Live!" *Ma'ariv*, May 6, 1974.

79. Ehud Sprinzak, "Gush Emunim: The Tip of the Iceberg," *Jerusalem Quarterly*, 21 (fall 1981); Gideon Alon, "MK Hendel Dubs US Ambassador 'Jewboy,'" *Ha'aretz*, January 1, 2002.

80. "You, Kissinger and the Telephone" (advertisement), *Ma'ariv*, August 15, 1975; "You, Kissinger and Jerusalem" (advertisement), *Ma'ariv*, August 19, 1975.

81. *Ma'ariv* correspondent, "Sharon: Interfere with Kissinger's Visit," *Ma'ariv*, March 3, 1975.

82. Amos Levav and Yosef Wachsman, "Demonstrators Burst in the Foreign Minister's Home in the Old City in a 'Warm-up' Demonstration in Advance of Kissinger's Arrival," *Ma'ariv*, August 21, 1975.

83. See, *inter alia*, Zvi Lavie, "'What Are They Shouting?' The Vice President Asked Begin," *Ma'ariv*, July 10, 1978; Shaiya Segal, "'Loudspeaker Noise' against Cyrus Vance," *Ma'ariv*, December 14, 1978; Yosef Tzuriel, "Gush Emunim Has Initiated Protest, Peace Now Readying to Respond," *Ma'ariv*, March 7, 1979; Baruch Meiri, "Demonstrators Burst the Chain of Police and 'Touched' Carter's Car—The 'Gorillas' Leapt into Action Immediately and It 'Was Only a Miracle They Didn't Open Fire,'" *Ma'ariv*, December 3, 1979.

84. Kook, "Arise and Live!"

85. Yohanan Fried at a debate at Rabbi Kook's yeshiva with *Shdemot* people, 1967 (precise date not stated), *Shdemot* (Tel Aviv: 1968), 16.

86. For elaboration see Idith Zertal, *Israel's Holocaust and the Politics of Nationhood* (Cambridge: 2005).

87. Moshe Hager on the Noontime program, *Kol Israel Radio*, June 6, 2004.

88. Hannan Porat at a debate at Kook's yeshiva with *Shdemot* people, *Shdemot*, 38. Porat is quoted as using the term *Judenrat* rather than *judenrein*. It is not clear whether this is his error or an editorial error.

89. O'dea, "Gush Emunim," 95.

90. Yoel Florsheim, "What Is the Land of Israel for the People of Israel," *Petahim*, 47–48, September 1979, 66.

91. Haim Y. Peles, "The Dialectical Development of the Zionist Idea," *De'ot, The Journal of Religious Academics*, 45, 1976, 333.

92. Zvi Freund, "Musings on the Wars of Israel in General and the Yom Kippur War in Particular," *Niv Hamidrasha*, Vol. 11, 1974, 172.

93. Quoted in Amnon Rubinstein, *From Herzl to Rabin: The Changing Image of Zionism* (New Jersey: 2000), 151–152.

94. Tal, *Myth and Rationalism*, 121–122, 125.

95. Shlomo Aviner, "Messianic Realism," *Morasha*, Vol. 9.

96. Yaakov Medan, "We Have Never Wanted to Rule over the Arabs," *Nekudah*, No. 216, July 1988, 25.

97.   Moshe Ben-Yosef (Hager), "In Favor of Transfer," *Nekudah*, No. 109, April 14, 1987, 16–17.

98.   For elaboration, see Zertal, *Israel's Holocaust.*

99.   Meir Seidler, "The Arabs Today Are Worse Than the Germans in the Nazi Period," *Nekudah*, No. 151, July 1991, 24–25.

100. David Rosenzweig, "Peace Is Made with Enemies, Not with Deadly Foes," *Nekudah*, No. 144, October 1990, 24–25.

101. Hillel Weiss, "By Force of Naïveté," *Nekudah*, No. 9, May 16, 1980, 12.

102. Hagai Ben-Artzi, "The Moral Attitude toward the Arabs," *Nekudah*, No. 84, March 1, 1985, 12–13.

103. Hannan Porat, "The Land of Israel in the Heart," *Al Hamishmar*, November 6, 1987.

104. Yoel Bin Nun, "Gush Emunim's Red Lines," *Davar*, June 21, 1987.

105. Menachem Fruman, "The Palestinian People Also Has a Place in the Greater Land of Israel," *Nekudah*, No. 142, July 1990, 36–37.

106. Uriel Ben-Ami, "Evaporating Leadership," *Al Hamishmar*, September 19, 1990.

107. Danny Rubinstein, *On the Lord's Side*, 75–76.

108. Shafat, *Gush Emunim*, 48–49.

109. Ibid., 108–109.

110. Ibid., 116.

111. Ibid., 120.

112. Haim Hefer, "With Them and Against Them," *Yedioth Aharonoth*, October 10, 1974.

113. Shlomo Shamgar, "The Heart Says Yes, the Mind Says No," *Yedioth Aharonoth*, October 10, 1974.

114. Quoted by Danny Rubinstein in "The Same Hills, the Same Heroes, but Where Are the Problems," *Ha'aretz*, August 7, 1995.

115. Aharon Megged, "The Phenomenon: Gush Emunim," *Davar*, December 12, 1980.

116. Kook, *Israel Paths*, Article 21, 148, 150–151.

117. For elaboration, see Aran, "Religious Zionism," 252–254.

118. Shlomo Aviner, *Questions and Responses Intifada* [Hebrew] (Beit El: 1989), 58.

119. Druckman, "Our Rabbi," 47. On this, Ravitzky comments in his book that the remarks of the senior Rabbi Kook concerning "the armies of Israel" were made about thirty years before the establishment of the state and referred to the community of the Jewish people (*Orot* [Jerusalem: 1963], 24), whereas his successor the younger Kook applied them to the concrete army.

120. Kook, "Arise and Live!"

121. Avishai Amir: "A Demonstrator: 'The Situation You Have Created Is Worse Than Exile,' Rabin: 'So You Can Go into Exile,'" *Ma'ariv*, January 30, 1975. Aran writes in his study about the younger Kook's "categorical and crude" language and refers to expressions like "impudent," "fools," and cruder epithets he applied to his political or religious rivals. Aran, "Religious Zionism," 283.

122. Kook, "Arise and Live!"

123. *Davar* reporter in Jerusalem, "Rabin on Gush Emunim: They Build Apartment Houses and We Have to Do Guard Duty There," *Davar*, August 5, 1987.

124. Nadav Haetzni, "The Founders Are Tired and Are Seeking Heirs," *Ma'ariv*, May 7, 1993.

125. Rubinstein, *On the Lord's Side*, p. 43; Rubinstein, "Same Hills."

126. Kotler, "The Fanatics."

127. For the Sebastia affair, see chap. I.

128. Yosef Walter, "And Thanks Again to Shimon Peres," *Ma'ariv*, September 20, 1998.

129. Nadia and Ruth Matar, "A Man without a Homeland," *Jewish Press*, quoted in Nahum Barnea, *Netanyahu's Days, Political Columns* [Hebrew] (Tel Aviv: 1999), 254.

130. Shimon Peres, "Why Emunim?" *Ma'ariv*, October 19, 1979. Peres expressed this regret more recently in an interview: "There are things I flog myself for. The settlements in the territories, to give an example, for which I co-share responsibility, were a big mistake in a substantial measure." Amira Lam and Amir Shoen, "I Shall Live to See Peace," *Yedioth Aharonoth*, April 20, 2007. In an interview with the Associated Press following his inaugural address as president of Israel, Peres went even further, saying, "We have to get rid of the territories." *Associated Press*, July 15, 2007.

131. Quoted in Rubinstein, *On the Lord's Side*, 149.

132. Israel Harel, "The Gush Emunim peace plan," *Yedioth Aharonoth*, September 8, 1978.

133. Shafat, *Gush Emunim*, 356.

134. Ibid., 288.

135. Rubinstein, *On the Lord's Side*, 43.

136. Peleg, *To Spread the Wrath*, 59.

137. Rubinstein, *On the Lord's Side*, 151.

138. Israel Harel, "People of Faith," *Yedioth Aharonoth*, September 8, 1978.

139. "By the 'Stockade and Tower' Method, but with a Helicopter and Arik Sharon—The Settlement of Elon Moreh Arose," *Ma'ariv*, June 8, 1979.

140. Yosef Tzuriel, "Politics Is Cracking Gush Emunim," *Ma'ariv*, July 22, 1979.

141. Israel Harel, "Gush Emunim: Religious and National—Non-party and Not Rightist," *Ma'ariv*, August 24, 1975.

142. Tzuriel, "Politics Is Cracking."

143. Conversation with Yuval Ne'eman, May 14, 2003.

144. Nadav Shragai, "The Settlers are Replacing the Kibbutz Members in the Knesset Too," *Ha'aretz*, April 26, 2004.

145. Eli Tavor, "Time Off," *Yedioth Aharonoth*, December 5, 1980.

146. Uriel Ben-Ami, "Blind Probing," *Davar*, October 7, 1987.

147. Rubinstein, *On the Lord's Side*, 160.

148. Mordecai Bassok, "Gush Emunim Has Decided to Renew Its Political Activity," *Al Hamishmar*, June 7, 1982.

149. Rubinstein, *On the Lord's Side*, 61.

150. Nadav Haetzni, "Gush Emunim: The Rabbis Will Determine Whether There Will Be a Split," *Hadashot*, May 11, 1987.

151. Uriel Ben-Ami, "Gush Emunim and Rabbi Kahane in National Unity," *Davar*, February 27, 1985.

152. Hephzibah Lifschitz, "Sabbath, the Torah Portion of The Life of Sarah, with Daniella Weiss," *Ma'ariv*, November 16, 1990.

153. Yael Paz-Melamed, "Red Lines, Parallel Lines," *Ma'ariv*, February 20, 1987.

154. "Gush Emunim: Balance of Power in the Narrow Secretariat," *Ma'ariv*, May 15, 1987.

155. Avinoam Ben-Yosef, "The Left Marker of Gush Emunim," *Ma'ariv*, May 12, 1987.

156. Uriel Ben-Ami, "The Genie Has Emerged from the Bottle," *Davar*, May 7, 1987.

157. On May 6, 2004, together with other settler women, Daniella Weiss attacked a group of women, members of Machsom ("Checkpoint") Watch who were taking a shift to watch proceedings at the Jitt roadblock. They hit three women, broke flags, ripped off badges, cursed, and threatened. Male settlers joined them and beat up the male driver, a Palestinian citizen of Israel. A complaint was filed with the police. Reported by Dafna Banai, May 9, 2004.

158. Lifschitz, "With Daniela Weiss."

159. Avshalom Ginnosar, "Daniella Weiss, Comet in a Wig," *Koteret Rashit*, October 28, 1987.

160. Nadav Haetzni, "Gush Emunim"; Nadav Haetzni, "Weiss and Levinger Attacked in Gush Emunim Organ," *Hadashot*, March 15, 1987.

161. Hagai Segal, "Yoel's Right," *Hadashot*, December 13, 1989.

162. Uriel Ben-Ami, "Thou Hast Chosen Us" and "I Have Chosen Us," *Davar*, November 11, 1986.

163. Uriel Ben-Ami, "Who Holds the Gush?" *Davar*, November 14, 1987.

164. Yedidya Segal, "Defenders of Mysticism," *Davar*, July 17, 1987.

165. Ben-Ami, "Thou Hast Chosen."

166. Arieh Stav, "Nevertheless, the Iron Wall," *Hadashot*, September 25, 1989.

167. Ravyehiya, "Gush Emunim—Whither?" *Yedioth Aharonoth*, May 11, 1987.

168. Aryeh Palgi, "There Will Not Be Peace with Half a People," *Al Hamishmar*, March 18, 1988.

169. Menachem Rahat, "Gush Emunim and Hakibbutz Haartzi Have Signed a Joint Document," *Ma'ariv*, June 4, 1985.

170. Ben-Ami, "Who Holds."

171. Vered Noam, "Now He Is a Mirror," *Nekudah*, No. 160, June 1992, 19.

172. Nadav Shragai, "Rabbi Bin-Nun: Gush Emunim Has Failed Spiritually," *Ha'aretz*, April 10, 1992.

173. Nadav Haetzni, "The Founders Are Tired and Are Seeking Heirs," *Ma'ariv*, May 7, 1993.

174. Yair Sheleg, "From Sebastia to Migron," *Ha'aretz*, March 12, 2004.

175. Ibid.

176. Tavor, "Time Off."

Chapter Five: A Moveable Death

1. For the sequence of events see *The History of the Haganah*, Vol. 2, Part I [Hebrew] (Tel Aviv: 1957), 304–340.

2. "On a Volcano" was the title of an article in the newspaper *Doar Hayom*. The leader of the Hashomer Hatzair movement, Meir Ya'ari, said in the Histadrut labor federation council, "One-hundred-fifty-thousand Jews are on a volcano. What is the

way out?" "On a volcano one doesn't build a viable structure that is intended to be a refuge for an entire people," said labor movement leader Moshe Beilinson.

3. This was the term that *Ha'aretz* used to describe the disturbances in Safed. The daily *Davar* adopted the term "city of slaughter," referring to the long poem that national poet Haim Nachman Bialik had written in 1904 reprimanding the fragmented, cowardly, and shortsighted Jewish society of the diaspora.

4. Avraham Shvedron, "The Bases of the Brith Shalom Ideology," in *The Outlook of Integral Zionism* (Jerusalem: 1931).

5. Chaim Bugrashov, "The Haganah Trial," *Ha'aretz*, September 10, 1929.

6. David Ben-Gurion, "Our Political Path after the Riots," in *We and Our Neighbors* (Tel Aviv: 1931), 213.

7. Idith Zertal, *Israel's Holocaust and the Politics of Nationhood* (Cambridge: 2005), introduction and chap. 1.

8. Gideon Aran, "From Religious Zionism to Zionist Religion: The Roots of Gush Emunim and its Culture," PhD diss., Hebrew University Jerusalem, 1987, 251, 256–57; see also Michael Feige, *Two Maps for the West Bank: Gush Emunim, Shalom Akhshav* [Hebrew] (Jerusalem: 2002), 43–44.

9. Elyakim Haetzni, "Fifty Years Later," in H. Barness and A Ehrlich, eds., *Collection of Articles, Testimonies and Pictures for the 50th Anniversary of the 1929 Massacre* [Hebrew] (Kiryat Arba, Hebron: 1979), 73.

10. Miriam Levinger, "The Hadassah Women's Words for the 50th Anniversary of the 1929 Massacre," in Barness and Ehrlich, *50th Anniversary*, 37.

11. "In Memoriam for Our Beloved Shammai Elazar Leibowitz of Blessed Memory," in *Hebron Since Then and Forever* [Hebrew] (Kiryat Arba, Hebron: 2002).

12. A correspondent for the national religious daily *Hatzofeh* reported that the settlers had defended themselves from a Palestinian attack. See "Riots Following Palestinian Disruption of Leibowitz Funeral in Hebron," *Hatzofeh*, July 29, 2002, and B'Tselem Report, 26.7.2002–28.7.2002, 5–9.

13. Jeffrey Goldberg, "The Zealots," *The New Yorker*, May 31, 2004, 48.

14. See *inter alia*, chap. 4 of this book.

15. Yuval Karni and Itzik Saban, "Love Bloomed in the Shadow of Bereavement," *Yedioth Aharonoth*, July 8, 2002.

16. Goldberg, "The Zealots," 48–49; the story appears in the Second Book of Maccabees, chap. 7, and in the Babylonian Talmud, Tractate Gittin, page 57-b.

17. "The Renewed Jewish Courtyard," *Yedion [Hebron]*, 26, June 15, 1989, 2–3, cited by Feige, *Two Maps*, 109–110.

18. Members of Breaking the Silence, established during the second intifada by demobilized soldiers who served mainly in Hebron, document on a daily basis settlers' transgressions and harassment of Palestinian inhabitants in an attempt to awaken Israeli conscience to the horrors of the occupation and the violent, immoral conduct of the settlers.

19. Aviv Lavi, "Defaming the Occupation," *Ha'aretz*, June 18, 2004.

20. "The Old Graveyard in Hebron," in *Hebron Since Then and Forever.*

21. Feige, *Two Maps*, p. 114.

22. From the Internet site of the Jewish settlement in Hebron: www.hebron.co.il, 2003.

23. For details of this incident, see the article by Tamar El-Or, "From Shiloh One Cannot See Iceland: The Event of Rahelim," in *Alpaiym* 7 [Hebrew], 1993, 59–82.

24. Feige, *Two Maps*, 150–151.

25. Hava Pinhas-Cohen, "Where End Meets Beginning," *Nekudah*, No. 188, September 1995, 42–43, 66.

26. This, even though it is clear that under traditional Jewish law it is possible in various circumstances to evacuate cemeteries. See *Sanhedrin*, p. 47-b: "It is permissible to move a grave that is harmful to the many." The Rambam also ruled thus. See Mishne Torah, Laws of Uncleanliness.

27. Nadav Shragai, "Another Meaning to the Grave by the Home," *Ha'aretz*, January 18, 1995.

28. Daniel Ben Simon, "The Lubavitcher Rebbe Was Also Mobilized against the Withdrawal," *Ha'aretz*, May 3, 2004.

29. Eli Bohadana and Itai Asher, "At Zero Range, with No Pity," *Ma'ariv*, May 3, 2004.

30. Semadar Shir, "They Will Stay by Their Mother Forever," *Yedioth Aharonoth*, May 3, 2004.

31. Ben Simon, "The Lubavitcher Rebbe."

32. Daniel Ben Simon, "The Road Not Taken," *Ha'aretz*, May 11, 2001; thanks to Dror Etkes for his comments and for the draft of his MA thesis.

33. Feige, *Two Maps*, 141–149

34. Hagit Rotenberg, "Clinging to Life," *Besheva*, January 8, 2004.

35. Ibid.

36. "Representative of Hebron House Owners Opposes Their Settlement Now," *Ha'aretz*, February 14, 1980.

37. Yehuda Litani, "Hundreds of Dunams Were Purchased Last Year in the Kiryat Arba area," *Ha'aretz*, February 7, 1980.

38. Eliezer Waldman, "The Song of Yehoshua," *Nekudah*, No. 4, February 8, 1980, 3.

39. Uzi Benziman, "The Government to Decide on Settling 5 Houses in Hebron," *Ha'aretz*, February 4, 1980.

40. Ibid.

41. Uzi Benziman, "Begin Might Bring Issue of Hebron Houses to the Knesset," *Ha'aretz*, March 24, 1980.

42. Shlomo Gazit, *Fools in a Trap: 30 Years of Israeli Presence in the Territories* [Hebrew] (Tel Aviv: 1999), 104.

43. Benziman, March 24, 1980, "Begin Might Bring Issue."

44. Hagai Segal, *Dear Brothers: The History of the Jewish Underground* [Hebrew] (Jerusalem: 1987), 11.

45. Noam Arnon in *Hebron since Then and Forever.*

46. Yehuda Litani, "Ariel Sharon Visits Kiryat Arba and Hebron: Liquidate Terrorist Organization at Its Outset," *Ha'aretz*, May 7, 1980.

47. Yehuda Litani, "If Its Neighbors Are Astute," *Ha'aretz*, May 9, 1980.

48. Ibid.

49. Yoel Marcus, "Washington Post: Eli Haze'ev Killed in Hebron Was a Member of Motorcycle Gang," *Ha'aretz*, May 8, 1980.

50. For more details of her killing and the aftermath, see chap. 2.

51. Gideon Meron, "Tirtza's Father Doesn't Cry: My Daughter's Death Must Strengthen the Nation," *Ma'ariv*, April 11, 1988.

52. Orna Landau, "Waiting for Revenge," *Ha'ir*, March 11, 1994.

53. Moshe Feiglin, *Where There Are No Men* [Hebrew] (Jerusalem: 1998), 92.

54. Ibid., 94.

55. Ibid., p. 90.

56. Michal Goldberg, "This Is How the Murderer's Grave Became a Pilgrimage Site," *Yedioth Aharonoth*, November 15, 1999.

57. Nadav Shragai, "Kach Supporters Planning Goldstein Memorial," *Ha'aretz*, February 24, 2002.

58. Nadav Shragai, "Legal or Not, Goldstein Loyalists Keep Coming," *Ha'aretz*, June 4, 1998.

59. On tanks, planes, and artillery as objects of sanctity and religious observance according to the younger Rabbi Kook, see chap. 4.

60. For the disturbances by the Hebron settlers following the murder of Shalhevet Pas, see the report by B'Tselem, the Israeli Information Center for Human Rights in the Occupied Territories, Jerusalem, October 2001, 7–9.

61. Shlomo Tsezana, "High Fire," *Ma'ariv*, March 28, 2001.

62. Emunah Elon, "Her Body Was Donated for the Rescue of the State," *Yedioth Aharonoth*, March 28, 2001.

63. Ronny Shaked, Yuval Karni, Itamar Eichner, Rami Hazut, and Zvi Singer, "The Weapon: A Baby's Corpse," *Yedioth Aharonoth*, March 28, 2001.

64. Oded Shalom and Guy Mei-Tal, "We Don't Mourn an Arab Child Who Is Killed," *Yedioth Aharonoth*, July 25, 2003.

65. Guy Mei-Tal and Zvi Singer, "Rabbi Kahana's Disciple, the Guru of the Hilltop Youth," *Yedioth Aharonoth*, February 19, 2003.

66. Nadav Shragai, Yehonatan Liss, Arnon Regular, and Amos Harel, "After His Release from Prison, Ozeri returned to His Illegal Outpost," *Ha'aretz*, January 19, 2003.

67. Guy Mei-Tal, Roni Shaked, and Eitan Glickman, "The Terrorist Knocked on the Door," *Yedioth Aharonoth*, January 19, 2003.

68. See footnotes 26 and 27 for this chapter.

69. Guy Mei-Tal and Amir Ben-David, "The Battle for the Corpse," *Yedioth Aharonoth*, January 20, 2003.

70. Ibid.

71. Ibid.; Ronny Shaked, "A Crazed Rampage," *Yedioth Aharonoth*, January 20, 2003.

72. Mei-Tal and Ben-David, "The Battle for the Corpse."

73. Daniel Ben Simon, "A Stronghold Loosened," *Ha'aretz*, March 28, 2003.

Chapter Six: Complicity

1. Central Command Entertainment Troupe, "Somewhere in the Valley," lyrics: Noah Warsauer.

2. Galili's remarks were quoted in a speech by Knesset member Rehavam Ze'evi in the Knesset. See Knesset Protocols, Vol. 133, Session of December 7, 1993, 1,645.

3. Ibid.

4. *Pieds noirs* was the term used for French settlers (colons) in Algeria.

5. Moshe Ozeri, *Kiryat Arba Is Hebron* [Hebrew] (Kiryat Arba: 1978), 17–18.

6. Knesset Protocols, Vol. 52, Session of June 12, 1968, 2,230–2,231.

7. Ibid.

8. For more on the discussions concerning the fate of the settlers, see Reuven Pedatzur, *The Triumph of Embarrassment (Israel and the Territories, 1967–1969)* [Hebrew] (Tel Aviv: 1996), 237–241; Hagai Segal, *Dear Brothers: The West Bank Jewish Underground* [Hebrew] (Jerusalem: 1987), 23–24.

9. Yehiel Admoni, *A Decade of Consideration: Settling beyond the Green Line, 1967–1977* [Hebrew] (Ramat Efal: 1992), 64.

10. Ibid.

11. Ibid.

12. Ariel Sharon with David Chanoff, *Warrior: The Autobiography of Ariel Sharon* (New York: 1989), 554–555.

13. From Katif Net, the Gush Katif Internet site, www.katif.net/history.php?un=2#_ftn2.

14. High Court of Justice Docket 302/72, *Sheikh Suleiman Hassein 'Ouda Abu Hilou Wahl and Others v. the Government of Israel*, Verdicts 27 (2), 169.

15. Ibid., 175.

16. Central Bureau of Statistics, *List of Locales, Their Populations and Their Symbols*, December 31, 2000 (Jerusalem: 2001).

17. Aharon Dolev, "'Let the Government Provide IDF Uniforms for the Pregnant Women and the General Staff Produce Military Diapers for the Babies,'" *Ma'ariv*, September 30, 1977.

18. Tuvia Mendelson, "The Face of the Gush," *Davar*, January 6, 1978.

19. Ibid.

20. Aharon Dolev, "Gush Emunim and the Government—The Conflict That Was Avoided (or Postponed?)," *Ma'ariv*, September 30, 1977.

21. High Court of Justice 606/78, 610/78, *Suleiman Toufiq Ayoub and Others v. the Defense Minister and Others*, Verdicts, 33 (2), 113.

22. Ibid., 125.

23. Ibid., 126.

24. Israel's Supreme Court (the highest appeal body) and the High Court of Justice are in fact the same legal body, the High Court of Justice acting as a special instance open for citizens' direct appeal in case of harm done to them by the state and its institutions.

25. High Court of Justice 390/79, *Izzat Mohammad Mustafa Dawiqat and Others v. the Government of Israel and Others* [Hebrew], Verdicts, 34 (1), 1.

26. Ibid., 7.

27. Amnon Barzilai, "Weizman Fears Problems with the United States and Egypt on the Question of the Autonomy," *Ha'aretz*, June 6, 1979.

28. Conversation with a former senior officer in the Civil Administration, March 17, 2004.

29. Ron Ben-Yishai, "We Will Separate from the Intifada," *Yedioth Aharonoth*, June 8, 1989.

30. These were Moshe Levy, Ehud Barak, Amnon Lipkin-Shahak, and Moshe "Boogie" Ya'alon.

31. Ruvik Rosenthal, "Contention Town," *Ha'aretz*, March 24, 1995.

32. Yosef Walter, "'A Long Day's Fight' Near Nablus; 100 Settlers Evacuated by the IDF," *Ma'ariv*, June 6, 1974.

33. Gershon Shafat, *Gush Emunim: The Story behind the Scenes* [Hebrew] (Beit El: 1995), 260–269.

34. Yitzhak Rabin, *Service Bloc-Note* [Hebrew] (Tel Aviv: 1979), 549–551.

35. Mordechai Gur in a conversation with Gershon Shafat, quoted in Shafat, *Gush Emunim*, 209. According to Shafat, "Gur never concealed his sympathy for us."

36. Shafat, *Gush Emunim*, 75–85.

37. Marnina Sendak, *The Attitude of the Jewish Inhabitants of Judea, Samaria and Gaza towards the IDF after the Diplomatic Agreements between Israel and the Palestinians, 1993–1997* [Hebrew], MA thesis, Bar-Ilan University (Ramat Gan: 1998), 53–54.

38. Ibid.

39. Interview with Edna Pe'er, broadcast on Army Radio, April 2, 1982. The transcript of the interview was published in *Ma'ariv*, April 2, 1982.

40. Ze'ev Schiff, "The Settlers versus the IDF," *Ha'aretz*, June 17, 1987.

41. Alistair Horne, *A Savage War of Peace: Algeria, 1954–1962* (London: 1977). The rights to publish it in Israel were purchased by the Israeli Defense Ministry; the Hebrew translation was published in 1989.

42. Gideon Alon, "MK Landau to Arens: The Senior Officers of the IDF and the Shin Bet Who Have Failed Must Be Replaced," *Ha'aretz*, December 4, 1990.

43. Ze'ev Schiff, "What has happened to the IDF during the Course of the Intifada?" *Ha'aretz*, June 16, 1989.

44. Nadav Shragai, "Indictment against 12 Inhabitants of Kiryat Arba for Rampaging in the Deheishe Camp Last Saturday," *Ha'aretz*, June 14, 1987.

45. Nachum Barnea, "Mitzna Travels," *Yedioth Aharonoth*, July 21, 1989; Schiff, "The Settlers versus the IDF."

46. Emmanuel Rosen, "This Time They Didn't Ask Mitzna to Stay," *Ma'ariv*, March 12, 1993.

47. Aryeh Shalev, *The Intifada: Causes and Effects* [Hebrew] (Jerusalem: 1991), 139.

48. Yossi Melman and Uriel Ben-Ami, "Rabin: The Settlers—A Burden on Security. The Settlers: Let Us Defend Ourselves," *Davar*, February 4, 1988.

49. Conversation with Amram Mitzna, February 10, 2003.

50. Ariella Ringel-Hoffman, "Taking the North," *Yedioth Aharonoth*, March 22, 1991.

51. Ibid.

52. Ibid.

53. Avi Benaiyahu, "Brutal Announcement by Gush Emunim to 'Eliminate the Chief of Staff' Stirs Up a Storm," *Al Hamishmar*, April 19, 1991.

54. Yoram Binur and Meir Turjeman, "Barak Won't Be Able to Move. Gush Emunim Has Targeted Him," *Ma'ariv*, April 19, 1991.

55. Zvi Lavie, "Sarid: Gush Emunim—A Mafia That Has Put Out a Contract on the Chief of Staff," *Ma'ariv*, April 21, 1991.

56. Nadav Shragai, "And the Holy One, Blessed Be He, Weeps in Secret," *Ha'aretz*, May 13, 1994.

57. Aryeh Dayan, "The Loneliness of the Major General," *Ha'aretz*, August 28, 1992.

58. Ariella Ringel-Hoffman, "GOC under Fire," *Yedioth Aharonoth*, May 22, 1992.

59. Zvi Gillat, "Katzover: Marshal Pétain Was Also an Officer—And a Traitor," *Yedioth Aharonoth*, March 24, 1995.

60. Ibid.

61. Nadav Shragai, "Katzover to Biran: In Lebanon Officers Said They Were Not Willing to Play the Game," *Ha'aretz*, March 21, 1995.

62. Sima Kadmon, "Words Champion," *Ma'ariv*, March 24, 1995.

63. Nadav Shragai, "Katzover to Biran: In Lebanon Officers Told the Government That They Are Not Prepared to Play the Game," *Ha'aretz*, March 3, 1995.

64. Zvi Singer, "Major General Ilan Biran in a Sharp Letter to Zvi Katzover: Get It into Your Head That It Is Thanks to Us That You Exist," *Yedioth Aharonoth*, March 3, 1995.

65. Ibid.

66. Ruvik Rosenthal, "Contention Town," *Ha'aretz*, March 24, 1995.

67. Itamar Eichner, "The IDF Provides Bodyguards, a Vehicle and a Driver to Levinger," *Ma'ariv*, October 3, 1994.

68. Arbel Aloni, "Reconciliation Meeting between the Major General and the Settlers Scheduled for This Evening," *Ma'ariv*, April 5, 1995.

69. Conversation with Michael Ben-Yair, April 24, 2004.

70. Conversation with Avraham (Beiga) Shochat, May 5, 2003.

71. From personal notes by Colonel (res.) Shaul Arieli, who in his capacity as deputy military secretary to the defense minister served as liaison between the minister's bureau and the Civil Administration on settlement matters. March 2003.

72. Nadav Shragai, "Wallerstein Will Watch the Baby," *Ha'aretz*, August 9, 1996.

73. Ithiel Ben Haim, "The IDF Will Hold a Huge Salute to the Yesha Settlers," *'Iton Yerusalaiyim*, October 23, 1998.

74. Ofer Shelah and Yoav Limor, "Interview with Major General Moshe (Boogie) Ya'alon," *Ma'ariv*, September 24, 1999.

75. Hagai Huberman, "Major General Kaplinsky to the Inhabitants of Binyamin: 'Yesha Settlers—The Real Heroes of the Current War,'" *Hatzofeh*, August 26, 2003.

76. Shlomo Tsazana and Avi Ashkenazi, "Soldiers' Rights for All the Volunteers in the Settlements," *Ma'ariv*, November 20, 2002.

77. Amos Harel, "The Men of the Alert Squads in the Territories Will Be Recognized as Soldiers If They Are Hit," *Ha'aretz*, November 26, 2002.

78. B'Tselem, *Foreseen but Not Prevented: The Israeli Law Enforcement Authorities Handling of Settler Attacks on Olive Harvesters* (Jerusalem: 2002).

79. Efrat Weiss, "President Katsav to the Settlers: 'Do Not Put the IDF to the Test,'" *Ynet*, March 2, 2004.

80. Amos Harel, "Bear Hug," *Ha'aretz*, December 22, 2000.

81. Shmuel Groag [architect and urban planner], "Appropriating Space: Planning and Non-planning in the West Bank as a Political Tool," from the Internet site of Bimkom: Planners for Planning Rights, http://www.bimkom.org.

82. Ran Edelist, "Carrot Man," *Yedioth Aharonoth*, May 29, 1987.

83. Eyal Ehrlich and Ori Nir, "Early Retirement," *Ha'aretz*, September 23, 1987.

84. Edelist, "Carrot Man."

85. Ehrlich and Nir, "Early Retirement."

86. Israel Landers, "Not Yet the End of the Intifada," *Davar*, June 21, 1991.

87. See B'Tselem Report, Yehezkel Lein, *Land Grab, Israel's Settlement Policy in the West Bank* (Jerusalem: 2002), and Peace Now reports.

88. A Peace Now report (at www.peacenow.org.il) mentions about a hundred new settlements that arose after the signing of the second Oslo agreement.

89. An official internal report diffused to higher Civil Administration officials, dated March 27, 2000. The authors got a copy of the document.

90. Ibid.

91. "Transport and Positioning of Moveable Structures (Mobile Homes), Order on the Matter of the Transport of Goods (Judea and Samaria) (No. 1252), 1988, and Regulations on the Moving of Goods (Transport of Portable Structures) (Judea and Samaria), 1993.

92. *State Comptroller's Report 54A for the Year 2003*, from the Internet site of the State Comptroller's Office: www.mevaker.gov.il.

93. Ibid.

94. Quoted in Amos Harel, "With Determination and Sacrifice, but Also with Restraint," *Ha'aretz*, June 10, 2004.

95. Moshe Hager in a conversation with Haim Zissovitch, on the *Midday* program, Israel Radio, June 25, 2004.

96. Hannah Kim, "Between the Lines: Will the Ground Shake under Migron," *Ha'aretz*, January 9, 2004.

97. Hannah Kim, "The Building within the Destruction," *Ha'aretz*, January 9, 2004.

98. The letter was written on February 24, 1998. An official internal report, March 2000.

99. Ibid.; May 20, 1998.

100. Baruch Kra and Nadav Shragai, "A-G Orders Freeze on Allocation of Funds to Settlement Councils," *Ha'aretz*, April 16, 2004.

101. Knesset Protocols, Session of January 28, 2004, from the Knesset site: www.knesset.gov.il/plenum/data/00291904.doc.

102. Conversation with Dina Yeshurun, Shavei Shomron, June 13, 2004.

103. From a conversation with a senior officer who served in the West Bank and asked to remain unidentified.

104. Arieli's notes.

105. Conversation with a senior officer.

106. Official internal report, March 2000.

107. Amos Harel, "The Defense Ministry Is Taking Steps to 'Launder Settlements' That Were Established in the Northern West Bank Without the Government's Approval," *Ha'aretz*, March 27, 1998.

108. Daniel Ben Simon, "Wayfarers' Prayer," *Ha'aretz*, Decemeber 8, 2000.

109. Official internal report, March 2000.

110. Testimony of a former senior officer in the Civil Administration who asked to remain unidentified.

111. Amos Harel, "Mapainik to the End," *Ha'aretz*, August 2, 2002.

112. Ben Caspit, "'Take Them Off,' was Barak's Word," *Ma'ariv*, June 14, 2002.

113. Lior Baron, Aryeh Bender, and Uri Yablonka, "Electricity and Water Should Be Cut Off from Illegal Outposts," *Ma'ariv*, April 2, 2003.

114. Shahar Ilan, ed., "The Price of the Settlements," September 26, 2003.

115. "The Soldiers Have Become 'Sheepdogs,'" *Yedioth Aharonoth*, September 22, 2003.

116. Ronny Shaked, "IDF Taxis," *Yedioth Aharonoth*, October 31, 2003.

117. From the army Internet site: http://www.idef.il/hebrew/organization/home-front/idnew.stm.

118. Ze'ev Schiff, "Settlers versus the IDF," *Ha'aretz*, June 17, 1987.

119. Yagil Levy, *The Other Army of Israel: Materialist Militarism in Israel* [Hebrew] (Tel Aviv: 2003), 343. For more on the way the military command perceived area defense, see chap. 7.

120. Schiff, "Settlers versus the IDF."

121. Ze'ev Schiff, "Fear of a Political Army," *Ha'aretz*, August 9, 1999.

122. Conversation with Yitzhak Mordechai, March 16, 2004.

123. Ibid.

124. Amnon Lord, "The Settlements Sew a Suit," *Makor Rishon*, January 3, 2003.

125. Ibid.

126. Ian S. Lustick, *Unsettled States, Disputed Lands: Britain and Ireland, France and Algeria, Israel and the West Bank-Gaza* (Ithaca and London: 1993), 265.

127. Jean Lacouture, *De Gaulle* (London: 1970), 176.

128. Lustick, *Unsettled States, Disputed Lands*, 287–289.

129. Ibid., 290–292.

130. Ibid., 296.

131. Ibid., 432.

132. Conversation with a former senior officer in the Central Command, March 12, 2003.

133. Stuart A. Cohen, "Portrait of the New Israeli Soldier," 1(4), *Middle East Review of International Affairs* (December 1997).

134. Levy, *The Other Army of Israel*, 340.

135. Ibid., 336.

136. Ibid., 337.

137. Yair Sheleg, *The New Religious Jews: A Contemporary Look at Religious Society in Israel* [Hebrew] (Tel Aviv: 2000), 69–75.

138. Ibid. Hagai Huberman reported in the settler newspaper *Besheva* that the commander of the Officers' School summoned the heads of the premilitary preparatory programs and the *hesder* yeshivas at the beginning of the summer of 2004, and told them that between 40 and 50 percent of the officer cadets are "religious guys." Huberman added that based on unofficial information in his possession, he estimates the proportion of religious officers at the junior ranks in the infantry at 35 percent, as compared to a maximum of 8 percent in the 1970s. "Thirteen percent of the graduates of the pilots' course in 2002 came from settlements," he said. See Hagai Huberman, "Crochet Beret," *Besheva*, July 8, 2004. Three of Eli's graduates were killed in combat during the 2006 Lebanon War.

139. Amos Harel, "The Prep Course Revolution: 85% Combat Soldiers, 30% Officers," *Ha'aretz*, December 11, 2003.

140. Ben Caspit: "The Eitam Law: The IDF Will Not Evacuate Settlements," *Ma'ariv*, February 17, 2004.

141. Harel, "The Gray Refusal of the Religious Soldiers," *Ha'aretz*, June 13, 2000.

142. Shafat, *Gush Emunim*, 209.

143. Nadav Shragai and Aluf Benn, "Settlers, IDF Clash during Removal of Illegal Outpost," *Ha'aretz*, May 18, 2004.

144. Sarah Leibovich-Dar, "How to Evacuate Settlers," *Ha'aretz*, June 27, 2003.

145. Amir Gillat, "The Bnei Akiva Leadership Rules: An Order That Is Contrary to Jewish Law Is Illegal," *Ma'ariv*, November 27, 1995.

146. Gillat, "Bnei Akiva Leadership Rules."

147. Shahar Ilan and Eitan Rabin, "Deputy Defense Minister Ori Orr Proposes Canceling the 'Hesder' Yeshiva Program in the IDF," *Ha'aretz*, Decemebr 11, 1995.

148. Shahar Ilan, "Rabbi Druckman: The Proposal Is Devoid of National Responsibility and Is Hypocritical," *Ha'aretz*, December 12, 1995.

149. Nadav Shragai, "Rabbi Goren Ruled in 1993 That It Is Necessary to Refuse to Evacuate Settlements," *Ha'aretz*, July 9, 1995.

150. Zvi Singer, "The Big Question: Who Allowed the Blood?" *Yedioth Aharonoth*, November 12, 1995.

151. Eitan Rabin, "Senior Personnel Directorate Officer: IDF Officers Must Not Kowtow to the Rabbis," *Ha'aretz*, July 9, 1995.

152. Shlomo Tsazana, "The Wording of the Rabbis' Call for Refusing Orders to Evacuate Settlements and Bases," *Ma'ariv*, July 13, 1995.

153. Zvi Singer, "The Hesder Yeshiva Heads Have Decided Not to Decide," *Yedioth Aharonoth*, July 14, 1995.

154. Shahar Ilan, "Porat: Fortunate Are We to Have Rabbis of Iron, Who Utter Words Like Spurs," *Ha'aretz*, July 13, 1995.

155. Avirama Golan, "Hebron Is Precious, but in a Category of Jewish Law," *Ha'aretz*, April 1, 1994.

156. Gideon Alon and Shlomo Dror, "Ben-Yair Asked to Check the Legality of the Ruling," *Ha'aretz*, April 1, 1994.

157. Shlomo Tsazana, "Yesha Rabbis Call upon Soldiers: 'Request an Exemption from Evacuating Settlements,'" *Ma'ariv*, October 15, 2002.

158. Itai Asher, "IDF Officer Refused to Take Part in Evacuation of Outposts," *Ma'ariv*, June 26, 2003.

159. Itai Asher and Uri Yablonka, "The New Refusers," *Ma'ariv*, June 30, 2003.

160. Nadav Shragai, "The commander of the Hebron Brigade Slams the Police, the Settlers and the Hebron Agreement," *Ha'aretz*, April 3, 2001.

161. Avihai Beker, "Pleasant Noam," *Ha'aretz*, May 5, 2000.

162. Nava Tzuriel, "Straight Schick," *Ma'ariv*, December 12, 2003.

163. A group of demobilized soldiers who took upon themselves during the second intifada to document Jewish settlers' misconduct and harassments of Palestinians, mainly in Hebron.

164. "Breaking Silence: Fighters Tell about Hebron," from a photography and video exhibition at the Gallery of the Geographical Photography School, Tel Aviv, June 2004; see www.shovrimshtika.org.

165. "Breaking Silence" report.

Chapter Seven: Everything Is Legal in the Land of Israel

1. Meir Shamgar, "Law in the Territories Held by the IDF," *Hapraqlit*, 23, (1967), 540.

2. Ibid., 541.

3. Notice concerning arrangements for law and justice, West Bank area, (No. 2), 1967, Provision 35 in *Collection of Notices, Orders and Appointments of the Command of the Area of Judea and Samaria*, quoted in David Kretzmer, *The Occupation of Justice* (Albany: 2002), 27; see also Amnon Rubinstein, "The Changing Status of the 'Territories': From a held Deposit to a Legal Hybrid," *Iyyuney Mishpat* 11, 1985–1986, 440–441.

4. See Yaakov Shimshon Shapira, *Knesset Protocols*, Vol. 49, Session of June 27, 1967, 2,420.

5. The Fourth Geneva Convention of August 12, 1949, relative to the Protection of Civilian Persons in Time of War. Israel deposited its ratification of the Convention on July 6, 1951.

6. Yehezkel Lein, *Land Grab, Israel's Settlement Policy in the West Bank* (Jerusalem: 2002), 7.

7. In an official letter from Yehudit Karp to the military advocate general in August 1993, quoted by Tova Zimuki in "The Deputy Attorney General in a Letter to the MAG: 'I Am Shamed by the Attitude towards the Arab Whose Son Was Shot'"; Tova Zimuki, "Karp to the MAG: 'We Were Like Sodom and We Resembled Gomorrah,'" *Yedioth Aharonoth*, November 16, 1993.

8. Rubinstein, "The Changing Status of the 'Territories,'" 440.

9. *Collection of Notices, Orders and Appointments of the Judea and Samaria Area Command*, No. 9, quoted in Rubinstein, "The Changing Status of the 'Territories,'" 441.

10. Benedict Anderson, *Imagined Communities: Reflections on the Origins and Spread of Nationalism* (New York and London: 1983).

11. Yehuda Zvi Blum, "Zion Redeemed in Law," *Hapraqlit*, 27, 1970–1971, 5; for a different analysis of this issue, see Yoram Dinstein, "And the Hostage Has Not Been Redeemed or—Rather Deeds Than Demonstrations," *Hapraqlit*, 27, 1971–1972, 519.

12. Eyal Benvenisti, *The International Law of Occupation* (Princeton: 1993), 3–6.

13. Trading with the Enemy Ordinance, 1939. The British government, which had controlled Palestine since the end of World War I in accordance with a League of Nations Mandate, passed this law close to the outbreak of World War II, and its characteristics resembled those of a law that was passed in Britain at the same time. Article 3 of the ordinance stipulated a prohibition on trade with anyone defined as an enemy. Article 9 authorized the mandatory high commissioner to appoint a custodian of enemy property and grant him enemy property by order. Enemy property, according to the ordinance, also included property owned by the enemy's subjects. Land was also included in the definition of property. Article 5 of the Ordinance (The Custodian), from 1939, which was issued by force of this ordinance, determined that the custodian must hold assets that were given him until the end of the war, and that afterward he must deal with the property in accordance with instructions received from the High Commissioner.

14. This emerges, *inter alia*, from the rulings in the cases District Appeals *The Council for the Assembly of Israel v. Al Ayoubi*, Verdicts 35 (4) and High Court of Justice ruling 97/79, *Abu Awad v. Commander of the Judea and Samaria Area*, 33 (30), 309, 312–313.

15. See the ruling in *The Council for the Assembly of Israel v. Al Ayoubi*, 192

16. Eyal Zamir and Eyal Benvenisti, *The "Jewish Lands" in Judea, Samaria, the Gaza Strip and East Jerusalem* [Hebrew] (Jerusalem: 1993), 49 (footnote 72).

17. Ibid., 53–54. Plia Albek, who was the head of the civil department at the State Prosecutor's Office and specialized in the matter of lands in the territories, on various occasions and at various times praised the Jordanian custodian's work.

18. Quoted in Kretzmer, *Occupation of Justice*, 83–85.

19. Meir Shamgar, "The Observance of International Law in the Administered Territories," *Israel Yearbook of Human Rights*, 1971, 262.

20. David Yahav et al., *Israel, the Intifada and the Rule of Law* (Tel Aviv: 1993), 22.

21. High Court of Justice 785/87, *'Afo v. Commander of the IDF in the West Bank*, Verdict 41(2), 4, although in High Court of Justice 13/86, *Shahin v. Commander of IDF Forces in the Judea and Samaria Area*, Verdict 41(1), 197, 207–208, Supreme Court President Shamgar notes with agreement with Israel's official position concerning the interpretation of Article 2 of the Fourth Geneva Convention.

22. High Court of Justice 61/80, *Haetzni v. State of Israel—Minister of Defense*, Verdict 34 (30), 595; refer to 54/82, *Levy v. Estate of Mahmoud Mahmoud*, Verdict 40(1), 374.

23. Zamir, Benvenisti, *The "Jewish Lands"*, 78. To this day thousands of laws have been promulgated in the West Bank, so much so that at present the law observed there bears greater resemblance to Israeli law than to Jordanian law.

24. High Court of Justice 393/82, *Jam'it Askan Alma'almoun Alta'ounia Almasoula v. Commander of IDF in the Judea and Samaria Area*, Verdict 37(4), 785, 792–793.

25. In this context see, *inter alia*, Hemda Golan, "Israeli Practice with Regard to Making International Covenants," in Robby Seibel, *International Law* [Hebrew] (Jerusalem: 2003), 373.

26. See, *inter alia*, High Court of Justice 358/88, *The Association for Civil Rights in Israel v. GOC Central Command*, Verdict 43(2), 529.

27. In this context see Ronen Shamir, "Landmark Cases and the Reproduction of Legitimacy: The Case of Israel's High Court of Justice," 24 *Law & Society Review* 781 (1990); Yoav Dotan, "Do the 'Haves' Still Come Out Ahead? Resource Inequalities in Ideological Courts: The Case of the Israeli High Court of Justice," 33 *Law & Society Review* 1059 (1999). In the Gaza Strip the Egyptians had no right or claim. The Supreme Court ruled that the laws of occupied territories continued to apply in Gaza until such time as a political agreement is reached. Here too the existing system of laws was identical to that which prevailed in the West Bank, and it included the Ottoman, Mandatory, and Egyptian levels, to which were added, after June 1967, Israeli military security legislation, the rules of international law, and Israeli administrative law.

28. Menachem Mautner (interviewer), "Interviews with Justice Meir Shamgar," in Ron Haris, ed., *The Book of Shamgar: A Life Story* [Hebrew], (Tel Aviv: 2002–2003), 163.

29. Ibid. Shlomo Gazit, the first to hold the position of coordinator of activities in the territories, relates that the General Staff, and especially the Military Government Department, had formulated as far back as 1963 guidelines for the eventuality of a war on the eastern front and for the eventuality of an occupation. He notes, however, that the emphasis was on the Gaza Strip more than on the West Bank. See Shlomo Gazit, *The Carrot and the Stick: The Israeli Administration in Judea and Samaria* [Hebrew] (Tel Aviv: 1984–1985), 21–22, 35, and *passim*.

30. David Shalit, "Even Menachem Begin Was against It," *Ha'aretz*, August 8, 1996.

31. Some of the senior people of the military government inside Israel served as first military governors of West Bank towns after their occupation or in other senior roles in the administration of the territories.

32. Harris, ed., *The Book of Shamgar*, 164.

33. Ibid.

34. Ibid., 172.

35. Ibid., "Preface."

36. Ibid., 225–226.

37. On July 1, 1975, Shamgar was appointed to the Supreme Court, after completing his term as attorney general. In November 1983 he was appointed president of the Supreme Court. During the years of his presidency, Shamgar presided over benches that deliberated various issues concerning the occupied territories, because "in important cases it is desirable that the president [Shamgar himself] sit in order to lead the deliberations and to voice his opinion." Harris, ed., *The Book of Shamgar*, 200–201.

38. Even when petitions from inhabitants of the territories were accepted, legal precedents were set like the one that permits the demolition of a house but postpones

its implementation in order to enable the Palestinian whose home is slated for destruction to bring his arguments before the military commander. On this matter see Shamir, *Landmark Cases.*

39. Harris, ed., *The Book of Shamgar,* 179.
40. Ibid., 172.
41. High Court of Justice, 302/72, *Hilou v. Government of Israel,* Verdict 27(2), 169.
42. Ibid., 175.
43. Ibid., 175–176, 178.
44. Ibid., 179–182. See also Leon Scheleff, "The Limit of Activism is the Green Line: On the Margins and in the Paths of the Rulings of the High Court of Justice in the Territories," *'Iyyunei Mishpat,* 17 (1993), 757–809.
45. Ran Kislev, "The Revealing Document" and "Dayan's Compromise," *Ha'aretz,* August 17, 1973, and August 19, 1973, respectively; see also Moshe Negbi, *Chains of Justice, The High Court of Justice in the Territories* [Hebrew] (Jerusalem: 1981), 12–18. The political storm that broke in the summer of 1973 around the "Dayan document" was erased from memory by the Yom Kippur War, which broke out a few months later.
46. Avigdor Feldman, "My Memories as a Dog in the Rafah Salient," *Hadashot,* March 30, 1989.
47. High Court of Justice 606/708, 610/78, *Suleiman Toufiq Ayoub and Others v. Minister of Defense and Others,* Verdict 33(2), 113 ; henceforth: *Beit El Plaint.*
48. Ibid., 116–117.
49. Ibid., 118.
50. Ibid., 119.
51. Yoram Dinstein, "The Ruling in the Matter of the Rafah Salient," *'Iyyunei Mishpat,* 3. 1972–1973, 934.
52. *Beit El Plaint,* 128–129.
53. Negbi, *Chains of Justice,* 45.
54. High Court of Justice 390/79, *'Izzat Muhammad Mustafa Duiqat and Others v. Government of Israel and Others,* Verdict 34(1), 1; henceforth *Elon Moreh Plaint.*
55. *Ma'ariv* reporter, "By the 'Tower and Stockade' Method—But with a Helicopter and Arik Sharon—The Settlement of Elon Moreh Arose," *Ma'ariv,* June 8, 1979.
56. *Elon Moreh Plaint,* 5–6.
57. Moshe Simon at a meeting of the expanded secretariat of Gush Emunim in Jerusalem, May 15, 1978.
58. *Elon Moreh Plaint,* 24; Negbi, *Chains of Justice,* 59.
59. *Elon Moreh Plaint,* 7.
60. Negbi, *Chains of Justice,* 61.
61. *Elon Moreh Plaint,* 11.
62. Harris, ed., *The Book of Shamgar,* 175.
63. *Elon Moreh Plaint,* 4.
64. Ibid., 17. Unlike his fellows on the Supreme Court, after his retirement Landau had no hesitation about openly supporting the idea of Greater Israel and participating in street demonstrations against the partition of the land and Jerusalem.

65. *Elon Moreh Plaint*, 11.

66. Negbi, *Chains of Justice*, 71.

67. "The Lands Trap: The Legal Situation," Gush Emunim document in the wake of the Elon Moreh case, December 1979, reproduced as an appendix in Zvi Ra'anan, *Gush Emunim* [Hebrew] (Tel Aviv: 1980) (emphases in the original).

68. Negbi, *Chains of Justice*, 74.

69. "The Lands Trap."

70. Aluf Benn, "The Settlements Have an Element of Temporariness, the Settlers Have No Right of Ownership to Their Homes," *Ha'aretz*, April 5, 2004.

71. Nachum Barnea, "Albek's Face, the State's Face," *Yedioth Aharonoth*, October 15, 1991.

72. Yaakov Galanti and Shlomo Tsazana, "Senior Police Sources: The Investigations of the Rabbis Will Not Lead to an Indictment," *Ma'ariv*, December 1, 1995; Shira Immerglick, Yaakov Galanti, Baruch Meiri, Menachem Rahat, Tal Shahaf, and Shlomo Tsazana, "The Assassin and His Brother Will Be Arraigned Today, the Indictment Apparently This Week," *Ma'ariv*, December 1, 1995.

73. Nadav Shragai, "Old City Rabbi: The View Is That Someone Who Hands Territories of the Land of Israel over to Gentiles Is Subject to *Din Rodef*," *Ha'aretz*, June 30, 2004; Nadav Shragai and Gideon Alon, "Calls to Fire Rabbi Nebenzahl Following his Remarks on *Din Rodef*," *Ha'aretz*, July 1, 2004; Nadav Shragai, "Rabbis Prefer That the phrase *Din Rodef* Not Be Uttered—Certainly in Public," *Ha'aretz*, July 7, 2004.

74. Zvi Gillat, "Dekel Doesn't Like Her," *Hadashot*, October 1, 1986.

75. Cited in Amiram Cohen, "The Mother of All the Settlements," *Al Hamishmar*, October 18, 1991.

76. Ibid.

77. Gideon Alon, "A Certified Surveyor," *Ha'aretz*, October 12, 1984.

78. Cited in Cohen, "The Mother."

79. Alon, "A Certified Surveyor."

80. Benn, "The Settlements Have an Element of Temporariness."

81. Gideon Alon, "Her Entire Estate Is in the Settlements," *Ha'aretz*, July 13, 1993.

82. Article 1 of the proclamation states: "The Israel Defense Forces are entering the area today and taking over control and the maintenance of security and civil order in the area."

83. Article 27 of the Fourth Geneva Convention, Article 43 of The Hague Regulations.

84. Remarks by the minister of police at the time, Moshe Shahal, at the Knesset Constitution, Law and Justice Committee, November 22, 1993, Protocol No. 118, 6.

85. Order in the Matter of Police Forces Acting in Cooperation with the IDF (West Bank Area), No. 52, 1967.

86. Order in the Matter of Security Instructions (Judea and Samaria Area), No. 378, 1970, which replaced a prior order from 1967.

87. Emergency Regulations (Offenses in the Administered Territories—Trial and Legal Aid), No. 52, 1967.

88. As implied in the remarks of Colonel (res.) Ahaz Ben-Ari, formerly head of the

international law branch in the military prosecution, cited in the B'Tselem report, *The Enforcement of the Law on Israeli Civilians in the Territories* [Hebrew] (Jerusalem: 1994), 16.

89. Article 12 (1), in *The Israeli-Palestinian Interim Agreement on the West Bank and the Gaza Strip*, September 28, 1995.

90. Article 1 (b2) of Annex 4, "Protocol Concerning Legal Affairs," of the *Interim Agreement*.

91. In this situation there is some damage to the principle of territoriality, whereby people who live in a certain territory are subject to the same legal system. See Amnon Rubinstein, *The Constitutional Law of Israel* [Hebrew] (Jerusalem: 1991), 105.

92. Article 3 of *The Order on Manner of Punishment (Judea and Samaria)*, No. 322, 1969, stipulates: "The calculation of the period of punishment and the decrease in the punishment of someone who is serving a prison sentence under a ruling by a military court will be subject only to orders of security law and not to the legal ordinances that establish rules in the matter of decrease in punishment for good behavior in prison."

93. Nadav Shragai, "The Soft Underbelly of the Prosecution in the Levinger Trial," *Ha'aretz*, May 9, 1990.

94. An investigative report by the Palestine Human Rights Campaign, *Israeli Settler Violence in the Occupied Territories: 1980–1984* (Chicago: 1985), 15–16.

95. Ibid., 17.

96. Zvi Bar'el, "The Legal Chase Season," *Ha'aretz*, November 25, 1983.

97. High Court of Justice 175/81 *Mustafa 'Anabi al Natsche v. Defense Minister*, Verdict 35(3), 361. For details of the case see *Report of the Oversight Team for Investigating Suspicions against Israelis in Judea and Samaria Headed by Deputy Attorney General Yehudit Karp*, Jerusalem, 1982, 10; henceforth *Karp Report*.

98. Ibid., 1–2.

99. Letter from the attorney general, April 31, 1981, quoted in *Karp Report*, 2.

100. *Karp Report*, 4–5, 8.

101. Remarks by labor faction chairman Moshe Shahal at a discussion in a joint meeting of the Knesset Constitution, Law and Justice Committee and Interior Committee on February 8, 1984. See Rafael Mann, "Alignment: The Karp Commission Should Function in a Permanent Framework in the Territories," *Ma'ariv*, February 2, 1984.

102. Baruch Meiri, "The Opposition to the Police among the Inhabitants of the Hebron Area and Kiryat Arba Is Tantamount to Civil Revolt," *Ma'ariv*, February 8, 1984.

103. Ilan Bachar, "The Settlers Are Preparing a 'Yesha Document against the Karp Report,'" *Ma'ariv*, February 13, 1984.

104. Yehudit Karp in an interview to Gideon Alon, *Halishka*, an organ of the Bar Association in the Jerusalem District, quoted in *Ma'ariv* (Gideon Alon, "Dastardly Acts Are Still Being Committed against the Palestinians and the Law Is Not Enforced"), August 8, 2000.

105. Avi Bnaiyahu, "No Police in the Territories—Settlers Involved in Cases of Palestinians' Deaths Are Hardly Investigated," *'Al Hamishmar*, July 4, 1988. For findings regarding police treatment of offenses against Palestinians attributed to settlers in

the years following the Karp report, see B'Tselem, *Law-Enforcement on Israeli Citizens in the Territories* [Hebrew] (Jerusalem: 1994), 58–72.

106. *The Report of the Official Commission of Inquiry in the Matter of the Massacre at the Tomb of the Patriarchs in Hebron* [Hebrew] (1994), 191–193, 250–251; henceforth *Shamgar Report*. Some years earlier Police Commissioner Aryeh Ivtzan acknowledged that "in the territories every administration officer is effectively a police commissioner in his own right. He can decide whom to arrest and whom to release." See Baruch Meiri and Ilan Bachar, "Ivtzan: In the Territories Every Administration Officer— A Police Commissioner," *Ma'ariv*, May 22, 1983.

107. Gideon Alon, "Rabin Will Decide Whether to Transfer Cases Against Settlers to the Military Courts," *Ha'aretz*, March 16, 1993; Gideon Alon, "Ben-Yair Is Convinced That Settlers Suspected of Security Offenses Should Be Tried in Military Courts," *Ha'aretz*, April 28, 1995.

108. Gideon Alon, "Rabin Rejects Ben-Yair's Proposal to Try Settlers in Military Courts," *Ha'aretz*, July 17, 1995.

109. Nachum Barnea, "Hebron Sector Commander: 'I Don't Sleep Nights,'" *Yedioth Aharonoth*, December 15, 1993.

110. For details of the cases, see B'Tselem, *Law-Enforcement on Israeli Citzens*, 79–80.

111. From the ruling of the appeals court, written by Judge Eliezer Goldberg, Appeal 175/88, *State of Israel v. Nissan Ben Yermiyahu Ishegoyev*, Verdict 42(2), 361; henceforth *State of Israel v. Ishegoyev*. It was not possible to know any detail about the victim, apart from his age (13). Even his name was not mentioned.

112. Article 298 of the Penal Code, 1977.

113. Severe Criminal Case (Tel Aviv), 461/83, *State of Israel v. Ishegoyev*.

114. *State of Israel v. Ishegoyev*, 461/83.

115. Harris, ed., *The Book of Shamgar*, 107–108.

116. Ibid., 368.

117. Eyal Ehrlich, "The Wallerstein Affair," *Ha'aretz*, March 25, 1988.

118. Ori Nir, Eitan Rabin, Nadav Shragai, and Gideon Alon, "Two Israelis Who Killed an Arab Youth Released; Another Killed in Gaza," *Ha'aretz*, December 1, 1988; Ehrlich, "The Wallerstein Affair."

119. Ehrlich, "The Wallerstein Affair."

120. Severe Criminal Case, 265/88, *State of Israel v. Pinchas Ben Moshe Wallerstein*, quoted in B'Tselem, *Law-Enforcement*, 83–84.

121. Eitan Rabin, "Clash between Settlers and the Army over Attempt to Position Two Mobile Homes at Rahelim," *Ha'aretz*, December 3, 1991.

122. Amnon Rubinsten, *Knesset Protocols*, Vol. 98, Session of January 2, 1984, 923.

123. Nadav Shragai and Eitan Rabin, "Yesha Council: Henceforth Anyone Who Is Stoned Will Open Fire; IDF: They Must Not Take the Law into Their Own Hands," *Ha'aretz*, March 3, 1993.

124. Report on a meeting with the commander of the army in Judea and Samaria, the newsletter of the Matteh Binyamin council, December 23, 1993. Wallerstein explained that "he prefers that settlers will be sent to jail but not to the graveyard."

125. Chronicle of "An Example of a Month of Violence" (October, 1992) can be found in B'Tselem, *Law-Enforcement*, 26–27.

126. Ibid., 23–25.

127. Ibid., 25.

128. These figures are from B'Tselem, *Tacit Agreement: The Policy of Law-Enforcement on Settlers in the Territories*, information sheet (Jerusalem: March 2001); henceforth: B'Tselem, *Tacit Agreement*.

129. Interview to radio military correspondent Carmela Menashe, *This Morning*, Radio Israel Second Channel, January 7, 1994, at 7:06, quoted in B'Tselem, *Law-Enforcement*.

130. For documentation of such cases, see B'Tselem, *Law-Enforcement*, 37–43,

131. "Breaking the Silence: Fighters Talk about Hebron," soldiers' testimony about their service in Hebron, from a photography and video exhibition, Gallery of the Geographical Photography College, Tel Aviv, June 2004. See www.shovrimshtika.org.

132. "Procedure for Enforcement of Law and Order with Regard to Israelis Who Break the Law in the Judea and Samaria Area and the Gaza Shore Area" [Hebrew], September 1998.

133. Nadav Shragai and Gideon Alon, "In a Meeting with the Yesha Council Rubinstein Refused to Rescind Procedures for Law Enforcement in the Territories," *Ha'aretz*, May 5, 1998.

134. Haim Shibi, "The American Administration Has Called for a Serious Investigation of the Murder," *Yedioth Aharonoth*, November 1, 1996.

135. Senior writers and commentators at the newspaper, among them Orit Shohat, Gideon Levy, Amira Hass, and others, followed the affair throughout its duration.

136. Former Attorney General Michael Ben-Yair claimed on a television program that the sentence was "utterly inadmissible." See *Personal Encounter*, Channel 3, January 27, 2001; State Prosecutor Edna Arbel admitted that it was a mistake to reach an arrangement with Korman. See Baruch Meiri, "The State's Prosecutor Admits: the Deal with Korman—A Mistake," *Ma'ariv*, January 24, 2001.

137. Yossi Levi, "Nahum Korman Who Killed the Palestinian Child Has a Criminal Record," *Ma'ariv*, February 22, 2001.

138. Criminal Appeal 3235/94, *Yoram Shkolnick v. State of Israel*, Supreme Court Verdict Vol. 51, 376.

139. Criminal Case (Jerusalem) 149/93, *State of Israel v. Yoram Shkolnick*, ruling of April 28, 1994.

140. The deputy president of the District Court, Judge Jacob Bazak, and Judges Yaakov Zemach and Ruth Orr, ruling of April 28, 1994.

141. Itamar Eichner and Menachem Rahat, "Wrath in Sussia: This Is a Perversion of Justice," *Ma'ariv*, April 4, 1994.

142. Dalia Shehori and Nadav Shragai, "Shkolnick's Attorney: We Will Appeal to the Supreme Court," *Ha'aretz*, April 29, 1994.

143. Presiding over the bench was Supreme Court President Aharon Barak, who was joined by Justices Mishael Cheshin and Yitzhak Zamir.

144. For this, see High Court of Justice 2713/95, *The Association for the Preservation of the Rights of Jews in the Land of Israel and Others v. Prime Minister and Defense Minister Mr. Yitzhak Rabin and Others.*

145. MK Zvi Hendel of the National Union faction responded to the attorney general's position: "The prosecution's reaction testifies to a double morality with respect to Palestinian terrorists and killers of Arabs, and thus undermines the rule of law." See Shmuel Mittelman, "Rubinstein: The Decision to Release Shkolnick—Unreasonable," *Ma'ariv*, March 22, 2000.

146. High Court of Justice 1920/00, *MK Zehava Gal'on and Others v. the Release Committee, Ma'asiyahu Prison, Prisons Service and Others*, ruling 54(2), 313, 323.

147. Ibid., 329. Justice Yitzhak Engelrad, in a sole dissenting opinion, agreed that the release committee had not sufficiently considered the extent to which Shkolnick represented a danger and therefore the decision should be revoked, but in his opinion it was not possible to determine positively that his early release could endanger public order.

148. High Court of Justice 89/01, *The Public Committee against Torture in Israel v. Release Committee, Ma'asiyahu Prison, Prison Service*, Ruling 55(2), 838.

149. Ibid., 872.

150. Ibid., 880, 884, 886.

151. See B'Tselem Report, *Tacit Agreement*, 5–22.

152. Amira Hass, Amos Harel, and Iris Baram, "Settlers Rampaged and Burned Greenhouses in Protest against the Murder of Roni Salah," *Ha'aretz*, January 16, 2001; Uri Binder and Shlomo Tsazana, "The Settlers' Revenge Campaign," *Ma'ariv*, January 16, 2001.

153. B'Tselem Report, *Standing Idly By, Non-enforcement of the Law on Settlers in Hebron, July 26, 2002–July 28, 2002* (Jerusalem: August 2002), 5–18.

154. Ofer Petersburg and Oren Meiri, "Wanted: Volunteers to Travel the Dangerous Roads," *Yedioth Aharonoth*, August 17, 2001.

155. Quoted in B'Tselem, *Standing Idly By*, 5.

156. Among other things, Sharon said that "the harassment of olive-harvesters must be viewed with severity; for the Palestinian farmers the olive harvest is a celebration and a cultural event." He promised that "all the necessary steps" would be taken "to prevent repetition of the incidents." *Ynet*, October 28, 2002, quoted in B'Tselem, *Standing Idly By*.

157. Amira Hass, "Trespassers on Their Own Land," *Ha'aretz*, October 16, 1998.

158. In January 1995, following the Palestinian terror attack at the Beit Lid junction, Prime Minister Rabin declared that it was necessary to separate Israel and the territories. All of the subsequent governments discussed the issue of separation, under various names, but on the ground practically nothing was done.

159. Yuval Yoaz, "The High Court of Justice Has Ordered Delaying the Construction of the Fence in the Area of Mevasseret," *Ha'aretz*, March 11, 2003.

160. High Court of Justice, 2056/04, *Beit Suriq Council and Others v. Government of Israel*, ruling of June 30, 2004.

161. Ibid., paragraph 1 of Justice Barak's ruling.

162. Ibid., paragraph 61.

163. Ibid., 86.

164. Amnon Abramowitz, *Ulpan Shishi*, Channel 2, July 2, 2004.

165. Moshe Cohen and Amir Rapoport, "Mazuz Scolds Fence Administration Head," *Ma'ariv*, July 2, 2004; Yuval Yoaz and Aluf Benn, "Mazuz and Mofaz Reprimanded Fence Administration Head for His criticism of the High Court of Justice," *Ha'aretz*, July 2, 2004.

166. Amnon Barzilai and Aluf Benn, "Assessment: Change in the Route of the Fence Will Also Be Required in Other Areas," *Ha'aretz*, July 1, 2004.

167. Ben Caspit, Amir Rapoport, Eliel Shahar, and Eli Bohadana, "Sharon: There Will Be No High Court of Justice Bypass law," *Ma'ariv*, July 2, 2004; Aluf Benn and Arnon Regular, "Sharon: Re-examine the Entire Route of the Fence in Accordance with the High Court of Justice," *Ha'aretz*, July 2, 2004.

Chapter Eight: The Pace of Apocalypse

1.   See, *inter alia*, Amira Hass and Baruch Kra, "The Visit by Sharon and the Likud to the Temple Mount Caused Rioting," *Ha'aretz*, September 29, 2000.

2.   Yossi Verter, "Sharon Will Come Down from the Tree—And Take Second Place," *Ha'aretz*, September 28, 2000.

3.   Nachum Barnea, "Not Sharon Alone," *Yedioth Aharonoth*, November 2, 2000. The reference is to the violence that broke out in the wake of the opening of the Western Wall tunnel in September 1996, after pressure from the mayor of Jerusalem at the time, Ehud Olmert. This violence left more than eighty Palestinians and Israelis dead. It should be noted that neither Sharon, who was responsible for the Temple Mount riots in 2000, nor Olmert, who was responsible for the events of the tunnel in 1996, paid a political price for their actions. On the contrary, both of them became prime minister.

4.   Sarah Leibowitz-Dar, *Ha'aretz Magazine*, January 23, 2004. In the interview, Spector related that Sharon's son Omri was strongly opposed to the plan to visit the Temple Mount and refused to accompany his father. Instead, Sharon took along his other son, Gilad, in the retinue. Not long after the events, the paths of the adviser and the man who became prime minister diverged.

5.   Gilad Sher, *Just beyond Reach: The Israeli-Palestinian Peace Negotiations 1999–2001* [Hebrew] (Tel Aviv: 2001), 290.

6.   Shlomo Ben-Ami, *Front with No Backing: A Journey to the Boundaries of Peace* [Hebrew] (Tel Aviv: 2004), 286.

7.   Amira Hass and Aluf Benn, "Barak Meets with Arafat; the Talks in the U.S. are Renewed," *Ha'aretz*, September 26, 2000.

8.   Sher, *Just Beyond Reach*, 281.

9.   Ibid., 282.

10.   Aluf Benn, "The Sharm Summit: Difficult Atmosphere at the Talks; Ben-Ami to Erekat: 'Calm Down, This Isn't an Appearance on CNN,'" *Ha'aretz*, October 17, 2000. When Barak was asked why he had not gone to all lengths to ask Sharon, with official reasons, to cancel the visit, he refused to respond. See Amir Oren,

"They Were Surprised When Their Warnings Proved True," *Ha'aretz*, October 3, 2000.

11. Ben-Ami, *Front with No Backing*, 286.

12. Sher, *Just beyond Reach*, 282.

13. Arik Sharon, "Koshering the Hangman," *Hadashot*, October 2, 1988.

14. Avi Shlaim, *The Iron Wall: Israel and the Arab World* (New York: 2000), 477, 543. Sharon had to depart from this view with the signing of the peace agreement with Jordan in 1994, which was supported by the Knesset in a 91–3 vote.

15. Danny Rubinstein, "Sharon's Visit to the Temple Mount Arouses Anger in the PA," *Ha'aretz*, October 2, 2000. See also Amos Harel and Avi Yissacharoff, *The Seventh War* [Hebrew] (Tel Aviv: 2004), 14.

16. Rubinstein, "Sharon's visit."

17. Baruch Kra, "Sharon and the Likud Faction Will Visit the Temple Mount Today," *Ha'aretz*, September 28, 2000.

18. Shaham's story is recounted in Harel and Yissacharoff, *The Seventh War*, 13–16.

19. Ibid., 16.

20. Amos Harel, "The Shin Bet Did Not Recommend the Cancellation of Sharon's Visit to the Temple Mount," *Ha'aretz*, October 12, 2000; see also Yossi Verter and Gideon Alon, "Sharon No Longer Discounts Joining the Government," *Ha'aretz*, October 4, 2000.

21. Rubinstein, "Sharon's Visit."

22. Amos Harel, "This Is How the Siege of Netzarim Junction and Joseph's Tomb Began," *Ha'aretz*, October 2, 2004.

23. Amira Hass and Baruch Kra, "The Visit by Sharon and the Likud."

24. "The Rosh Hashanah Riots/The Conflagration: Diary of Events," *Ha'aretz*, October 2, 2000; "The Official Summation of the Or Commission Report," *Ha'aretz*, September 2, 2003.

25. See, *inter alia*, Ben-Ami, *Front with No Backing*, 293–294.

26. Ben-Ami, for example, believes that things could have turned out otherwise had it not been for a miserable sequence of events, which could not have been expected at all, in which right at the beginning of the events Jerusalem District Commander Yair Yitzhaki, "one of the best and most cautious officers I have known," was wounded in the head by a stone and replaced by his "hot-headed" deputy, David Krause. Krause ordered the police, in response to the rioting, to break into the Temple Mount/Al-Aqsa Mosque compound, an order that Yitzhaki, according to his own testimony, would never have issued. Police Commissioner Yehuda Wilk was not there at the time but on his way to Tel Aviv. He turned his car around and arrived in alarm at the site of the event, "in order to confirm, in retrospect, the dimensions of the disaster." When Ben-Ami was informed of what was happening, he ordered an immediate withdrawal from the Temple Mount and restraint from any shooting. Conversation with Shlomo Ben-Ami, August 10, 2004. See also Ben-Ami, *Front with No Backing*, 292–293.

27. This version began to be formulated in the first days of the uprising, and official

Israeli spokespersons cast the full responsibility for the events on Arafat. See, for example, Aluf Benn, Sharon Gal, Amos Harel, and Amira Hass, "Israel: Arafat Is Responsible for the Riots; the IDF Is Concentrating Tanks in the Territories," *Ha'aretz*, October 2, 2000.

28. Akiva Eldar, "His True Face," *Ha'aretz*, June 11, 2004; Yoav Stern, "A Baseless Conception," *Ha'aretz*, June 13, 2004; Yoav Stern, "Hitler Also Promised Quiet," *Ha'aretz*, June 16, 2004; Danny Rubinstein, "The True Assessment Fulfilled Itself," *Ha'aretz*, June 16, 2004.

29. Yossi Beilin, *Manual for a Wounded Dove* [Hebrew] (Tel Aviv: 2001), 161.

30. Nitzan Horowitz, "Concern in the United States about Loss of Control and Escalation," *Ha'aretz*, October 2, 2004.

31. Rubinstein, "Sharon's Visit."

32. See Aluf Benn et al.: "Arafat Is Responsible."

33. See Ben Caspit, "Israel Is Not a State That Has an Army, but Rather an Army That Has an Adjunct; the IDF Determines and Carries Out Its Policy," and "The Army Will Decide and Approve," *Ma'ariv*, September 13 and 16, respectively. Caspit, citing sources in Israeli military intelligence, wrote about the firing of 1 million bullets during the first days of the intifada. Others spoke of 1.3 million bullets.

34. Ben-Ami, *Front with No Backing*, 319.

35. Caspit, "The IDF determines."

36. Ari Shavit, "Yaalon: People Are Coming from Your Side, and Really Undermining You," *Ha'aretz Magazine*, August 30, 2002.

37. Cited in Caspit, "The IDF Determines."

38. Shavit, "Yaalon: People Are Coming."

39. Ibid.

40. On Israel's porous border, see A. B. Yehoshua, "The Necessity of a Border," *Ha'aretz Magazine*, February 8, 2002; Adriana Kemp, "The Border as the Face of Janus: Space and National Consciousness in Israel," *Theory and Criticism* 16, 2000, 13-43; Idith Zertal, *Israel's Holocaust and the Politics of Nationhood* (Cambridge: 2005; originally published in Hebrew in 2002), 184-186.

41. As early as right after the terror attack on Dizengoff Street in Tel Aviv in October 1994, Prime Minister Rabin spoke about the need for separating from the Palestinians, not just for a few days, as was the rule after each terrorist act, but rather as a principle. See Gideon Alon, "Rabin: Israel Wants to Separate from the Palestinians Not Only in a Closure of Several Days, but as a Worldview," *Ha'aretz*, October 20, 1994; see the prime minister's "Speech to the Nation" on Channels 1 and 2, January 23, 1995, which was quoted in all the newspapers. See "Rabin: We Will Persist on the Way of Peace, Because There Is No Other Alternative," *Ha'aretz*, January 24, 1995.

42. See Yeshaiyahu Fullman, *The Story of the Separation Barrier; Was It Life Sacrificing?* [Hebrew] (Jerusalem: 2004), 89-90.

43. Aluf Benn and Eitan Rabin, "Rabin Wants to Establish a Security Separation Line between Israel and the West Bank, East of the Green Line," *Ha'aretz*, October 24,

1995; Aluf Benn, Eitan Rabin, and Gideon Alon, "Rabin Is Establishing a Committee to Formulate a 'Separation Plan' between Israel and the West Bank," *Ha'aretz*, October 25, 1995.

44. Orit Galili, "How Is It They Never Thought of This Before," *Ha'aretz Magazine*, March 3, 1995; Aluf Benn, "Shahal Presented the Separation to Rabin; at Its Center Is the Establishment of 18 Crossing Points and the Restriction of the Passage of Vehicles. The PM: Separation of Traffic in the Gaza Strip Will Not Prevent Suicide Attacks," *Ha'aretz*, April 12, 1995; Eitan Rabin, "18 Crossing Points to Be Established Along the Separation Zone; No Separation in the Jerusalem Municipal Area," *Ha'aretz*, April 12, 1995.

45. Fullman, *The Story of the Separation Barrier*, 90-91. See also Ori Orr (who at the time was chairman of the Knesset Foreign Affairs and Defense Committee), "Just a Sedative," *Ha'aretz*, April 12, 1995.

46. During the course of 1998 the Netanyahu government decided to build a barrier in sensitive areas along the line, but the decision was never implemented.

47. *State Comptroller's Report Number 48 for the Year 1997 and the Accounts of Fiscal Year 1996* (Jerusalem: 1998), 1,019-1,030.

48. Aluf Benn, "Barak's Plan—A Palestinian State in Half of the West Bank," *Ha'aretz*, December 12, 2000; Amos Harel, "A Security Fence Will Be Erected Along the Green Line," *Ha'aretz*, December 26, 2000.

49. Fullman, *The Story of the Separation Barrier*, 97–98.

50. This testimony appeared in a special B'Tselem report on the roadblocks, "This Isn't Security. This Is Humiliation" (Jerusalem: 2003).

51. One example among many: Shlomo Lahat, "Breeding Grounds for Hatred," *Ha'aretz*, January 5, 2004. Lahat was formerly a brigadier general in the army and for many years the mayor of Tel Aviv. See also Yoav Shamir's film *Roadblocks*, (Tel Aviv: 2003), as well as the activities of the Council for Peace and Security against the route of the fence, among other things, in the petitioning of the High Court of Justice.

52. Interview with Lieutenant General Moshe Yaalon, *Yedioth Aharonoth, Sheev'a Yamim Magazine*, July 4, 2003.

53. *State Comptroller's Report on the Subject of the Seamline Zone* (Jerusalem: July 2002), 36.

54. Ada Ushpiz, "The Revolt of the Secular in Karnei Shomron," *Ha'aretz*, September 26, 2003.

55. Israel Harel, "From the Bar-Lev line to Sharon's," *Ha'aretz*, February 28, 2002.

56. Pinchas Wallerstein, head of the Binyamin regional council, was opposed to the barrier and argued that if it was built the army would not be able to act on its eastern side and therefore in fact Israel's security would be harmed. Daniella Weiss argued that any kind of separation plan is contrary to the idea of Greater Israel. Others argued that the agreement to the barrier was only tactical and temporary. However, the majority in the Yesha Council supported the building of a fence, and council chairman Bentzi Lieberman called on the council to determine a route that would be as distant as possible from the Green Line. See, *inter alia*, Nadav Shragai, "Disagreement in the Yesha Council on Question of the Separation Fence," *Ha'aretz*, June 7, 2002.

57.   Ushpiz, "The Revolt of the Secular."

58.   Arieh Haskin, "Defining the Eastern Fence," *Nekudah*, No. 269 (March/April 2004), 74-76.

59.   Ari Shavit, "Courting Disaster," *Ha'aretz Magazine*, June 5, 2003.

60.   Avi Primor, *Terror als Vorwand* (Düsseldorf: 2003), 148-149.

61.   Aluf Benn, "Is Sharon Fulfilling His Own Vision?" *Ha'aretz*, October 24, 2003.

62.   Aluf Benn, "'State Land' Loophole Allows Appropriation," *Ha'aretz*, September 26, 2003.

63.   Population figures are based on the population estimate at the beginning of 2004, based on a 1997 census. See also www.pcbs.org; the information is taken from B'Tselem Information Sheet, "Not All It Seems: Preventing Palestinians Access to Their Lands West of the Separation Barrier in the Tulkarm-Qalqilya Area" (Jerusalem: June 2004).

64.   Ibid.

65.   The segment of the fence around Salit penned in 6,000 Palestinians. In order to leave their homes and return to them the Palestinians need eleven different permits, whereas the newcomers of Salit move about unhindered. See Lily Galili, "Seamier and Seamier, This Seam-Line," *Ha'aretz*, February 13, 2004.

66.   Fullman, *The Story of the Separation Barrier*, 160.

67.   See for example the testimony of Palestinian farmers from villages in the area of Tulkarm and Qalqilya in the B'Tselem Information Sheet "Not All It Seems."

68.   Arnon Regular, "Kibbutz Member Seriously Injured by IDF Gunfire during Fence Protest," *Ha'aretz*, December 28, 2003; Arnon Regular and Amos Harel, "About 35 Palestinians and One Israeli Wounded in Demonstration against the Fence," *Ha'aretz*, March 3, 2004; Arnon Regular, "How Not to Disperse Demonstrators," *Ha'aretz*, April 14, 2004, and, on the same date, "Soldiers Move from the Territories to the Demonstrations and the Orders to Shoot Change," *Ha'aretz*; Amos Harel, "Ongoing Nightmare for the Military," *Ha'aretz*, April 14, 2004; Yehonatan Liss and Arnon Regular, "Violent Confrontation between Demonstrators against the Fence and Police," *Ha'aretz*, June 27, 2004; Arnon Regular, "IDF Killed Boy of 13 in Nablus; Dozens Wounded in Demonstration against the Fence," *Ha'aretz*, June 11, 2004, and more.

69.   See the position of the research team on Jerusalem at the Jerusalem Institute for Israel Studies, the head of which, Yisrael Kimchi, has said that the wall in the Jerusalem area is "a desperate step" that will not provide security and will rather do severe damage to both the Jewish and the Palestinian populations. Daliah Shehori, "A Barbed Wire Jerusalem," *Ha'aretz*, December 25, 2003. See also Uri Elitzur, "The Spirit of the Fence," *Yedioth Aharonoth Weekend Magazine*, September 3, 2004. Also see the organized protest against the route of the fence by key people in the Council for Peace and Security, all of them former senior officers in the army and the security agencies, who were partners to a petition to the High Court of Justice against the route of the barrier.

70.   Ze'ev Schiff, "The Bluff Goes On and On," *Ha'aretz*, October 31, 2003.

71. This was also the opinion, uttered by many former senior army officers during 2005–2006, who discovered the weakness and futility of state violence only after having been demobilized.

72. Aluf Benn, "The Whoops, We Made a Mistake Government," *Ha'aretz*, December 2, 2004; Aluf Benn, "Repeated Test for the Fence," *Ha'aretz*, September 8, 2004.

73. Prime Minister Sharon defined the Hague ruling as "pure evil." See James Bennet, "Sharon's Wars," *New York Times Magazine*, August 15, 2004.

74. Aluf Benn, "Attorney General Urges Sharon to Consider Adopting Geneva Convention," *Ha'aretz*, August 24, 2004. According to the report, in the wake of the World Court ruling the attorney general appointed a team of senior jurists at the Justice Ministry to examine its implications. The team recommended applying the convention in the territories. Benn wrote that if the recommendation was accepted, there would be a long-term and consistent turnaround on the part of Israel, which had always negated the applicability in the territories of the Geneva Convention. He added that Israel rejected in particular the argument that the settlements are in contravention of the provision in the convention that prohibits transfer of population to the occupied territory.

75. Danny Rubinstein, "On the Ground, the Fence Already Defines the Settlement Blocs," *Ha'aretz*, February 5, 2006; Ehud Olmert in Various Media Interviews; see for example Romesh Ratnesar, "Is Ehud Olmert Feeling Lucky," *Time*, April 17, 2006.

76. Amira Hass, "This Is How the State of Israel is Crumbling the West Bank into Enclaves"; "Restrictions on Movement Have Split the West Bank into Enclaves"; "The State Has Created Four Kinds of Enclaves," *Ha'aretz*, March 24, 2006.

77. Nadav Shragai, "Top Marks for Talk," *Ha'aretz*, May 3, 2001.

78. Shalom Yerushalmi, "Careful, Arik: The Prime Minister Has to Neutralize Tremendous Pressures from the Right and from Within the Likud in Order to Prevent a Disaster," *Ma'ariv*, July 23, 2001.

79. Ze'ev Schiff, "PM Ready to Move Gaza Settlers," *Ha'aretz*, March 19, 2001.

80. Nadav Shragai, "Top Marks."

81. Sima Kadmon, "Ariel Sharon: Interview," *Ma'ariv*, July 8, 1994. "Today, when I see how they are using this issue to weaken Israel's staunchness in the matter of the Golan Heights and in the matter of Judea and Samaria," said Sharon twelve years after the destruction of Yamit, "I think that this was a mistake. The issue of taking down settlements should not have been accepted under any circumstances."

82. Elyakin Haetzni, "Where Does Arik Sharon Stand?" http://www.gamla.org.il, December 7, 1997.

83. Yaakov Medan, "A Passive Refusal to Obey Orders," *Nekudah*, No. 269 (March/April 2004), 22.

84. Aluf Benn, "Settlements: The Guidelines are More Flexible Than the Government's Declarations," *Ha'aretz*, May 1, 2001.

85. Motti Basok, Aluf Benn, Daniel Sobelman, Amira Hass, *Ha'aretz* staff, and agencies, "Sharon Wants NIS 1.5 Billion for Settlements," *Ha'aretz*, May 6, 2001;

Shimon Schiffer, "Sharon Has Hogtied Peres: Don't Discuss the Settlements," *Yedioth Aharonoth*, May 1, 2001; Benn, "Settlements: The Guidelines"; Nadav Shragai, "Sharon Praised, and the Settlers Kept Quiet," *Ha'aretz*, July 2, 2001.

86. Yuval Karni, "30 settlements Have bBeen Established during the Sharon Government," *Yedioth Aharonoth*, June 26, 2001.

87. Daliah Shehori, "Settlement Freeze Is Already in Force," *Ha'aretz*, June 26, 2001; Meretz MK Mossi Raz said that "Peres doesn't know what he is talking about." Raz reported that construction in the settlements was continuing at an accelerated pace and that since the beginning of May tenders for the building of 746 housing units beyond the Green Line were issued.

88. Ibid., Gideon Alon and Aluf Benn, "Peres: The Settlements Are Thwarting the Achievement of Peace," *Ha'aretz*, July 14, 2001; Amos Harel, "Sharon Does Not Want a Confrontation with the Settlers at the Outposts," *Ha'aretz*, June 27, 2001.

89. Shlomo Tsazana, "Yesha Leaders Agree to Evacuate Uninhabited Outposts," *Ma'ariv*, July 4, 2001; Gideon Alon, Amos Harel, and Nadav Shragai, "Sharon to Labor Heads: Evacuation of Outposts Near," *Ha'aretz*, July 5, 2001; Nadav Shragai, "Ben-Eliezer Gives Settlers the List of 14 outposts That Will Be Evacuated," *Ha'aretz*, July 6, 2001.

90. Nadav Shragai and Amos Harel, "Settlers Remove Outposts but Number Is Disputed," *Ha'aretz*, July 1, 2002; Yehuda Golan and Shlomo Tsazana, "Ben-Eliezer: 20 Outposts Will Be Evacuated in the Coming Days," *Ma'ariv*, June 25, 2002.

91. Mazal Mualem and Nadav Shragai, "MK Zvi Hendel: 'All the Evacuated West Bank Outposts Were Fake Outposts,'" *Ha'aretz*, July 9, 2002. "We assumed in advance that the moment would come when this very great Zionist move would not go by quietly and we would have to give a bit of a whore's fee to the Moloch of hatred of the settlers," Handel said. He added that "if [Defense Minister Ben-Eliezer] goes for the inhabited outposts, the problem will be with the prime minister."

92. Daniel Ben Simon, "Rubble-Rousers," *Ha'aretz*, October 25, 2002. Dror Etkes, head of the Peace Now Settlement Watch unit, said that Ben-Eliezer ignored most of the outposts that were detailed in the lists he received from Peace Now. "The dismantling was one big bluff," Etkes said. "In the territories there is a creeping process of illegality that over time has become the norm." Authors' conversations with Dror Etkes during 2004.

93. Shlomo Tsazana, Yoav Limor, and Eitan Rabin, "The Battle for Havat Gilad," *Ma'ariv*, October 20, 2002.

94. Relating to the period during which he served as interior minister in Barak's government, Haim Ramon said that the headquarters officers at the Civil Administration, the great majority of them settlers, treated the territories as if they owned them. Ramon admits that he approved budgets for illegal outposts as long as he was convinced that the money was essential for the inhabitants' basic needs, especially when it came to children. Conversation with Haim Ramon, September 20, 2004. Pinchas Wallerstein said that during the period of Barak's government the attitude toward the settlers was friendlier and better than under Sharon's government. "Nowadays they

don't let me move water tanks into an outpost, something that would not have happened ever during the period of Barak and Ben-Eliezer. Every monetary outlay for the outposts was approved and was done in accordance with the law and procedures," said Wallerstein. Conversation with Pinchas Wallerstein, September 20, 2004.

95. See, *inter alia*, Nadav Shragai, "Despite a Promise to Bush: Sharon Signed an Evacuation Order for Only Five Outposts," *Ha'aretz*, August 16, 2004.

96. Ze'ev Schiff, "Losing Control over the Outposts," *Ha'aretz*, June 25, 2004.

97. Nadav Shragai, "An Outpost and Another Outpost—This Is How We Create a Jewish 'Settlement Continuum,'" *Ha'aretz*, September 6, 2004.

98. Conversation with a settler at Migron who asked not to be identified, September 20, 2004.

99. Ze'ev Schiff, "Two Fronts of Settlers," *Ha'aretz*, October 8, 2004; Ze'ev Schiff, "Security vs. the Settlements Budget," *Ha'aretz*, September 5, 2003.

100. Prime Minister's Office, Media Branch, *The Prime Minister's Speech at the Herzliya Conference* [Hebrew], December 18, 2003.

101. Army Radio, June 22, 2004.

102. Israeli electronic and printed media, March 8 and 9, respectively. On March 10 the Office of the Prime Minister published the report. It states, among other things, that the Housing Ministry supplied at least 400 mobiles to illegal outposts; that the Defense Ministry approved positioning of trailers to start new outposts; that the Energy Ministry connected outposts to the electricity grid. In the years 2000–2004 the Housing Ministry paid NIS 72 million for the establishment of outposts. Thousands of outpost demolition orders wait to be implemented, the report states.

103. At the State Prosecutor's Office they reject this term, which they say is accompanied by an attitude of forgiveness and romanticism. Sources there, who refused to be identified by name, told us, "These are criminal, violent youngsters, who scorn all the democratic frameworks and institutions. Many of them are narcotics addicts. They constitute a real danger to Israeli democracy."

104. Nadav Shragai, "Nowhereland," *Ha'aretz*, November 1, 2002.

105. Natan Alterman, "The Land at Biria," *The Seventh Column*, Book I [Hebrew] (Tel Aviv: 1975), 358-359.

106. Yair Sheleg, "The Settlers Think Again," *Ha'aretz*, October 24, 2002.

107. Amos Harel and Nadav Shragai, "12 Illegal Outposts Dismantled So Far," *Ha'aretz*, October 11, 2002.

108. Avirama Golan, "Danger in the Hills," *Ha'aretz*, January 4, 2001.

109. Shlomo Tsazana, "The Hill of Dispute," *Ma'ariv*, October 21, 2002.

110. Hagai Huberman, "Titus, You Have an Heir," *Hatzofeh*, October 20, 2002.

111. Gideon Alon, "Dichter: There Are Dozens of Extremists Who Might Act to Assassinate Sharon," *Ha'aretz*, July 21, 2004; Gideon Alon and Yuval Yoaz, "Dichter Warns: Worsening of Extreme Right's Actions; Mazuz Will Discuss Incitement," *Ha'aretz*, July 5, 2004; Yehonatan Liss, Gideon Alon, and Yuval Yoaz, "Hanegbi: There Are Already People Who Have Decided to Assassinate a Minister or Prime Minister," *Ha'aretz*, July 7, 2004.

112. Sharon first spoke directly to the media about the evacuation in an interview with Yoel Marcus. "This vacuum . . . cannot go on forever. So as part of the disengagement plan I ordered an evacuation—sorry, a relocation—of seventeen settlements with their 7,500 residents, from the Gaza Strip to Israeli territory." See Yoel Marcus, *Ha'aretz*, February 3, 2004. However, in various conversations before then and in his speech at the Herzliya Conference in December 2003, Sharon had revealed his intention to carry out a unilateral move.

113. In April 2004 Sharon told William Safire of the *New York Times*: "Back in November, so many plans were around, from the Saudis, from Geneva, from the Arab League, and I saw we could not resist those pressures without a plan of our own." See Safire, "The Sharon Plan of Disengagement," *New York Times*, April 4, 2004. In an interview with *Ha'aretz*, Dov Weisglass expanded on this: "The Geneva Initiative garnered broad support. And then we were hit with letters of officers and letters of pilots and letters of commandos [letters of refusal to serve in the territories]. These were not weird kids with green ponytails and a ring in their nose. . . . Really our finest young people." See Ari Shavit, "The Big Freeze," *Ha'aretz Magazine*, October 15, 2004.

114. Ariel Sharon at the Likud Knesset faction. In his talk he used the word "occupation" four times. See Gideon Alon, "Sharon Amended: Not 'Occupied' but 'Disputed' Territory," *Ha'aretz*, May 28, 2003; Yoel Marcus, "Escaped from the Stable," *Ha'aretz*, May 30, 2003; Israel Harel, "As If He Had Undergone a Religious Conversion," *Ha'aretz*, May 29, 2003; Hagai Huberman, "Sharon Is the Palestinians' Best Propagandist," *Hatzofeh*, May 29, 2005. In his appearance at the Knesset Foreign Affairs and Defense Committee a few days later, Sharon said that "when I used the expression 'occupation' I meant that it is not desirable to rule over a Palestinian population." It was Attorney General Elyakim Rubinstein who protested against the word "occupation" and noted that the legal position of all the governments of Israel since 1967 in the matter of the territories was that the territories are "disputed" and not "occupied" territories.

115. Prime Minister's Office, Media Department, *The Prime Minister's Speech at the Herzliya Conference* [Hebrew], December 18, 2003.

116. Nachum Barnea and Shimon Schiffer, "An Interview with Sharon: 'I'm Disengaging and That's It,'" *Yedioth Aharonoth*, September 15, 2004.

117. Shavit, "The Big Freeze."

118. Quoted in Uzi Benziman, "The Hudna Came before Its Time," *Ha'aretz*, June 6, 2003.

119. Uri Elitzur, "Migron and Herzliya," *Nekudah*, No. 267 (December 2003), 3.

120. Uri Elitzur, "All Its Sailors Have Fallen Asleep," *Nekudah*, No. 269 (March/April 2004), 2; Gonen Ginat, "The Skinheads' Demonstration," *Hatzofeh*, May 14, 2004; Naomi Eldar, "To Think That What We Have Built Will Disappear," *Makor Rishon*, March 12, 2004; Nadav Shragai, "Senior Religious Kibbutz Figure on the Person Responsible for the Disengagement: There Were Also Bureaucrats in the Holocaust," *Ha'aretz*, July 23, 2004. "Like after the pied piper of Hamlin, like after

Shabtai Zvi, even the best people are following him without saying a word, right into the river . . . so alarming and incomprehensible is Sharon's running amok, as though he has been haunted by a dybbuk to destroy everything that is sacred and essential to the very continuation of existence," wrote Haetzni in "The Pied Piper of Hamlin," *Nekudah*, No. 269 (March/April 2004). For the elaboration on the abuse of the Holocaust by the settlers, see Zertal, *Israel's Holocaust*, chap. 5.

121. Ariella Ringel Hoffman, "What Arik Has Built Even Arik Cannot Put Asunder," *Yedioth Aharonoth, Weekend Magazine*, July 11, 2003.

122. Nadav Shragai, "Old City Rabbi: According to the View, Anyone Who Hands Territories of the Land of Israel to Gentiles Is Sentenced to *Din Rodef*; Chairman of Yesha Rabbis: The Knesset, the Government or the High Court of Justice Are Not Entitled to Decide on Evacuation," *Ha'aretz*, June 30, 2004. In matters that are contrary to the way of the Torah, said Rabbi Dov Lior, like the uprooting of settlements in the Land of Israel and handing them over to strangers, "neither the king decides, nor the Knesset, nor the government nor the High Court of Justice, which has become the Holy of Holies here." Evacuating Jews from the Land of Israel is tantamount to a decree that cannot be enforced on a Jew who observes Torah and the commandments, and it is like a decision by the Knesset to legislate a law that will move the Sabbath to Tuesday," said Rabbi Lior.

123. Nadav Shragai, "Split in the Yesha Council Because of the Signatures of Three Members on a Covenant on the Rules of the Struggle," *Ha'aretz*, July 28, 2004; Nadav Shragai and Aluf Benn, "Yesha Council Heads: Without a Referendum on the Disengagement—We Will Support Refusal to Obey Orders," *Ha'aretz*, September 12, 2004. Professors for National Strength published a release that determined that an order to "transfer" Jews is "a crime against humanity and blatantly illegal and it is compulsory to refuse to carry it out." On this *see* Yitzhak Zamir, "A Statement That Stirs Abandon," *Ha'aretz*, September 9, 2004.

124. Ze'ev Schiff, "Sorry, We Didn't Win," *Ha'aretz*, October 1, 2004.

125. William Shakespeare, *Julius Caesar*, Act III, Scene ii.

Bibliography

Books (English)

Aronson, Geoffrey. *Israel, Palestinians and the Intifada: Creating Facts on the West Bank.* New York: 1990.

————. *Settlements & Israel Palestinian Negotiations.* Washington: 1996.

Ashrawi, Hanan. *This Side of Peace.* New York: 1995.

Aviner, Shlomo. *The Making of Modern Zionism: The Intellectual Origins of the Jewish State.* New York: 1981.

Baker, James. *The Politics of Diplomacy: Revolution, War and Peace, 1989–1992.* New York: 1995.

Beilin, Yossi. *Touching Peace: From the Oslo Accord to a Final Agreement.* London: 1999.

Ben-Ami, Shlomo. *Scars of War, Wounds of Peace.* New York: 2005.

Benvenisti, Eyal. *The International Law of Occupation.* Princeton: 1993.

Demant, Peter. *Plowshares into Swords: Israeli Settlement Policy in the Occupied Territories, 1967–1977.* Amsterdam: 1988.

Friedman, Robert. *Zealots for Zion: Inside Israel's West Bank Settlement Movement.* New York: 1992.

Gazit, Shlomo. *Fools in a Trap: 30 Years of Israeli Presence in the Territories.* London: 2003.

Golan, Matti. *Road to Peace: A Biography of Shimon Peres.* New York: 1989.

Gorenberg, Gershom. *The Accidental Empire: Israel and the Birth of the Settlements, 1967–1977.* New York: 2006.

Horne, Alistair. *A Savage War of Peace: Algeria, 1954–1962.* London: 1977.

Karpin, Michael, and Ina Friedman. *Murder in the Name of God.* New York: 1998.

Kretzmer, David. *The Occupation of Justice.* Albany: 2002.

Lustick, Ian. *Unsettled States, Disputed Lands: Britain and Ireland, France and Algeria, Israel and the West Bank/Gaza.* Ithaca: 1993.

Newman, David. *The Role of Gush Emunim and the Yishuv Kehillati in the West Bank.* Thesis submitted for dissertation, Durham Univ., 1981.

Primor, Avi. *Terror als Vorwand.* Düsseldorf: 2003.

Rabin, Yitzhak. *The Rabin Memoirs,* expanded ed. Berkeley: 1996.

Ravitzky, Aviezer. *Messianism, Zionism and Jewish Religious Radicalism.* Chicago: 1996.

Ross, Dennis. *The Missing Peace: The Inside Story of the Fight for Middle East Peace.* New York: 2004.

Rubinstein, Amnon. *From Herzl to Rabin: The Changing Image of Zionism.* New Jersey: 2000.

Sharon, Ariel, with David Chanoff. *Warrior: The Autobiography of Ariel Sharon.* New York: 1989.

Solomonica, David Doe. *Gush Emunim: Faith Transformed into a Political Social* Movement. Pittsburgh: 1989.

Sprinzak, Ehud. *Brother Against Brother: Violence and Extremism in Israeli Politics from Altalena to the Rabin Assassination.* New York: 1999.

Swisher, Clayton E. *The Truth About Camp David: The Untold Story About the Collapse of the Middle East Peace Process.* New York: 2004.

Teveth, Shabtai. *Ben-Gurion and the Palestinian Arabs: From Peace to War.* Oxford: 1985.

Weisburd, David. *Jewish Settler Violence: Deviance as Social Reaction.* Pennsylvania and London: 1989.

Zertal, Idith. *Israel's Holocaust and the Politics of Nationhood.* Cambridge: 2005.

Books (Hebrew)

Alpher, Yossi. *And the Wolf Shall Dwell with the Wolf: The Settlers and the Palestinians.* Tel Aviv: 2001.

Alterman, Natan. "The Land at Biria," *The Seventh Column,* Book I. Tel Aviv: 1975.

Aviner, Shlomo. *Questions and Responses Intifada.* Beit El: 1989.

Barnea, Nahum. *Netanyahu's Days, Political Columns.* Tel Aviv: 1999.

Bar-On, Aryeh. *Personal Imprint: Moshe Dayan in the Six Days War.* Tel Aviv: 1997.

Ben-Ami, Shlomo. *A Front Without a Rearguard: A Voyage to the Boundaries of the Peace Process.* Tel Aviv: 2004.

Ben-Dov, Shabtai. *Prophecy and Tradition in Redemption.* Tel Aviv: 1988.

Benziman, Uzi. *Prime Minister Under Siege.* Jerusalem: 1981.

————. *Sharon: An Israeli Caesar.* Tel Aviv: 1985.

Bramson, Yosef. *Days of World: The Forcing End.* Jerusalem: 1980.

Feige, Michael. *Two Maps for the West Bank: Gush Emunim, Shalom Akhshav.* Jerusalem: 2002.

Feiglin, Moshe. *Where There Are No Men: The Struggle of the Zo Artzenu Movement Against the Post-Zionist Collapse.* Jerusalem: 1997.

Fullman, Yeshaiyahu. *The Story of the Separation Barrier: Was it Life Sacrificing?* Jerusalem: 2004.

Gal-Or, Naomi. *The Jewish Underground, Our Terrorism.* Tel Aviv: 1991.

Gazit, Shlomo. *The Carrot and the Stick: The Israeli Administration in Judea and Samaria.* Tel Aviv: 1985.

Haris, Ron, ed. *The Book of Shamgar: A Life Story.* Tel Aviv: 2003.

Harnoy, Meir. *The Settlers.* Or Yehuda: 1994.

Klein, Menachem. *Shattering a Taboo: The Contacts Toward a Permanent Status Agreement in Jerusalem, 1994–2001.* Jerusalem: 2001.

Kook, Abraham I. *Lights.* Jerusalem: 1963.

————. *Lights of Holiness.* Jerusalem: 1964.

Kook, Zvi Y. *Israel's Paths.* Beit El: 2002.

Lein, Yehezkel. *Land Grab: Israel's Settlement Policy in the West Bank.* Jerusalem: 2002.

Levy, Yagil. *The Other Army of Israel: Materialist Militarism in Israel.* Tel Aviv: 2003.

Naor, Aryeh. *Begin in Power, Personal Testimony.* Tel Aviv: 1993.

————. *Government at War: The Government's Functioning in the Lebanon War.* Tel Aviv: 1986.

————. *Greater Israel: Ideology and Policy.* Haifa and Lod: 2001.

Negbi, Moshe. *Chains of Justice, High Court of Justice v. the Israeli Government in the Territories.* Jerusalem: 1981.

Neriah, Moshe Zvi. *Religious Judaism and the State.* Tel Aviv: 1952.

Ossetzky-Lazar, Sarah, and Assad Ghanem. *Between Peace and Equality: The Arabs in Israel During the Labor-Meretz Government.* Givat Haviva: 1995.

Pedatzur, Reuven. *The Victory of Embarrassment: The Eshkol Government's Policy in the Territories After the Six Day War.* Tel Aviv: 1996.

Peleg, Muli. *To Spread the Wrath of God: From Gush Emunim to Rabin Square.* Tel Aviv: 1997.

Ra'anan, Zvi. *Gush Emunim.* Tel Aviv: 1980.

Reshef, Tzali. *Peace Now: From the Officers' Letter to Peace Now.* Jerusalem: 1996.

Rubinstein, Danny. *On the Lord's Side: Gush Emunim.* Tel Aviv: 1982.

Schwartz, Dov. *The Theology of the Religious Zionist Movement.* Tel Aviv: 1996.

Segal, Hagai. *Dear Brothers: the History of the Jewish Underground.* Jerusalem: 1987.

Seibel, Robby, ed. *International Law.* Jerusalem: 2003.

Shafat, Gershon. *Gush Emunim: The Story Behind the Curtain.* Beit El: 1995.

Sheleg, Yair. *The New Religious Jews: A Contemporary Look at Religious Society in Israel.* Tel Aviv: 2000.

Sher, Gilad. *Just Beyond Reach: The Israeli-Palestinian Peace Negotiations 1999-2001.* Tel Aviv: 2001.

Tal, Uriel. *Myth and Rationalism in Contemporary Judaism.* Tel Aviv: 1986.

Weissman, Aliza. *The Evacuation: The Story of the Uprooting of Yamit's Settlements.* Beit El: 1990.

Zamir, Eyal, and Eyal Benvenisti. *The "Jewish Lands" in Judea, Samaria, the Gaza Strip and East Jerusalem.* Jerusalem: 1993.

Articles

Cohen, Stuart A. "Portrait of the New Israeli Soldier." *Middle East Review of International Affairs* I(4) (Dec. 1997).

Dotan, Yoav. "Do the 'Haves' Still Come Out Ahead? Resource Inequalities in Ideological Courts: The Case of the Israeli High Court of Justice," *Law & Society Review* 33 (1999).

Shamgar, Meir. "The Observance of the International Law in the Administered Territories," *Israel Yearbook of Human Rights* I (1971).

Shamir, Ronen. "'Landmark Cases' and the Reproduction of Legitimacy: The Case of Israel's High Court of Justice," *Law & Society Review* 24 (1990).

Sprinzak, Ehud. "Gush Emunim: The Tip of the Iceberg," *Jerusalem Quarterly* 21 (Fall 1981).

Newspapers, Periodicals, and Electronic Media (English)
Ha'aretz English Edition
Jerusalem Post
Midstream
The New York Times
The New York Times Magazine
The New Yorker
The Washington Post

Newspapers, Periodicals, and Electronic Media (Hebrew)
Al Hamishmar
Besheva
Channel 2, The Second Authority for Television and Radio
Channel 3, Cables
Davar
Doar Hayom
Dvarim
Ha'aretz
Hadashoth
Ha'olam Hazeh
Ha'tzofeh
IDF Radio
Israel Radio
Iton Tel Aviv
Iton Yerushalaiym
Kol Ha'ir
Koteret Rashit
Ma'ariv
Makor Rishon
Nekudah
Yedioth Aharonoth
Yesha Rabbis Newsletter
Ynet

Archives
Hakibbutz Ha'meuchad Archive
Israel Galili Archive
Knesset Archive
Labor Party Archive
Rabin Center for Israel Studies Archive (Sprinzak Collection)
State Archive
Yad Eshkol Archive

Human Rights Organizations Reports

B'Tselem Reports, 1994–2006

Israeli Settler Violence in the Occupied Territories: 1980–1984, an investigative report by the Palestine Human Rights Campaign (Chicago: 1985)

Official Reports and Publications

Report of the Investigation Commission on the Matter of the Massacre at the Tomb of the Patriarchs (Jerusalem: 1994)

Knesset Protocols

State Controller Annual Reports, 1984-2004

Statistical Yearbooks for Israel

Interviews

Ed Abbington
Shaul Arieli
Yossi Beilin
Shlomo Ben-Ami
Ahaz Ben-Ari
Benyamin Ben-Eliezer
Michael Ben-Yair
Arie (Lova) Eliav
Amiram Goldblum
Eitan Haber
Israel Harel
Noah Kinarti
Amnon Lipkin-Shachak
Amram Mitzna
Yitzhak Mordechai
Yuval Ne'eman

Moriah Ozeri
Shimon Peres
Haim Ramon
Mossi Raz
Tzali Reshef
Talia Sasson
Uri Savir
Shimon Sheves
Avraham (Beiga) Shochat
Yoel Singer
Ehud Sprinzak
Matti Steinberg
Pinchas Wallerstein
Philip Wilcox
Dina Yeshurun

Index